MEN *Freeing* MEN

EXPLODING THE MYTH OF THE TRADITIONAL MALE

edited by
Francis Baumli, Ph.D.

NEW ATLANTIS PRESS · JERSEY CITY

To Fred McKinney,
who on his deathbed
showed me the path.

Published by New Atlantis Press
473 Pavonia Avenue, Jersey City, NJ 07306.

Typography by *Paragraphics*, New York City.

Fourth printing, September 1991. Printed in the United States of America.

Library of Congress Cataloging-in-Publication Data
Main entry under title:

Men freeing men.

  Includes bibliographies and index.
   1. Men—United States—Addresses, essays, lectures.
2. Masculinity (Psychology)—Addresses, essays, lectures.
3. Men—United States—Sexual behavior—Addresses, essays,
lectures.   4. Father and child—United States—Addresses,
essays, lectures.   5. Sex role—United States—Addresses, essays,
lectures.   I. Baumli, Francis, 1948–
HQ1090.3.M46 1985   305.3´1´0973   85-21487

ISBN 0-9615480-0-2

ACKNOWLEDGMENTS

The editors would like to express their gratitude to all the contributors and to the several publishers of their works for their kind permission to reproduce the material in this collection.

Chapter 1

"Child of the Glacier": © 1980 by *American Man Magazine*.

"Loneliness": From *The Rule Book*, by The Men's Project, Kansas City, MO. Under preparation.

Chapter 2

"Opening": © 1983 by Jed Diamond. From *Inside Out: Becoming My Own Man*, published by Fifth Wave Press, P.O. Box 9355, San Rafael, CA 94912. (All subsequent selections by Jed Diamond are taken from this same book.)

"Prostitution As Male Humiliation": © 1976 by Herb Goldberg. From *The Hazards of Being Male*, under the management of Sanford J. Greenburger Associates Inc.

"Learning to Tarry, Touch, Talk": © by Sun Features, Inc.

"Men Are Learning to Listen to Their Bodies": © 1979 by Richard Haddad.

Chapter 3

"One Afternoon At Happy Hour": © 1979 by Otis L. Adams, III.

Chapter 4

"Women as Well as Men Share the Illusion": © 1979 by Richard Haddad.

"Isn't the Home Where Our Values Originated?": © 1979 by Richard Haddad.

"Men Up Against Women's Emotions": © 1983 by Otis L. Adams, III.

"John Brockett, of Millersburg, Missouri": From "Societal Pressures Inhibit Male Character Expression," *Columbia Missourian*, mid-March, 1982. © 1982 by *Columbia Missourian*.

"How to Recognize the Earth Mother Trap": © 1976 by Herb Goldberg. From *The Hazards of Being Male*, under the management of Sanford J. Greenburger Associates Inc.

"Signs for Recognizing a No-Win Situation": © 1979 by Herb Goldberg. From *The New Male*, published by William Morrow and Company, Inc.

"Constructive Fighting," "What is the Playful Relationship": © 1983 by Herb Goldberg. From *The New Male-Female Relationship*, published by William Morrow and Company, Inc.

"Her Husband's New Sex Life": © by Sun Features, Inc.

"Living with Mom and then Dad: A Matter of Personality, Not Gender": Originally published in *Transitions*, Spring 1983.

Chapter 10

"Family Violence and Women's Lib": Originally published in MEN'S 8 (May & June 1982): 6.

"He Wasn't Such a Bad Guy": Originally published in MEN'S 8 (July & August 1982): 6.

"Man Beaten To Death...Film at 11:00": © 1982 by Fredric Hayward.

Chapter 11

"The Draft": © 1978 by Otis L. Adams, III.

"The Man's Unpaid Role: Bodyguard and Protector": © 1981 by Fredric Hayward. From "Opening Address: National Congress for Men."

"We Who Are About to Die": © 1982 by Fredric Hayward.

"Women Want to Serve": Orginally published in MEN'S 8 (March & April 1982): 5.

"The Expendable Male": © 1980 by Fredric Hayward.

Chapter 12

"Kids Are Smoking—Why Don't We Care?": © Sun Features, Inc.

"Men and the Macho Ideal": © 1980 by the Coalition of Free Men.

Chapter 13

"Men Are Disadvantaged Too": © 1979 by Richard Haddad.

"Female Chauvinism": © 1979 by Richard Haddad.

"Concepts and Overview of the Men's Liberation Movement": © 1979 by Richard Haddad.

"Female Emotion and Feminist Logic": © 1983 by Otis L. Adams, III.

"Feminism and Male Guilt": © 1983 by Otis L. Adams, III.

"Today's Male Feminists": © 1979 by Richard Haddad.

Chapter 14

"The Trouble With Men's Issues": © 1983 by Otis L. Adams, III.

"Stereotyped at 13: The Frustrations of Being a Young Male": Originally published in *Transitions,* Spring 1983.

"Boys Will Be...Men": © 1982 by Fredric Hayward.

"Men Are Turning to Other Men": © 1979 by Richard Haddad.

"Men's Liberation and Human Liberation": © 1979 by Richard Haddad.

Author's Acknowledgments

I will not list the people to whom I owe the most gratitude here: the authors whose works are contained within these pages. They made this book possible. Over and above their literary contributions, I thank these writers for their personal support. More than once there were dark hours when their encouraging phone calls lifted my spirits and allowed me to believe that eventually it would be finished.

I also want to thank the many authors who submitted for this book, but in the end, could not be a part of it. Space limitations necessitated excluding many excellent manuscripts.

There are people close to me whom I have already thanked. My daughter Dacia deserves both gratitude and special consideration, given that she quite justifiably had trouble understanding why Daddy was working on a book that would help fathers learn to play with their children, when that very book sometimes kept her own Daddy from playing with her. To my dear friend and wife, Abbe Sudvarg, I owe a debt that is immeasurable, and paradoxically, qualified. Let me explain. I have sometimes been amused, and other times embarrassed, by books on men's liberation in which the author thanks his wife for her support, encouragement, and for typing the manuscript. Well, Abbe lent dialogue, encouragement, support, love, and a rare understanding. For all this I am grateful. But she did not type the manuscript. I am grateful to myself that I neither felt the need, nor had the presumption, to ask her for this.

Dr. Herb Goldberg deserves special mention because of his initial involvement with editing manuscripts, and his help with the introductions for this book. And I must thank my friend, Dr. Patricia Linit, who provided emotional support during many a pseudocrisis.

And there are other people who helped in their own, unique way. I thank James A. Cook, Peter T. Cyr, Henry Esposito, Sam Femiano, Chris Griffith, Carl H. Hays, Alfred E. Koenig, Suzy Morse, Jack Paradise, O.A. Robinson, Mitsuko Shimomura, Arthur Shostak, Dr. John Small, and Josephine Williams.

Organizations were also helpful. I am deeply grateful to the many ways I was helped by the Coalition of Free Men, Divorced Dads Incorporated, The Men's Experience, Men's Rights Association, Men's Rights Incorporated, MEN International, the National Congress for Men, the National Organization for Changing Men, and Realia. I am especially indebted to the publishers, editors, and staff of *American Man, Brother, Changing Men* (formerly *M.: Gentle Men for Gender Justice*), *Contemporary Philosophy, Divorced Dads Inc. Newsletter, The Humanist, Journey-Men, Legal Beagle, Men's News Magazine* (formerly, *MEN'S*), *Options,* and *Transitions.*

Finally, I must especially thank my publisher, Ted Stevenson. His belief in the ideas this book contains, and his loyal crusade to make it available to the public, have been inspiring and gratifying. I am fortunate to have met him.

Contents

Section I: Discovering Ourselves

Section II: When Feelings Become Issues

Preface

Over and over I have been struck by how issues in women's liberation and men's liberation are complementary. For example, the women's liberation movement has attempted to gain access to economic and political power—arenas that traditionally have belonged to men. The men's movement has attempted to gain access to the domestic and parenting spheres—areas that have traditionally been under the strict control of women. Similarly, while women are becoming more assertive, men are becoming more receptive. Women are discovering new dimensions of their sexuality, men are learning to be more sensual. Women are exercising their intellects, men discovering their emotions.

Not only are the issues complementary, the very *process* of engaging those issues has also been complementary. The women's movement has been visible, vocal, well organized, and a media darling. The men's movement, however, has been relatively invisible, soft-spoken, held together by loose networking, and has generally been neglected by the media.

Women have needed strong, aggressive, dynamic role models to help them come out of the home and enter the public domain with their issues. They have eagerly looked to individual women for support and especially for leadership. Those who could provide such powerful leadership and articulate women's feelings into communicable issues became the bestselling authors—authors who, in effect, became celebrities: Gloria Steinem, Betty Friedan, Adrienne Rich, Susan Brownmiller, and many others.

But men? Their journey toward gender liberation has taken a different path. The man who pretends he can say the final word on gender issues, whether it be on a talk show or in a book, sounds too much like a character from the same old script. And if he tries to do it by himself, if he alone tries to shoulder the burden, then he unwittingly but inevitably assumes the old macho warrior role —hammering out the issues all by himself. Thus doing it alone, he denies one of the most important facets of men's liberation—contact with other men. Eschewing such comradeship—and the trust that goes along with it—he simply perpetuates the established macho style, a mindset which leads to competition, loneliness, stress, and dogmatic posturing.

The women's movement needed celebrities because a large part of its task involved self-assertion in a competitive environment. Hence, the women's movement has produced many spectacularly assertive individual authors who have written best-sellers.

In the men's movement, the problem is more or less reversed. Men have never lacked for assertive individual leaders. What they needed was a way to discover and share an awareness of their *collective* interests, as opposed to the apparently exclusive *individual* interests that have previously kept men competing with each other. In the process of men's liberation, then, finding a kind of collective voice (within which individuals can find the support necessary to make innovative statements) has been essential. Hence, in the process of men's liberation, there has been a need for a collection of men's writings which reflects the unique nature of men freeing themselves: men *sharing* themselves through their writings and *showing* what it means to be *one man freeing himself in the company of other men.*

This collective body of literature—a few books, but mostly essays, short stories, and poetry—has existed for some time. It has for the last several years been growing in maturity and volume. Now the time has at last come to make this body of literature available to the public. Hence, this anthology.

This anthology reflects the process of men freeing themselves, but just as importantly, it can help further this process. For one thing, it can help bring men together. It does provide a collective voice of men speaking together—disagreeing, compromising, accepting one another. It thus helps achieve a relaxed, supportive atmosphere in which intimacy with other men can be fully explored.

There are other ways this anthology offers a unique view of the issues of men's liberation. Even as the movement progresses, it remains encumbered by a pervasive homophobia. The homophobic man responds to both the topic and the author with a fearful uncertainty. A book about friendship written by one man thus tends to be a setup. But an anthology, in which more than fifty men are writing about similar issues, and many of them very clearly extolling the value and desirability of friendship with other men—this is not so frightening, and even for the cautious reader is something worth looking into.

Just as importantly, a piece of collective literature can provide long-needed encouragement for men. Traditionally, men's role models have been so remote, so unreal (witness Teddy Roosevelt, Babe Ruth, John Wayne, Clint Eastwood), that they have promoted images men can never live up to. Initial inspiration by such men tends to lead to bitter disappointment. Today, men know that they need a new kind of role model: people who are not heroes, but are courageous enough to talk about their feelings and risk doing something about those feelings. Such men are to be found within the pages of this book.

An anthology can also communciate emotions in ways that a book by one author never could. Men are trying to cast off the old armor that has kept their feelings locked away inside them. They are beginning to unlock those feelings. But feelings are confusing to men. To enter their realm is to enter a domain that is frightening, bewildering, and sometimes erratic. (Succumbing to them seems like stepping into chaos.) To risk going down this road, men need to hear how other men have done it—what their experiences have been. But no man walks this road exactly like another. Each man has his own unique turmoil. If he looks to other men for comfort, it is important that he look to more than one man. One man's voice might confuse him. Another man might demand too much. Another man's message sounds foreign. But another man says it just right! And now he understands a little bit better. Another small step has been taken. Soon, perhaps another writer—who earlier scared or confused him—will be his next teacher.

This anthology's voices—of men cooperating, encouraging, sounding the beat of many drums so that individual men may find their own step—can help men in the process of freeing themselves in ways that a book by a single author cannot.

The division of this collection into two parts reflects the twofold nature of the liberation process for men. The first section, "Discovering Ourselves," deals primarily with the inner man. In it, emotions are given birth, are nurtured and struggled with, and, ultimately, accepted. The second section, "When Feelings Become Issues," recognizes the crucial fact that not all of the difficulties men experience emanate from inside themselves. There are "real world" issues that must be articulated, engaged, and resolved, with a combination of courage and forgiveness. The necessity of doing battle on so many fronts—even as we are learning to divest ourselves of the emotional armor in which we've been so long imprisoned—makes the path to liberation that much more challenging. But the ends—self acceptance and true equality—are equally important, and to lose sight of either would diminish the value of the quest.

For all these reasons, this book was designed to serve as a guidepost to men just starting out on the journey of masculine liberation. But it has also been carefully organized as a compendium of men's issues, and for this reason, can serve as an ideal text for the ever-increasing number of men's studies courses currently cropping up around the nation in colleges and universities. Such a text has thus far been lacking, and college instructors have complained that in order to fully cover the wide variety of topics in men's studies, they have had to piece together a reading program from as many as a dozen books. And even then the coverage of issues is sketchy and discontinuous.

This current anthology, during the entire course of its preparation, has been intended to fill those gaps and in one volume cover the whole gamut of men's issues with detail, depth, and emotional honesty. The more personal articles in Section I lend themselves to classroom discussion. The more scholarly articles in Section II challenge the student to articulate the issues. At the beginning of the course, the students might say, "I don't know how to explain it, but I don't think I'm all that privileged just because I'm a man." By the end of the semester, he will be able to explain it—whether to friends, in a discussion with feminists, or in other college courses.

To digress briefly: I said that this book is comprehensive. I must qualify this statement. Despite my best efforts, I was unable to get sufficient articles of high quality to have sections on aging and on men of color. Perhaps my lack of success in these areas points to current limitations in the men's liberation movement. Perhaps we do not have the desire, or the courage, to come to grips with the process of aging in a personal, honest way. And perhaps the boundaries— both explicit and subtle—that separate the races in our culture have not been examined sufficiently by the men's movement. Whichever is the case, I hope that a future edition of this book can include writings on these issues.

So...this book should appeal both to the man seeking to liberate himself and to the college instructor. I also believe this book has a great deal to say to women and feminists.

A dictum popularly espoused by feminists over the last two decades asserts that no man should even *think* of offering an opinion on women's issues until he has spent a couple of years reading women's literature. I would not impose such a stringent obligation on women and feminists, but I do believe that for those women who are willing to do their basic homework, this book, because of its candor, passion, and careful scholarship, is an excellent place to begin.

Reading this book can help women better relate to the men in their lives. It can even help women help men—because yes, just as many a profeminist man has devoted his life to the women's cause, so also the men's movement welcomes the help of interested dedicated women.

Feminists especially can profit from reading this book. It can show them that men indeed have problems—something many feminists would just as soon deny. And it can mirror to them some of the excesses and distortions of their own movement, and thus perhaps help them better travel the road to their own liberation.

One final comment: An anthology is a compendium of writings, put together —in this case—by a single editor. What has happened to this editor in the process of putting it all together?

This task has taken four and one-half years of his time, consuming at a minimum twenty hours per week. In preliminary work, he read thousands of articles and short stories, more than one hundred books on men's liberation, and every existing anthology on the topic. For him it was a trial of the spirit, an odyssey into his own soul, and a wonderful adventure with other men.

The labor, at last, is done. May we all share the fruits.

Francis Baumli

Section I:
DISCOVERING
OURSELVES

INTRODUCTION

In the best sense of the word, liberation for men means growth and redevelopment of a man's intimate or "human" side. While social conditioning and role pressures stunted women's growth to a point that a women's liberation movement was needed, similar pressures have distorted and impaired men's life experiences. Masculine conditioning has, to a great extent, destroyed men's motivation and ability to develop and place a priority on the personal, self-caring, playful parts of their lives.

Many men who are defined as successful by society resemble machines. At their best, these men are high-performance machines that function impressively for a period of time within the structure of their work role. Viewed from a distance, their power and accomplishments seem admirable, even enviable. But viewed up close, these men are sadly lacking when it comes to achieving, much less sustaining, true intimacy. Their lives are empty and even desperate in personal areas. Removed from their work context, they are lost. They live a life of externals: jobs, success, and image. But they have a seriously impaired capacity to look inside to see what they themselves need as persons. They are like powerful engines, racing at high speed without any oil. They will soon burn out—self-destruct on the inside by constantly defending and proving themselves. Before long they will go out of control, speeding headlong toward the destruction of their family lives, their bodies, and the support of people around them who otherwise might give them love and intimacy.

Even in our society, saturated as it is with popular psychology books and self-awareness workshops, the notion that men need liberating has been a matter of only mild and bemused interest. Too often, it has been a target for ill-willed reactions, distortions, and even mockery. For those of us who have been active in the process of men's liberation, it has been an uphill effort—and one without precedents. We have not had role models. There has not been anyone to help by telling us how they got through the struggle. Still, we have tried to become aware of the insidious and frightening undertow of traditional masculinity in order to understand its nature and make changes. And it must be admitted that men still have a long way to go before they will be ready to take off the destructive armor so many wear. It will take a good deal of time and work before the thrust toward dehumanization and destruction that seems to be the psychological lot of most men can be blunted, parried, or turned around.

But some men have begun the process of awakening. They want to be free of their destructive cultural programming. Some have come to this new awareness because their lives were drastically affected by the women's movement. Others have decided that they are no longer willing to define themselves as people only through the kind of job they have. They are no longer willing to measure their masculinity by their sexual performance, or to be denied the precious experience of active fathering. They are rejecting the role pressures that have forced them to become chronically competitive, "successful" providers. They are acknowledging, examining, and confronting the realities and grotesqueries of their traditional marriage experience. They are recognizing the self-destructive vulnerability and loneliness that come from placing all their emotional well-being in the keeping of one woman who may at any time turn against them in rage and accusation. Even the most resistant and "macho" of men are beginning to realize the emptiness of a life devoid of close relationships with other men. These men too are rebelling against the conditioning that makes every other man a competitor and potential enemy. They crave the experience of a loving and caring friendship, and have begun testing the terribly difficult, but wonderfully rewarding, possibilities for closeness with other men.

It is true that the psychological pressures and mandates of masculinity have had a horrendous impact on men's lives. Men have been separated from their inner experience and an awareness of the *process* of their lives. But some men are no longer willing to be satisfied with emotional numbness and the terror of lonely masculinity. They are looking inside themselves, and reaching out to each other. They are discarding much of the conditioning that has stifled them. And in doing so, they are discovering some parts of themselves that they never knew were there.

In the four-year process of collecting and sifting through the writings submitted for this book, I have been moved to laughter and to tears, to delight and rage, by the men who shared their writings with me. Sometimes they disturbed me deeply. Other times they comforted me. Sometimes I did not like what I read or I disagreed with the point of view. But the raw emotion, the jarring candor, the painful confessions, and the joyous affirmation meant that through it all I had to acknowledge, empathize, and accept the reality and authenticity of each man's experience.

I am heartened by the prospect of living in a society that is finally making room for a new kind of male experience. And I am excited by what this means: very simply, that there are individual men who are out there, and here around me, with whom I can find comfort, share friendship, and enjoy, as we all—both men and women—continue the arduous but fulfilling task of creating ourselves anew.

Chapter 1:
The Process of Reclaiming Ourselves

CHILD OF THE GLACIER

M. Adams

One Sunday morning in the spring of 1961, my family had invited our next-door neighbors to go to our church with us. I was nine years old.

After parking the car, the seven of us were walking the several blocks down St. Paul Street to the church. My mother, my sister, and the woman from next door walked and chatted together, while my father and I, the man from next door and his son walked silently behind. It was a bright spring day and I was full of a child's energy. I decided that I wanted to be the one to point out our church to the visiting neighbors, and I began to run ahead of the group to do so. I never got the chance; as I ran ahead, my father grabbed my wrist and yanked me back violently, hurting my arm and almost pulling me off my feet.

"Never walk in front of the ladies!" he said sternly, still holding my arm. "That's not polite! Always walk *behind* the ladies!"

Immediately, two thoughts came into my nine-year-old mind. First, I wondered why in the world men should have to walk behind women, and I decided that I didn't like that rule. Then, it occurred to me that my father would never have yanked on my sister that way, no matter *what* she had done. From that moment on, I hated—consciously—anything that anyone expected from me simply because I was male.

I imagine I was one of the first masculinists. . .or at least one of the youngest, for it was with a *conscious* awareness and a *conscious* opposition that I mentally noted and logged every form of discrimination against males that I encountered for the remainder of my childhood.

At that age, it was athletic expectations and the training in points of etiquette that plagued me. I was expected to participate in every boy's sport, to *want* to participate, and to do *well*—or at least to keep on trying until I *could* do well.

5

Whenever I tried and failed, I was mocked and chided; whenever I said I wasn't interested and refused to try, I was severely scolded. Girls, I could see, were not expected to perform in these capacities, and though I could never quite see what it was that they were doing on the other side of the playground, it always looked a lot more interesting, a lot more imaginative, a lot more creative. . .a lot more fun.

In addition to "walking behind the ladies," there were such customs as opening doors, pulling out chairs, having to stand whenever a woman entered or left the room, and having to pay for things. The "ladies first" syndrome always made me fiercely angry. The old "I can hit you but you can't hit me back because I'm a girl" routine angered and humiliated me beyond description. That boys were always dealt much more severe punishments for a given act than were girls would throw me into a rage. It was significant to me that these unfair customs and punishments were condoned and administered by adult *women* as well as by adult men. No matter how many times my parents and teachers told me that these things were traditional and correct, none of it made sense to me and I couldn't tolerate any of it. Though these were conscious sensibilities, I learned quickly never to express them to my elders, who considered them naughty and maladjusted.

From about the age of eleven, the pragmatic ramifications of sexism became more serious: any task or chore involving physical strength or exertion was automatically to be done by males; any task or chore involving risk or danger was automatically to be done by males. Meanwhile, I continued to catalog, in my mind, all of the sexist attitudes, policies, and laws that I had observed or experienced. Sometimes, I would try to talk about these ideas to other kids my own age. None of them understood, none of them were interested. In the course of growing up, they had managed to adjust, and they didn't seem to care.

During those pubescent years, I discovered that the sore spot on my life created by etiquette was malignant, and that it festered and grew, with the coming of adulthood, into something horrible called "chivalry." Chivalry dictated that men risk their lives for women, and accept death outright if it meant saving a woman. It was a fearful moment when I realized that the term "innocent women and children" no longer included me. It was at the age of fourteen that I decided to strike the word "coward" from my vocabulary. The word and the concept were entirely sexist to me, and had no meaning.

I entered high school in 1967. I was growing closer and closer to the Viet Nam war. At age fifteen, I began to have an obsessive, maniacal fear of the military draft. The urgency of the draft/war situation prompted me to start expressing my beliefs about sexual equality. I did so compulsively, crazily thinking that if I convinced enough people that I was right, the wheels of sexism and war and selective service would grind to a screeching halt just before my eighteenth birthday. I would try, in my own confused way, to describe a society where men and women would be truly equal. I always tried to demonstrate that the advantages of such a system would be tremendous for *both* men and women. I had been able to figure out the more basic, obvious aspects of women's liberation on my own, and I never failed to include them in my argument. But this was in

6

1967, and not even the current wave of the women's movement had reached our part of the world then; of course, nobody shared my views, nobody really even understood, and most people thought I was crazy.

There was little else in my life at that time to offer any solace or diversion. These were my adolescent years, and my avant-garde outlook on sex-roles played havoc with my concept of sexuality. There was the normal emotional bind created by the clash between my sexual attraction for women and the Mariological guilt-complex instilled in all young men. While I was trying to convince myself that I shouldn't feel guilty about my sexual desires, the whole thing was further complicated by a feeling of deep hurt that women did not seem to return those desires (to men in general). I not only wanted girls, and felt guilty about it, but I also wanted for them to want *us,* and was insulted by the fact that they didn't.

There were some girls who were more sexually free and aware, but they invariably favored the macho-jock types, and regarded me as a waste of a male body. Those girls who intellectually preferred more sensitive boys were almost always extremely prudish, which served only to aggravate my sexual guilt. Despite the fact that my sexual feelings were completely heterosexual, I began to realize that there were certain aspects of the female sexuality of which I was jealous. Women seemed to have a purely aesthetic sexuality, while the male sexuality was mostly functional, more directly related to role performance. Certainly, I was able to see that the aesthetic value placed on women had been taken to a dreadful extreme, and that women suffered some brutal consequences for it. Nevertheless, it was easy to see that, in ways both passive and active, women *enjoyed* the aesthetic nature of their sexual image. The male "aesthetic" was really just another measure of their capacity to live up to role expectations; men didn't really enjoy any of the kind of sexual attention that women got. It occurred to me that in terms of sexuality, men and women needed to move *toward* one another; women moving away from the aesthetic extreme that made them sex-objects, and men moving away from the opposite, functional extreme that made them objects of risk, strength, and performance. I would have liked to have been a little more of a sex-object, myself! But I didn't dare express those feelings then, not in 1967.

High school phys. ed. was, for someone like me, pure hell. The expectations were bad enough, in addition to having to put up with the usual bullying from most of the other boys in the class. I was labeled a "sissy" and mocked accordingly, but they could see that I was different breed of sissy. I was an angry, *assertive* sissy—something they had never seen before—and for that they hated me. The teachers were perplexed to hear blunt expressions of what I thought about their sessions of mindless semi-violence. It was less fear than pure contempt that I showed for sports like football and lacrosse. I told them that I saw no reason why I or anyone should be required to participate if they didn't want to. The bullying would often become violent—it was a pretty miserable time for me.

Finally, in the winter of 1968, when it came time for the annual four-week period devoted to wrestling, I rebelled. I refused to wrestle. I told the teacher that I would *not* wrestle, and that furthermore, I would not even don my gym-suit. The teacher warned me that if I did not wrestle, he would fail me for the entire year. I told him to go ahead and fail me—a pretty bold move, considering that the Baltimore County Board of Education had just passed a law requiring every student to pass three out of four years of high school phys. ed. in order to graduate. There were so many things in life upsetting me at that time that I didn't even care. I attended the first wrestling class in my street clothes, stand-ing over in a corner of the room. During his verbal introduction to the study of wrestling, the teacher said, "Boys, wrestling is important, because this is the kind of thing that's going to get you ready for the rice-paddies." I was so shocked and offended by the remark that I left the classroom, left the gymna-sium area and went and sat in the library. I never attended another of that teach-er's classes again. I failed the course.

That was basically the state of my life in 1968. The daily headlines of Viet Nam had me terrified to be approaching what was supposed to be the prime of my life; sexually, I was confused and hurt, and three times a week, I had to wor-ry about whether or not I'd be leaving the boys' locker room in one piece. I had begun to develop a deep, underlying resentment towards women for not hav-ing to go through the same things. I knew women weren't directly to blame, but the resentment was only natural; I saw them as being completely free of all of the things I hated about my own life. Of course, they had their exclusively fe-male problems of which *I* was free, but from my side of the fence the grass on their side looked considerably greener. The only thing that kept me stable was my relatively conscious awareness of my own feelings, and my attempts to express them. Then, something totally unexpectedly happened. Like a hurri-cane, the women's movement was suddenly upon us.

My immediate reaction to feminism was intense indignation. With Viet Nam and the draft forcing every young American boy into choosing between war, jail, and exile, and with what I considered to be all of the other injustices of the male condition, it was hard for me to take the idea of "women's liberation" seri-ously. This feeling didn't last long, however; I had basically believed in libera-tion for both sexes all along. It was the anger, the hostility, and the unyielding stubbornness of their point of view which continued to make me wary of fem-inists' ideas.

The uni-directional forcefulness of their assertions blotted out all other points of view on sexual roles and stereotypes. Women were victimized by soci-ety in every way. Men were to blame for all evil conditions in the world. Men greedily shared all of the world's rights and privileges, all of the glory and dig-nity, while women were denied everything, had no advantages, and were treated like slaves. It was not that I doubted the validity of these points of view, but I could see that they only told half of the story. I hoped that these new fem-inist ideas would begin to make people see what I had been trying to tell them about men, and about people in general.

Surely, amidst the waves of feminist ideology, it would be mentioned that men, too, were stereotyped, that they were forced into a role-image and ex-pected to fulfill it. Surely, it would be pointed out that men, too, were treated

8

as objects, as death-risk objects, physical strength-objects, success-objects. Surely, it would be noticed that society was always much more sympathetic and forgiving of women, and that women were free to express sensitivity and emotion, while men were treated much more brutally, dealt far worse penalties in life, and were not allowed to be emotionally free. Surely, it would be brought out that women, with their own attitudes, beliefs, and behavior, contributed to the existence of sexism in the world as well as men.

But just as surely as I thought everyone would realize these things, no one did; feminist theory was being accepted by the social intelligentsia as cold, hard fact. And, just as surely, I began to lose my one foothold in sanity, my own conscious, coherent point of view, and my ability to express it. Everything I had ever believed, my every thought, my every point of view, everything I had ever tried to express was lost, drowned-out in the roar of feminism.

I looked around me, trying to see some manifestations of the ghastly horrors that feminists were complaining about. What I saw was men being allowed their special "privileges" only as a result of constant victory and success. Male "privilege" was given only as a kind of reward for fulfilling male role expectations, like giving a trained animal a cracker for successfully performing a trick. Women, meanwhile, were being loved, supported and protected by men at all costs—even at the cost of the men's lives. Not very many women seemed to act as though they felt particularly "oppressed" in this situation, either. I and my other male friends were faced with the options of the Viet Nam war, going to prison, and going to Canada. The girls we knew in high school, however, seemed to be pursuing a number of more benign options: getting married, going to college; all of the girls who had decided to try and get good jobs seemed to be getting them. Where did all of this feminist theory apply? I didn't doubt that it applied somewhere, but it certainly didn't seem to apply in my experience.

My bitterness and resentment towards women deepened. Not only did they seem to live an existence which I envied, but they had stolen away my point of view. On top of that, the one-sidedness of the women's movement seemed to be leading us toward "unilateral" liberation, a society where women were to be freed from their role and men were not.

I became obsessed with these issues; I thought about nothing else. I began to brood constantly. The impending doom of Viet Nam multiplied my anxiety a hundred times. My great emotional need for girls and romance in my life came up against my anger and hostility toward them, rendering me unable to relate to them at all. I became unable to concentrate on school work. I stopped doing homework. I started cutting classes. Eventually, in my junior year in high school, I stopped going to school entirely. That year, I was truant over eighty days, forging notes from my parents to the school explaining my absences, and ultimately falsifying my report-card to keep my truancy a secret from my parents. Incredibly, I continued these deceptions for a year and a half before getting caught.

During that time, I spent most of my days sitting and wandering by myself in the forests of Glen Arm, in which I had played and hiked since childhood. I was using the time to try and keep a grip on who I was and what I believed. I painfully contemplated every situation in life that I could think of, deciding what I would do and trying to take everything to its ultimate implications, ramifications, and conclusions. I questioned everything—sex-roles, middle-class values, life. Sometimes, sitting in the woods, I would go into fits of deep depression or acute anxiety, over Viet Nam, or over my irresolvable love/hate attitude towards women. I was going through the agonizing process of developing a practicable, personal philosophy. I don't mean to give the impression that this was the moralistic speculation of a young philosophical prodigy; this was the compulsive, obsessive turmoil of a highly disturbed young man. But I would never go back and change any of it, for in that process, I became somebody. And I did it utterly alone. I was sixteen years old.

The lies could not go on working forever, and I was eventually caught and made to go back to school, where I was scheduled to repeat the eleventh grade. The daily pressures of schoolwork aggravated my anxieties, just as before, and the need for some kind of diversion became stronger than ever. I found it in a group of friends who were essentially juvenile delinquents.

They were the perfect diversion for me. They were totally amoral, and cared about nothing in life. They made fun of everything and everybody. Their universal response to any topic was a barrage of obscene language and crude jokes. Their attitude made me laugh, and took my mind off of my obsessions.

Unfortunately, I started to become one of them. My association with them alienated many of my regular friends, and I started spending more and more time with the gang. We would run around together and get into mischief, setting off firecrackers under people's windows, and pulling the valves out of people's tires. I suppose I felt like I was getting back at the world. Finally, two of us got into serious trouble when we burglarized an office building. The diversion had gone too far.

After the legal crisis with the police was over, both my parents and the Board of Education decided that I should see a psychiatrist. The school board referred me to one. When the psychiatrist told me to talk to him about myself, it didn't take me long to get around to my philosophy on sexual equality. As I explained to him about how I believed that sex-roles were bad, he looked very interested; he nodded frequently, and took some notes. All the while, I was thinking that I had finally found someone who understood, someone who might even agree with me. When I had finished, I sat back and waited for his reply. He looked at me and said, "Tell me, did your mother ever cross-dress you when you were little?" He was surprised and disappointed when I told him that she had not. He was sure that he had found the source of my aberration.

Once, when I was upset about Viet Nam and the draft, I told him that I didn't believe that I should have to take on that responsibility just because I was male. There were many women who were stronger and tougher than I was, and who furthermore *believed in the war*. Why shouldn't one of them go in my place? His answer to this line of logic was to tell me that I shouldn't have such a "low opinion" of myself. Another time, when I was angry, I asserted the idea that I simply *did not want* to go to the Viet Nam war. I told him that I didn't need a moralistic reason, I simply didn't want to. *Women* were allowed *not to go,* even if they supported the war! Nobody told them it was ignoble for them not to want to go. Why should it be so for me? He replied with a little parable:

"If a fireman is sitting in the fire house, and receives a phone-call reporting that there is a fire in his precinct, and then he hangs up the phone, and sits and smokes a cigar before going out to answer the fire-call. . .what would you say to that?"

"I'd say that the fireman isn't doing his job," I said.

"Yeah, that's what I'd say, too," he said, snidely.

I was outraged at the implication of that little bit of nonsense! I told him angrily that I did not agree that, because I was male, I was automatically a cosmic "fireman" in the "precinct" of life!

I saw that same psychiatrist regularly for about a year and a half. I was growing dangerously close to draft age, and spent most of the sessions crying the blues about how I knew I could never hold up physically, mentally, or emotionally under a military experience. I finally convinced him to write the draft board a letter telling them not to draft me. The draft board acknowledged receipt of the letter, but months later, I found out that they had *ignored it!* Their secretary told me, "The doctor just didn't tell us enough about you." Ultimately, the only thing that saved me was my Selective Service lottery number, 257. To this day, I have never gotten over the fact that, after all of the anguish I went through, I had absolutely no control over my own destiny. The only thing that had saved me was pure, fool luck.

College was such a welcome relief from high school that for about a year or so, my spirits changed. My grades were good, and I started dating a girl I had met in high school who seemed to like me. (We subsequently became engaged to marry.) My disastrous high school career and my brief tenure with the gang of delinquents seemed like bad dreams. I was pretty sure I wasn't going to be drafted, and there were even some encouraging-sounding things coming out of the mouths of feminists. They were saying things like, "If you liberate women, you automatically liberate men, too."

Liberate men? Sounds good to me! I didn't really like the idea that liberation for men would come only as a by-product of feminism, but it was better than nothing. At least it sounded like an acknowledgement that men needed to be liberated from something.

I decided to start actively supporting the women's movement. For several months, I passed out feminist literature, sat in feminist booths, and collected feminist funds. I spread the feminist gospel to all of my friends, and, most importantly, always treated women as equals. I waited patiently for some sign of reciprocation. Nothing happened. Not really. Every now and then, someone would say something about the alimony issue, proposing that women should have to pay alimony, too, if the situation warranted it. That was it. That was all the men's liberation I heard. I decided to wait, give it time.

Over the next year and a half, my relationship with my steady girlfriend deteriorated and ended, due to intense personal conflicts involving the interplay of love, guilt, anger, and selfishness. Our skirmish was so severe that I actually lost

11

a job in trying to meet her demands for my time before I finally broke up with her.

I was traumatized by the experience. It had been difficult, even with all of the trouble she caused me, to break that emotional bond. There was also the social embarrassment of breaking the engagement. I went into a period of depression. I was also angry about losing my job. Worse, I had still not seen any signs of the alleged reciprocal liberation for men which was supposed to grow out of the women's movement.

The old anxieties started to return, so much so that I eventually dropped out of college. I got a job working in a bookstore which I quickly grew to hate. It was 1973.

That year, sexism again took an obsessive hold on me. The woman's movement had advanced on many fronts; attitudes and laws were changing radically to suit them. This was all well and good, but the prevailing point of view had not changed at all: women were victims, and men were to blame. These ideas were still being asserted in so rigid a fashion that the men's lib point of view was precluded by it. It was confusing for me, because I did, after all, *support* feminism and its proposed reforms. It was only the movement's blind refusal to accept a co-existing point of view to which I objected. I wanted the women's movement to succeed, but deplored its ideology and methods.

Worse yet, their singular point of view was now being espoused on a mass scale; feminism had invaded and infested the media. Television had become a feminist circus. All of the "progressive" comedy shows such as *All in the Family* and *Maude* showed women venting their righteous anger on the men, who were all depicted as chauvinist buffoons. Dramatic crime shows dealt primarily with women rising through the ranks and with women's problems, usually in a way that strongly implied that men didn't *have* any problems. In the store where I worked, there were whole sections of books dealing with women's issues; never did it occur to anyone that there might be such a thing as men's liberation issues. Everywhere you turned, there was sympathy for women in their oppression by the big, bad males.

Most painful to me was the wildly growing syndrome of "unilateral" liberation. When the women on the comedy shows displayed sexist attitudes towards men, it was shown as perfectly acceptable. It was perfectly natural that men should still have the same old role expectations imposed on them. On the crime dramas, lady cops were allowed to righteously give orders and assert their equal rank, but almost never had to pay equal consequences for doing so; and if a plot called for a character to die, it was ninety-nine times out of a hundred a male.

Frighteningly, laws started to display the same hypocritical trend: in spite of the rights supplied to women by the various state and federal civil rights acts, the draft laws called for only males to register; many states still had (at that time) laws making alimony payable to women only; women were still rescued first in times of emergency; and in matters involving insurance policies, men could be discriminated against on the basis of statistics, but feminist groups were seeing to it that women could not be, not even on the same basis.

What was it they had said . . . ? "If you liberate women, you automatically liberate men." It wasn't true. It had sounded good, and I had believed it, but it hadn't worked. No one can be truly liberated until he has confronted his own problems, gotten in touch with his own anger, and expressed those things from his *own point of view*. It wasn't enough just to have things changing from someone *else's* point of view. Men had to discover their own, and had to express it, make it known. A separate men's movement would be necessary. I realized that now.

In my obsessed state of mind during this period, I had once again begun trying to express the notion of men's lib. This time, I was even more frantic, more desperate than before, feeling that I was being thwarted by feminism at every turn. I babbled out my ideas angrily, compulsively, to everyone I met. Several friends started giving me some obvious advice. "Why don't you *do* something about it?" they would ask. "Why don't you start your *own* movement? Why don't you write your own book?" It was, of course, an idea which had occurred to me. Perhaps they were right. Perhaps I should try to act upon my environment. Being active in that way might be therapeutic, and I might actually get something started.

In the summer of 1973, I began to try to put some of my thoughts down on paper, and to do research for what I thought might turn out to be a book of some sort. I also began to talk to people who were active in the women's movement to see if there was a chance of giving some talks here and there.

In early 1974, I gave a talk at the Towson State College Women's Center. They were basically a hostile feminist audience, but I thought that I had gotten a few vital points across:

"Men, too, are forced into a role, with often brutal expectations. They are also oppressed."

"But that's *their* fault! Men made things the way they are! They do it to themselves!"

"Which men? Show me the men! Point to the man who 'made things the way they are.' I didn't have anything to do with it, and neither did any of my friends, nor any man I know. We were all raised in this society just like you. And women display sexist attitudes too, and thereby contribute to its existence."

"Yes, but that's because they were *conditioned* to do those things by men."

"No, not by 'men'; by society. Men are conditioned to do the things that they do, too! Men are not chauvinist pigs when they're born; they're *taught* to be that way by their mothers and fathers and teachers and all of society."

Hmmm . . . they had never thought of it like that before.

I started talking about the war.

"Men make all the wars!" was the inevitable response. "They do it to themselves."

"I didn't make the war. None of the boys who are fighting it made it. They are as innocent as any woman; in fact, many are *more* innocent than many women. I never contributed so much as a positive thought to the war, and yet many women actively support it politically. I understand that Margaret Chase Smith had something to do with introducing the Selective Service Act of 1967 into Congress. There are women in Congress who officially support the war. And

13

what about all of the women who voted for Richard Nixon? *Who* makes the wars?"

Hmmm. . .They were impressed enough, despite their hostility, to invite me back for another talk. I thought I was getting somewhere. After cutting through the "it's all the men's own fault" idea, I was able to discuss many issues directly. They would always parry every idea with some feminst parallel, in a kind of game of one-upmanship. I found myself having to draw my own parallels just to keep them from getting me off the track. Husbands, as well as wives, were often the victims of beatings. Men, as well as women, suffered great emotional trials, including guilt, and self-abasement, from the traditional concept of love and romance. I found that the phrase, "as well as women" was my greatest weapon. With that qualification, they would listen to my points of view. I thought the talks had been a success.

The book project was to be, emotionally, my undoing. Because of the prevailing feminist viewpoint and the way it made people react to the idea of men's lib, I felt that one of the book's main goals would be to refute the idea of the single viewpoint. To this end, much of my research was being done among feminist literature. I felt it was necessary to take their theories and draw parallels, to show that there were co-existing theories that were equally valid. Unfortunately, I was not able to handle such close contact with feminist theory. The things I read in those books dangerously aggravated my inner anger. The narrow-minded, short-sighted, sometimes deluded claims they made about the male/female conditions would infuriate me, sometimes into an outward rage.

Other research for the book included interviews and questionnaires, which I conducted and passed out on college campuses. They were designed to reveal prejudiced attitudes towards men, and to show that people did indeed make certain demands exclusively of men, and had many exclusive expectations of them. There was also a marked emphasis on revealing the trend toward "unilateral" liberation, my particular pet peeve.

Another research project involved audience reactions to what I called "reversible dialogs." I got some drama students at the college I had attended to perform short dialogs before a dozen or so different sociology classes. The dialogs would always involve some sort of conflict or argument between a man and a woman; either a domestic quarrel, involving jobs, money, children, etc., or some sort of conflict involving concepts of love and romance. The dialogs were performed before half of the classes, and then the players *reversed speaking parts* and performed the same dialogs before the second group of classes. The idea was to show that in any situation involving a conflict between a male and a female, people would almost always sympathize with the woman. The dialogs were genderless in their address; either part could be spoken by either character. The members of the audience were then asked to write down their responses: with whom did they sympathize, and why?

The results of the interviews, questionnaires and dialogs proved (at least to me) that my ideas were correct. They showed that men were truly the victims of prejudiced thought, discriminatory attitudes, in general, oppression. I felt that I had won the theoretical arugment with feminism.

14

Contrary to what one might think, this *shattered* me. I suppose there had been, throughout the years, a part of me that secretly hoped that none of it was true. Maybe things weren't *really* that bad, maybe it really *was* me, after all. Maybe the world wasn't such a bad place. . . .

But the research for the book clinched it. It was all true! I was seeing all of my worst life-long fears coming true before my eyes, affirmed by the people all around me.

The questionnaires showed the basic stereotype: men should be strong, silent, successful, protective, and victorious in all things. In the responses to the "reversible dialogs," a large majority of people, both men and women (usually more than seventy-five percent of each audience) sympathized with the female character—regardless of which part she read—in the dramatized cross-sexual disputes.

Most horrifying to me was the affirmation of the tendency toward one-sided liberation. Yes, said the women I interviewed, women were just as good as men, and could do everything that men could do, and men shouldn't be so presumptuous as to think otherwise; but, when it comes time for someone to risk dying or being physically injured, men should do that, because it's better for those things to happen to a male than to a female. Why? Well, because, it's just *always* been like that, that's why! Yes, men should still have to pay for everything on dates, even though women should have equal job opportunities and equal pay. Why? Because, it's just *common courtesy,* that's why!!! Yes, women should be allowed to reject their traditional sexuality and start being sexually freer in the ways that men have always been, but no, men should not expand their own sexuality to include aspects which have been traditionally considered feminine, because *that* would destroy the old sexuality *completely,* men would lose their masculinity, and that would spoil everything. An astounding number of women expressed these inconsistent views, consciously, casually, as though they saw nothing wrong with them.

I was unable to bear these realizations of my fears. I was in a constant state of anger and disillusionment. I began to consciously hate women. I think I may have started to go a little mad. The narratives in the manuscripts for the book became more and more laced with resentment. I realized that I could no longer trust myself to be objective, either in the research or the writing. In a frenzy, I drove to a far side of town, rented a safe-deposit box, stuffed all of the notes, manuscripts, and books I had used into it, and abandoned them. It was for the sake of my own mental and emotional health. To make matters worse, I finally received some feedback from a couple of different people on the talks I had given at Towson State. It seemed that the general consensus of opinion among the people who heard me talk was that I was crazy. I hadn't accomplished a thing.

It was still 1974. My hatred of my job, on top of all of my other responsibilities, caused me to "drop-out" again. I walked off the job on a busy Saturday morning. The same day, I was hired as a salesman at a camera store directly across the mall from the bookstore.

Then, an amazing thing happened. I married the wife of one of my best

15

friends. Their marriage had broken up suddenly, and the woman and I, who had been friends since high school, started seeing each other as friends. I helped her through the aftermath of her first marriage, and she helped me to calm my own anxieties. The friendship grew into an intimate relationship, and then into a marriage.

This, in many ways, was the most stable period in my life. I went back to college and received excellent grades. I stuck with the same job. My obsession with sexism took a back seat in my life for a while. There was, however, one significant thing about my relationship with my wife of which I was consciously aware. My feelings for her had never been accompanied by the sensation of strong romance, by that feverish, all-consuming feeling of "falling in love."

I had experienced that sensation twice before in my life. It was a beautiful feeling, of course, but it also partly consisted of a need to *serve* a woman, to constantly look after her and do things to please her in a way that denied myself. Both times that it had happened to me, it had been completely unrequited from the start, which had caused me a lot of pain; both times, I chose to play the part of the rejected martyr, and carried a torch for both women for years. This, I think, had helped to fulfill the strange need within me to love someone through self-denial. In any case, I did *not* have these feelings for my wife. This much tamer brand of love had grown out of friendship, and the romantic fever was absent. I couldn't decide whether that was good or bad.

Unfortunately, the old need was still there, because the fever struck me again —this time, through a woman with whom I worked and saw regularly. Once again, it turned out to be unrequited from the start. I had put myself back into the same spot where I had been twice before. It meant pain and anguish, but it was fulfilling some sort of bizarre need. I tried to keep it a secret from my wife, but she could tell from my odd behavior that something was very wrong. She eventually confronted me and asked me if I was in love with someone else, and I had to tell her what had happened.

Understandably, she was deeply hurt. That, along with other factors from both of our viewpoints, caused the marriage to break up. With both the unrequited love and the end of my marriage weighing me down, whatever defense mechanism had been protecting me from my obsession with sexism began to fail. The anxieties returned. *Again,* I dropped out of college. The repeating pattern in my life was not undeniable: unrequited love/acute anxiety over sexism/dropping-out. This time I even entertained thoughts of suicide—the ultimate drop-out—though they were probably not serious. Where in the world was I headed?

Newsweek magazine may have saved my life. In January, 1978, the magazine's cover caught my eye at the grocery store. There was a cartoon of a man washing dishes at the kitchen sink. The caption read, "How Men are Changing." I decided *not* to buy it and read it. I assumed that it would just be like all of the other articles with similar titles, men reaffirming feminist principles: Oh, what terrible chauvinist pigs we've been; now we see the errors of our ways, and we are willing to be good little boys and do whatever the feminists tell us. My wife (from whom I was now separated), however, did read the article, and she called

16

me and told me to read it. "It sounds like the kind of stuff you've always talked about," she told me.

I went to the library, requisitioned the back issue, and read the article. Sitting in the library, I almost wept. Here were men talking about *men's liberation*. Here were other people who *shared my point of view!* Men *needed* to be released from the pressures of their role, the article said, *for their own sake!* The article even mentioned the shock and consternation men had experienced as a result of the women's movement, and the hurt and confusion of "unilateral" liberation. And, as if all of that weren't joy enough, some men had actually *organized,* and formed a men's lib group called Free Men. And if *that* wasn't enough, the group was founded in Columbia, Maryland—*thirty minutes from where I lived*!!!

The article also referred me to a remarkable book: *The Hazards of Being Male,* by Dr. Herb Goldberg. With this book, Dr. Goldberg became the first person to coherently lay out and discuss the male point of view on liberation from the sex-roles. I was overjoyed to see that he discussed the same points that I had been trying to express since I had been a teenager, many of the same points I had tried to express in my own aborted "book." Dr. Goldberg, of course, discussed them with the qualifications and understanding of a psychologist, and with the calmness and objectivity of a person a hundred times better-adjusted emotionally than I. He touched on all the issues: emotional suppression, the pressure to succeed, crime and punishment. . . . He even defined and gave a name to the self-denying, guilt-ridden way that I had always related to my girl-friends. He called it the "Earth Mother" complex, and it was apparently common, almost universal, among men. After reading the article and the book, I began to feel—perhaps for the first time since childhood—*happy.* There were other people like me. I wasn't crazy.

I contacted the group in Columbia, and became a member. I'll never forget the first meeting I attended. I met other people who shared my beliefs. I could express my feelings simply and they immediately understood. I didn't have to spend hours trying to cut through feminist theory, and then hours more trying to explain my own. The years of frustration had not been in vain. I began to feel better about life. I began to calm down.

The acid-test of my re-adjustment to life came recently, when I was at a party. At one point, I was sitting more or less by myself, and I tuned in on a conversation taking place off to my right. It was a feminist discusssion; some women were denouncing the ancient Japanese tradition of having the woman walk behind the man.

"Can you imagine how degrading it is?" one woman was saying to the men in the group, "What a feeling of inferiority that gives somebody?" Everyone in the group solemnly agreed that this was truly degrading. The woman continued, "It's so typical of men to set themselves up as superior. . . ."

In years past, I would have exploded. In years past, I would have impulsively babbled a lot of angry counter-arguments. I would have acted crazy. This time, I just smiled. My mind went back, almost twenty years, to that nine-year-old kid who was knocked down by his father for daring to walk in front of the ladies.

I called over to them. "You're right," I said. "It *is* degrading to have to walk behind someone. Only *I* know that from *experience!*" They looked at me as if I were out of my mind. They didn't have the slightest idea what I meant. I laughed out loud at the expressions on their faces. I didn't bother to explain. The movement was coming. . .they'd understand soon enough.

Sitting there at the party, my thoughts turned inward. I had been through a lot of bad experiences since that Sunday in 1961, but I had come through alive, and was feeling better. I realized that I had lost a lot of self-respect over the years by continually dropping out of things. I had dropped out of schools and jobs. I had dropped out of my own attempt to start a men's movement back in 1973 and '74; and I had dropped out of dozens of other smaller, personal projects throughout life. There was one thing, however, that I had not dropped, not even for a second—my beliefs in sexual equality. I had held onto them through all of the fear and anguish, through the frustration and anger; through all of the trials I had carried them with me, and they were unscathed.

Suddenly, I laughed to myself, because I had just realized an enormous irony. I had done an incredibly "macho" thing. In terms of my sexual philosophy, I had defended myself against all odds. I had staunchly faced every enemy of the cause, and, when defeated by them, had gotten up and faced them again. I had stood up to parents, phys. ed. teachers, the school board, psychiatrists, feminists, a demanding fiance, and had been ready to take on the draft board and the U.S. government.

I had even, in one very important way, stood up to Earth Mother. Though I had needed her and sought after her, I had never relinquished my principles of equality before her. She had cast me out many times for my unacceptable beliefs, and I had always gone back to her, but not even she could make me stop believing in what I knew was the truth. Sometimes, I think my constant attempts to bring her back into my life were born less of a need to serve her than they were of a need to *fight* her.

I had not come through without some battle scars. I was twenty-eight years old, with a menial job and no college degree. I had a lot of residual anger towards women, and a neurotic, irrational fear of war and the military draft which would probably stay with me all my life. My need for Earth Mother had destroyed my marriage, the only healthy relationship I had ever had with a woman. But things were changing, and the potential for things to come seemed unlimited.

The day after the party I drove out to Glen Arm and returned, for the first time since my high school days, to the natural beech forest where I had spent so many hours as a tormented adolescent. I wanted it to be there, in that same place, where I would consummate these new, positive feelings I was having about life and the future.

Standing there, alone with the smell of the earth and the leaves, my mood was lifted into a kind of transcendental state. I felt like I had lived through some sort of epic ordeal. It was spring, and there were wildflowers in the woods. I was reminded of one of my favorite quotes from Robert O. Petty: "We, too, are children of the glacier. . . . And when we find the first wildflower in the spring, we sense that primal knowing—somehow, we too, survived the glacial snows."

We, too, are children of the sex-roles, a social glacier suspended for a thousand thousand years in the midst of our evolutionary environment. I have lived through some of the snows. I have seen the first flower of the new, liberated spring, and it is a group called Free Men.

The glaciers of sexism are receding, and the human race has, again, survived.

SOME THOUGHTS ABOUT MY FEELINGS

Dan Logan

My emotions are the most authentic expression of who I am.

But until recently, I couldn't even identify my feelings—much less express them.

I was overly intellectual—always trying to understand, afraid of feeling. I retracted, distracted, and abstracted myself from the emotions, because I found them intractable.

Wearing my career as though it were armor, I was uneasy whenever personal subjects came up in conversation, and relieved when the subject changed to work.

I couldn't make delicate distinctions about what was best for me, because I operated like a robot—responding to what I thought other people wanted. Playing the part of the "real man," I expended considerable energy in shielding myself from being like a woman.

There was a whole different person inside my skin.

I was so isolated that I thought I was the only one in this predicament. (I had only my fantasies and images to tell me what other people were like.)

My men's group showed me that it's unusual for a man to share his inner life.

I'm relearning how to be friends with men.

A member of my men's group gave me his business card and asked me to call him at work. I considered this very "forward." Overcoming my discomfort took a week.

I enjoyed that conversation and subsequent ones with him. But I still get the jitters before phoning him just to talk.

I told my wife about a very intimate men's group meeting. She said, "Did it ever occur to you that you're the only member who doesn't know the other guys are homosexuals?" None of them were—but I didn't sleep that night.

A second night of insomnia followed my viewing a film about male homosexuality, designed for medical students, at a sexuality workshop. The tenderness of the gay men's kissing and caressing in bed shattered my comforting illusion that they only have sex in public bathroom stalls.

Being around an attractive woman makes me feel small.

Emotionally naive as an adolescent, I had little sense of myself—who I was or what I wanted. I thought I could get that sense by attaching myself to a woman.

No wonder I was afraid of girls—they meant so much to me. And if I ever got close to one, I risked losing what little sense of autonomy I had.

Whenever I had a crush on a girl, I'd have fantasies about being a sports or music superstar who would impress her. I would hit the three-and-two pitch with two out in the last of the ninth to win the seventh game of the World Series. In these fantasies, I always saw myself as implacably strong and in control—impenetrable by emotion.

The fantasies became more and more fantastic, and they were endless. But no matter how much I pumped myself up with them, the fear never went away.

I learned to rate women from one to ten and fantasize about using them sexually. Reducing women to numbers and objects seemed to help me control my feelings about them.

In this respect, I didn't need to be more "sensitive" towards women. I was already more sensitive than I could handle.

My most appealing sexual fantasy is that I'm overwhelming a woman—as much as dealing with a good-looking woman overwhelms me.

I was emotionally inexpressive with women. It was too frightening to consider opening up about my feelings with them.

Also, I expected them to read my mind—one of my mother's functions when I was a baby. When I was hurt or angry, I'd pout, hoping a woman would come to my rescue. She almost never did.

In the past few years of my happy marriage, I've had little urge to chase women—and this worries me. Am I still a man?

Developing awareness of my emotions in therapy has been psychological detective work.

I've stopped ignoring the signal sensations—changes in breathing, muscles tightening, heart pounding. Then I've tried to match them up with feelings— which at first was a guessing game.

Untangling is often necessary, since I'm frequently experiencing multiple emotions. And my feelings are likely to change from moment to moment.

I've been jotting down notes about one such case of the mysterious feelings —those surrounding reading books.

As with a new friend, I fear commitment to a book—reading the early pages skeptically, doubting the premise and style.

Often I'll read a passage, but the information doesn't register. This seems to represent fear that the book will change the way I see the world—all good books do.

Once I give in to the book's attraction, I read eagerly—until very near the end. Then I slow down, leaving fifty pages or so unread. I've formed an attachment to the book and don't want to miss it.

I've been reading the last fifty pages lately—anxiety is less compelling when you're conscious of it.

When I get uptight, I'll try to figure out what I'm feeling. This usually disengages the tension, like opening a combination lock.

Like big game, my emotions attack when wounded.

I reject the rejection: I don't care what you think, I say. What I mean is I do care.

It's OK for a man to show anger, but not hurt.

My emotions control my behavior.

I've learned that suppressing them doesn't work. They'll only express themselves in a different—often destructive—way.

When my intellect is pushing me to do something I hate, my bad back lets me know.

Growing up, I considered myself an extremely sensitive boy. I used to brood about that—it seemed unmanly.

Now I think a boy can be both strong and sensitive.

There are two ironies about my emotional isolation.

The first is that I thought I was being tough. Actually, it takes courage to confront emotions. I didn't have the guts to be emotional.

The second irony is that I attempted to control my emotions by not dealing with them. In reality, I couldn't control them, because I didn't have the slightest idea what they were.

I used to be preoccupied with success; now I'm more absorbed in self-discovery. My chief focus used to be outside myself; now it's inside.

I've come to the conclusion that I have a right to my feelings.

I didn't consider learning about my feelings "liberation." I see it as a reconciliation with my humanity, which my forbears must have bartered long ago for "manhood."

LONELINESS

Jerry Medol

It's not simply a fact that if you're a worthwhile person, then you won't have to start over in your life. It's not simply a fact that if you're a good person, then nobody'll split on you. And it's not simply a fact that if you're doing the best you can, it's gonna be okay. Doing the best we can may have nothing to do with what the other person needs and may have nothing to do with the way other people see our validity. We ourselves, including me, get trapped in the dilemma of making a choice between keeping faith with what we believe, or enduring the loneliness of not having people in our lives with us. The experience of loneliness is like a mini-death . . . it's a small experience of dying . . . it's like being without, not having a sense of my own validity, not having other people in my life to help make it okay.

ONE OF THE MOST MADDENING TIMES OF MY LIFE

Robert A. Sides

One of the most maddening times of my life has been the last three or four years. Not only have I been driving myself crazy in a search for the "perfect career," but I have felt, to paraphrase Alice in her Wonderland, "furiouser and furiouser." What really has hurt me has been the almost universal response of men: anger is "wrong," "too negative," or *"counterproductive"*—to use the corporate euphemism. Many times what this means is that you won't score with women unless you pretend to be happy all the time. So I have felt pretty much alone these years, and not a little worried about the circuits in my bio-computer, and the health of my heart.

Feeling alone and lonely only compounds the frustration and pain of repressed anger. It's hard to keep walking down the road alone, feeling you have an ice cube up your ass, like a prophet-pariah.

A lot of men, even the ones "up" on all the current pop-psych books, self-help courses, biofeedback fads and "support" societies are nevertheless content to deal with women in old-style ways. That is, the female as passive prey and the male as impassioned hunter (or "pray-er"!). The usual footnote is that these men don't believe for a moment in women's liberation. Instead they pretend to, humoring the women long enough to fuck them—and then split. It's a cynical worldview, perhaps, but in some ways it's more realistic than mine. And certainly the macho men get laid more, and the women *do* respond to their macho machinations.

Then there are the men who are themselves becoming preliberated females; that is, self-effacing, second-class citizens in the oriental tradition. Daunted by today's (untested) superwomen, these male feminists exude the same kind of self-hatred exhibited by those religious masochists who say, "Help me, O Lord, for without Thee I am but a dollop of shit." But there is no converting the True Believer; changes, if they come at all, must first begin *inside* a person. Unfortunately for all-too-many men, the inside is enemy territory, filled only with danger and best avoided altogether. So, with no gut-level radar, the mind works overtime and conflicting messages get intellectualized. If such emotionally dessicated men remain dedicated to the view that women are Madonnas and males their lowly lackeys, no "rational" talk will dissuade them. They need to "go out of their minds" and into their feelings. . .apparently a too-terrifying leap of faith for most men.

But then I think of the women who say they seek a "vulnerable" man; and run from him in terror when he appears! The *emotions* they seek in men are slight tears forming in the eyes of a junior V.P. as he sees the sunset on Roman ruins, where he has flown them both on his company tab. The women definitely don't want the man who is sobbing out of control, boogers cascading down his cheeks, because his world no longer makes sense. *That* display is all-too-real and presumes upon her to be the supporting one for a while. Too adult a task for her.

Real emotions, we read, are not very neat or polite. Too often, we are coerced into expressions so tame that the body still retains the tension after the verbal declaiming. The same people who tell you to lower your voice when you're angry, to not flex your muscles in "mock battle" displays (that, in fact, *keep* animals from *real* combat!), are also the ones that are forever shocked to learn that the universally acknowledged "nice boy" down the street is also the heinous chain-saw murderer, the mass killer, or random sniper. Why don't we learn? From Reich to Rolf to primal therapy to ulcer/heart attack experts, the message is the same; unexpressed emotions turn inward and ravage the body. Soon the ulcerated patient can't "stomach" his job any more and the chiropractic patient *feels* his marriage is too much a "pain in the neck" to bother saving. We glibly say that the mind and body are one; then we separate them. You jog your body like you do your dog. And you verbalize your feelings like a computer; saying "Ouch," with all the compassion of a computer, as your dog is run over by a truck. Perhaps if we sometimes lost our tempers, if we lost our patience a bit more, we'd have less stress-sick male patients.

Yet we have men with "extra muscle" in a culture that prevents normal use of them in daily life. We are too often all-revved-up-with-no-place-to-go. Sedentary businessmen must turn themselves off until they get to the squash court. Even then, the emotions stay buried while the body gets worked out. (If pure exercise were the only key to mental health, ditchdiggers would be gurus!) No wonder we men lose so much spontaneity! Every spontaneous outburst becomes a source of economic or social punishment. So we often deal later with what happens now. For example, maybe premature ejaculation is not "premature" at all; maybe it's one way for "gentle" men to finally say, physically, what they can't or won't say psychologically: "Me first, this time!"

Personally, I'd like to see a National Emotions Week. I'd like to see people really let go: scream at bosses, tell kids to take a leap, and even call the president and insist he insert a bat where the sun can't shine. I'll bet the supposedly "endless" outpouring of feeling would last only three days, people would feel 100% better, and real change would finally begin.

But in reality we deal with symptoms. Behaviorists try to analyze our problems into separate steps and then eliminate them sequentially by assorted "techniques." So, stuttering finally stops, and six months later an eye tic begins. Or we try to "understand" it all away, "mellow" people to death with "active listening." But there is never any real change—one that doesn't require constant vigilance lest the dreaded "feelings" surface again.

Men must learn to vent anger and pain and sadness in *emotionally* satisfying ways or forever deal with the consequences. Which is worse: to be thought of as a bit "loonie" or to stay Mr. Nice Guy who just "happens" to beat the wife and kids every day? And do women *really* prefer to run away from men who yell at them into the arms of stoical men who might rape them?

Guilt has been called "anger stood on its head." Perhaps it is also anger staying *in* the head, not being expressed vigorously with body, soul and voice. Men are supposed to suffer nobly, silent, and endlessly. . .until enough tension builds up for the next war. Slapped, we are to turn our cheeks. Baited, we are to restrain ourselves. We are to be modern-day, "detached" high priests, somehow above "petty quarrels." Transcendental.

So, while we are giving Ph.D.s to our heads, we give grammar school training to our bodies. Even those giving Ph.D.s to their bodies usually abandon their feelings at the kindergarten. When emotions arise they shunt them all to their brains, hoping their bodies won't notice. Only the body is not so stupid. When anger comes up, for example, and they try to absorb it intellectually (or so it's hoped), ulcers grow and blood pressure soars. Sometimes, too, they will blindly punch out, having neither the restraint of the martial artist, nor his full commitment to action. More often these men flounder in-between. . .and suffer doubly.

Now, men are *thought* to be allowed anger in their limited masculine emotional repertoire, but it's just not true. They are however, "allowed" to be hostile or violent or guilty provided they accept being called Animals or Bastards or Wimps. Real anger is apparently too positive a feeling for mere men. And we won't even mention true pain or sorrow. That, we are told, is too, too taboo.

What happens to the man with no tears? He becomes a sterile desert, dried up in the very regions he needs to sustain himself. And women, by and large, do *not* help him. Women have a very strong conditioning effect on men, despite their wish to be seen exclusively as Victims. Despite their *words* about wanting men who can cry, most women *act* quite differently. They judge a crying man to be out-of-control, a loser, someone unable to cope. For a woman needing a stronger daddy-figure to protect, decide, and provide for her, this man with tears is Bozo.

My experience has not shown that women want much more of a man than a wolf in sheep's clothing. The "honesty" women want of men seems to be the laundered kind. The other honesty is too real. She wants to know that though

24

you've slept around, you'll settle down with her; that your career questions are only, "How much money can I make?" not, "Do I want out of this Rat Race?"; that while you mouth non-violence, and would never hit her, you will kill any man she baits, protecting her "honor."

No wonder men tally numbers. If you can't have quality, at least have quantity! The truth of the liberated woman is as reliable as the "Immaculate Conception." There is so much we are expected to be unilaterally responsible for. It's unfair. It's upsetting. There is *much* for us to be angry about. And I prefer to be obnoxious, and off the wall, and a son-of-a-bitch about it rather than swallow feelings and have it lead to tensed muscles, headaches, stomach cramps, ulcers, colitis, and ultimately colonic cancer. . .emotions going, literally, from the head to the *other* extreme. Whether it's the Big "C" of cancer or the Big "H" of heart attacks, we men should be deciphering the obvious message: "Give us emotional liberty. . .or you'll give us death!"

We must encourage each other to be more viscerally expressive, to take chances. Too often we start out wanting this, but then read "just one more book" and end up putting so many conditions on the "right way" to emote that we never really do. It's like trying to have the book-perfect orgasm. We men have read too many books. What we need to do is to start acting crazy for a while, and begin trusting ourselves. Better to talk out loud to yourself in a public place and become free of group pressure, than to always be cautious and never jump in the water.

I agree with those who say impulsiveness has its drawbacks. But men are hardly too spontaneous. Let women cry or scream a little less. Let *them* read the books. We need to throw more tantrums, get into the place where the "wild things dwell"—emotions! *We* need to leap more before we look. Our hesitation has been our painful loss.

So forget all that repressed "nurture-nagging" and just start to trust that nature. The life you save must be your own!

Chapter 2:
About Our Sexuality

HIDDEN FEARS

WISING UP TO PENIS SIZE:
Does She Want Six Inches of One of
Half a Dozen of the Other?

Francis Baumli

Over the last decade, more than one wag has said, "Contrary to Freud, it's men, not women, who suffer from penis envy." Of course we all know that men worry about penis size. But there's one question I'd like to raise with people and get some straight answers on. Namely, does penis size really matter to women?

Yes; I know that people who think they are sexually sophisticated are going to say, "Look; don't go bothering us with your private insecurities. Hasn't that myth been laid to rest?"

Well; I wish it were that simple. But you see, I'm very contaminated when it comes to this worry. I grew up exposed to a lot of conditioning to the contrary. I heard all the stories about "giving her six inches" when I was at an age—maybe 13—when I didn't have half that much, even though I was already supposed to be getting my quota of "ass." I read the porno books about men with huge penises, and about women going into hysterical adoration at the sight of such organs. It seems, if memory serves, that the women were always moaning, "Give me more! Give me more!" while the man's gargantuan penis was already so far up her I was worried it might plug a heart valve.

Then there were the locker-room episodes, infrequent to be sure, but spelled out clearly enough to leave some rather indelible impressions. The men who matured quickly always had bigger penises, while some of us didn't have much more than a wee-wee. And what was worse, the damned wee-wee in question always seemed to shrink and get smaller when we were nervous about its size —which was just about all the time.

Later there were the jokes. For example:

"The man, whose wife had recently divorced him, went to a restaurant alone to have dinner. Across the room he saw his wife with her new lover. Instead of leaving, he sat there for the next hour, fuming and cursing, tossing down one drink after another. Finally, unable to bear it any longer, and with several drinks already under his belt, the man got up and went over to their table. 'And how,' he asked sarcastically, 'does your latest man here like your old, worn out pussy?' She looked up at him coolly and replied, 'Just fine, once he gets past the old worn out part.'"

Of course, there were sayings to the contrary that might have been reassuring. A few examples are:

"It's not the size of the wand, it's the magic in it."

"It's not the size of the meat, it's the rhyme of the beat."

"It's not how deep the well is, or how long the rope, but how you dangle the bucket."

These aphorisms never gave me much comfort. Not being a well-endowed man, I carried quite a few insecurities into my early sexual experiences. Most of the time I didn't say anything about my insecurities, and it seemed that the women I had sex with didn't have any problem with my size. But occasionally I talked about the question with lovers, and usually heard pretty much the same stock answer: "Size doesn't matter at all. It's stimulation to the clitoris that counts."

Of course that's what all the pop-psych literature had told me, too. But I felt suspicious of some of these answers. Partly because they sounded so contrived —as if the women were saying what they were supposed to say, rather than what they really felt (sic).

I began feeling suspicious for other reasons, too. For example, a woman I was very close to was once telling me about one of her early lovers, and how huge his penis was. I felt insecure—even jealous. I asked her if size matters, and she said that no, it doesn't. Yet, I couldn't help but notice the earlier appreciation in her voice when she was describing the size of his organ.

Was I being overly sensitive? Or just picking up on something she wasn't quite willing to own up to?

Then there were some very explicit things other women said that didn't help either. For example, shortly after getting married, my first wife told me how her mother jokingly asked about me, "Is he well-hung?"

After my divorce, a woman I was in love with was telling me about a former lover. Her exact words were, "He was so exciting. He had the most beautiful, golden body! And the biggest penis!"

And one of my female friends quit dating a man, "Because he's so little you can hardly feel it."

There was another woman friend I was considering being lovers with, until an evening I spent with her and some of her friends. She said about a man we all knew, "God; I don't see how any woman would want to sleep with him. His penis is so small." I asked her "how small?" and was rather horrified when she spread her hands to show a length that was larger than mine. Needless to say, I

27

decided to avoid ever exposing myself to this woman.

Also, a good male friend told me how his current lover likes making love with him because his penis is so much larger than her former husband's.

Another woman friend commented about a former boyfriend, "His penis was so small I didn't even like him to be in me. Fortunately he could do fabulous things with his tongue."

And in an encounter group, which was made up of an equal number of men and women, three of the five women bravely confessed that while penis size makes no difference to them in lovemaking, large penises definitely have more aesthetic and erotic appeal.

Then once at a party, a woman—with two M.A.s behind her name, and a university position—upon hearing me allude to the topic, began calling me, "Weensy," in a loud voice, teasing me unmercifully for the rest of the evening.

Also, there was a bad situation with a female counseling psychologist I worked with. A client had come in wanting to deal with insecurity about his penis size. It turned out that this counselor thought that eight inches was average, because her husband's penis was about ten inches long. She was giggling about the matter with another female member of the counseling staff, adding a story about how a few years ago she went to bed with a man whose penis was so small, "I couldn't keep from laughing! It was so funny I just couldn't help myself!"

And there have been instances when I've heard women joke about men with "pencil dicks." Only once could I get a woman to elaborate on this preference. She said, "It's diameter and not length that counts. I mean, the ones that are about the diameter of a cigarette really don't stimulate me. It takes a large-diameter penis to do that."

"What's a *large* diameter?" I asked.

"Oh, you know, just...uh, large," she laughed. My further questions only embarrassed her. The end result was that I didn't collect any information.

All in all, my experience with the true confessions of women I've come in contact with suggests to me that the opinion among women on whether or not size matters is just about evenly divided. I've wanted to talk to men about this issue, but so far there have been only three men who were willing to openly discuss it. I brought the topic up to a men's consciousness-raising group I was in a few years ago, and they immediately broke out in laughter. And quickly went on, one by one, to claim that it's something they *never* worry about, one man even saying, "God; if I were any bigger, I think I'd be embarrassed."

Was I the only one bothered by such questions? But then, something about that initial laughter left me wondering. It seemed a little too quick, and a bit too loud for me to believe there wasn't some insecurity behind it.

Maybe the most troubling thing about this issue is the constant barrage of mixed messages we men get. On the one hand, men say they aren't insecure about penis size, but jokes and quick denials of insecurity make such claims suspect. And while many women say that penis size doesn't matter, all a man needs is a set of ears to hear many women contradict this view.

Hoping for some new light on the issue, I eagerly read part of an article called, "Body Parts" in *Esquire* (June 1981, pp. 42–43) by Priscilla Flood, their executive editor. She recounts a situation where she was gathered with several women friends, all of them tipsy on wine, when she broached the big question. Here's the response she got:

" 'Of course it matters,' they chorus. 'Bigger *always* feels better.' "

But Ms. Flood is not so easily convinced, and probes the question more deeply. . .she then gets an array of explanations which to me sounded like the women were trying to beat an embarrassed retreat from their true feelings.

One woman, after the initial response, goes on to say that size matters only when you don't love the man, or only when, " 'you tend to look at him more objectively, more as a pleasure machine.' "

What do we men conclude from this? That size counts only as long as we are sex objects? How comforting.

Another woman says that size doesn't matter, " 'once you're reassured that he can function okay.' "

In other words, don't worry about size; just worry about getting it up.

A third woman laments, " 'I remember being terribly disappointed with a man I knew because his penis was small. I really liked him—loved him, in fact —but the sex with him never was very good. He was inhibited by his size even though I did everything I could think of to make him feel he was good in bed.' "

I read this statement over several times, and I never could quite figure out if the only problem was *his* insecurity, or if her initial "terrible disappointment" had been, or had caused, part of the problem, too. Which causes me to suspect that if I feel confused about this whole matter, then a vulnerable man making love with this woman for the first time very well might have been even more confused. Not to mention insecure.

And a fourth woman opines, " 'The only time it really matters is when you're [first] getting to know a man.' "

Oh really? If that's the case, how are you ever going to convince him that it *doesn't* matter later on?

And a fifth: " 'As long as a guy's within the normal range, it just doesn't matter.' "

Which brings us back to the original question. What the hell is normal? And if nobody knows—neither men nor women—then being told that we're okay if we're normal doesn't clarify a damn thing!

Ms. Flood herself seems somewhat bewildered by the double messages, and concludes the issue by saying, "I leave you with the assembled company's first response. *In vino veritas?*"

So where *do* you go for reassurance? Out of fairness, let me say that many women I talked to have vowed that no, it really makes no difference at all. And I believe them. But a lot of women have said that it *does* make a difference. And many women, while saying that it doesn't matter, gave me the impression that it does. Often it seemed that they were just saying what they thought they were supposed to say, because they didn't want to admit that they might have feelings to the contrary. After all, they wouldn't want to be accused of being sexist or of objectifying men's bodies. Maybe they would rather we believe that only men are worried about things like breast size or penis size.

I'd probably feel less threatened by women's concerns about penis size if they were more up-front about what they think. But this constant ambiguity of, "Why, we never think of that, because it's the clitoris that needs stimulation," coupled with, "Of course it matters!" makes one wonder who is telling the truth, *if* anybody is, or whether these women are even sufficiently in touch with their bodies and desires to know what they really want.

Regardless, it's a question we're all very concerned about. I've seen such a confusing variety of statistics about the percentages of men and women who are, or are not, concerned about penis size that I won't even bother to here list the data. It's all so inconsistent it ends up being meaningless.

So that leaves me pretty much where I began. It remains a question. A question that is broached coyly by the sex magazines over and over, but never gets answered because it seems that no one knows how to collect the data. Or maybe people are afraid of the answers. What, after all, are we insecure men going to do if we find out that a goodly percentage of women *do* care about size?

And a question broached just as often by the physiology and anthropology books is, of course, what really *is* the normal size. Again, data varies so much that not even a secure six-year-old boy would trust it. Often the lengths are given in centimeters instead of inches—even in the American books—as though the authors would rather you go scratching with a pencil than discover the truth. Or, maybe they've guessed that you'd rather not find out the truth. I mean, what would you do if you found out what you've suspected all along—that, oh my God, mine *is* smaller than average! Or, what would happen to those lusting ladies (let us hope they are few) should they find out that the average really *is* smaller than they thought, and that henceforth they're going to have to start dealing with the "new scarcity."

And, oh, yes; one final point: It's very easy to write a witty, somewhat scatological article about the problem, isn't it? But you, the hungry reader, want something more. You want some personal testimony.

Okay; here goes. Yes; I feel very insecure about the size of my penis. I've only in the last three or four years been able to sometimes believe that maybe it's close to average in size. Although, of course, I'm really not sure.

I do know that it goes through a lot of variations in size. It tends to be small when I'm tired, smaller when I'm nervous, big when I'm horny, bigger when it's hard, and even bigger when I'm about to come.

Whew! How was that for a testimonial? Courageous, huh?

"Not enough!" comes the snide accusation. "Come on Baumli. 'Fess up. How long is yours?"

All right. What's there to lose when I have so little to start with? By last measurement, it was, when hard, exactly 5⅞ths inches long. (*Please* editors, print this right, and don't make it smaller than it is!)

I told a male friend—one of the three I've discussed the topic with—about this. He replied, "Yeah; and I'll bet you had the ruler jammed back into your body as far as it would go when you measured it."

"Well; not quite," was my (honest) comeback.

But he wouldn't tell me how long his is.

I did go on to tell him that I was afraid to buy some of those new, "Snug-Fit" prophylactics: *Made for men who are just a little bit small. Or who want a more sensitive fit.* The fact is, I admitted, I was afraid I'd discover that even they were too large.

As for diameter, well, it never occurred to me to measure this little attribute until the writing of this article. So—if it won't offend my more squeamish readers for me to acknowledge this—I admit that I stopped midway in the writing of this very sentence to stimulate myself to an erection and pull out the ruler. If memory serves me correctly—I say correctly, because I was distracted from my initial purpose while doing the measuring and went on to do something else—it was 1½ inches in diameter at the base of the shaft, 1¼ inches across at the middle, and 1⅝ inches at the head.

There. I've done it. I've brought my penis out of the closet and am finally proclaiming (certainly with no immodesty or pride) that it doesn't even measure up to six inches.

But one final confession is in order before the denouement. I have to admit that were my penis an inch longer than it is, I probably would never have been concerned enough about the topic to even bring it up. I also have to admit that were my penis an inch shorter than it is, I probably wouldn't have had the nerve to write this article.

Actually, it was pretty hard writing this article as it is. But I read somewhere that as a man gets older, his penis gets shorter. So I thought I'd better get mine on record while I still have something left to write about.

THE FLY
(A True Story)

Robert D. Nagle

It was a strange evening. Maybe its strangeness goes beyond that evening. There were four of us. Dolly is my woman friend, companion, bailer-outer from all kinds of trouble, etc. Then there is Charlie—tall, thin, mild mannered, quiet, tolerant and intelligent—altogether a loveable human being. And of course there is Pushy. She had been nicknamed Pussy since childhood, but when I got to know her well, and when I recognized the term as a woman's crotch, I changed it by inclination to Pushy, and it stuck. Everyone knew her as Pushy, by name as well as by actions. She had a charm all her own. And it was both loud and pushy and entirely lovable to some of us. She was five feet five or so, blond, gray-green eyes, voluptuous to some, charming to others. And, I am thoroughly sure, obnoxious to many others.

I will not describe both Pushy and Dolly physically, because to describe one of them is close to describing the other. Most people who did not know them,

31

who saw them together, thought they were sisters. In a very real sense they were sisters. (Don't get all excited. This is not one of those cases where I mistake Pushy for Dolly. De Maupassant already did that—and he did it well). I am Abe, big, dark-haired, Russian.

Charlie and Pushy used to take turns keeping me up all night. One would take a nap while the other talked. Then they would switch. But Pushy didn't really need any help from Charlie. She could carry on a monologue all night long without trouble.

We all loved each other. I still do, for that matter. But not like that. We were not into each other's pants. We were just very close. And each of us had a great deal of love for the other three. We planned things together. And we lived many many wonderful interludes together. Any of us could get as obnoxious as we felt like without fear of offending any of the others.

Okay, to the story. It was a warm, lightly breezy summer evening in rural Missouri (that vacuum between NYC and SF) when we parked the car off the country road and walked over the ridge to Charlie and Pushy's home. Charlie was moving lazily on the patio swing, a beer in his hand.

"Hello, Charlie," I say. "How the hell are you?"

"Hi, Abie," he says. "Want a beer?"

"What are you doing?" I ask.

"Waiting for you," he replies. "Sit down," he says, and he gets up. "Want a beer, Dolly?" he asks.

"Sure," she says. He walks in to get us a beer. The house is built into a hill, so that one side of it is visible, and comparatively open. This gives them light and easy access.

I looked around at the available chairs, then sat where Charlie had been sitting on the swing.

Dolly says, "Abe, behave yourself. Charlie was sitting there. You get up and let him sit down."

To which I reply, "Aw, shit." I remain in my seat. Charlie comes out of the house, hands us each a beer, and finds himself a seat. He is keenly aware that I have purposely taken his seat—I can tell by the slight smile at the corners of his mouth, almost imperceptible. He will no doubt find adequate means to get even later on. But by then he'll be drunk, kindness will overcome him. And he'll reject the idea of getting even.

Enter Pushy.

"Hey Abie, what the hell are you doing? Fuck you, ha ha. Hi, Dolly, how are ya? Hey, hey Charlie, go get me a beer." Yakity yakity—as stated, no brass band needed.

"Hi, Pushy; Hi, Pushy." Both of us.

Charlie returns with Pushy's beer. She is seated in the chair he got out of, one arm leaning on the edge of it with her hand open so Charlie can put the can of beer in it.

She and Dolly are talking about guys who can't get it up, all the while laughing. Charlie and I look out over the beautiful view.

Dolly says, "Maybe it is psychological more times than not."

"Hey, Charlie, did you hear that?" Pushy shouts. "Maybe that's your problem. You fucking nut without a hard-on. Maybe you just ain't got what it takes upstairs."

Charlie continues to stare out into the beautiful view. If he is hurt by what Pushy is saying, he doesn't show it. The almost-grin plays on his face.

"Jesus Christ, Pushy. Let up on my friend," I say. The light is growing dim. "Why, he's got a hard-on right now."

"That's not a hard-on," Charlie says, "that's a beer can."

Dolly bursts out laughing. She says, "Use it anyway, Charlie. She won't know the difference."

"You can fuck me," I say to Charlie. "I won't make fun of you." Nobody laughs. Fucking nerds.

"Thanks, Abie," Charlie says.

Three beers' time and Pushy starts the push.

"Hey, we gotta go to this bar in town. I just found out about it. It's a really neat place, Abie. Come on, let's go. Let's party. Come on you party poopers. Hurry up! I'm leaving."

Reluctantly, but not entirely so, we pile into the car. Charlie drives.

We pull up in front of this beer joint that has to be well over one hundred years old in a town of about the same age.

"Well, shut the thing off," Pushy shouts at Charlie. "Let's go. Let's party."

We enter the old wooden structure. The inside appears about like the outside —worn and somewhat neglected. There is a pool table over to one side in the rear, and a long bar across the length of the room on the other side. A very few people, primarily local farmers, are scattered here and there.

"Let's have some beer here!" Pushy shouts as we amble toward the bar and take seats near the far end.

Pushy gets into a conversation with this seedy character who says he lives down by the river in a tent—claims to have been in the military—or maybe it was prison he was talking about—for the last few years. He says he's thirty-seven years old. "That's nothing," Pushy says. "Abie here is thirty-nine."

"Thanks, you fuggar," I say under my breath.

"That's right," she says loudly—as she says everything, "he's thirty-nine years old."

"That so," this guy—Carl is his name—says. They are obviously trying to out-do each other. "Well," he says, "you ought to see my tattoo."

"Oh, yeah," she says, "I'll bet you've got a goddam tattoo."

"I have," he says, "right on the head of my dick."

"She-it," Charlie says, laughing from the periphery.

"Lessee," Pushy demands. The guy stands directly opposite her behind the bar. They are down at the far end of it. She leans up so she can see over the bar. Charlie wanders off to the pool table.

"You really want to see it?" he asks conspiratorily. "It's a great big fly, gets bigger and bigger."

"Hey, Dolly," Pushy says, "this guy claims he's got a big fly tattooed on his dick. Wanna see it?" Dolly looks off at Charlie over by the pool table laughing.

"Great big? A great big fly?" Dolly laughs.

"All right," Carl says. "I'll whip it out right here if you don't believe me."

"Aw shit you will!" Pushy challenges.

The bartender, a not much, looks over and smiles.

"Look here then!" Carl says. He unbuttons his fly and pulls his nine-inch dick out of the opening. He pulls back the foreskin and, lo and behold, a fly is tattooed on the head of his penis.

Pushy's eyes bug out. She laughs, and does not take her eyes from it. "Goddam, it is a fly," she exclaims. But her eyes are not bugging out this way only because it's a fly she's staring at.

"Hey Charlie," Pushy hollers, laughing. "Get over here." She has to coax him. He finally leaves the pool table, cue in hand, and comes over to the bar.

"My God," she says. "Look at it!" She is obviously getting hyper, even for her. Finally, unable to hold it back any longer, she exclaims, "What a dong! Don't you wish you had one like that, Charlie, you puny little fuggar? No wonder you can't make it," she says.

"Want to step outside?" Carl asks her, his enormous dick still in his hand.

"Sure," she says. "It beats the hell out of Charlie's two-inch pea shooter."

"Want to play pool?" Charlie asks me, trying his best to ignore the putdown.

I head for the pool table. "Sure!" Pushy hollers. She grabs the cue and heads for the pool table. Pushy and I start playing pool together while Charlie and Dolly talk at the bar. The game takes forever. The only pool player I know who is worse than I am is Pushy. She leans so far over the edge of the table her breasts get in the way of her shots.

Carl, who is still at the end of the bar with his dick in his hand, finally gives up. He tucks his tattoo back into his pants and then wanders out of the place. Before the night is over the four of us are good and loaded.

During the entire trip back to the cellar house, Pushy keeps on riding Charlie, comparing his dick with Carl's, etc.

Finally Charlie cries out in pain. "Nobody loves me!"

"I love you," I say.

Later that night we are all about to hit our respective sacks. I walk by Charlie and Pushy's bed on my way from the bathroom. I throw a typical greeting at them in case either is awake. "I don't care if we are love birds. I hate you, I hate you, I hate you. Let's get the fuck out of here." No response. I head for the couch to join Dolly, who is also sound asleep, but somehow I end up on the floor next to it.

The next thing I hear, sometime in the middle of the night, is a row. By the time I am awake enough to realize what's going on, Charlie is sitting at the kitchen table putting his rifle together. Then he jumps up suddenly, points the rifle at Pushy, then throws it down on the table and heads for the door, knocking Pushy down on the way.

"Where you going?" Pushy asks. "It's four-thirty in the morning!"

"I'm going to go where somebody loves me," he replies, dashing out the door.

That was the last I saw of either of them.

JEALOUSY

OPENING

Jed Diamond

We played together like three little kids, my wife, my friend, and me. We laughed and joked, went out to eat, had ice cream together. It felt like a family, playing with the brother and sister I never had. When Lindy suggested we all go camping together I was excited to deepen our family ties. I wasn't prepared for the pain of what followed.

We found a campsite and spent time lying out in the sun and walking along the river. Later in the afternoon Lindy and I got into one of our philosophical discussions about "open marriage" and what it would be like if we were sexual with someone else. Maybe someday it would be right for us.

"I hope you'll let me know if you and Lenn ever decide you want to be sexual." Like in 20 years or so I thought to myself.

"We do," said Lindy brightly.

"Oh really," I said calmly, feeling like I'd just been kicked in the balls. "Well, let's talk about it."

Lenn arrived and the sharing began. They both wanted to make love with each other, but didn't want to hurt or threaten me. I admitted that even though we'd been talking about it for some time, I was shocked and fearful of the reality of the situation. But on the other hand, I felt this might be the time to experience the reality of what we'd been talking about for so long. We'd been feeling like one big family and maybe this was the time to extend the sharing to sexual intimacy.

Lenn left us alone and Lindy and I walked and talked. She seemed so loving and supportive. I really felt her love for me and her desire not to hurt me. She said she felt ready to open up our relationship and have sex with Lenn. She felt it would enhance our relationship and not hurt it. The more we talked, the more open and expansive I felt. My fears gradually calmed down.

We agreed that I would stay with the kids in the tent and she and Lenn would spend some time in the woods, and then Lindy would return and spend the rest of the night with me. It all seemed so romantic and noble. "Dutiful, liberated husband stays with the children while wife and friend make love in the woods. She returns after 20 minutes to say it was nice but doesn't at all compare to making love with you. Husband and wife make mad passionate love the rest of the right, and the three friends walk off into the sunrise the next morning."

In the tent alone I found my heart pounding wildly. "I'm not sure I made the right decision, but there's no turning back now. I'll practice the new meditation I just learned and it will soon be over. Lindy will be back here with me and our relationship will be firmer and more loving than it has ever been."

The night was quiet and dark, the tent was warm and cozy and I felt comfortable hearing the children quietly breathing. But then I began to hear sounds from outside, quiet at first, then louder. "Oh God I can hear them. She's getting fucked and loving it. I'm scared. I'm going to lose her. She'll want to stay with him and won't want to come back to me."

But then it quieted down, except for my heart which I couldn't seem to slow down. In just a little more time and I'd be OK and it would be over. "Shit, there it is again. She's calling out his name. Please God, make it stop. Make it go away. Make me not hear it. . . . Quiet again. How long has it been? Has it been 20 minutes or two hours? She's got to come back to me now."

I heard them again, the screams, the moans, and it was driving me crazy. I couldn't stand it anymore. All I could see was my wife slipping away, and I was a little boy again and my mother was in the next room and I heard them making love and I knew she was going to leave me and run off with him, and I was going to die.

"They're trying to drive me crazy and I've got to get out of here. I've got to get away from the sounds. I've got to make them stop. But I can't. If I go out and stop them I'll never know if she would have come back and if I break my agreement to wait here I'll lose her for sure. God, more sounds, over and over and over. Won't it ever stop? Oh God, please stop them, please, please, please."

But it didn't stop and I had to do something or go mad. I ran out of the tent in the dark calling, "Lindy, Lindy, I can't take it anymore. Please help me." They called to me from the dark and I followed her voice to their love nest, sobbing uncontrollably. They scrambled into their clothes and Lindy held me close. I felt safe. But then I realized I was in the middle of their love space and the place smelled of sweat and sex and I wanted to spit on them and leave. But I didn't have the guts and I hated myself for my weakness.

We sat together in the back seat of the car, three lost souls, each wrapped in our own thoughts, facing the grey morning.

DEALINGS WITH A DOUBLE STANDARD

Brad Hollister

The most important personal statement I can make about my dealings with female sexuality is that I do not yet have my act together. I believe, in fact, that this is the *only* interesting statement I can make, so I'll make it at some length. Afterwards, some commentary.

I'm thirty-seven years old. My sexual history is fairly standard for my generation. I was raised in the Midwest, in an urban setting that felt rural. It was on the fringe of the Bible Belt. Literally nothing was available on the AM radio dials on Sunday except for hollerings about damnation and such. As I was growing up, I can remember three or four instances of sex information talks from my parents, whose forced attempts to be natural made me nervous. Most of my information and attitudes came from the streets, reading, and the general milieu, which was, in the current terminology, sex-negative. I went to a high school for exceptional students, intensely competitive, where academic performance was almost an obsession. Your social standing was dictated by your grade-point average, and being competitive, I ended up with the supersmarts. Very few, if any, of my peers had sexual experiences in high school. There were occasional rumors that a few guys were getting laid across the river, but we dismissed this as just talk. No one had ever gotten pregnant in my high school and there was certainly no hope for such an event in the elite crowd that I traveled with.

I dated and even made out a little bit, which was quite an accomplishment. The girls in school all dressed exquisitely. It was difficult to imagine them being sexual, in the same way as I felt sexual when I fantasized or masturbated. I would have sworn at the time that those girls didn't defecate. Sex, in short, had unreal qualities for me.

Sexual reality became sharpened somewhat during my stint at college, where sexual experience was almost a graduation requirement. There was an awful lot of messing around, and three or four years of that will liberalize a person. However, my own college sexual experiences were limited by my fear of getting a woman pregnant (this was in the pre-pill era), and my knowing that, being the responsible fellow I was, I would feel obligated to marry in the event of pregnancy.

My first sexual experiences occurred with Barbie during my senior year. I was very much in love with Barbie and wanted to marry her. During the middle stages of our relationship, when I was still a virgin, Barbie told me that she was not. She had experimented with a boyfriend once at age nineteen. That bothered the hell out of me. I felt emasculated by the fact that she had more sexual experience than me. Her behavior did not fit with my pervasive double standard and my romantic notions about women, especially the one I wanted to marry. I stewed and fretted badly for a couple of months, and then got over it. We did not, however, get married.

I did get married the next year, to Katie, whom I met the summer after graduation. It was a common-sense decision. I knew I'd be working my tail off in graduate school, with strong needs for companionship and support but with little time for dating, so I wanted to be married. My reasons for wanting to marry Katie, with whom I did not have much of a romantic attachment (nor she with me), were that she had a wonderful ass, was unusually supportive, and was a person I respected a lot. I am surprised that, being the romantic and impulsive person that I am, I could ever have made such a careful decision, though it was probably the best decision I ever made.

When I got married, and for our first three years, I accepted without question the traditional ideology of marriage, including sexual fidelity. In retrospect, I am again amazed at myself for this show of passivity. I have since then literally made a living out of intellectually dismantling all sorts of social institutions, but it did not occur to me, those first few years, to scrutinize the institution of marriage.

At any rate, the normal marriage thing lasted only a few years. At the end of that time, I found myself excessively horny. My sexual relationship with Katie was satisfactory, but other women began to look exotic. Also, I fell in love with other women once or twice during that time, tried to deal internally with the limitations on relating to them which my marital ideas imposed, and managed to become miserable in the process. I was having problems. I talked to male friends. They encouraged me to have outside affairs, but pointed out that my doing so might well mean that Katie could do so too. I didn't like that. Katie was a virgin when I met her, which pleased me. Her sexual exclusivity with me seemed a large part of the basis of our relationship. I told her so several times during those initial years; I remember saying that if she ever had intercourse with another man, I was sure it would shatter me.

"It feels okay for me," I said to my male buddies, "but not for Katie."

"But that's a double standard."

"I know it's a double standard."

"Well, how can you justify that?"

"Moral ideas don't have to have rational justification. My sexual double standard is just as inherently defensible as an egalitarian one. I don't need to defend it," I replied, contortedly.

"I'm not comfortable with that idea."

"I'm not comfortable with this conversation."

"Obviously."

I resolved my dilemma by having two secret affairs. They were neat and sweet and did wonders for my self-esteem and outlook on life. I also did some thinking about marriage and open relationships. I gave my wife a couple of Rimmer's novels, which were, at the time, virtually the only available literature on open relations. My own experiences, plus absorbing some of Rimmer's utopian ideas, helped me to cope with the idea of Katie going to bed with someone else. A while after my second affair I told her everything, in a pleased-with-myself manner. She blew her lid, told me she couldn't handle any more expeditions, and asked me to stop. Which I did. But I encouraged her to do some sexual exploring on her own. She did not react well to that idea. Prospects for utopia were dim.

The turnabout came almost a year later, when Katie gleefully announced that she had initiated an affair shortly after our talk, and had continued it without my knowledge to the present moment. I was astounded. I knew that she enjoyed keeping secrets, but this was of major proportions. Another immediate reaction was my increased respect for her; I had no idea she was capable of starting an affair and managing it secretly.

I did not experience any jealousy or ego deflation. I was shaky and shocked for a day or two, but that soon passed. I knew the guy—David—slightly, whom Katie was seeing. My social sensibilities were not shocked by the fact that David was our gardener. Nor was I disturbed to learn that David was a much better lover than I was. Katie's affair increased her erotic value for me. We tried out a few things David had taught her.

There followed several years of immersion in open relationships. I experienced only slight and occasional jealousy, and was downright smug about my togetherness. We were beginning to talk to other people who were into open relationships, and I knew that most people experienced considerable difficulty moving through the opening process. Katie sometimes did, though I didn't, with minor exceptions. I would get slightly uptight when she got independent and didn't check out how I felt about her activities. And I once or twice felt a territorial twinge when her male friends got possessive about her. When I got intensely involved with a friend named Yvonne, I remember feeling threatened by the idea of Yvonne's having any other sexual contacts. But she did, and I handled it well. On the whole, my problems in dealing with my wife's or lover's sexuality were minimal.

And I remember some joyfully liberating moments. After her relationship with David, Katie had a long dry spell. She was distraught. One night she came home very late from a weekly encounter group. I was already in bed.

"Where have you been?" I was very curious.

"I've been fucking all night with Steve! We just started kissing after the group, then made love. It was really neat! It made me horny, and I want you to make love to me."

No secrets this time. Katie was excited, aglow, alive, and joyous. She jumped in bed on top of me and we made love. I was so glad for her.

I remember camping trips together, we and our lovers; groups of us lying quietly in bed and talking; my bringing a female friend to our house one evening when Katie was with Don, who is now her present husband. The bedroom door was closed, and in the middle of the living room floor we were amused to see two separate but very close piles of clothes.

I think it was relatively easy for me to accept Katie's sexuality because I was married to her and knew her so fully as a human being. There were other factors, of course. I was the one to initiate outside contacts; I had ideals; our relationship, though open, was communicative and carefully structured; I never felt intense romance with Katie. But, in the main, I experienced her so intimately as another person that her sexual desires seemed only natural to me.

I felt very pleased with the ease and thoroughness of my sexual liberation. I had exorcised the Midwest. I even went slightly public about it. I started teaching a sex class (I'm a university professor). I also became active in the leadership of an alternative lifestyles organization.

Our experiences led eventually to new and incompatible visions. For me, our lifestyle was terribly exciting. I wanted to move on to trying a bunch of us living together in a group marriage. Katie eventually decided that she liked me better as a friend than a lover, found our lifestyle stressful, with continual packing and unpacking of overnight bags, and wanted to spend more time with Don. We had an amiable divorce. That our marriage was sufficiently stimulating and growth-producing to encourage us to dissolve it is not, for us, a sad story.

Which brings me to Dennie, who is an altogether different story.

39

I met Dennie during my last months with Katie, and gradually fell intensely in love with her. Dennie was twenty-eight years old, and had not been married. She was physically attractive, bright, sociable, sweet, and sexually diffident. Especially the latter. It took me six months to get to bed with her. Six months of sending flowers every week, lunches, trips together, visits. . .without pressure on my part during that time for sexual intimacy. I am extraordinarily persistent in all things, but in Dennie's case I should get gold medals.

Our physical relationship, once started, developed slowly. Dennie seemed very physically shy and inexperienced. She was nervous about being intimately touched. She had never made love during her period. She had never made love during the daytime or with the lights on. And so on. I applied the same nondirective tactics to the development of our physical relationship as I had to getting there in the first place, and we slowly developed the closest, most exciting sexual and sensual relationship I've ever experienced. I was delighted. Dennie was positively blooming.

When Katie and I split up, Dennie and I continued to see each other. After a few months, we moved in together. We decided to be monogamous for a while and develop our relationship, and perhaps eventually get married. During our courtship, Dennie had not, to my knowledge, been seeing anyone else. She showed no interest in other male relationships. Our communication in the present seemed very good. Dennie seldom talked about her previous involvements. She said once that she had no sexual experience until age twenty-four, which I could easily believe. I had the general impression that she had been sexually intimate with only two or three men before she met me. I didn't much care.

Then came the fatal moment. Dennie had been getting romantic letters from a guy named Robert, who was a prominent sex researcher. She was nervous about my reading them. I finally demanded to know what was going on. The ensuing dialogue, to be repeated many times over the next few months, went somewhat as follows:

"I met Robert at a convention one night, and had such a good time with him that I stayed and had sex with him. He's been writing me ever since."

I was stunned. . .not only by the fact that Dennie had had a one-night stand, but that her manner of speaking about it was so clipped and matter-of-fact.

"I don't understand. Did you really like Robert?"

"No, I didn't like him very much. He's so vain. He talks about himself all the time."

"Well, why did you go to bed with him?"

"He was attractive, and I was lonely and horny."

"Have you had many other experiences like that?"

"Yes, quite a few. I've gone to bars quite a bit, and hustled guys. You have to look after your own needs. I was honest with them. I would tell them after I brought them home that I was just using them, and they said they were just using me, and we both knew that would be it after the morning."

"What made you decide whether or not to sleep with somebody?"

"I'll sleep with anyone who's attractive. And if they're persistent enough, if they ask two or three times, I'll go home with them. Sometimes I would be the one to call a guy up and ask him to come over, and we would just ball."

"I don't understand why you did so much of this. Did you have strong sexual needs, or what?"

"No, I just didn't see any reason why not. I figured if boys could do it, I could do it, too."

"Have you had such experiences while you were going with me, that you haven't told me about?"

"Yes, there was Mick and Larry. I met Larry traveling in Mexico. He wasn't interested in me and I wasn't interested in him, but we did have sex together one night in his camper."

"If you weren't interested in him, what did you have sex for?"

"It was his birthday. And he asked me to."

My God.

I had never been so shocked, hurt, and angry in my life. I had been with some sexually active and outspoken women, but had never heard of such behavior, or heard sexual experiences talked about so flatly and coldly. And to hear all this from the sweet, shy girl I was in love with went through me like a knife. I felt stunned, betrayed, hopelessly confused, hurt, angry, separated from reality.

I didn't show Dennie any of this. In the first place, I didn't want her to think I couldn't accept her. In the second place, I am very much the strong, silent type who needs to be self-reliant, especially about working out my feelings. In the third place, I was a self-proclaimed sexually liberated male. I had my pride to think of.

I worked on my feelings in privacy for a month or two. But I couldn't cope at all. I could hardly think of anything else. I tried to image what her experiences had been like, and ended up with recurrent nightmarish fantasies that made me break out in chills and sweat. I pounded the walls to relieve my anger. Every time I saw an attractive male on the street, he became a sexual threat. Every time I saw a camper, I got a sinking feeling in my stomach. My whole attitude toward sexuality suddenly changed. The Midwest was resurrected. I felt uncomfortable even watching two people hold each other, because I pictured Dennie doing so indifferently with someone else. I didn't like women or sex any more. Dennie's touches and lovemaking became filled with confusion for me. I found pleasure in her body and touch, but not without pangs that made me grit my teeth. Her touches didn't feel as intimate any longer. I imagined they had been easily shared with everyone, and became angry. I believe my worst feelings stemmed from violated proprietorship—apparently any male could have access to Dennie's body by asking two or three times. I felt my intimacy with her had been devalued.

I was doubly upset at my inability to cope with my feelings. I had always been able to recover equilibrium in a day or two; I was dismayed that this problem was taking longer. I became depressed, and finally shared my feelings with Dennie. I'm sure keeping everything to myself and stewing so long made matters worse.

My best defense, in previous cases of jealousy or double-standard uptightness, had been to enter as fully as possible into my lover's experience with another person, to share her needs and joys. I asked Dennie to try this with me, to share more fully. That didn't work; it merely resulted in variations on the above dialogue. Although her experiences were not dissimilar to sexual behaviors I had occasionally engaged in, or that I had accepted in Katie when we were together, they somehow seemed alien to me.

After a few months of little progress and Dennie's pleading, I made the ultimate sacrifice and went to therapy. That was a hard nut to chew. I tried avoidance and relaxation techniques to stop my fantasies and desensitize my feelings about past behavior. That helped, but not much.

I had never felt so bad for so long. I am generally an upbeat guy with a sense of humor who snaps out of things quickly. The only comparable negative experience I've ever had was facing my comprehensive exams in graduate school, which gave me stomach aches for months. This was worse. I was chronically depressed, my self-esteem had dropped, and I didn't like the way I was feeling and behaving with Dennie. That was difficult for a guy who is used to liking himself. Dennie and I agreed to try working things out for a year, and then split if there wasn't enough progress.

We separated around the end of that time. The precipitating incident was seeing one of Dennie's past lovers in a supermarket. I came home in such an agitated state that I threw my wallet and keys through the side of the kitchen cabinet. There are still two holes in the cabinet. I was shocked at my own violence, and decided to leave.

There is still some kidding around the house about the day I threw my wallet and keys through the cabinet. My current roommate, who does not believe that such a mild-mannered guy as myself could get violent, and who also does not believe that it is possible to throw leather through plywood, asks me frequently to be sure to let him watch next time I throw things. It is interesting to me that I am pleased by the physical prowess of the act. Maybe I could have played for the Yankees.

The astute reader, or maybe just about any reader, will have been suspicious about the discrepancy between my initial impressions of Dennie and her own callous self-descriptions. A clarification would be helpful, although, since this article is about my dynamics and not about Dennie's, it will be brief. Dennie's personality and behavior were exactly as I had first perceived them. Her bald and cold self-descriptions were distortions which resulted from the following: 1) Occasionally men had conned her badly to get her to bed, then left her. She had dealt with her resultant deep hurt by becoming matter-of-fact when rationalizing these episodes to herself or others. 2) She had not been accustomed to communicating about her sexual experiences to anyone, and certainly not to her lovers. She felt inadequate about communicating in this area, and so initially chose not to communicate with me at all. And when we did communicate, she had only the mannered vocabulary of her singles culture as a descriptive medium. 3) She imagined that I would feel better about our relationship if she minimized the importance of all her past lovers.

It took me a year and a half to figure all that out. I was a little dense. Figuring it out has helped me recover my former mental outlook and sexual attitudes, as has separation and being with other women. Dennie and I have of course experienced significant growth as the result of our relationship; but the cost seems much too high. The fact remains that my residual or not-so-residual hang-ups about double standards and negative programs about female sexuality have made an untidy botch of the most loving relationship I have ever experienced. I feel very badly about this. I do not blame Dennie or my parents or my high school or the Midwest. . .or myself. I would like to shape up, however.

To end the story on an upbeat note, I can say that I'm rather back on my feet. Dennie and I still love and see each other. She has had two other intimate relationships since we separated, which she has shared with me and which I feel fine about.

One of them has been a renewal of her relationship with Robert. Over the past year Robert and I have talked over the phone and corresponded, and I have formed some good feelings about him. I've felt no jealousy about him, sexual or otherwise. He came in town to visit Dennie one week, and we met each other. I spent an evening with Robert, then part of the next evening with Robert and Dennie together. I've seldom liked anyone so well and so quickly as Robert, or met anyone so similar in intellectuality and temperament. He seems to have similar feelings about me.

The first evening Robert shared with me some of his problems with a double standard and with female sexuality (as a noted sex researcher, he's supposed to be sexually liberated also). The second evening Robert and Dennie and I talked about our mutual relationships, and about our limitations on our capacity to love each other. It was honest and gentle and loving. Robert and I hugged each other feelingly when he left. That was a high.

I have had no homosexual experience or interest. As possible lovers, men are just too hairy. But there seems to be something about a man honestly sharing with me an intense love for the same woman that brings out my tenderness and physical feeling for him. That could be the biggest high yet.

I want to close by sharing some general perspectives and feelings about this business. I've had some important learnings as a result of my experiences with Katie and Dennie. The learnings go something like this:

I am no doubt going to continue to be surprised by life and surprised by my own reactions to it.

I am not *always* going to like myself, and I am going to have to live with that fact.

Life, as the psychologist Richard Farson says, is a dilemma to be experienced, not a problem to be solved. I'm not going to like it. Or, if you'll excuse mixing in Jack London, I am a biological organism, I am human, I am a piece of yeast upon the ferment, and I am prone to diseases, jealousy problems, and grouchiness from lack of sleep.

I doubt that I'll ever totally get rid of my double standards or occasional jealousies. I do think I can learn to keep such feelings from crippling my relationships, and instead use them as an index to what I'm feeling.

Such learnings, and my story in general, may not strike anyone as insightful or new. And indeed they are not. It's merely that I've been obtuse and arrogant.

43

This is somewhat significant because, as the world sees it, I should have my act together. I am, after all, a university professor with a doctorate in psychology. I teach a class in human sexuality. I have been a visible leader in the alternative lifestyles movement—publishing, speaking, leading organizations. I think these activities create the impression that I've surmounted human frailties in the sexuality area, which must make some people feel envious and inferior. The fact is, I share the same human frailties as everyone else.

I have an agenda for my life which has only one definite priority. I'd like to be able to love my mates thoughtfully and gracefully, without jealousy or possessiveness, sexual or otherwise. . .I think also without rules, obligations, expectations, or insecurities. Other concepts of love do not seem meaningful or liberating to me. It's something to work toward.

I sometimes get impatient with my men friends, or those in the men's movement in particular, for avoiding issues of double standards and sexuality. I don't think there's anything more important or more scary for us to face. I also get impatient with those who claim biological impediments to eliminating sexual jealousy and possessiveness. I rather cynically attribute these sentiments to lack of successful personal experiences. I will attest for my part that we're in for a struggle, to put it mildly. Let's get on with it. We're going to have to go through that struggle, and it's well worth it. I have sometimes been to the mountaintop, and seen the valley beyond.

I DON'T WANT TO BE FIXED

Jed Diamond

Little by little, I was beginning to release the image I had of myself that demanded that I be able to handle anything, including my wife being sexual with others. In the past a man of strength would knock her around if she even thought of being disloyal. The new man of strength, I believed, would learn to conquer his anger, subdue his jealousy, control his confusion and fear.

To fail at this was to acknowledge that deep within I was a monster living only for myself. The new dragon to slay was this beast within. Yet another voice was beginning to say, "What's wrong with being weak?. . .what's wrong with saying I want a woman who is sexual with me only?"

Lindy wanted us to go to a sex therapist. If we could just get that part of our relationship fixed up, she was sure everything else would fall into place. It was a very strange experience for me. We tried to pick someone who was "enlightened" and could understand all our open relationship issues without judging one of us as being bad or wrong. The last time we had seen a therapist, the man seemed to have a subtle bias towards men and had a difficult time relating to Lindy, particularly her outside sexual activity. We picked a woman this time, hoping to find someone more objective. Lindy thought she was great. She praised Lindy for her courage in following her own instincts and developing her sexuality in a way that was right for her.

This time the little voice in me was getting stronger. "What about me, what about my feelings, what about my sexuality? Is this the price I have to pay for living in a society biased in its advice on behalf of men? Now I'm expected to say 'OK, now it's your turn to walk on my head, to hell with the way I feel, if it works for you it must be right.' Well fuck that shit. There's got to be a better way than going through life trading off who will play the role of victim to your mate's oppressor. I'm getting tired of looking deeper and deeper inside to find the problem that I've got to get fixed. I'm tired of being fixed."

SEXUAL ANGER WITH WOMEN

MALE ANGER AND MALE SEXUALITY

Robert A. Sides

Women don't really expect or accept our anger. They aren't ready for it. They think all emotions are *their* exclusive territory. They'd have us believe only they can get angry at Brooke Shields and only because of yet-another image hyping women as "sex objects." Never mind that a woman—her mother—is directing the media butt-blitz. Never mind that women are the buyers of the pants. (Of course they don't like to talk about the *panting* men they hope to attract by such pants). What irks me most is the fact that women cannot believe men would get p.o.'d seeing this 16-year-old sexpot yank them around who then whispers, on talk shows, that she really is still a virgin!

So why is she sticking her ass in our faces? I mean, don't taunt us unless you're going to deal with the heat, too, sister! Imagine the feminist furor if a man dangled a promotion in front of their career-oriented eyes only to whisper off stage, "Pssst! I really don't have any jobs to give them, heh! heh!"

THE MALE PERSPECTIVE—THE MALE EXPERIENCE:
View From a Man in His Fifties

Ardus

Sex is very important in my life but means little to my wife. A large part of this is my fault because of my apparent lack of showing love. I sometimes feel I should have never gotten married, that I was not meant to be married to one woman. However, these feelings have nothing to do with the deep love I have for my wife. She is a good woman, a fine mother and a loving grandmother. I don't deserve her but I am very glad that I selected her to marry and bear my children. She does, however, have many sexual hang-ups, some the same as I was taught thru' religious beliefs at home. I do try to discuss them with her but she has been unable to discuss them freely with me, so we get nowhere.

To really have fun in sex I find that when I know I am pleasing the woman then it is really great. It is even greater when the woman is able to give of herself freely without hang-ups. If these two things are present then sex will be great. I know that I can never be a one-woman man sexually.

PROSTITUTION

YOU PAY FOR EVERY PIECE YOU GET

David C. Morrow

(The male situation is so bad it merits an article like mine, which is intended both as a desperate prescription and a Swiftian essay on the relations between the sexes. It is very gentle and tolerant compared to the vituperative rantings of feminists who demand mass castrations and free handouts.)

You always pay for every piece you get. You probably first heard this aphorism when you were in junior high school, and still don't want to admit that it is the profoundest truth about the condition of the American male. It's as cruel a fact as military slavery, and far more basic and pervasive; sometimes war is necessary and it always ends, but your payments for love's illusion leave you eternally desperate even in your most intimate moments. You ask yourself again and again: is there a way out?

The way girls started growing attractive in junior high school promised to give the pleasure of companionship a new dimension. Just a passing glimpse of a breast, a shoulder, or a smooth thigh could take away your breath. The lines of calves and the silken suppleness of a neck, scents of powder and perfume, made you want more.

These new sexual feelings were given broader social meaning within the context of a childhood of both live and media examples depicting femininity as mysterious and inexplicable. These examples forced male "politeness" to yield to girls' whims and immaturity, and ended up causing us to feel worthless compared to females. To enjoy their mere presence, you now realized, you had to be less than yourself. Now you had to learn how to put an apparent status and economic value—i.e., women on their pedestals—before your hopes for self-fulfillment.

You also realized that girls had all the advantages, including that of your **not** being allowed to say they had any. And this realization, given its built-in silencer, ended the opportunity for any real honesty with females. Instead you had to accept, or at least live with, the female myth that women are socially and mentally disadvantaged (another part is that they are superior) and that they needed your protection. Believing or pretending to believe those myths provided access to girls; and since you competed with other boys for them, you not only had to accept these myths, but also, to keep from being a loser in the competition for women, you had to avoid sharing opinions you might have held which would have gone contrary to these myths.

Male-female relationships could still survive. Sort of. There were those steady relationships with girls who really did like you (some of these relationships became marriages) and who also wanted to be sure they always had a partner to show their score in female competition. Most of these steady relationships broke up, usually when the girl, her genuine feelings still strong enough to give her an appearance of confused irrationality which could soothe her conscience, gain sympathy, and keep open the possibility of a later reconciliation should she "change her mind," succeeded in interesting a boy with more prestige than her steady.

If you didn't marry young you learned to protect your feelings by hiding them. If you liked yourself, your knowledge, however tacit, that women rated you in terms of your material value, combined with their ambivalent behavior, caused you to despise them, but hide your contempt from yourself by intense idealization of the feminine nature.

At some point, of course, women learned well that they could use you through sex and by manipulating your idealization; as a result, they were threatened by any insights you might have had into their motives. Meanwhile, other men derided you as "queer" if you showed interest in any female characteristics not strictly anatomical, unless, of course, you were "in love," in which case your interests were private. Thus, you could be outwardly aware only of women's sexual possibilities, and learned to take their individual natures only as proof of female irrationality, since as real persons they deviated from the idealized image you had to consider them in terms of.

Under these chaotic emotional circumstances, how else could you seek companionship, intimacy, and tenderness except through sex?

You came to know a few girls who would have sex; at first they seemed very unlike those who avoided sex. But later experience would prove that they weren't free, but rather neurotically stuck in preadolescence. If you got involved with one of them you ended up fixing her car, doing odd jobs around her place, and taking up the slack she'd leave at work or school, all in exchange for sex that became less and less frequent as she continued making new men friends. By the time she had you doing favors for the guy she really cared about —a coarse, brutal fellow who insulted her and slapped her around, which behavior signified high status to her primitive soul—you were trying to tell yourself that it was your high level of self-respect which allowed you to endure her insults.

And there were some women around who sold sex. They were the subjects of many of the first dirty jokes you learned; and if you'd already visited a couple of them, you knew that they were pretty much like the other girls you had casual sex with—the only difference was that with these you paid money. And the game was simpler; in fact, their only game with you was business: you paid one of them, she did what you asked, with whatever apparent feeling you bought or she chose to show. And that was it; no strings.

What you really wanted, though, were genuine feelings and shared experiences. But you didn't get these from neurotics, hookers, or women to whom you presented a false appearance of accomplishment to impress them. As a result, sex remained the only admissable route to closeness. And since a steady supply of closeness is always desirable, after awhile you joined the ranks of other married couples.

You probably weren't aware of all the problems and responsibilities marriage would involve, but as long as the two of you weren't totally incompatible, it seemed worth the trouble. You could fall naturally into your long-programmed role of providing for her, long accustomed to the imperious female assumption that she deserved the world on a silver platter.

But your wife—the woman to whom you gave your life and labor—most likely took a different view. She was always alert for more rewards, knew that there were scads of willing men, and if she didn't already know it when she took you down the aisle, she soon found out that whatever she does, you are the one who will be held legally and financially responsible for the consequences of her actions.

That means she can sidestep female competition. Maybe she can't land that rich, powerful or glamorous foreigner all women really want, but she can get the same quantity of benefits by having you and a couple of other ex-husbands running the support treadmill. Maybe that's why she soon dumps you.

So, now, after you're dumped and on your own, what postdivorce lessons are you going to learn as you sit brooding in the shabby little efficiency which is all you can afford? What do you conclude as you struggle to get over her smug cruelty, the glow of pride radiated by judge and lawyers, the scarcely disguised joy of other men? Well, you could do the expected and customary thing and blame yourself. You could reaffirm your belief in the myth of female irrationality to avoid facing the fact that you lost out to more successful men, and worse, that the person to whom you turned for companionship and affection was all along coldly evaluating and using you as an economic resource.

Or you could examine your experiences to discover the common factor in female behavior toward you. You could use what you find to help yourself and other men. You already know what you're looking for. You've known it at least since junior high school, even though you've couched it in a dozen rationalizations. What compels a girl to accept one date and not another, compels a woman to file half a dozen divorces in ten years, and takes another woman up onto a sleazy stage where she fellates donkeys? In his autobiography, *My Wicked, Wicked Ways,* that rich glamorous foreigner, Erroll Flynn, stated that money is women's prime motive. If *he* didn't know, who would?

It should be apparent now that a woman's motive as a female is to trade sex and companionship for men's property and status. Women's competition for the most desirable men, or those men's property, causes them to adopt various strategies, overt and covert, cultural and personal. Women thus are just as promiscuous and hedonistic as men; but their strategic, money-oriented sexual behavior is what gives them ultimate control over male sexual behavior.

Now you see into the so-called mysteries of the female mind. Why, for instance, do women marry jerks and pricks despite their insistance that they want thoughtful, gentle, considerate husbands? With the covert motive supplied, the rule is this: only if a woman has several suitors of the highest socioeconomic standing which her body and personality can attract will she choose the one who is most gentlemanly. But if she has as suitors a prominent asshole and a gentleman of lesser economic means, she will choose the asshole. Later she can easily divorce him, sue for alimony, and still be maintained in his economic lifestyle.

So what do *you* do? Well, just think back to how the Victorians, those venerable fellows whose wisdom is unjustly maligned, advised a young man to get well established in his career and buy a house before getting married so he could adequately support a family. That's good advice today. A man who waits until after he is established before thinking about marriage will have the economic bait to attract quality females, but since his properties are in his name and were acquired before marriage, a woman's major temptation to divorce is absent. Too, a job steadily and conscientiously performed by a man before marriage will be fairly secure even in the event of a divorce, since the boss would blame the wife for any disruption.

Waiting also lets female competition give you a better selection of women. Since females aren't as particular as men about their mates' age, you'll be able to marry a young woman without much trouble if that's what you want. On the other hand, available women your own age know that men often prefer younger women. Hence, if they're smart, women will take advantage of opportunities for being friends with males, realizing that friendship and understanding are men's real needs.

But if you're wondering what to do for sex while you're getting yourself set up, keep in mind that great-grandpa had the answer to this, too. The Gay Nineties were famed for their abundant, often luxurious whorehouses. You'll find plenty of the same, in one guise or another, in the yellow pages. There are still plenty of those professionals from whom you learned a lesson or two, ladies who gave you what you wanted for pay, no games, no strings.

If you have negative feelings about seeing prostitutes, then maybe you still don't understand the situation. Venereal disease and legal embarrassments may concern you, but don't bother feeling guilty unless you use a weak or desperate person against her will.

But don't worry—in this day and age you aren't using a woman against her will in a whorehouse. Anyone who suggests that you are is trying to shift to men the responsibility for a situation originating in women's desire to live off men. Some women choose the strategy of marriage as one permanent investment or as several successive investments whose gains add up, while other women prefer payments in cash, goods, or services from many partners. Either way, whether under the guise of marriage or in the aboveboard transactions with a prostitute, it adds up to the same thing: women selling sex. You wonder which type of woman is the real whore. Regardless, you will find that the prostitute who *admits* she's a whore is a lot more trustworthy when you're making the transaction.

So if you really understand the game and consider the sexes equal, you won't feel guilty or even ashamed. Prostitutes choose their life strategies, many are in fact married and use both strategies with or without their husbands' knowledge, and the responsibility for it is theirs. You didn't make them do it, they want your money, and if the situation doesn't meet their psychological needs you can be sure they'd never have gotten themselves into it in the first place.

By visiting prostitutes you will in the long run save money, enjoy much pleasure, and improve your ability to deal with women. When you date a straight woman, you don't know what or how much it's going to cost you because she's trying to get the most she can for as little as she can give. You may or may not get sex, and you know, given the odds, that she probably won't make a suitable wife for you. But you do know that you'll pay a prostitute, and you know you'll get sex, and you know there's a possibility she might turn out to be a suitable companion. Unlike their arrogant sisters, these ladies will be polite, tolerant, and usually willing to meet your needs because they want your business and have no legal or other lasting hold on your money.

During the years you spend getting economically established, you will become acquainted with a variety of women. This will enable you to observe many different female types, drawing useful observations, and losing any fears or self-consciousness you may have. With women demythologized in your mind, you will see them as persons.

When you marry, you will be better able to make your wife happy and respond to her problems. She will be perfectly glad you're experienced, especially if she thinks that of all the female rivals out there, she's the one who finally succeeded in making you monogamous. It's a situation she'll be reluctant to jeopardize, because it flatters her ego at the expense of the people who really matter to her, i.e, other women. And she needn't ever know you planned it that way all along.

PROSTITUTION AS MALE HUMILIATION

Herb Goldberg, Ph.D.

Feminists have expressed the idea that prostitution is an exercise in male chauvinism, one that results in the degradation of the female wherein she is simultaneously being exploited by her customers, her pimp, and the police.

While there is merit to this argument, there is still hardly a more humiliating, self-annihilating and less satisfying experience for a man than a visit to a prostitute, an experience that thoroughly reinforces the hateful self-image of himself as a despicable animal.

To be sure, not all prostitutes are the same. Some are more sensitive, supportive, and emotionally attuned than others. However, even under the best of conditions a man tends to leave this experience with his worst conscious thoughts about himself as a person confirmed.

A friend of mine was describing his first sexual experience, which happened to have been with a prostitute. He was fifteen years old and living in a time when sex with a girlfriend was still not common. The prostitute he went to was not a high-class call girl, nor was she a streetwalker. Appointments were made by telephone and the customer rang the apartment buzzer three times as a signal to let him in.

I came into her apartment on West End Avenue in New York City. There was one older dude sitting in the kitchen and another guy waiting in the hallway. She was in the bedroom screwing but came to the door. She told me to wait in the kitchen with the older dude. We sat there waiting our turns and trying to avoid looking at each other—obviously we both felt ashamed to be there.

Twenty minutes later she called me in. She asked me for my ten dollars first. After I got undressed she washed me like a baby with soap and water and then put a rubber on me and believe it or not started to blow me with the damn thing on. I couldn't feel a thing. About two minutes later, at the most, she asked me if I was "ready" yet because she couldn't spend all day with me. Before I could answer, she got on her back, spread her legs and put some saliva in her vagina to lubricate herself. As soon as I was inside she started going "ooh" and "aah" trying to convince me, I guess, that I was really turning her on. Meanwhile, she wouldn't even let me kiss her and she wouldn't let me put my fingers into her. She said that she was too sore. In the middle of her "oohing" and "aahing" the telephone rang. She answered it while I was still inside of her and casually made another appointment for that day—she even gave the guy instructions on how many times to ring the bell.

When she got done with her phone call she asked me impatiently if I was "finished" yet. When I said "no" she got pissed off. She told me that I better hurry up. This was only about nine minutes and one phone call after I had come into the room. Finally she got me to come by removing the rubber and jerking me off. Then she hustled me out of the room and made me put my clothes on in the hall.

Listen to Laurie, a twenty-three-year-old prostitute, who expresses the contemptuous attitude that many men will receive during a visit to a prostitute. Her techniques were described by a writer who had interviewed her:

She insists that she be allowed to wash a man whom she is about to sleep with—"With me it's none of this 'You go into the bathroom. . .and wash yourself' stuff, 'cause they don't do it. They'll sprinkle a little water and say they're clean," she says contemptuously, "but they're not." It's hot water and soap with Laurie and she maintains that it is indeed necessary. . . .

Following her clinical ministrations, she magically clicks on the role of a John's 'long lost lover.' That's part of being a hooker: "You have to act like you're in love with them and tell them how good it is. . . I have no sensation or feeling, no nothing. . . . Most of them make me sick, though," she says.

The manner in which Laurie perceives her customers is indeed humiliating to the male.

Not surprisingly, a good proportion of the customers of prostitutes are not single men with no women but married men. The married men who frequent prostitutes are all too often men who are trying to live up to the demands of a "meaningful relationship" and who have become super self-conscious in their inhibited sensitivity, "gentleness," and restrained behavior with their wives. They are starved for a moment of spontaneous, nonobligating, aggressively free sexual abandon. They go off and buy it, but the price is further damage to their already negative male self-image.

The answers to this problem are, of course, fairly complex and difficult to sort out. Many men have been so negatively conditioned and inhibited that they no longer seem to be able to be spontaneously sexual in an intimate relationship. This harks back to early memories of being called "horny" or feeling like an animal because they aggressively lusted after a "nice" girl. Surely, the changes in the male psyche will require a revolution in the evaluation of his sexual patterns and desires.

PORNOGRAPHY

WOMEN AND PORNOGRAPHY

Robert A. Sides

Of course the women who pose always say, "We only did it for the money." A curious defense. It's supposed, I guess, that men do whatever they do for their health (or, as it turns out, their unhealth!) and never the money. And the feminists' defense sounds a lot like a prostitute making big bucks and then damning the institution for being solely sexist and in *male* terms! Would we listen to a tycoon who damned Big Business from his yacht circling Tahiti? I mean, heifershit! Women make choices to play the sexual game, too, be it in porno, prostitution or what goes for "regular American" versions. They get something from it. They create it as much as anyone else does. To poo-poo their active involvement away is to assume no man is ever born with a rusty spoon in his mouth, no woman with a gold one in hers. Women have choices, whether they want to be responsible for them or not.

Men who have been cowed by the Feminist Lament have double trouble. They have the original pain itself and then the pain of suppressing it as they defer to the little ladies.

Once again the message is clear and sexist: men's feelings do not count. They are expendable, like male bodies. Only women suffer. Only women's problems are significant and real. This must amuse the men buried in the national cemetery. Their no-less-silent brothers above ground should be a little less amused by the bamboozlement of Femthink.

Is the woman who gets paid to make love to an attractive man to be pitied more than the man who opts for buying that celluloid fantasy of sexuality because female resistance and sexual blackmail have worn him down that much?

SOMETHING ABOUT PORNOGRAPHY

Eugene V. Martin

I'm really sorry I agreed to write something about pornography. I took on the commitment fairly casually—or so it seemed to me. In fact, I was unaware of how important the issue is to me, how emotionally involved I am, and how difficult I would find the task of expressing myself publicly about personal sexual matters.

To get started, I read—or tried to read—some of the feminist articles and a number of women's "letters to the editor" on pornography. Many times before, I've learned a great deal from women in the movement against sexism and I approached these articles anticipating that I would find important insights and useful ideas.

I found myself having great difficulty getting into these writings. I kept losing the line of thought. The ideas seemed overly abstract and the feelings came across as campaign rhetoric. Perhaps I could have tried harder to hear the concerns behind the positions but I was hearing messages for sexual repression and couldn't imagine finding common ground.

So I tried to explore ideas with a few close female friends. I imagined we would explore some ideas that were puzzling me: why do liberated women welcome the public exploration and development on the one hand and yet object to photographs of naked women and men? Why is it alright for *Cosmopolitan* to use sexually stimulating photographs of women to sell itself and a myriad of products and services, but morally repugnant for *Hustler* to do it? Is the concern really focused on what part of the anatomy is visible? Who is really being exploited by men's magazines like *Hustler* and *Playboy*—the well-paid models, women who never see the magazine, or millions of men who pay a lot of money to look at anatomical details common to all women?

(I also wanted to complain about some "dirty" tricks—like *Ms.* using a photo of an adult bookstore as the primary illustration for an article on the female sexual slave trade which nowhere mentions pornography—and note the irony that this article ends next to an advertisement for posters and photographs of "the male nude.")

I was wrong. We didn't discuss anything. We fought. I was astonished by the intensity and seeming inflexibility of the exchanges that occurred. I heard diatribes about "kiddy" porn when I wanted to talk about consenting adults, and I got generalizations about "men" when I was concerned about me. I didn't feel understood or even listened to.

Then I started to hear myself. I heard myself debating words rather than seeking to understand ideas. I felt critical and defensive. And, even to my own ears, my arguments sounded abstract, rhetorical, and difficult to follow. We were saying articles on pornography at each other!

I was very shaken and dismayed by these experiences. These are respected and loved friends, colleagues, and allies and suddenly I could see no common ground. I felt dismayed and self-doubting and at the same time angry and injured. I have often heard of "the war between the sexes" but I have never before seen myself so vividly as a combatant; never before had so intense a sense of how deeply entrenched are the battle lines, how extensive the no-man's-and-no-woman's land And I have rarely before felt quite as wounded and helpless with my sources of support enlisted "on the other side." How terrible, I thought, when wounded combatants are the only available negotiators for peace. How desolate when the individual's sanctuary of love and sex is also the very battlefield in the gender war. Woe is me! If I want to be loved for myself I must openly present myself and risk the vulnerability of intimacy with my "enemy."

Suddenly I felt elated and vastly relieved. I had found common ground. It is precisely the risking and the vulnerability. Sex is an area of great vulnerability for almost all of us. My friends and I hadn't been attacking each other's views on pornography as much as we had been protecting ourselves.

I've come to know some of the ways I respond to situations where I feel vulnerable, needy, and not as adequate or competent as I think I should be. Then, I find myself judging others, usually critically, doubting their self-assessment and looking for hidden motives.

I start to view their activities solely in terms of my needs, feelings, and values, without any empathy for how their situations may differ from mine.

Now I began to understand the articles on pornography and my own reactions—or I think I did. My guess now is that when the topic of sexual stimulation comes up, a number of us have been sufficiently wounded to have lost the capacity and will to empathize with others' experiences. In real pain we can only report on the atrocities we've seen, heard, and felt. These reports—appearing to be cognitive discussions—are one of the few ways some of us have for publicly saying "I'm hurt." After all, how loudly should I shout for help when the enemy is hereby?

Sure, I'm projecting my reactions and issues onto others—perhaps there's no validity to any of this except for what I'm saying about who I am and how I experience. But the more I observe, the more comfortable I get with the idea that the key issue in the current public debate about pornography is in our personal experience with sexual arousal. I hasten to add that I do believe most emphatically that there are a number of exceptionally important related issues and problems such as the protection of children, freedom of expression, economic and sexual exploitation, the affirmation of joy, sex education, our acculturation to violence, and lots more! These are real issues affecting public policy and decisions, and action is required. They are also issues that have been with us a while and you can get a good argument on either side of whether we're learning and doing better or not. Perhaps it's worth exploring the issues underlying all of them.

I think sexual arousal and pleasure are close to if not at the center of these issues—at least for me they are. My idea—fantasy, if you will—of utmost sexual pleasure is what might occur if I were feeling high in self-esteem, joyful, physically fit, centered and whole in my body, aware in the here and now, and if I were with a woman similarly awake and alive. Each would see the other as peer, each responsible for our own pleasure and delighting in pleasuring the other, fully open within the limits of our personal awareness to being known. Each of us would know and be comfortable with our own capacities for tenderness, vigor, passivity, and aggression. Each of us would find the other attractive in those ways that would most turn us each on. And with all that going for us we would play and communicate uninhibitedly without goal or distraction!

Do you have the internal permission to have that much fun? I sure as hell don't. Even when I am reasonably OK with everything else (and that fantasy lists almost every psychological issue I've got!) I find I am very fearful of unrestrained passionate joy; "reckless" seems to naturally accompany "abandon."

I think that what happened to me when I was "discussing" pornography was that I was getting into all the hang-ups and tensions I have about sex and pleasure, and rebounding into protective intellectual "discussion" which was in turn defensive and more focused on my anxieties than on the interaction at hand. It also seems likely to me that some process similar to this was occurring with my friends.

And so I come to a modest proposal—less polemic, more sharing.

I believe there is a tremendous difference between sharing how we experience our lives and taking allegedly rational, cognitive positions. I learned from the women's movement about the incredible power of emotional sharing for securing both personal and social change. The sharing provides us with essential data about what is real for humans and what are only social conventions that merit reexamination. The sharing fosters our empathy, deepens our communication, generates creativity for problem solving, facilitates mutual effort and models the changes we seek in a progressively expanding yet internally nurturing process.

Position taking, however, reminds me more of mounted men in chain mail, being sent to do battle in a medieval tourney so that God can signal his position on philosophical matters by designating a champion. Think what you will of that process, the blood and human pain was real; when I find myself arguing I always feel a curious sense of detachment, of unreality.

Perhaps you can see a different way but I find myself now believing that the only way we will begin to understand pornography and do whatever needs to be done to promote a nonsexist, nonexploitative, nonrepressive, sensual and joyful society will require a great deal more sharing in a much less judgmental and much more caring atmosphere.

Please know that I have great respect for people who take direct action in support of their ideals and I am not asking others to stop their "antipornographic" campaigns. (I don't think my request would help.) Instead I would invite them to share their experiences and feelings—as well as their positions—so that we can begin to hear/see/feel others' concerns.

Now I feel a little trapped. I've invited the sharing—which means me first. I don't know how far I want to go but I'll try a little and see what happens.

I always had a lot of fears and inhibitions about sex. To start with, I didn't like my body—too fat, not muscular, not strong, mediocre coordination. I didn't feel very "manly"—I was terrified of being beaten by my peers because I was afraid I could not take the pain, and worse yet, I would be revealed as a coward. I also assumed there was something wrong with my lack of competitiveness because I couldn't take the games and sports and academic contests seriously. I felt very stupid about "girls." I watched the "popular" kids and the dating game from afar and felt congenitally deficient that other boys seemed to know what to do and when to do it, but I didn't. I never heard sex discussed openly, publicly, positively, or joyfully. It was always an activity of dubious morality, frightful consequences, considerable mystery, and social controversy. I was supposed to be good at it without asking how and it scared me silly. I was also supposed to be uncontrollably eager; and although I chafed at the general social assumption that I was like those other boys whose lust overrode all sense of propriety and morality, I felt deficient in virility.

To my ignorance, misinformation, self-doubt, unrealistic expectations and fear I added a whole variety of inhibitions, undeveloped tastes and lack of awareness! Whew! I could detail the picture more but I'm sure you get the point. Exploring and rediscovering my sexuality feels like and is reclaiming a substantial part of myself and resurrecting the potentials of my life in a very important way. The issue for me is self-acceptance and wholeness as well as pleasure and orgasm. I'm happy not to be sixteen anymore—not the way I did sixteen, anyway. But the sense of risk remains as my focus shifts away from my previous fear of failing to perform and centers more on my awareness of how I can take care of myself emotionally and physically. There are important learnings left for me in the fantasies I concoct out of nude photographs. I am learning to recognize my desires and to accept myself. And I feel attacked and threatened when anyone passes judgment on what provides me pleasure.

Until I knew this I couldn't begin to empathize with the concerns of those who fear the porn I enjoy. I have known enough of the pain of the exaggeration and repression of male sexuality to know that there must be equal pain from the denial and suppression of female sexuality. Just as I make access to pornography symbolic of sexual freedom, I can guess that my sisters are seeing in pornography all the threats of sexual slavery of every sort.

Is there more to this than memories—long-standing patterns evolved through many generations of people like us who had no contraception better than repression and the forcible separation of sex and pleasure, men and women who had none of the technologically supported options that we enjoy? It seems more reasonable to me that we're likely to be in the midst of learning than it is to assume that there is an ancient and ongoing patriarchal conspiracy. So I'd like to hope that we can learn to drop the enemy postures, the name-calling and blaming. Not to concede positions nor to relinquish concerns, but to accelerate the mutual resolution that is the only way out of this unwinnable and costly war.

Well, I'm sorry I couldn't write that article for you. I just don't have any positions I'm sure enough to defend. And I still have no taste for fighting for its own sake. I do feel much better for having had a chance to get this stuff off my chest —I really appreciate your patience in listening to all this and hope it makes some sense to you.

A REPLY TO EUGENE MARTIN'S "SOMETHING ABOUT PORNOGRAPHY"

Francis Baumli

The problem doesn't seem to be pornography *per se,* but whether we can dialogue with women and other men about it. Whether we can realize that our sexual vulnerability—hurt as it has been—can be talked about without first insulating it behind a wall of rhetoric, statistics, and accusations.

Maybe I can put this in my own words: It seems to me that *in most instances a moral issue is the mentalistic counterpart of an emotional hurt.* Hence it is important, if we are to deal well with an emotional hurt, that we remain loyal to a language of feeling. In doing so we have to avoid moralizing, finger pointing, and intellectualistic verbiage. We each need to talk about our own hurt, and about whether it is in the best interests of the person we're speaking with to avoid a similar hurt.

My personal feeling is that pornography does exploit women. But I'm not talking with women right now, so I'm not interested in pursuing that claim. I'm talking to you, and to other men. And I want to tell you how pornography has hurt me. And why I believe it can hurt you.

I too grew up feeling isolated, lonely, and fearful about sex. Pornography was a handy masturbatory outlet for the loneliness, although it provided only temporary relief. But I don't want to knock pornography for this. The real question is, did pornography do anything for my ignorance about sexuality? Did it bring me any closer to the sexual pleasure I really wanted to attain?

Your statement about what utmost sexual pleasure would be for you, and the kind of relationship which might provide that pleasure, is well put. I'm sorry you don't have the internal uninhibited permission to actually have that kind of pleasure. I don't have it either—at least not all the time. Sometimes I get close though. And I'm happy with getting close.

For a long time, however, I wasn't close at all. I was too concerned about virility, potency, how long I could last, etc. This period of my life was very miserable. And I feel a lot of anger toward the forces that conditioned me to be so ignorant about my own sexuality and about women. Pornography was one of those forces. Only one, I say; yet a very crucial one.

That's why I feel upset when you talk about the important learnings you hope to get from the fantasies you concoct from photographs of nude women. But then, I want to be careful with what I say here. I have nothing against such photographs or fantasies if they are realistic. In other words, if the photographs you use are of a wide variety of female bodies—if they include women of different ages, some with and some without "well-shaped" bodies, in different sizes and proportions, all of them looking more or less natural, then I have no reason to think such pictures are pornographic. And I feel that maybe you'll get something good out of your fantasies. But if the photographs are the kind that appear in the "girlie" magazines, I'm afraid your fantasies are setting you up for more confusion and ignorance. Because real women, when they take their clothes off, don't look like the posed, idealized, i.e., distorted, bodies in those pictures. And if you think they do, I'm afraid that your attempt at dispelling your ignorance about women's bodies, or moving closer to a fully satisfactory sexual experience, is going to end up creating unreal images. Images which, I fear, will leave you even more lonely and frightened because they have distanced you further from what you're after.

Not only women, but men also, suffer from treating women as sex objects. The glut of pornography on the magazine racks gives a man ready access to finding out what the nude female body supposedly looks like. Opening the magazines, he sees picture after picture of nearly perfect bodies, each woman smiling invitingly or posed provocatively. What the reader doesn't realize is that many things have been done to lengthen, thin, curve, and idealize these bodies. The faces are made up; toenails and fingernails are painted. Stretch marks, blemishes, veins and scars are brushed out by the photographer. High heels lift up the calf and make the legs appear longer; legs are held together or crossed in standing poses to give more curve to the hips. The belly is pulled in, the breasts are pulled up by raised shoulders or held up by arms crossed under them. The chin is cocked down and the eyes seductively turned up. The hands are spread stiffly as if about to clutch for a man's turgid penis. And the faces have about as much character as pictures of babies on Gerber cereal boxes. Little wonder that many men experience something on the order of shock when they begin having sexual experiences with real women. The female body looks twenty pounds heavier than it does in the pictures, the breasts seem to sag, the legs seem short and squat, the skin isn't so smooth, and the woman's physical imperfections show out in pimples and scars and stretch marks and varicose veins. And most of all, there is a person with a unique personality and sexuality, whose face registers emotion, expectations, pleasure, and disappointments.

In other words, Eugene, don't hurt yourself like I and a lot of other men have. I spent quite a number of years pursuing sexual knowledge with pornographic pictures. All I did was heighten my ignorance, and distort my ability to appreciate natural-looking, real female bodies. If you want to use photographs, okay; but make sure they're not stylized, idealized, or youthanized.

I hope by now you see my point: that pornography can hurt men too. Just as much as it hurts women.

With this realization, I have begun to see that there *is* a common ground for discussion of this topic with feminists. I find this common ground when instead of fleeing to the safe but unproductive domain of mental, moralistic issues, we share our emotional hurt. In this way we can cathart without accusing, be angry without blaming, and address the problem in a constructive way. In other words, because our vulnerability doesn't feel so threatened, we can open up our sexuality to one another again, and this time feel comforted and somewhat healed. In this kind of atmosphere, a great deal of learning about each other's sexuality can take place. And sometimes we even feel what you referred to as, "the internal permission to have that much [sexual] fun."

THE PERFORMANCE OR THE PLAY?

THE PURITAN

Arthur Winfield Knight

I was brought up
to believe
in the work ethic.
When we are together
I begin by thinking
we should not be
doing this
in the afternoon,
your naked body
next to mine.
There are things to do.
When I pucker
your right nipple
with my thumb and finger
you tell me, seriously,

59

"You don't do that
very often;
it must not be
much fun."
You laugh when I do.
It all seems silly:
you worrying about
the size of your breasts
and me about the work
I have not done.

IMPOTENCE

Arthur Winfield Knight

I went soft
before I got into you
this afternoon,
and now I sit
watching Walter Cronkite,
getting the news.
Lying in bed
you asked me
what I was thinking,
but it was
too grim to tell you.
For the thirty-third day
Americans are being held
hostage in Iran,
and I listen to Cronkite
speculate as to what
Ayatollah Khomeini will do,
but no one knows.
The rate of inflation's up
more than twelve percent,
but I'm down. I'm down.
In the town where
your parents live
twenty-seven hundred
steel workers have been
laid off, Cronkite says.
"And that's the way it is."

one bucketful of orgasms doesn't

Francis Baumli

She said she had orgasms
one upon the other like infinite
waves of ocean currents
crashing in the surf
never stopping.

But with me she was cold
"You don't make waves"
she said, hard eyes glinting
like broken moons in black waters
full of angry corpses.

Like infinite waves, she said,
but couldn't get her pelvis right
couldn't even make ripples
cause I don't make waves,
but how could I
when everywhere my kisses went
she wasn't even wet.

breast milk don't mix with little boy's tears and pee and virgin semen

for Meredith

Francis Baumli

I came once already
ain't it enough?
you moaning grab my scrotum
but I can't cause your cunt
smells like stale cig smoke
and sour wine
I won't say anchovy
that'd be sexist so
I'll stick to sour burgundy
and say your nether lips
stink like your lungs

61

you want my penis once more
but I just ain't interested
you faked an orgasm when I came—
I know, but I couldn't say it
knowing you'd deny it and
get by with it,
besides you won't take off your jewelry
even when you're naked it
distracts me makes me think of
picks and shovels and caskets
your body dead someday
gold metal on gray skin
but dead skin's maybe prettier than
kissing my way past lip gloss
three layers of deep blush
foundation paste, do you think
I'm supposed to be a hog
snout rooting for the goodies
no matter if it tastes like chemical dung,
and thanks for the hard kiss you practiced
while reading harlequin romances,
now after your chewing kiss of a tongue bite
one deep breath please
so I can choke on
your thick perfume that smells
like a drunk's puke on white begonias

no don't go fumbling
it ain't there, no hard-on yet
so you turn over and reach for the wine glass
your ass sags soft wrinkles
someday like my mother's

she's the one who
spanked me when I touched myself
spanked me again when I cried those
wet tears from the first spanking
yelled when I peed the bed
changed my wet dreams to nightmares
and cut farts
muffled by her girdle
when she'd turn out the light
saying "sweet dreams!"
for the company to hear

nice and easy yes please no I don't know but pretend you won't

Francis Baumli

A man goes for the down there zone
because it's up to him
he's supposed to since he's past
buttons snaps clasps and
she's still kissing and moaning
so even though he's scared he goes for it
and she wants it, but watch out
she's scared now she coos
says no, please no, she adds
the please to let him know
she loves him and oh she's so helpless
she's got to say please
plead with him to not whet
her fragile passion.

So she says no but
don't mean no
but then maybe she does
she's not sure,
and maybe he ain't sure
would like to say no
since he's scared too
but can't say no
cause then he'd be a wimp
and she can't say yes
cause then she'd be a whore
so she says no and don't mean it
entirely but partly does
and he says yes and don't mean it
entirely but he says it
you wonder why she's
the one says please
and he doesn't.
Could be this is why
when I want or a woman wants
or we both want to do the, you know—
go to bed together and

do what we want
I'll say let's be gentle
take it slow and easy
maybe nothing genital
just our bodies loving each other
and see what happens. . .

And she nods eagerly, she's relieved
I think, and glad I'm gentle
considerate of our feelings
not the rapacious macho kind
not the kind who takes and runs
not Mr. feel 'em finger 'em fuck 'em leave 'em,
they're so glad they bare skin quick
spread legs before I'm hardly beside 'em
grabbing my penis my balls my. . .
but then it doesn't seem mine
and my penis doesn't like it either
gets scared and small
and I say no let's go slow,
sure baby she says and rubs me harder
what's wrong baby she groans,
like she's been practicing these words so she can
rub my softness against her hard pelvis
nothing's wrong I'm just shy I say
she says sure it's okay we'll get it up
and works harder on what I'm not down there
and I'm wondering if I should
get up and leave, or maybe. . .
but then she'd think I'm a wimp
though I already think she's a bitch
and I know sure as I know anything that
she was thinking all along
me saying let's go slow and be easy
was just my way of getting her in bed
which allowed her a way of pretending
she ain't the one who wants it too
though once she's in bed
she of course will cooperate
sort of go along with it
be fired up now she's given in
though she never believed I meant it when
I said let's go slow and be easy

thought it was just my way
and now she doesn't understand
sits up angry, says what's wrong—
ain't I enough—where you comin from?

I could say I ain't comin' from anywhere
and you ain't goin' nowhere
but I don't, I'm quiet
wondering if a different sort of
man would just hit her in the mouth
but then I think a different sort of
man would just poke it in
wouldn't of said let's go slow and be easy
in the first place, would have
got her drunk
told her he loves her
told her he'll marry her
gone ahead and fucked her
even though she said no
and if she liked it she could have
cooed how it feels good
and if she didn't like it
she could have said she was raped.
I just want to leave
walk out on her, let her
leak a few tears
I ain't free and I ain't easy
and all this sex she did to me
after I trusted her and was
vulnerable and took risks
is all *against my will*
so I guess *I* got raped
she didn't stick any penis in me
but neither do most male rapists I hear
they rape with the threat of sex the attempt
and I got raped with the attempt
to make me the threat I wouldn't be
I hope she folds her legs up
like a dead spider
that's how bad
it stung.

LEARNING TO TARRY, TOUCH, TALK

Jim Sanderson

Male understanding of female desires and needs has come a long way in the past quarter-century since Kinsey first opened the bedroom door. Suddenly women were speaking up. In the late '50s, you could hardly glance at a magazine or newspaper without reading some complaint about male louts who didn't know the meaning of foreplay, didn't care whether a woman was receptive or not.

Men quickly learned that lesson. Simple trial and error did the trick. A woman who was approached slowly and lovingly became a more enthusiastic partner.

Then the emphasis shifted to orgasm. Every woman had a right to one—or more. This seemed fair to most males, and they went to work with a vigor. A male is goals-oriented; just tell him the production quota and he'll deliver. Today, it's debatable whether the female orgasm is not more important to the man than the woman herself.

For many a man the first question after he catches his breath is: Did you? And the next is: How many? The questions imply an uneasy combination of generosity—he really wanted it to be good for her—and a need to measure his sexual power. A generation ago, males gloried in the number of their own orgasms; today it's more socially acceptable to compute hers.

SEX WITHOUT WOMEN

Jed Diamond

I began doing some of the exercises in a book on sexuality I had gotten at the Center for Human Sexuality in San Francisco. The exercise on masturbation was interesting. The instruction was to concentrate attention on the sensations in my own body rather than fantasizing. At first, I found it difficult to get turned on at all without looking at pictures, or reading, or picturing some sexy scene in my mind. Gradually, I found the feelings pleasurable, but not highly stimulating, a kind of low plateau of sexual turn-on. I fantasized some scene and the turn-on increased. I returned to just touching myself and focusing on my physical sensations and the turn-on settled at a higher plateau. I eventually had an orgasm which was very nice and spread through my whole body. For the first time, I became aware that fantasies take me away from my own body. The orgasm is intense but over very quickly, and is very localized around my penis. When I concentrated more on the sensations in my own body, the pleasure seemed more total.

I liked the process of getting to know what felt good to my body, not just the stimulation of the fantasy in my mind.

MEN ARE LEARNING TO LISTEN TO THEIR BODIES

Richard Haddad

Men are learning to listen to their bodies in matters of sex. They're learning that there are times they feel like making love and times they don't; that there are some partners who stimulate them physically and others who do absolutely nothing for them. They do not feel compelled to perform at any time with any partner—to "prove" their masculinity in bed, and they're discovering that their blind obedience to the male mandate to perform was what often led to the torture of sexual dysfunction. They no longer think of sex as something a man does "to" a woman; they insist on a sexual partner who is willing to accept responsibility for her own sexual pleasure, relieving the male of the burden to "satisfy" her and somehow enjoy the experience himself.

Chapter 3:
The Game of Dating

ON WOMEN HAVING IT BOTH WAYS

Robert A. Sides

How dare women demand something from men unequally! How dare a woman ask another human being to do what she's not willing to do herself! I've heard more adult, "successful" women act like two-year-olds when you suggest that they go out and actually call a man for a date than I can shake an E.R.A. petition at! My God, it's as if you're asking them to act equal or something. The universal response: "Ooooooooh! We aren't ready for *that*!" I guess if they don't have, literally, a "federal case" going for them, they just can't hack equality. They are counting on our Ms.-guided chivalry: "There, there, little women. You don't have to do that. You can be selective in your perception of equality. You can have only the benefits of change with none of the cost!"

Sorry. And no thanks. If women can convince me that they can take the heat of an executive position, then they've also convinced me that they can do something a 13-year-old boy MUST: namely, get on the horn and take some risks. He's supposed to face rejection over-and-over-and-over again for the rest of his life. Surely a 45-year-old woman can do it once!

ONE AFTERNOON AT HAPPY HOUR

M. Adams

(One afternoon after a discouraging job interview, the author found himself in a foul mood and at an expensive bar in one of Baltimore's business districts.)

Woman: Hi there. Are you all by yourself?

Me: Yeah, I'm all by myself. I only hang with the best crowds.

W: That's a nice necktie. It looks really good on you.

M: Really? Thanks. This is the first time I've worn a tie in ten years.

W: You're not serious!

M: Sure I am. I just interviewed for a job. A book I read told me the tie would help.

W: Well, then, this must be your first time in here, because they won't let anybody in without a tie.

M: So they tell me. Say. . . how come they let *you* in? *You're* not wearing a tie!

W: You're funny! I like a man with a sense of humor.

M: Women always tell me I'm a million laughs when they get to know me.

W: Oh! You've known a lot of women, then?

M: Well, I've lost count, but I'd estimate that over the past fifteen years I've known at least two or three. I think I even touched one of them, once.

W: You're being silly!

M: But you like a man with a sense of humor.

W: Yes. And you know what else I like?

M: Hmmm?

W: I really like your car.

M: My *car??*

W: Yes! I noticed you drive up. It *was* you, wasn't it? Didn't you park in the lot around the corner?

M: Well, since that's the only public parking lot within ten blocks, it was either park there or park down by the harbor and ride the bus up here.

W: Oh, silly! It's *not* the only parking lot around here!

M: But it's the one that everyone in here uses.

W: I suppose. Anyway, I really do like your car.

M: That lot's *full* of beautiful, expensive cars. Why mine?

W: Well, of all the beautiful, expensive cars, I just happened to like it best.

M: You like that particular model, huh?

W: Yes, but I don't know much about cars and I don't really know their names. What exactly is yours?

M: A Camaro.

W: *That's* right! I remember, now. Yes, I love Camaros.

M: I lied.

W: What?

M: I lied. I have an eleven-year-old Volkswagen.

W: You do??

M: Uh-huh. Guess you didn't notice me drive up, after all.

W: That was a dirty trick!

M: Well, don't feel too badly. At least you were able to correctly identify which necktie was mine out of all the neckties in here.

W: Now you're being nasty. Are you angry at somebody, or something?

M: Only at the whole world, babe.

W: Awww. . .that's too bad. Do you want to talk about it?

M: Talking about it only seems to make the whole world angry right back at me.

W: Awww. . .Look, why don't you buy me a drink and we'll talk about it.

M: You want me to buy you a drink??

W: Yes, I'd be delighted.

M: You'd be delighted? I suppose *that's* reasonable. . .I'd be delighted, too, if someone bought *me* a drink.

W: Well, are you going to buy me one, or not?

M: I don't think so. That's disorienting to me.

W: Why?

M: Because I thought *you* were being the aggressor, here.

W: Does that bother you?

M: No, not in and of itself. It's the part about *you* asking *me* to buy *you* a drink. *That* bothers me.

W: Why?

M: Because. . . isn't the instigator supposed to take the responsibility for buying?

W: Not any more; not necessarily. That's old-fashioned. These days, women are claiming the right to approach the *guys*. Open-minded men don't mind the idea of equality.

M: But that's not equality!

W: Sure it is! Men have always been free to approach *women*. Why shouldn't women have that same freedom?

M: But men *haven't* been free to approach women and say, "Will *you* buy *me* a drink?" Whenever men approach women, it has to be, "May *I* buy *you* a drink?" Who approaches whom isn't the whole issue.

W: But *guys* pay for things! That goes without saying!

M: Well, it doesn't seem right for women to be both the agressors *and* the beneficiaries. You're only taking the equality halfway.

W: Well, I can certainly tell that *you* haven't been in many singles bars.

M: That's the nicest thing anybody's ever said about me.

W: So. . . I can't talk you into a drink?

M: You mean talk me into *buying* a drink? Nope, sorry. It isn't fair for you to have the best of both worlds. I believe in *real* equality. The aggressor buys—at least the first round.

W: Now *that's* not fair. I mean, I'd be taking a real risk. Suppose I bought the first round and then the guy decided to leave—or saw someone else he liked better. What would I do, then?

M: Gee, I don't know. Why don't you ask one of the fifteen million men in this country who just had that happen to them in the past five seconds?

W: What you're saying is a little odd. Whoever heard of men *expecting* women to buy them drinks?

M: No one, apparently.

W: Right! And besides, you men have all the money.

M: We do? That's a relief! And here I thought I was broke. Do you know where I can go to pick up my share?

W: You know what I mean! Men make lots more money than women.

M: And if they wind up spending it on women, then who's got it?

W: What? Oh, you're weird.

M: Thanks. You're not so bright, yourself.

W: Hmpf! No wonder you've only known two women in fifteen years. Did *they* buy you drinks?

M: No. . . back when I knew them, *none* of us had any money.

W: But now that's all changed. You're obviously a successful business-man. Surely you can spring for one lousy drink for an attractive lady!

M: "Lady" is a euphemism. I never liked euphemisms.

W: What?

M: Forget it. It's something I read in a book, once. If you've never read that book, consider yourself lucky.

W: Was that the same book that said to wear a tie to your job interview?

M: Yeah, sure. Now, what were you saying?

W: I was saying that you're obviously successful now. You can certainly afford to buy me a drink.

M: You could certainly afford to buy *me* one, too.

W: Ah, but as I said, you probably make more money than I do.

M: I'm sure I don't. How much do you make?

W: Only eighteen thousand a year.

M: That over *twice* what I make!

W: What!? That's impossible. That would mean you only make nine thousand dollars a year!

M: Seventy-eight hundred. I'm not a successful businessman, I'm a retail salesclerk. I make minimum wage.

W: You're kidding!

M: Nope. The gumball machine by the door of our store makes more money than I do.

W: Then what are you doing in *here*?

M: It looked like a nice place. I was all dressed up and I wanted to treat myself to a drink after a tense job interview.

W: Didn't you know this was a singles bar?

M: No, I didn't. Why? Is it a prerequisite at a singles bar for a man to have a salary which matches or beats that of any woman who might sit next to him so that she'll be able to rationalize bumming drinks off him?

W: The only prerequisite is to have a good time. Are you having a good time?

M: Impossible on minimum wage.

W: Still, you could afford one drink for little ol' me. . .?

M: Unbelievable! You're *still* trying to get me to buy you a drink, in spite of the fact that you now *know* that you make over twice the money I do.

W: Well, that's just because I have faith that you'll get this new job. Is it a good job?

M: Relative to what? Minimum wage or 18-K?

W: Does it threaten you that I make more than you do?

M: No, that fact alone doesn't threaten me at all. To have a total stranger come up to me and say, "Please spend money on me for no reason except that you're male and I'm female," threatens me terribly.

W: It's threatening to your male ego?

M: No, not to my "male ego." It's threatening to my sense of fairness . . .and to my human dignity.

W: My! Aren't we getting serious!

M: No, we're getting drunk.

W: *You're* getting drunk. I'm getting *nowhere.*

M: Well, try the next guy down the bar. Maybe he'll have a nice tie, too.

W: You're more of a challenge.

M: Challenge?? You don't even *like* me, for God's sake.

W: I didn't say that.

M: Of course you didn't *say* it. That would be very poor mooching strategy.

W: You think I'm a moocher?

M: Either that or the *owner* of this place! Why else would you persist at this point? We're obviously not right for each other.

W: Oh, you're just mad at the world, remember? Look, why don't you just buy me a small glass of wine and you can tell me about it.

M: Do you think we'll ever see each other again after tonight?

W: Maybe. Do you plan on coming in here a lot?

M: I don't *ever* plan to come back.

W: Then I guess we won't.

M: Then why should I buy you a drink? Why should I spend money on someone I never saw before and will never see again—especially when she makes twice as much money as I do?

W: Well, for Pete's sake—I mean, at this point, I've sat and talked to you for quite a while, now. It's only polite for you to treat me to a drink.

M: I owe you a drink because you *sat and talked* to me?? What, have you got a goddam taxicab meter in your pocket, or something? Do you charge by the minute or by the word?

W: You certainly have a negative way of looking at things. I'm just trying to say that it would be considered proper at this point for you to buy me a drink.

M: Because you sat and talked to me? You're saying that your company is worth *money*??

W: To a gentleman it would be, yes.

M: Oh, *shit*!

W: Hey, I don't like that kind of language.

M: Uh-oh! Is there a surcharge for bad language?

W: God! You're an odd one, all right.

M: What a concept! You sit here of your own free will, uninvited, and now I'm in your debt. Hey, you know what? That's not such a bad idea!! I like it!! I've just decided that *my* company is worth money, too! And since I'm so "odd" and I'm such a "challenge," I've decided that my time is worth *twice* as much as your time! We challenging, minimum-wage types have to make up in profits what we lack in volume, y'know?

W: Quiet down! You're being foolish.

M: I'm just trying to be a successful businessman. So anyway, since being with me is worth *twice* as much as being with you, that means that *you* now owe *me* a drink! HEY, BARTENDER!!!

W: Stop! What are you doing??

M: SHE'S GONNA BUY ME A DRINK!! I'LL TAKE SOMETHING REALLY EXPENSIVE ON THE ROCKS!!!

W: I'm not buying you anything!! Cut it out!! You're being a real asshole!!

M: Whoops! Bad language!! MAKE IT A DOUBLE!!!!

74

W: Oh, Jesus! I'm leaving!! You're *crazy*!!!

(She storms out of the bar)

Bartender: I'm sorry, man, but I missed what you said just then. It's so busy in here that I really couldn't hear you.

M: It doesn't matter.

W: You're new, right? I've never seen you here before.

M: Just passing through.

W: Well, listen, I ought to warn you that that lady you were with is a real vulture.

M: It's O.K. I brought my BB gun.

W: I *mean* it, man. She's a heavy. I couldn't help but notice the way she walked out of here just now. What the hell happened? What got her so pissed-off?

M: Beats me. Maybe she just doesn't like Volkswagens.

THE SENSITIVE MAN: WHY IS HE SO UNDESIRABLE?

Robert A. Sides

When it comes down to the nitty-gritty, the man always has to approach the woman. Suddenly, listening to Simon and Garfunkel seems a liability for men. Women can listen to all that soft, "mushy" stuff—they can afford to—because they never have to *also* face the hard, "tough" stuff. They don't have to turn off the music and their wide-open sensibilities in order to go out and take some risks. So. . .sensitivity has unequal consequences for men.

Women say that they want "sensitive" men, but it's not often clear just what they mean by that. Usually it means they want men to "sense" what the women want and give it to them without complaint. Men's own needs are to remain in limbo, their lives in hell. Well, if sensitive, feeling men are really so desired by women, why aren't they being pursued? Why do Bold women become Demure when they have to get off their duffs and do something?

Who's kidding who? I read an article recently which shows the true colors of hip-talking women and those who try to slide out of present-day assertiveness by saying the Next Generation will be different. The piece spotlighted junior high-school girls and their sociosexual attitudes. The message to men: Give Up All Hope, Ye Who Enter Into The World Of These Women!

Even at their tender ages, the girls had hardened views about The Place of Boys. They had already distinguished between the Clammy Hands and the Cool Hands. As a savvy young miss, you were to only "fool around" with the Cool-Handed Lukes.

But, hey, it's the clammy-handed guys that *aren't* masking their feelings! The message is clear: the "price" of these waifs is the suppression of male feelings. If you want some simple attention and affection from your female peers, you have to become super mask-uline. You cannot show fear to people who themselves never face what is scary. Do these girls want male "persons," or controlled, moneyed, older "actors" shamming their roles?

It's easy for women to tell men how to act when they themselves never have to face those same trials. I just get weary of their lamenting that they have no power when they *have* the power to say Yes or No. If that isn't power, what does the word mean?

Feminists have been dishonest with us. They say they want Sensitive when they mean Successful. Mr. Wonderful is really Mr. Warrior. And they have said *they* free themselves (and wonder why men cannot do the same), but they conveniently leave out the fact that they have had halfway houses, books, courses and support groups, too. Men don't have those options. Men only have a history of being rewarded for stoicism, being punished for being spontaneous, open, excited, etc. Yet he is to go from being an Emotional Island (a prison "penal" colony!) to Caring Continent with no support and even hostility from women who were helped themselves. Real men are not in demand. Rocky I, II, and III, the fleshed out Rock-of-Gibraltar are what attracts women. Or haven't you noticed?

WHO GETS THE VALENTINES?

Arthur Murray

We all, men and women alike, enjoy being told that someone loves us. But we don't all receive this privilege equally. *The Guardian,* one of London's major newspapers, on Valentine's Day, published a list of Valentine messages: 78% were from men and only 22% were from women.

Chapter 4:
Women in Our Lives

THE GENDER DANCE

WOMEN AS WELL AS MEN SHARE THE ILLUSION

Richard Haddad

Women as well as men share the illusion that men rule the world. The role of women as the primary transmitters of social values (including sexist ones) is not generally acknowledged by either sex, perhaps because it upsets the balance of power, or threatens the male ego, or plays on the male's primal fear of the power of women. I think also that the oppressor label flattered rather than offended the average male, strengthened his illusion of power, and confirmed his manliness.

So we were told that men were the social villains, and we believed. We were told that women had suffered one indignity after another at the hands of power-hungry, insensitive male beasties, and we agreed. We were told that not only was the condition of women in our society terrible, but that the male role was one of privilege and advantage, a veritable bed of roses—and we applauded. Men had systematically exploited women over the eons for their own advantage, we heard, and now they must make it up by wearing sackcloth and ashes and chanting *mea culpa*; and we replied only, "When does the penance start?"

What a strange development that we should suddenly decide that only the female has been handicapped by sex-role limitation; that we should forget that sexism is and always has been a double-edged sword.

EXPLORING THE MALE MACHO TRAP

Roy U. Schenk, Ph.D.

FIRST ENCOUNTERS

"Chauvinism is the attitude that one group of people is superior to another group of people." Therefore, "Male chauvinism is the attitude that men are superior to women." "Women are oppressed by male chauvinism." "Macho behavior is male chauvinism in action."

These were some of the messages I and millions of other men were confronted with in the late sixties and early seventies from women calling themselves feminists. And these feminists spoke in no uncertain terms of the need for equality—for equal opportunities for women.

Clearly there was evidence that women were seen and treated as being inferior to men both economically and politically. For myself and multitudes of men, this evidence became an additional source of guilt to add to our already extensive guilt-burden.

DISCOVERING FEMALE CHAUVINISM

Yet, in listening to messages about male chauvinism and women's oppression, one thing quickly became clear to me. These feminists were presenting women as the innocent, virtuous victims of evil, violent men. Clearly they had an image of themselves and of all women as morally superior to men. And yet these were the same women who had told me that the attitude that one group of people is superior to another group is chauvinism.

Whether it was innocence, naivete, or just plain stupidity, I believed these feminists when they spoke of their commitment to achieving equality. And so I pointed out to them, at first tentatively but later with increasing insistence, that their attitude of moral superiority is female chauvinism. They totally rejected my observations. And I finally came to realize that for most of them "equality for women" meant eliminating women's disadvantages while retaining as many of women's advantages and special privileges as possible.

SUPERIORITY: COMPENSATION FOR INFERIORITY

In trying to understand the effects of superiority and inferiority on people, an important discovery for me was the writings of Alfred Adler concerning compensation. Adler states that "the striving for superiority and the feeling of inferiority are naturally complementary." In other words, a person or group that feels inferior will necessarily strive to compensate by developing ways they can feel themselves to be superior.

And suddenly it all made sense! Men feel morally inferior to women and so they compensate by developing economic-political areas they can feel superior in. As time went on I came to realize that there are other areas in which men are seen as inferior—such as nurturing and sexuality. I chose the term "spiritual" to encompass these male inferiority/female superiority attitudes. In contrast, I selected the term "material" to encompass the female inferiority/male superiority attitudes which include economic and political areas.

I describe this Vicious Circle of Male/Female Negative Interactions in Figure 1.

FIGURE 1. THE VICIOUS CIRCLE OF MALE/FEMALE INFERIORITY/SUPERIORITY[1]

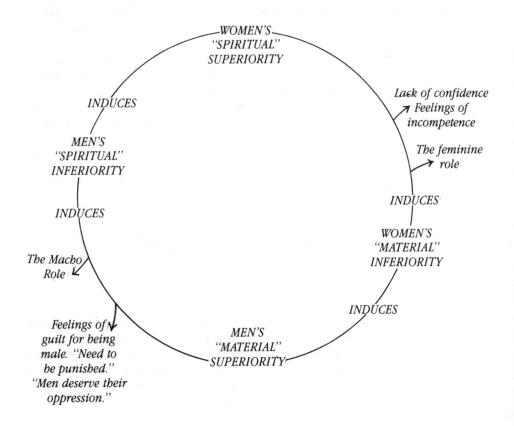

---

[1]For a more complete discussion of this issue and related issues, read Roy's book, The Other Side of the Coin: Causes and Consequences of Men's Oppression (P.O. Box 9141, Madison, WI 53715: Bioenergetics Press, 1982; $5.75). © Roy U. Schenk.

OUR MOTHERS

ISN'T THE HOME WHERE OUR VALUES ORIGINATED?

Richard Haddad

Isn't the home where our values originated, and isn't it the most important of the institutions where the values of any society are passed on from one generation to the next? The men who make our laws and who enforce them in our courts, who run our governmental bureaucracies and private corporations: where did their values originate? And where were those values first reinforced?

Consider that after spending our first five years learning about the world on our mothers' knees, we were sent off to elementary school—part of another social institution—where for the next five or six years we were more likely than not to have a woman as teacher. What do you think that taught us about the world? Exactly how important *are* men in society's scheme of things if it was not thought necessary for them to be around while we were growing up—while our minds were being molded and we were forming the worldviews which will govern most of our personal decision-making for most of our lives?

LIBERATING THE WOMAN IN ME

Jed Diamond

I'd been saying for a long time that we wouldn't understand male/female relationships until we explored the reality that both men and women are born of a woman who in our early experience was all-powerful. A man grows up to marry a woman who he is "supposed" to dominate, but who he is deeply dependent upon and frightened of losing. A woman marries a man she is "supposed" to be subservient to, but who she deeply feels superior to.

MIXED EMOTIONS ABOUT WOMEN

MEN UP AGAINST WOMEN'S EMOTIONS

M. Adams

Society begins to emotionally disable men from the moment they are born, and by the time they are grown they are practically helpless against emotion used by women as a manipulative tool. To challenge the average man emotionally is essentially like challenging a paraplegic to a dance contest.

NOTES FROM THE HUMAN LABORATORY: A POSTMORTEM REPORT ON EVOKED RATIONALISTIC POTENTIALS VIA EMOTIONAL MANIPULATION

Francis Baumli

Ever since we were born, we have been told that men are rational and women are emotional. Recent theories about brain bicamerality have embellished this idea by describing the left cerebral hemisphere as primarily logical, analytical, and masculine; the right hemisphere as emotional, responsive, and feminine. The bicamerality theory has been picked up by people in very diverse fields: learning disabilities psychologists speculate about how to stimulate right brain functioning during early childhood so that children can grow up to be more emotionally healthy, psychiatrists speculate that insufficient contact with the right hemisphere may be one cause of schizophrenia, and even modern-day Indian gurus like the Tantric Buddhist, Bhagwan Shree Rajneesh, claim that it is the feminine propensity of the right brain which may best lead a person to enlightenment.

It does not require careful reading to notice, even in the technical jargon of the neurologists and the inspired invocations of the gurus, that there is a common motif which surrounds the bicamerality fad. Namely, that because the right brain governs the *feminine* aspect of our personality, it is therefore *superior.* It intuits the world directly, and because it has a natural sympathy for other human beings, it is selfless, sacrificing, and given to being virtuous and moral. The left brain, however, being *masculine,* is somehow *inferior.* It is coldly rationalistic, indulges in sterile logicizing about the world, allows a callous attitude toward human suffering, and fosters violence and war for the sake of economic gain, the pursuit of power, and the triumph of patriarchal values.

Within this context, we are told that although all men and women may have more-or-less the same cerebral potential, men are ruled by that sterile, brutish left hemisphere, while women are loyal to the fecund, gentle right hemisphere.

As a researcher in neurology, I could argue about many of the presuppositions underlying the bicamerality theory. It is true that self-consciousness seems to be primarily located in the left hemisphere; but as for the other claims about how emotion is indigenous to the right hemisphere, and logicizing to the left hemisphere—these are questionable. Recent studies of brain function with electroencephalograms (EEGs) more global than have customarily been used, show that there is not as much bifurcation of function as has often been presupposed.

But I don't want to here argue a neurological point. I want to look over some of the implications that stem from the bicamerality fad. Implications which claim that feminine, emotional functioning is superior to masculine, rational functioning. Implications which further claim that it is men who fostered and further their tendency to overrationalize the world, and that women have done nothing to contribute to this tendency, but rather, do everything they can to make the world a more emotional, i.e., more benevolent, place to live in.

Yes; males are overly rational; we men are rather aware of this. Women are more emotional than men; this also is likely true. But we of the men's liberation movement are trying to throw off our sterile, rationalistic view of the world by being more at ease with our own emotions, and by helping other men with their emotions. In the course of this learning process, we sometimes look to women as role models to help us. Unfortunately, however, we often find that we cannot learn from them as much as we had hoped for.

Of course, this sometimes is because we are encountering an unfamiliar, somewhat fearful realm. But there is a further difficulty. Sometimes our reluctance is occasioned, and perhaps warranted, by our ability to discern that while friendly, nurturing emotions are part of women's repertoire, there is a whole bag of other emotions which can be used as weapons against men.

Let me give an example:

Not long ago, a woman I felt very close to had accused me of acting in a certain way, and I felt the accusation was inaccurate. I felt so misunderstood that all I could do was feel hurt, bewildered, mistreated, and frustrated in trying to figure out how to clarify where I stood with her.

It isn't necessary to here go into all the specifics of our interchange. Suffice it to say that I finally felt so angry that I confronted her with my feelings. And, optimistic person that I am, I was truly hoping to work through the misunderstanding.

But I didn't get very far. Not because I was afraid of being emotional, and not because she didn't respond to me emotionally. Rather, our exchange had scarcely begun when she laughingly explained away her perception of me, and consequent accusation, with this statement: "It was just sort of an intuition, and it kind of came out spontaneously. Besides, it was based on what you were saying."

This is all. A very simple statement.

But for some reason I felt totally stymied by that comeback. It was like the argument was over. Nothing more to be said. I was ready to confront her about something that had hurt me, and suddenly it seemed to have disappeared. But somehow I felt it hadn't disappeared. I wanted to deal with it, yet now I couldn't locate the object of my frustration.

Later I went home and wrote down what she'd said, word for word. I pondered it over. I brought logic, reason, analysis, and all those masculine tools to bear, and dissected what she'd said with the interest of an anatomist working on a cadaver. It was gruesome work, and I probably sullied my own emotions in the process. But it was interesting, and I discovered some things. Here's how I dismembered her statement:

"It": notice how she depersonalizes what happened. There's no mention of "I said," or, "I meant."

"was just": she's ducking out here by trivializing what was a big deal to her before, because now I'm ready to confront her about it.

"an intuition": and here is a real weapon. Intuitions are insightful, and by their very nature have a claim to truth. Furthermore, they are the province of women's perceptivity, which men are blind to and therefore cannot argue with. Also, intuitions have a sanctity which makes them inviolate to logical suspicion or scrutiny.

"and it": again, she depersonalizes what I'm upset about.

"kind of": this is like her earlier "sort of." More elusiveness. No wonder I'm chasing shadows.

"came out": yes; nothing like a passive, intransitive verb to further the confusion. It's not something *she* did. Actually, her judgments happened on their own; in fact, issued from her mouth as if by their own volition.

"spontaneously": how do I argue with that? Spontaneity is a virtue that children, artists, and saints have. It's something everyone wishes they could have more of, and it's such a brief, momentary bubbling over of one's authentic personality that only a pedant would argue with what it gives forth.

"Besides": as if I'm not already confused enough, here comes the excuse—the exculpation—which will exonerate her from all involvement.

"it": this is the third time that what I'm upset about gets allocated to a gender-neutral, impersonal pronoun.

"was": the second time the past tense has been conveniently used. What I'm upset about happened in the past, not the present. That makes it easier for her to deal with it, and reminds me that I might be better off if I just let the past alone and lived in the here and now.

"based on what you were saying": And here is the grand conclusion. The summary which says it all, and dismisses it all.

Turns out I was the one who really set up the misunderstanding. It was all based on what I said, not on our long and difficult interaction. She had just reacted to my action. And reactions usually don't have to be accounted for; or, if they do require accountability, the reactor need only point to the actor.

83

Suddenly everything was my responsibility. I had started it all, hence I was responsible for her reaction, and responsible for how her reaction affected me. And now all I had to do was go home and figure out how it was that what I'd said in the first place caused the problem. Once I had that figured out, I of course could solve my problem by myself. Meanwhile, she gets off the hook.

Okay; end of autopsy.

But, just to make my point a little stronger, or in case you, my loyal reader, would like to understand from a more personal standpoint how this sort of exercise feels, let me give you something to work with. The following are four statements I garnered from recent interactions I've had with women. They may appear innocuous or funny at first reading, but they aren't dissimilar to the one dissected above. Go ahead; take them apart like I did. You'll very likely find yourself getting squeamish before you're finished.

1. "I know we both agreed to not talk about it 'til later. But I was just throwing that out as a possibility. Now I've decided I need to discuss it. And you're being inflexible."

2. "I know that's what I said. But it's obvious I must have felt differently."

3. "I don't normally act this way. Apparently you bring it out of me."

4. (In this last example I was talking with a woman—a married counseling psychologist—and she was telling me about an affair she was having. I asked her how her husband felt about it: "Does it hurt him? Or have you told him?")
Her answer:
"Oh, he knows. He just doesn't ask."

Yes; I am fully aware that all this is an exercise in rationalistic futility. That's my point.

But I also have a further point.

Women say that we men are *too* rational. Granted. But I believe men sometimes turn to overly rationalistic ways of dealing with women's emotions *because* we are bewildered by their ways of communicating about emotions, and thereby feel so stranded and alone with the emotions we ourselves want to communicate that in our attempts to escape the confusion and hurt we use anything we hope will help us. As a result, we often overcompensate by relying on the rational tools we are familiar with.

My point is that if men are overly rational in their dealings with women, it is women who sometimes enable this masculine fault. And one of the most effective ways they do this is by using emotions wrongly. Women are the supposed experts at emotion. And when referring to their expertise, they like to talk about emotions that involve nurturing, honesty, intuitive directness, and love. But I believe we men are starting to recognize that the emotional realm can also be used as weaponry when women hide behind its vagueness and elusiveness. In short, perhaps women are also the experts when it comes to *misusing* emotion.

Let me return briefly to my example. Some weeks after the exchange, I went to a third person who had talked to my woman friend about our upsetting interchange, and discussed what had happened. When I mentioned to this third person what I had *initially* felt accused of, and how for me it had never been resolved, this person said to me, "She told me she was just using it as ammunition against you. You mean she never told you that?"

I was stunned. Not so much by the dishonesty, but by the fact that she could have been aware of what she was doing, aware of the responsibility she was evading when she dismissed my confrontation, and yet so effective at confusing me.

What was I to think—much less feel?

Really, I don't have a neat conclusion drawn from all this. But I do feel I have a right to speculate:

Yes; women know emotions and can use them better than men can. Culturally and traditionally, emotions have been their domain. They are so familiar with this domain, moreover, that they can use it to good ends, when they wish, and, with just as much facility, use it to wrong ends. But—and this is so crucial —because we men have difficulty dealing with emotion, because women have told us for so long that we are bunglers at emotion, we do not even trust ourselves enough to call them at their game. And when we do, we are at a disadvantage because we have to speak an emotional language we are just learning.

The example I used is just one instance of the frustration I have experienced when trying to work through emotional situations with women. I chose it because it was so upsetting, because I did myself damage by trying to deal with it rationalistically, and because, given what I later found out, it illustrates so well those instances when women are fully aware of what they are doing when evading emotional responsibility—instances when they are aware of how much manipulative power their familiarity and facility with emotions can give them over men.

I said that my rationalistic analysis did me damage. This is only partly true. It also showed me how women's emotions aren't always so pure and angelic. As a result I am somewhat more cautious about automatically trusting women in that realm.

I also said that we men are just now learning how to feel and how to talk about our feelings, and that compared to women in this domain, we are somewhat at a disadvantage. But like I said, we are learning.

And we of the men's movement are learning well. We have been accustomed to the direct, specific language of rational logic. But we are learning that reason by itself is insufficient to the requirements of life, and sometimes does damage to ourselves and others. We are trying to undo that damage, avoid the logic that can be used as weaponry, and value the workings of the intellect only for the good it does.

As we men learn to deal with emotions, I think we will value their intrinsic indeterminateness or vagueness, and yet be loyal to the necessity of communicating them directly and responsibly. We will not very quickly become so agile with our emotions that we can play elusive war games with them. But then, perhaps it will be to our advantage to avoid learning such things. And what gives us advantage can also be to the advantage of women, if they will consent to put aside their own weapons.

JOHN BROCKETT, OF MILLERSBURG, MISSOURI

Michael Cox

John Brockett, of Millersburg, Missouri, says when he visits his cousin they typically behave in a playful fashion. Such behavior peeves his wife, although he and his cousin communicate more freely when they "act just as children would." Brockett says, "Our behavior is non-threatening and non-destructive, but my wife gets very upset and doesn't want to be around when we're doing it."

PASSIVE MAN, WILD WOMAN, AND BEYOND

Jed Diamond

With Sheila, I was able to take my own space, but wasn't able to be nose-to-nose with her and say, "I hear your fear, but I'm not going to buy into it." Part of my need to be away from her during the week was that I wasn't yet aware enough and secure enough always to stand up for myself when I was with her. Damn, I hated to admit it. When I was with Lindy, I gradually gave up bits and pieces of myself over the period of 10 years that we were married. In the year after we separated, I reclaimed a lot of my power, my desires and sureness about my own needs and rhythms. But how much power did I really express when I felt under pressure from a strong woman? It definitely was in a relationship with a woman that I still had the most trouble. I'd been able to face the draft, face policemen wielding clubs, face the Hell's Angels when they rode their motorcycles through our peace march. So I wasn't exactly Mr. Milktoast in most situations. At work, I'd been seen as strong and honest, one of the few people who could consistently stand up for himself and others against the administration. But with the significant woman in my life, I still felt scared. Why couldn't I be as strong at home as I seemed to be everywhere else in the world?

RELATING WITH THE WOMEN
WE TRY TO LOVE

HOW TO RECOGNIZE THE EARTH MOTHER TRAP

Herb Goldberg, Ph.D.

1. You feel alternately sentimental about her, then bored, suffocated or engulfed.
2. You feel guilty about depriving her and not giving enough of yourself.
3. You believe that you're working and doing the things you do primarily for her.
4. You believe that she's a more giving and more selfless person than you.
5. You're sure that she has no sexual fantasies or desires toward other men.
6. You feel guilty whenever you're having a good time that doesn't include her.
7. You kiss her on the forehead in fatherly fashion rather than on the lips, in a more sensual way.
8. You are exhilarated when you see her cooking for you or smell the clean laundry.
9. You feel you have to hide your sexual fantasies about other women from her because she'll be "deeply hurt" and "shocked."
10. You're sentimental about what a "good" woman she is and how lucky you are to have her standing behind you.
11. You're glad she's not one of those "women's libbers."
12. You're amazed at how she is like you—she always wants to have sex when you do, she likes the exact same vacation places, and enjoys the same kinds of activities. Everything you like she seems to like.
13. You like the quiet life with her apart from other people, because with her as a friend you don't need any other people to be close to.
14. You need her in order to feel that you're a man.
15. You're amazed that she loves you in spite of your faults and the other terrible things about you.

SIGNS FOR RECOGNIZING A NO-WIN SITUATION

Herb Goldberg, Ph.D.

1. It's hard to pin her down to specifics of any kind—a date, plans for future meetings, how she really feels, what she thinks or what she's been doing. If you press the issue and demand specifics, she withdraws, tells you that you're

smothering her and suggests that perhaps it would be best to end things completely. Out of fear, you back off and let *her* establish the rhythm and nature of the interaction.

2. She makes dates and shows up late, with ever-changing excuses, or she forgets to show up at all. Of course, you're always there on time. Occasionally, when she forgets, she may have forgotten so completely that if you never mentioned it, the broken date might have escaped her memory altogether. Clearly, she is not "there" for you, and you are no longer central in her consciousness.

3. She does not remember the nuances or subtleties of your preferences, your habit patterns and issues of importance to you, while you, on the other hand, seem to remember *every detail* of hers. Whether it be a food preference, a seating preference, a critical matter you are involved in and have told her about, [whatever,] she seems oblivious. Your feelings are constantly being hurt by this, but if you tell her that, she responds with annoyance over your "spoiled," "little boy" expectations. "If you want me to remember, remind me. I have other things on my mind. Don't expect me to think of everything. I'm not your mother," might be her response.

4. On occasions when she tells you that she really cares about you or even that she loves you, you have a sense of unreality, a feeling that it's too good to be true and that the bubble will burst momentarily, which it almost always does.

Indeed, if in a romantic moment on the telephone she indicatesd this love, if you follow up her statement with a request to be with her right away or even very soon, she almost always has an excuse for why that would be impossible.

5. Frequently when you are with her, she seems distracted, preoccupied and resistant to being touched. Rather than feeling welcomed when you come close, you sense that you're intruding on her, even though she may deny it. If you ask her why she seems so distant and cold, she tells you that it has nothing to do with you. It's just the mood she's in.

6. When the two of you are together, you feel that you're giving out all of the energy, and that, indeed, if you did not take responsibility for initiating and maintaining conversation or deciding on activities, little would be said or done because she is relating to you in a passive, detached, low-energy way.

7. When in a moment of extreme frustration and exasperation you say, "Maybe it would be better for us to stop seeing each other for a while," her response is calm, casual agreement. She might say, "Maybe we should. I don't like the fact that I bring this out in you. I obviously can't be what you want me to be, what you really seem to need." You then retract your threat.

8. There is no sense of continuity in the relationship. Each time you meet, it's almost like starting at square one. You feel no development of solidity or momentum, and after each time together, no matter how good it seemed, you sense that there might not be a next time.

9. You are obsessed with thinking about her. You *rehearse conversation with her in your head* and premeditated strategies for holding on to or interesting her. While nothing else seems important except being with her, you're often too insecure even to telephone her without your heart racing while questioning whether you really should call or whether you're just making a nuisance of yourself and driving her away. *You've lost your spontaneity and balance, and it's been replaced by premeditation, an overly deliberate scheming and manipulation born of insecurity.*

10. You're constantly showing off to her, trying to prove yourself worthy in ways you don't ordinarily do—talking about how much money you just earned, how well you handled a situation, how successful you've been at work and so on. This reflects your very low self-esteem when in her company.

11. You catch her in little lies and distortions of the truth. If you confront her with this, she always succeeds in evading admission and may even make you feel guilty for not showing more trust.

12. You're anxious around her, and certain self-destructive habits intensify. You find yourself constantly reaching for cigarettes or alcohol, sipping coffee, spilling drinks, clumsily bumping into things, dropping dishes, scraping your car in parking lots and in conversation frequently putting your foot in your mouth. You drive faster, stop exercising and become more belligerent with men who you think are coming on to her. All the things that in your more balanced periods you control and know better than to do you find yourself doing.

13. Like a child, you find yourself constantly asking everybody for advice, information and answers to help you deal with her. Underneath, the real message that you give off is that you're looking for reassurance and want people to tell you that everything will work out all right.

14. You focus on and magnify any little sign that allows you to tell yourself, "She wouldn't have said or done that if she wasn't planning to stay with the relationship." Your search for such indications and clues is insatiable.

15. Many parts of you emerge that you usually hold other people and even yourself in contempt for, such as possessiveness, clinging, suspicion, insecurity, jealousy, manipulation and the never-ending need to prove yourself in front of her. You withdraw energy from other relationships and from activities and pursuits that are important to you. You even feel uncomfortable and distrustful around male friends when she's around, because you think they're interested in her and that she might find them more attractive than you.

You think every man is interested in her. When you see her in conversation with other men, it generates anxiety and suspicion in you, because you suspect she's establishing a liaison. When you mention this to her, she becomes enraged, tells you you're being paranoid and that she resents your watching her.

16. You're constantly the one doing the apologizing. No matter what the conflict, you are left feeling at fault. She seldom acknowledges that she has done anything to create the problem or to hurt your feelings. The responsibility for problems always seems to be yours.

17. You give up things that are important to you—activities, friendships, work—to be with her at *her* convenience. You might even move to another city just to be with her, even though she wouldn't do the same for you. You are somehow always available and flexible in regard to getting together with her, while she is always having a hard time figuring out when she can fit you into her crowded schedule.

The meetings, therefore, always seem to be structured to accommodate *her* schedule and desire, not yours. You feel unable to change that, because you sense that her motivation to be with you is less than yours to be with her, and that if you pressure her in any way, she'll sever the relationship and you won't be able to see her at all.

18. You accept progressively more outrageous behavior on her part and self-degrading behavior on yours. You go along with things alien and humiliating to you to the point that you might even consider supporting her boyfriends if she wanted to have them move in with you and her. In short, you'll do and accept almost anything if you believe it will make the difference between holding and losing her.

19. While you're constantly thinking of little ways to please her—gifts to give, places to go, surprises and so on—she rarely, if ever, does the same for you.

20. She encourages you to take more freedom, do more things without her, even to see other women. However, you can't think of anything you want to do or anyone else you want to be with.

21. Sex, particularly "good sex," occurs only when *she* wants it. Even then you may get a sense that she's not really there with *you*. When you're turned on and she's not, you're left feeling like a demanding, lustful animal, the insensitive, "horny" one, and nothing you do can turn her on.

22. No matter what she does or says and no matter how objectionable her behavior, you put her on a pedestal and excuse her, thinking she's the most perfect, sensitive and incredible woman in the world. Obvious facts to the contrary are ignored or disregarded. *Clearly, you are addicted to your fantasy of her.*

23. You're terrified of doing *anything* to displease or anger her. The relationship feels so tenuous to you that you feel anything negative could trigger her into leaving you. Indeed, arguments often lead to a threat from her that "we ought to end things completely right now. I don't want to hassle anymore." You apologize.

24. Many times when others are around, you feel as if you weren't there, or even that you're an intruder. Specifically, she may begin to talk to someone and forget to introduce you, or not include you in the conversation at all, leaving you standing there uncomfortably.

25. She doesn't call you or want you around when she's feeling bad, even though you tell her you'd like to be there for her. She tells you, instead, that she needs to be alone when she's blue or depressed.

26. She seems to say the very things that make you feel hurt or rejected. For example, you speak of love and she says she's not sure there is such a thing— that it's all really just immature dependency. When you speak of intimacy and relationships, she philosophizes about how people are afraid of freedom and don't know how to give each other space.

27. Your mood swings are volatile in relation to her. When she says something reassuring, you're elated and energetic. Desperation, loneliness, anxiety and apathy set in whenever she is cold or in any way seems to indicate a lack of interest in the relationship.

28. No matter how much you pursue clarification, you're never really sure of where you stand with her. When you ask her how she's feeling toward you, the answer is either evasive or an angry, "Stop asking me!"

29. She is always surprising you. She telephones just when you've given up or even resigned yourself to never seeing her anymore. Then, when you think things are becoming more solid, she doesn't call when you expect her to or are sure she will. There's constant unpredictability that keeps you off balance.

30. You're obsessed with her during the day and are constantly struggling against the impulse to call her, to talk or to tell her that you love her. When you do, she often puts you on hold, tells you she's busy, just on the way out or talking to somebody, and asks you to call her back in a few hours. You don't want to ask her to call you back, because you sense that she won't, so you say yes. When you do call her back, sometimes she's not even there.

31. She seems oblivious to your down moods. When you're hurting, she doesn't seem to notice your pain.

32. You're constantly having to explain what you *really* meant. Or you're interrogating her about the *real* meaning of something she said. Either way it's as if there is always some tension and distrust, a sense of walking on eggs that you'd like to avoid but can't seem to.

33. You rarely laugh around her spontaneously. Instead, discussions with her tend to be heavy, intellectual and grim in their intensity, as you are seemingly always and endlessly discussing and analyzing "our relationship."

34. She's always telling you she needs time, freedom and space to be alone, to collect herself and to think things over. She rations out the amount of time you can see her, and the amount of time seems to progressively decrease.

35. She considers your endless gropings for affection and reassurance to be infantile, and she tells you they make her uncomfortable.

36. Your intuition tells you that you're not central in her life, that she doesn't love you and that the relationship is doomed—and YOU'RE RIGHT! To fully accept this is very painful, but to continue to deny it will be self-destructive.

CONSTRUCTIVE FIGHTING

Herb Goldberg, Ph.D.

The capacity to develop a friendship by articulating, managing, and resolving conflict, for the male, requires an absence of defensive aggression—the need to always be right and the tendency to view issues in black-and-white terms. For the female, it is necessary to directly experience and own her autonomous aggression, including her power strivings, so that she no longer perceives herself as a victim and morally superior, and rids herself of the destructive and erroneous equation between being "nice" and being constructive and feminine.

Once that is achieved, conflict will be recognized as a constructive, inevitable, and necessary part of the development of an authentic friendship. The striving to be nice and to make peace will be unnecessary once the process of resolving conflict is altered so that it is no longer experienced and engaged in destructively. Therefore, in the new male-female relationship, conflict will be seen as a necessary, helpful process for creating authentic intimacy, because it generates genuine, mutual knowing and a clarification of issues. Efforts to deny resistance, anger, and differences will be seen as destructive. The repressed feelings create a dangerous undertow, and are factors in the development of psychosomatic and psychological illness, as well as the contamination of the interaction with indirect manifestations of aggression.

It is the nice, peaceful couple that denies aggression and fears fighting that is the couple in trouble, rather than the couple that freely engages in equal, direct, give-and-take encounters when conflict arises.

The key indicator of a new process in resolving conflict will be the absence of painful, round-robin accusations. Instead, fights will be about genuine issues and differences and they will be resolvable with goodwill. Both partners will be able to hear each other objectively and empathically and will not, therefore, distort the problem or overreact. Feelings of guilt and victimization will not be present and fighting will not be seen as a hurtful process to be avoided, but as one that generates greater intimacy and friendship.

New male-female relationships, in the beginning stages, will be replete with conflicts over decision making, control, money, social issues, responsibility allocation, and the existence of other intimate relationships, but will steadily progress to a calmer state as conflicts are worked through and the partners get to know each other as separate people. These relationships will begin with considerable conflict because of an honest acknowledgment of differences, and will progress steadily toward a more comfortable, harmonious state, rather than beginning without conflict in a romantic high and ending in an atmosphere of irreconcilable differences.

His aggression will not be exaggerated and hers will not be denied. Therefore, fights will not be avenues for discharging accumulated rage, but will be over genuine issues.

In the new male-female relationship, there will be no desire to win for its own sake or to justify oneself. Rather than vindication, the goal will be the genuine resolution of difference. Both partners will be sensitive to the objective facts as well as the less rational emotional nuances.

HOW TO RECOGNIZE A CONSTRUCTIVE FIGHT IN THE NEW MALE-FEMALE RELATIONSHIP

The ways couples fight are as varied and personal as their lovemaking styles, and will evolve and change as the new male-female relationship becomes more intimate. The process of conflict resolution will involve a clear definition of issues, hearing each other accurately, and providing feedback to ensure that the other person's thoughts and feelings were correctly heard.

The friendship-generating process of conflict resolution will be characterized by the following:

- *Bonding:* The end of a fight will be accompanied by a greater sense of intimacy and closeness than before.
- *Nondefensiveness:* The fight itself will be free of any attempt to define who is at fault or who is more responsible. Blaming and feeling guilty will not be present. Instead, the emphasis will be on resolving the issue and taking responsibility for one's share in maintaining the problem.
- *Reason and emotion combined:* The fight will be neither a battle of logic nor a great emotional display. Rather, it will be characterized by empathic objectivity.
- *Nonrepetition:* The issues fought about will have a new and fresh sound and will not be a replay of previous, identical fights nor even a variation on familiar old themes.
- *Absence of intimidation:* Neither person will be afraid of the other, nor will they create an artificial crisis or threaten to end the relationship in the middle of a fight. Both partners will be clear, open, strong, flexible, and supportive.
- *Authentic issues:* Fights will have a satisfying feeling because they will be focused on genuine, identifiable issues and differences. They will not be personal attacks or "straw man" fights that disguise deeper conflict.
- *A sense of being more fully known:* Each partner will have the satisfying experience of feeling more known and real to the other after the fight.
- *Closure:* The end of a fight will be charcterized by a clean feeling in which both partners feel heard and the problem is successfully worked through.

WHAT IS THE PLAYFUL RELATIONSHIP?

Herb Goldberg, Ph.D.

There is an unfortunate misconception about playfulness in the man-woman relationship. "Playful" is thought to be next of kin to "irresponsible." To want to play is supposedly to want to be a child.

Paradoxically, from a psychological perspective, it is the serious orientation or process in a relationship that is irresponsible. The serious orientation is a manifestation of repression and role playing in the name of being approprate or loving or mature, and a general denial of inner experience that is inappropriate to one's image. It makes the interaction fragile, self-conscious, and explosive. *It is irresponsible because of the great mass of unconscious or defensively blocked inner life that throws the relationship out of conscious control. The relationship controls the couple, who become its victim. Love is suddenly and unpredictably transformed into hostility.*

Playfulness is an elusive concept because it exists in process, not in content. Anything can be play, and conversely activities that should be play are not when they are transformed by gender defensiveness into something serious. Two different people can be doing the same activity: for one, it's play; for the other, it's onerous. *Playfulness is, to a large extent, a product of the absence of*

93

defensiveness, and the capacity for it develops as men and women move be-
yond masculine-feminine interaction to a nondefensive relationship where
they are together because they want to be, rather than because they need to be.

Certain characteristics of play can be defined and doing so is useful for understanding the new male-female relationship. One of the fundamental characteristics of play is that it is not goal directed. It is engaged in for its own sake. Dr.
Arthur Koestler pointed out that the more soiled an activity becomes with
other motives, the less likely it is play.

Psychologist Eric Plaut, in a paper titled "Play and Adaptation," described
play as "a pleasurable, freely chosen, intrinsically complete, and noninstrumen-
tal activity."

Psychologists K. Sylva, J. Bruner, and P. Genova defined it similarly: "The
essence of play is the dominance of means over ends."

The whole person, capable of being playful and in the moment, has been
termed process oriented. In her book *Sex Roles and Personal Awareness,* Dr.
Barbara Lusk Forisha wrote, "Process-oriented individuals are less bound by
roles in general than other people. They are less bound by their personal and
cultural past. Less energy is tied up in maintaining the self that has been, or in
constructing the self that might be. Such individuals are more completely, honestly and authentically in the present."

Dr. Mihaly Csikszentmihalyi of the University of Chicago described the experience of adult playfulness as one of "flow," which means a "merging of action
and awareness, a loss of self-consciousness, and a goal of continued flowing
rather than an external reward."

Translated into the daily world of the new male-female relationship, one
aspect of playfulness is that it is not a symbolic relationship based on defensive
needs, but instead a relationship based primarily on the pleasure of being together, on *the experience itself.* It requires that the man and woman not need
each other for security or defensive reasons, but choose to be together simply
because they want to be. The primary reward is the flow, the energy exchange
generated by the interaction.

Play as a basis for the new male-female relationship is far removed from the
traditional, serious man-woman relationship, which is always instrumental and
mutually exploitive. He is chosen primarily for his functions, and she for hers.

The symptoms of traditional neurosis (which also characterize the polarized
relationship), such as anxiety, conflict, tension, hostile eruptions, desire to escape, psychosomatic illness and compulsive activity, can be seen as originating
in a person's deep awareness of being engulfed by the oppressiveness of seriousness and the underlying hunger for growth, expansion, play, and getting out
of the trap. Unable to do that, both men and women begin to become more
self-destructive and hostile toward each other.

Yet generation after generation has glorified the work obsession as a virtue
and ultimate validation. Parents transferred their play repressions to their children. They rewarded the offspring who worked hardest and took on the greatest responsibilities earliest. These children were looked on with favor as the
best and most mature. Parents could be truly proud of them. These parents

94

were extinguishing in their children the play capacity that, if maintained and expressed, would threaten to expose their own frustration and unhappiness over not being able to let go and be playful.

Men and women alike are victims of this. The cultural preoccupation with growth, as the widely heard plaint of the past ten years, is an expression of a powerful, subliminal awareness of something lost that is struggling to reemerge. I believe that to be the capacity for playfulness.

Seriousness as the dominant tone of life, in or out of a relationship, may, in an enlightened human atmosphere, be recognized as one of the major symptoms of the pathology of socialized gender defensiveness.

However, the individual's resistance and inability to become playful cannot be blamed totally on society, as some tend to do. By confusing *effect* with *cause,* one comes to blame the pressure of economics, family life, religious orientation, and social context for blocking the capacity for pleasure and play. *Playfulness is a way of perceiving, experiencing, and relating to the world, not something that has to do with society's external reality. Indeed, reality is relative to it.*

The strong motivation to acquire wealth, for example, requires the same serious defensiveness that represses playfulness. *The paradox of wealth is that the very same process that facilitates its acquisition also may destroy the capacity to enjoy it.* The person who believes he or she can buy pleasure and still play is confusing content with process. Distraction and stimulation can be purchased, but not the consciousness of play, which requires the antithesis of the defensiveness that is the driving force behind acquisition obsessions.

Playful consciousness is not nonmaterialistic or antimaterialistic. Rather, it simply keeps materialism in perspective so that there is motivation for acquiring only enough material security to fulfill real needs and not imagined and distorted ones.

THE COMPONENTS OF THE PLAYFUL NEW MALE-FEMALE RELATIONSHIP

Intrinsic Attraction

The relationship is motivated principally by the pleasure of the other person's presence and not his or her function. This person is an end, not a means.

Mutual Knowing

Both people feel known and recognized by the other, in the way they know themselves to be. There is no sense of being on a pedestal, of being idolized, distorted, or magnified by the other person's needs.

Stream-of-Consciousness Relating

The verbal interaction flows. Conversations are personal, connected, unintellectualized, and engaged in easily and spontaneously. There is no conscious self-censorship or concern about avoiding certain topics, being misunderstood, or saying something that shouldn't be said.

There is no need to maintain an image and therefore there is a sense of freedom in response and expression. This does not imply uncontrolled self-indulgence, but rather that any self-control will be based on voluntary restraint rather than fear of exposure of one's thoughts or feelings.

Transcendence of Gender Defensiveness

No behavior or response is repressed because of its reflection on the masculinity of the male or the femininity of the female. The interaction is gender free, person to person, as between two intimates of the same sex.

Authentic Attraction and Interaction Based on Want Rather Than Need

The decision to come together and be together is based on the pleasure of being in each other's presence, rather than on defensive motivations. Sexuality, for example, becomes spontaneous experience free of feeings of responsibility, defensive proving, and need for affirmation that one is loved that cause it to become *work* and eventually a source of fear and distress in traditional relationships. The greater the gender polarization, the greater the insecurity and defensive clinging, which make it impossible to come together out of passionate desire.

The Maintenance of Separate Identities

As the fusion of identities occurs, the energy and stimulation of being with another person is lost. Gender defensiveness produces the kind of fusion that results in feeling as if one is talking to oneself rather than to another person. As this happens, boundaries disappear and the capacity for flow is lost. The degree of playfulness potential is correlated with the security and strength in the definition and maintenance of separate identities. *Genuine* interest in each other can only exist under such conditions.

Mutual Acceptance

The capacity to know and be known is related to the absence of mutual judging and control. Conversely, the need to present an image instead of the reality of oneself grows in proportion to the fear that one will be judged.

The capacity to accept another person is also contingent on full awareness and acceptance of oneself. The more defensive one becomes in the quest to be "perfect" rather than fully real, the more critical one will be of others. As all people become more authentically human and whole, I believe, the full complexity of inner experience will be found to be similar and available for all.

Objective Love and Admiration for One's Partner

If one's partner were not one's mate, one would want him or her as a friend anyway, because one objectively loves and admires that person—in terms of aesthetics, values, intellect, and the overall delight experienced in each other's presence.

SIGNS OF THE PLAYFUL RELATIONSHIP

Energy in Each Other's Presence (The Absence of Toxic Fatigue)

The relationship increases the energy of each person rather than draining it.

Typically, repression of feelings and thoughts, plus unconscious barriers constructed to defend oneself against the toxic impact of the other person, are the destroyers of energy flow. A sign of a playful partner is a continual, reciprocal flow of energy with no feeling drained or emotionally fatigued.

Conversational Flow

The verbal interaction is easy, unself-conscious, continuous, of a stream-of-consciousness type, and ever changing. There is little self-monitoring, intellectualizing, or deliberate effort to communicate.

The Stamp of Personal Identity

Celebrations and events are continuously created and experienced according to inner feelings rather than the demands of ritual and social pressure. External structures and supports are used to facilitate and enrich, but are secondary. Holidays and special events become tools for self-expression rather than acting as mandates for creating "joyful" experiences that are unfelt.

Laughter

You know you're in the midst of a playful relationship if there is easy, spontaneous laughter, not based on jokes or "making each other laugh," but rather on a sharing of perceptions, separate visions, and individual consciousness.

Naturally Good Habits

Self-destructive, compulsive habits such as smoking, alcoholism, drug use, television addiction, and overeating can be seen as manifestations of a need to numb oneself or escape from the here and now. In a playful relationship, such compulsive habits or escapes will not be present. Instead, alcohol, drugs, and so on, to the extent that they are indulged in, will be there as conscious choices, and never as a compulsive need.

Liking Yourself

In a playful interaction you find that you really like yourself. Even things about yourself that you might at other times judge negatively are experienced with benign acceptance and good humor. In general, you feel yourself to be eminently sane, validated, and functioning optimally when you're with your partner. There is no feeing observed, evaluated, or analyzed.

In the playful relationship you do not feel an urgency to change yourself or to work on your hang-ups *though you are constantly open to input and feedback*. You feel appreciated for who you are; you like yourself and your desire is only to grow and learn more about yourself and thereby broaden the vistas of the relationship.

Generosity of Spirit

The result of liking oneself, being nonjudgmental, feeling good in the here and now, and experiencing energy and laughter is an atmosphere best described as generosity of spirit. Specifically, you let each other get away with the idiosyncrasies and imperfections that are typically subject to attack and criticism in a nonplayful or serious interaction. You are not constantly watching each other for slip-ups in behavior or speech.

GETTING THERE: THE PATH TO THE NEW, PLAYFUL MALE-FEMALE RELATIONSHIP

The capacity for the playful relationship involves a process of growth and is not an either-or phenomenon that can be gained in immediate how-to fashion. The following dimensions are directional signs for the growth process that makes the playful relationship possible.

From: *What* you are, based on your symbols

To: *Who* you are, based on how you relate

From: Intellectualizing and abstractions

To: Stream-of-consciousness, unself-conscious, unmonitored communication

From: Behavior motivated by have-to's

To: Spontaneous, freely chosen (want-to) behavior

From: Seriousness, intensity, and dutifully trying to meet expectations

To: Laughter, lightness, and self-motivation

From: Ritual (how it "should" be)

To: Creativity (how it expresses you)

From: A focus on past and future

To: Being in the present

From: Rigidity

To: Fluidity

From: Being externally programmed

To: Being internally motivated

From: Concern about gender appropriateness (Is this masculine or feminine behavior?)

To: Freedom from sex-role self-consciousness

From: Clinging dependency

To: Being together when and because you want to be

From: Being careful and self-protective

To: Being transparent

From: Security as the prime motivation for being together

To: Enhancement and enrichment as prime motivation

From: The need for external stimulation

To: Fulfillment based primarily on the experience of the relationship

These dimensions are part of a movement in relationships toward authenticity. They do not imply selfishness or "doing your own thing," but rather a consciousness designed to avoid the buildup of repression, resentment and rigidity.

The liberated relationship of the future will not succeed, nor should it, if it is humorless, mutually judgmental, intellectualized, polemic, perfectionistic, critical, and toxic.

I like the way Dr. Michael Novak, distinguished professor of religion at Syracuse University, expresses it: "Play, not work, is the end of life. . . . Play is reality. Work is diversion and escape."

THE MARRIAGE EXPERIENCE

FOR MARK: A WEDDING TOAST

David P. Faas

A silver noose around his finger
offers fifty years of swinging
from a branch
he never built;
But he is happy this way:
it is his solitude's execution;
it is his moment of kisses;
it is his honeymoon of silence
to centuries of civilization.
This giant step to a doublebed,
a calendar of clean sheets
flapping on the clothesline
like the cliche of time
in a forties' movie,
announces his life
like a headline some
coffee-sipping editor issued
for a painstaking deadline.
But he is happy this way:
before the static screen of events
and canned laughter,
after the repeated episodes
of winning bread
and spaghetti on Wednesday
to save a few coins
for that spring splurge
to Disneyworld
with daughters in strollers
and sons in sunsuits
crying tears that stick
in cotton candy on the corners
of their curled mouths.

A silver noose around his finger
throttles impossible others:
a life of crime,
of devout intelligence,
of causes lost

99

in the broad bays of the commonplace.
Tradition's son whoops it up
one last night
before they come for him in the humid garden.
He prays for no cup's passing,
but downs the bitter nectar
that must taste sweet when there's nothing else to swallow.
Deaf to the lynch mob of matrimony,
a bachelor,
groomed by twenty-five years
of waiting
for the bugles and the hounds
and slash of the trap door
dropping down,
      drops down.

IT'S OK TO BE WEAK

Jed Diamond

Another blast of insight: Lindy was very much like my mother. Outwardly strong and self-sufficient, she had difficulty allowing herself to be vulnerable. She was not very accepting of weakness in others, particularly men. I realized that a lot of her support which I so praised—getting through school, facing the draft and deciding to go to Canada, standing up to the mental health director— was support to be strong. Get out there and fight. When I said, "I'm tired of fighting, of being strong all the time. I want it to be OK if I'm weak," Lindy had difficulty.

A BIRTHDAY FANTASY

Perry Treadwell, Ph.D.

For the fourth time in the past half hour George Hampton stood up and walked to the window. He looked out over the parking lots and shorter buildings to the mountain rising some twenty miles away. But he didn't see the city or surrounding countryside at all. He was rehearsing the telephone call again.

"What if they laugh at me?" he mused. "What if they say no? What name did I decide to use? Which number should she call me at?" George had been around this track a hundred times in his mind. He wasn't getting anywhere.

"Damn, I'd better do it before Sally comes back from lunch," he resolved and picked up the phone. Looking down at the card he pecked away at the buttons.

"Hello, A-One Dating Service, can I help you?" a bouncy girlish voice replied to the second ring.

"Hello. . .yes, I'm. . ." George paused. He couldn't remember what name he decided to use. "I'm. . .I'm new at this," he blurted out. (He was going to be so suave, so in charge and he had already blown it.)

"Well, what do you want?" asked a more businesslike, bored voice belonging to the same woman.

"Let me tell you my fantasy and see if you can do something for me." George was desperate enough to blurt anything out. "You see I want to celebrate my birthday." (He wasn't going to tell her it was his forty-fifth.) "And I want to do it in a special way. I want a woman about 35" (young and vivacious but still experienced), "about five four," (shorter than his five eight so she could lay her head on his chest), "black hair," (he had a fetish for dark women like Veronica Hamel on Hill Street Blues; his wife was light blond), "and thin but not skinny. It's okay if she's married. . . ." (He figured she wouldn't be doing this because she had to but because she enjoyed it.)

When he paused the voice on the line asked, "When do you want her?"

"Next Wednesday," he replied. "I want to meet her at 'Reggies' for drinks about six-thirty. Then we'll go to dinner, a play or symphony and then 'Johnny's' for dancing. . . .She's got to be able to dance the forties stuff, then we'll go to the Plaza Hotel. . ."

"Sir," the voice interrupted, "I must tell you we don't make sexual dates, this IS NOT A CALL GIRL SERVICE." The voice was firm and well rehearsed.

"Yes, I know," he replied quickly. "But I want the liberty to negotiate what happens the rest of the evening. . . ." George paused for some reply. (He envisioned them finishing a bottle of champagne together before slipping into a king-sized bed. As the light streamed in the next morning he would awake to see this beautiful creature peacefully curled up next to him. He would call for breakfast and maybe they would make love once more before parting. . . forever.

"Sir, how can your date reach you?" the voice interrupted his dreams.

"Please have her call 378-6798, say she is from the. . ." (pause) "the Action Rental Company and ask for George."

"Sir, you will be called this afternoon or tomorrow. Is there anything else?"

"No, I don't think so."

"Thank you for calling A-One. Have a good day." Click.

George stood up and walked to the window again. He felt exhilarated, excited. He anticipated the evening all over again and wanted it to happen NOW. Would someone really call him? What if no one called, what if he was out, what if Sally intercepted the call, what if. . .what would his date look like?

The mountain in the distance appeared larger now. "I've got to share this with Frank." He turned to call Frank but stopped in the middle of a push button. Frank didn't understand.

Last Thursday, over a pitcher of beer, Frank had said, "I don't understand why you can't do all that with Helen. Why you have to do it with someone you don't know. . .don't even want to know."

"That's the whole point, Frank." George repeated words to himself. "I'll learn all I need to know the first three hours. It's all the excitement of a new date, new feelings and smells and touch. Just like those dates before we were married. But the anxiety is gone. I don't have to perform, to play a game, to try to seduce her. Just be myself."

George had hurried on, "I read somewhere that brains, even brains of old people, need constant stimulation to remain functional. Maybe this is my way of hyping my brain. . .you've got your soccer."

Frank had divided the rest of the pitcher between their glasses without looking at George. "And I don't have to make any commitment to this woman. We are together to enjoy the evening. There's no past, no future, just now. For one time in my life there'll be just now."

Frank had gotten up, drained his glass and replied with appropriate sincerity, "You do what you have to, George. You know you have my support. . .if not blessing. But I still don't understand."

George lowered the phone on the cradle and ambled back to the window noticing that the mountain was beginning to look like a single breast. He really didn't understand either.

HER HUSBAND'S NEW SEX LIFE

Jim Sanderson

I was talking to Scott, a 46-year-old man who six months ago suddenly sold his prosperous retail business and who, just a week before his 25th anniversary, told his wife he wanted to move out of the house to live as a single man.

Question: A wife always assumes that only another woman could have provoked such a massive upheaval.

Answer: I tried to convince her that I hadn't fallen in love with someone else, but that I had rediscovered sex, among other things.

Q: This sounds like the old "male menopause" cliche.

A: That phrase angers the hell out of me. A lot of men my age discover they've been systematically starved of powerful sex for years, and they decide to do something about it. It's not a last gasp clutching at fading virility. You find that sex isn't the same as when you were an 18-year-old kid, but it's about four times better than you've been doing with your wife lately. There's no reason not to have good sex all your life.

Q: The novelty of a new partner is always exciting, expecially with a younger body.

A: No, all that wears thin pretty quickly. Wives claim this in self-defense; if all he wants is a young body then obviously the problem isn't theirs, and they don't have to do any changing.

Q: How did your relationship go wrong?

A: After the first couple of years it's the woman who controls the sexual level of the marriage. My wife almost never denied me sex; she just got less enthusiastic about it. Women assume that sex is something mechanical with a man; if he doesn't ask for it then he must not want it. But the older a man gets the more he needs to have a woman want him, provoke him. Desire is the big turn-on, not a young body. I had to re-sell my wife on the idea every time and at the end we'd drifted down to about once a month.

Now I've met some women who haven't given up on sex. They're playful and inventive and even aggressive sometimes, and they have tremendous orgasms. This is the ultimate male euphoria.

Q: You weren't a selfish lover at home, then?

A: I tried everything to please her. The turning point came after the kids arrived. I think she began to see her primary role in life as a mother, not a wife, and certainly not as my mistress.

Q: Mothers are often just plain too tired, especially with young kids.

A: Yes, I know all that, and I tried to make allowances.

Q: Maybe those endless 14-hour days at work that you talk about gave her the feeling you were cutting her out of your life, that you didn't need her. A wife who doesn't feel loved also has a hard time acting seductive.

A: When a marriage breaks up it's always the man's fault, isn't it? When I told her I was moving out of the house I said I wasn't blaming her, I just thought we had to live apart for a while and think about what we wanted to do with the rest of our lives.

Q: How did she react?

A: First she couldn't believe it, and then she was furious. She actually thought we had a pretty good marriage going. After all, we'd survived 25 years and a lot of people we know hadn't. She saw a couple of lawyers but never has actually filed for divorce. She hasn't even put me through all the legal hassle of a formal separation agreement, for which I'm grateful.

Q: Is she dating other men?

A: Apparently she's had a couple of affairs, which must have raised her consciousness some about men. She's also gone back to work, although I still put money in our joint checking account. I cooked dinner for her a couple of times at my place, but we ended up with a lot of tears and reproaches. Now we just talk on the phone.

Q: What do you talk about?

A: It always starts off with something about the kids in college, or my mother, but then we get a little more personal. I think we're trying to feel each other out about what kind of mutual interests we have that could last the rest of our lives. The other day she asked me to a concert. I never had much time for music but now I do. We're also talking about a trip to Mexico. I think she's wooing me a little—and that's a wonderful experience.

Q: You sound like you might like to resume the marriage.

A: I don't know if it's possible. Still a quarter of a century is a long time—I've shared most of my adult life with this woman. Her body is as sweetly familiar to me as my own. If we can re-create some kind of sex life, and if we can find some new common ground in other areas that we never had before, then maybe we have a chance. I'm a different man now, six months later; maybe she's a different woman.

Chapter 5:
Men with Men

FRIENDSHIPS

HOMOPHOBIA

Tom Williamson

Homophobia means fear of others like oneself. The men's movement has claimed this word for itself by redefining it to mean one man's fear of getting emotionally or physically close to another man. The overcoming of homophobia is not to be confused with anything homosexual. Rather, it is to be likened to the way European men greet with a warm hug, in contrast to the way American men exchange a brief handshake.

It means that it is all right for fathers to hug and express positive emotion toward their sons. It means that, in conversation, instead of concentrating on the "how-to" of sex, one expresses how one feels about it. It also means that we be tolerant of and sensitive to the problems other men face, even though those problems may not be our own. And it means that men must be supportive of other men who are less able, and it means that men should never have to be embarassed to ask for help or to admit that they have a problem.

WHAT GOOD ARE MEN?

Jed Diamond

Lindy went away for the weekend with a friend from San Francisco. I spent the weekend learning to run with a runner named Mike Spino in Golden Gate Park. I felt so alive and part of the flow of the world. I experienced Saturday night alone, felt some loneliness, but also excited to be just with me. I met a man in a bar and we talked in an open, friendly way. I realized how few men friends I had in my life, how much had revolved around women. It was nice to just be friendly with a man in a bar, rather than seeing him as a potential competitor for some woman I had my eye on.

I used to envy women I would see in bars who were with a group of women friends. They looked like they were truly enjoying being together, not just waiting to meet a man. The men I'd seen had one hand on a bottle, one eye on the conversation they were having with the guy next to them and the other eye and all of their attention on the women walking by.

It was a real treat for me to "forget" about women for awhile and talk to another man.

The following week I called up my friend Les and asked if he'd like to go out for a drink with me. It turned out to be a delightful evening. We talked about ourselves and our lives, our work, and our women. I realized I'd rarely ever spent an evening with a man, or any time for that matter, where we weren't doing something. I had known Les for several years and never knew he played the organ. Slightly drunk, I followed him into the darkened church where he played on Sunday. I sat in the pews while Les played some Bach selections in the dark. That truly was the most unusual Saturday night date I had ever had.

GETTING TO KNOW OURSELVES WITH OTHER MEN

LIBERATING MALE SEXUALITY

Rick Blum

Life-events, at their best, and lovemaking, at its best, share similar dynamics. The time is right; all energies are drawn into harmony. Our resistances are easily seduced by the appropriateness of the moment. The impossible becomes pos-

Acknowledgment: with appreciation to Betty Dodson and Tom Sargent

sible: pain and fear dissolve under the gentle massage of love and pleasure. An all-absorbing climax leaves excited and satisfied hearts to notice that nothing is now the same as it was.

I shared in such an event during the second weekend in September. After years of requests, Betty Dodson, the author of *Liberating Masturbation* and the originator of the "Body Sex Workshop," agreed that the time was finally right for her first all-male workshop. It was with embarrassment, fortunately tempered by enthusiasm, that she recalled having previously said that "women should teach women, and men should teach men." Her solution was the intention that we all learn from each other and we did.

To understand what it was like to participate in her workshop, you have to know something of Betty. She is unique. Compact, strong, and radiant, she seems to have a sexual relationship with reality, and the attraction is mutual. While a noted feminist, she is as free from any countercultural mindlessness as she is free from conventional mindlessness. I found her to be open, loving and a prime example of the joyous sensuality of which she speaks. To meet her was to experience instant feelings of safety and acceptance. Her delight in my group's opportunities for freedom and caring tolerance for our areas of inhibition formed a reliable center from which to make our explorations.

A "Body Sex Workshop" consists of about ten naked people together in a room, each of us rediscovering a unity between body, sexuality, and sense of self-worth. People look at themselves and others; people massage themselves and others; people talk about themselves and about masturbation. In Betty's groups, as opposed to the less controversial version which we have been offering at the New England Sex Forum, people also masturbate together.

The benefits of this group for women have become legendary. Body-image improves remarkably; ability to experience pleasure increases dramatically.

But, as a man, I wondered seriously before the workshop if I would be able to gain much from it. Like the others, I was used to being naked with other men in locker-rooms since youth. I could certainly masturbate already, and looking at my genitals would hardly be a new experience for me. Surely, men are already personally sex-positive, I considered. While we tend to expect restrictions in women, we seldom take them seriously for ourselves. Sexual experiences are, for men, more often a sign of pride than of shame. The purpose of a Body Sex Workshop for a woman in our culture was clear to me. For a man, I wondered.

As I powerfully discovered, the attitude toward my sexuality which I have been trained to have is hardly positive, just as aggressiveness is not assertiveness, bravado is not confidence, and violence is not communication.

To illustrate, Betty suggested, at one point, a somewhat embarrassing exercise which had us moving as we do in "missionary position" sex, only without anyone on the "receiving" end. Our responses to the exercise surprised her: "I don't understand, you're all doing it!" She began to relate to us how, at the women's groups, there is always a degree of hesitation about the exercises. Some might just watch. Others might cautiously investigate the movement. But, not us: we were fucking the air as if we wanted to. Suddenly, it hit her: "Oh, of course, you're men: you're afraid *not* to!"

You couldn't ask for a more cooperative group of people than a group of men at a sex workshop. We had each been thoroughly trained to instantly refuse to "chicken-out" of anything, especially anything sexual. In addition, our group included a variety of therapists, who "should" be even more willing. We had to be sophisticated and brave and so we immediately followed orders. This one-hundred-twenty-pound woman had only to quietly suggest an activity, and her large students jumped into their best approximation of her wishes. Our clothes were off quickly. Immediately, Betty had us straining to straighten our Western-ized backs, making outselves dizzy with yogic breath-of-fire exercises, coopera-tively examining our genitals before we even knew what we were looking for, obediently humping the air to music, and even swinging our hips in the most unmasculine fashion.

Tom Sargent, a sex-counselor at the New England Sex Forum, is a delightful rogue whose input was central in helping to transform the workshop into a men's group. His first contribution, however, was an eight-inch rubber penis which he gift-wrapped for Betty with the fervent wish that she not feel left out in a room full of naked men. She graciously accepted the offering but had little use for it, I'm sure. The fact was that she had ten live penises, and their owners, at her command.

We sometimes had no initial idea what an exercise was about; we acted out of the cultural rules which legislate male attitudes towards sexuality. Yet, the exercises themselves were often well-designed to break those rules. Something was beginning to happen. Among other things, we were laughing at ourselves quite a bit.

It took us a full day to get afraid. Since men are not allowed to have doubts, it required half of the workshop for us to begin to share them. For women, who are ordered to be afraid by the culture, the best approach is to move away from fears in this type of workshop. For men, it is particularly liberating to spend some of the time sharing our fears in an accepting environment.

So, while women fear sex, we discovered that men fear fear. Other compar-isons became apparent. While women pressure themselves for orgasms on demand, we seek erections at will. While women are more comfortable with nudity among their own sex, heterosexual men are terrified of touch among their own sex. I soon realized that we men had our share of work to do.

But it didn't feel like work. It felt like a celebration. The first day was fun and "light" in atmosphere. Laughter, time, and mutual acceptance were establishing a safe-culture for what we were about to do.

The second day of the celebration included three difficult activities. We each were to give and receive a group-massage, full-body. We each were to have the chance to give the others full-body hugs, naked. And, we all would masturbate at the same time, a "circle jerk." As the day progressed, each of us experienced a central surprise consisting of two simultaneous facts. First, each of us ex-pected most or all of these activities to create intense distress. Second fact: they didn't.

Usually they would have, and now they didn't. We enjoyed ourselves thor-oughly. This shift gradually taught me what it is like to really be sex-positive, what it is like to say "yes" to ourselves, to our sensuality, and to others.

I noticed a sense of closeness, amazing and unique for me, steadily increasing among us that second day. As this comfort and caring grew, another feeling noticeably lessened, a feeling that I usually keep around as a substitute for a relaxed affirmation of my male sexuality. My aggressiveness drained, and I was no longer interested in fighting myself and other men. I was loving myself and other men. That was supposed to make me lose my masculinity and it didn't. In fact, in increased my confidence.

As I hugged other men, I could feel their bodies against my body, sometimes their penises against my own. Rather than anxiety, I felt relieved at the freedom of including my genitals in my comfort. I felt easy, and relaxed, a sensual being expressing affection with another. Pleasure surrounded me and was accepted within. There was no argument, no censoring of my sensations. My violence was at rest, my paranoia inoperative. Without it there was nothing to prove and nothing which I needed to have proven.

How can I relate that experience of closeness felt with other men and its freeing effects? The source of our celebration was ourselves—our sexuality, our humanity. It was simple. There we were, in a room full of naked, relaxed male bodies. Sensual music and delicious incense in the air. Almond oil was circulated and we reclined. Each man began to give himself a gift of pleasure. I caressed and explored my body, enjoying the fact that others were doing the same. I had been concerned that I might not be able to feel sexual sensations in the company of other men. Now I recognized that I was giving myself a new permission to celebrate my sensations. I could hear the deep breathing and the pleasure-sounds of the others, hear them increasing. I realized that my envelopment by a roomful of pleasure was increasing my own, and that the same was happening to the others. Orgasms came in waves, a domino effect, with one man's groans likely to set off the ejaculation of a man next to him.

Meanwhile, our bronze goddess, with her vibrator active between her strong thighs, stood in electric heaven above us, gyrating in beautiful ecstacy at the sight of her ten admirers, who lay at her feet absorbed in a myriad of sensations and fantasies.

We called it "jerking off," but it was not. Male masturbation, like all male sexuality, tends to be violent and cold. Now we were loving ourselves, giving ourselves an exquisite moment of aliveness. Techniques varied among us, and fluctuated in each of us, and the constant was the feeling of comfort and caring with the others and ourselves.

Compare this to the original "circle-jerk." What is the objective? Speed! Conquest and self-violence masquerade as sexuality for most males. The result is that we never get to enjoy it. We rob ourselves of our own pleasure just as effectively as women rob themselves. We distress ourselves over our pride and performance, and miss the joys of sensual exploration, sensitive response, and enthusiastic self-love.

I sensed that every man in that room would now be a better lover for it. Love of self, of men, and of women now seemed so obviously connected. This love appeared to be in stark contrast to my frequently violent relationship with

108

other men, with my own body, and with my sexuality. Such discomfort would *have* to make me a lousy lover. I was clearly glimpsing what it is like to replace violence with affirmation.

The violence that I feel toward other male bodies leads me to treat myself roughly as well. I cannot caress myself, relax with my own sensuality, because I do not like men. Treating myself roughly and insensitively, it is not difficult to guess how I will relate to women. It is all connected, and the workshop demonstrated this in the experience of each of us.

As I felt ease with the sensual presence of the other men, I reconnected to a peaceful passion toward my own body. Sex roles faded as my masculinity seemed easy and natural. I could see this happening to the other men as well, and our way of relating to Betty, and our discussion of sexuality, became receptive and lucid. Sensitive to ourselves, we felt naturally sensitive to women and their needs.

There are some facts about human behavior which help me to identify the above experiences, and which give us some definite indications about our sexual alternatives. It has been well established in psychological experiments that fearful responses can be extinguished by stimulating certain other incompatible responses. So, when people are afraid, they can lessen their fear by refocusing on other types of feelings. Two feelings that work remarkably well in counteracting fear are none other than anger and pleasure. Either one will usually work well.

This gives me some definite clues about what I do with my fears. Remember that fear is forbidden to me by our culture, especially in sexual situations. I have learned to counteract this fear with anger and aggression, which is also suggested to me by the culture. Taking this choice robs me of the other alternative. Our supposedly unbreakable cultural conditioning broke apart. Connecting to our sensuality and affection, our aggressiveness became unnecessary. We no longer feared our fears: they eroded under streams of pleasure.

I have always found sources of fear to be legion for myself as a man. Invulnerability is legislated to me: any confusion panics me. Vulnerability, self-doubt, sadness—each are inevitable, and yet, even in small doses, each feels self-destructive. While self-control is my expectation, I seldom achieve it. My sexuality certainly laughs at any attempt at control. It has, at times, left me cringing inside at the spontaneous reality of that which happens to have stimulating associations for me and that which doesn't.

I have been trained to dominate, and the world now asks that I equalize. Either attitude leaves me guilty for violating the other. Women are in the same predicament; and so, if I am dominant, a woman may resent me, and if I am not, she may lose her sexual response to me.

My guess is that other men are in precisely the same spot. My personal choice is to learn to do something new in refocusing from these many other sources of sexual fear—I now choose to use pleasure instead of anger, and it works.

As it turns out, we would do well to return to popularity those bumperstickers which read, "Make Love, Not War." It was pure delight to watch the other men at the workshop. Smiles became uncomplicated and warm. A con-

109

fident gentle masculinity radiated from clear and steady eyes, as they looked directly into mine. Strong hands periodically reached out for me, friendly and flexible, confirming a message of communion which had woven us into easy comradery.

I am exhilarated at the possibilities of substituting pleasure for defensive combat in the conquest of my fears. I have found that I can be sexually creative and exploratory, and be sensitive to receiving sexual feedback from my partners, not needing to already know it all. I no longer need to try to order about my penis, telling it to be hard or soft. I can know and enjoy the entire range of my own passions, even when I don't wish to always act upon all of them. I now make love in an entire range of complementary styles, depending upon the moment's pleasure. Gentle, slow, and receptive have all been added to my repertoire. I am finding that an increasing number of men can also testify to the delight of these options.

On the other hand, just imagine the Body Sex Workshop which I have so glowingly described, if it were run according to our usual aggressive alternative. We could have sat far away from each other, never looking at each other, except for an occasional glare. We each could have bragged about our sexual expertise, worrying secretly whether the others weren't lying. We would have been embarrassed by the exercises and so could have "studded" them up. We could have found some way to make rotating our hips look macho, or else convince everyone that it was too "queer" to do. We wouldn't get to laugh, except at others. If necessary, to avoid looking scared, we might have consented to hug other men. This could have been performed in a manner that resembled an A-frame house, and with a lot of backslapping. To cover up any enjoyment of the physical contact, we could have seen who could most effectively squeeze out the breath of his partner. Our circle-jerk could have, of course, been timed, although even the winner would not have felt his orgasm. In fact, he would most likely be having a premature ejaculation. If pressured into giving the massages, we could have seen how much the massagee could "take," simultaneously demonstrating our powerful (and aching) fingers. We would each have come away angry, lonely, and, most of all, frigid.

In exaggerated form, this example illustrates what it means to be sex-negative. "Frigidly" we do not experience our orgasms, even though we have them. Women avoid sex with fear, as they have been trained to do. Men avoid sex with anger. While the above illustration sounds absurd, it describes exactly what our cultural training would tell us to do. Now, in the Body Sex Workshop, with people like Betty Dodson and Tom Sargent clarifying our choices, not being stupid, we chose pleasure. In daily life, we are not so lucky. Our unaware cultural programming is constantly telling us to act according to the above description. Without some careful, though joyful, intentionality, we men are indeed sex-negative—frigid, if you will.

Betty said, at the end of the workshop, "Men will be able to relate to women when they can love men." The accuracy of her insight is now clear to me. That an all-male workshop could be run by a feminist without a hint of conflict is one demonstration. And our shared feelings were the essential proof. By reach-

110

ing out to our sensuality, by letting in our gentleness, by touching softly and confidently, we resurrected our tranquility, our human warmth, and our pleasure.

We came away with a sense that we had shared an experience with a significance that went beyond our small group. The dream of male liberation glided in from the previously impossible heights to become a tangible reality right in our midst. This reality, and the freedom which it offers, is as near as the nearest pleasure.

GAY RELATIONSHIPS

THE MEMOIRS OF A SISSY

Tommi Avicolli

SCENE ONE:

A homeroom in a Catholic high school in South Philadelphia. The boy sits quietly in the first aisle, third desk, reading a book. He does not look up, not even for a moment. He is hoping no one will remember he is sitting there. He wishes he were invisible. The teacher is not yet in the classroom so the other boys are talking and laughing loudly.

Suddenly, a voice from beside him: "Hey, you're a faggot, ain't you?"

The boy does not answer. He goes on reading his book, or rather pretending he is reading his book. It is impossible to actually read now.

"Hey, I'm talking to you!"

The boy still does not look up. He is so scared his heart is thumping madly. But he can't look up.

"Faggot, I'm talking to you!"

To look up is to meet the eyes of the tormentor.

Suddenly a sharp pencil point is thrust into the boy's arm. He jolts, shaking off the pencil, aware that there is blood seeping from the wound.

"What did you do that for?" he asks timidly.

"Cause I hate faggots," the other boy says, laughing. Some other boys begin to laugh, too. A symphony of laughter. The boy feels as if he's going to cry. But he must not cry. Must not cry. So he holds back the tears and tries to read the book again. He must read the book. Read the book.

When the teacher arrives a few minutes later, the class quiets down. The boy does not tell the teacher what has happened. He spits on the wound to clean it, dabbing it with a tissue until the bleeding stops. For weeks he fears some dreadful infection from the lead in the pencil point.

SCENE TWO:

The boy is walking home from school. A group of boys (two, maybe three, he is not certain) grab him from behind, drag him into an alley and beat him up. When he gets home, he races up to his room, refusing dinner ("I don't feel well," he tells his mother through the locked door) and spends the night alone in the dark wishing he would die. . . .

These are not fictitious accounts—I *was* that boy. Having been branded a sissy by neighborhood children because I preferred jump rope to baseball and dolls to playing soldiers, I was often taunted with "hey sissy" or "hey faggot" or "yoo hoo, honey" when I left the house.

To avoid harassment, I spent many summers alone in my room. I went out on rainy days when the street was empty.

I came to like being alone. I didn't need anyone, I told myself over and over. I was an island. Contact with others meant pain. Alone, I was protected. I began writing poems, then short stories. There was no reason to go outside anymore. I had a world of my own.

> In the schoolyard today
> they'll single you out
> Their laughter will leave your ears ringing
> like the church bells
> that once awed you. . .[1]

School was one of the more painful experiences of my youth. The neighborhood bullies could be avoided. The taunts of the children living in those endless row houses could be evaded by staying in my room. But school was something I had to face day after day for some two hundred mornings a year.

I had few friends in school. Some kids would talk to me, but few wanted to be known as my close friend. Afraid of labels. If I was a sissy, then they would be sissies, too. I was condemned to loneliness.

Fortunately, a new boy moved into our neighborhood and befriended me; he wasn't afraid of the labels. He protected me when the other guys threatened to beat me up. He walked me home from school; he broke through the terrible loneliness. We were in third or fourth grade at the time.

We spent a summer or two together. Then his parents sent him to camp and I was once again confined to my room.

SCENE THREE:

High school lunchroom. The boy sits at a table near the back of the room. Without warning, his lunch bag is grabbed and tossed to another table. Someone opens it and confiscates a package of Tastykakes; another boy takes the

---

[1] *From the poem "Faggot," by Tommi Avicolli, published in* GPU News, *September 1979.*

sandwich. The empty bag is tossed back to the boy who stares at it, dumb-founded. He should be used to this; it has happened before.

Someone says, "Faggot," laughing. There is always laughter. It does not annoy him anymore.

There is no teacher nearby. There is never a teacher around. And what would he say if there were? Could he report the crime? He would be jumped after school if he did. Besides, it would be his word against theirs. Teachers never noticed anything. They never heard the taunts. Never heard the word, "faggot." They were the great deaf mutes, pillars of indifference; a sissy's pain was not relevant to history and geography and god made me to love honor and obey him, amen.

The boy reaches into his pocket for some money, but there's only a few coins. Always just a few coins. He cleans windshields at his father's gas station on Saturdays and Sundays to earn money. But it's never much. Only enough now to buy a carton of milk and some cookies. Only enough to watch the other boys eat and laugh, hoping they'll choke on their food. . . .

SCENE FOUR:

High school religion class. Someone has a copy of *Playboy*. Father N. is not in the room yet; he's late, as usual. Someone taps the boy roughly on the shoulder. He turns. A finger points to the centerfold model, pink fleshy body, thin and sleek. Almost painted. Not real. The other asks in a mocking voice, "Hey, does she turn you on? Look at those tits!"

The boy smiles, nodding meekly; turns away.

The other jabs him harder on the shoulder, "Hey, what'samatter, don't you like girls?"

Laughter. Thousands of mouths; unbearable din of laughter. In the arena: thumbs down. Don't spare the queer.

"Wanna suck my dick, huh? That turn you on, faggot!"

What did being a sissy really mean? It was a way of walking (from the hips rather than the shoulders); it was a way of talking (often with a lisp or in a high-pitched voice); it was a way of relating to others (gently, not wanting to fight, or hurt anybody's feelings). It was being intelligent ("an egghead" they called it sometimes); getting good grades. It meant not being interested in sports, not playing football in the street after school; not discussing teams and scores and playoffs. And it involved not showing a fervent interest in girls, not talking about scoring or tits or *Playboy* centerfolds. Not concealing pictures of naked women in your history book; or porno books in your locker.

On the other hand, anyone could be a "faggot." It was a catchall. If you did something that didn't conform to the acceptable behavior of the group, then you risked being called a faggot. It was the most commonly used put-down. It kept guys in line. They became angry when somebody called them a faggot. More fights started over calling someone a faggot than anything else. The word had power. It toppled the male ego, shattered his delicate facade, violated the image he projected. He was tough. Without feeling. Faggot cut through all this. It made him vulnerable. Feminine. And feminine was the worst thing he could possibly be. Girls were fine for fucking, but no boy in his right mind wanted to be like them. A boy was the opposite of girl. He was not feminine. He was not feeling. He was not weak.

Just look at the gym teacher who growled like a dog; or the priest with the black belt who threw kids against the wall in rage when they didn't know their Latin. They were men, they got respect.

But not the physics teacher who preached pacificism during lectures on the nature of atoms. Everybody knew what he was—and why he believed in the antiwar movement.

SCENE FIVE:

Father: I wanna see you walk, Mark.

Mark: What do you mean?

Father: Just walk, Mark.

Mark: (Starts to walk) I don't understand.

Father: That's it, just walk.

Mark: (Walks back and forth)

Father: Now come here.
(Mark approaches; father slaps him across the face, hard)

Mark: What was that for?

Father: I want you to walk right now.

Mark: What do you mean?

Father: Stop fooling around, Mark, I want you to walk like a man.

Mark: Dad, I . . .

Father: (Interrupting) Don't say another word. Just get over there and walk right—walk like a man.[2]

My parents only knew that the neighborhood kids called me names. They begged me to act more like the other boys. My brothers were ashamed of me. They never said it, but I knew. Just as I knew that my parents were embarassed by my behavior.

At times, they tried to get me to act differently. Once my father lectured me on how to walk right. I'm still not clear on what that means. Not from the hips,

---

[2] *From the play* Judgement of the Roaches, *by Tommi Avicolli, produced in Philadelphia at the Gay & Lesbian Coffee house, the Painted Bride Arts Center, and the University of Pennsylvania; aired over WXPN-FM in four parts; and presented at the Lesbian/Gay Conference in Norfolk, VA, July 1980.*

I guess; don't "swish" like faggots do.

A nun in elementary school told my mother at open house that there was "something wrong with me." I had draped my sweater over my shoulders like a girl, she said. I was a smart kid, no complaints about my grades, but I should know better than to wear my sweater like a girl.

My mother stood there, mute. I wanted her to say something, to chastise the nun, to defend me. But how could she? This was a nun talking—representative of Jesus, protector of all that was good and decent.

An uncle once told me I should start "acting like a boy" instead of a girl. Everybody seemed ashamed of me. And I guess I was ashamed of myself, too. It was hard not to be.

SCENE SIX:

Priest: Do you like girls, Mark?

Mark: Uh-huh.

Priest: I mean REALLY like them?

Mark: Yeah—they're okay.

Priest: There's a role they play in your salvation. Do you understand it, Mark?

Mark: Yeah.

Priest: You've got to like girls. Even if you should decide to enter the seminary, it's important to keep in mind God's plan for a man and a woman. . . . [3]

Catholicism of course condemned homosexuality. Effeminancy was tolerated as long as the effeminate person did not admit to being gay. Thus, priests could be effeminate because they weren't gay.

As a sissy, I couldn't count on support from the church. A male's sole purpose in life was to father children—souls for the church to save. The only hope a homosexual had of attaining salvation was to remain totally celibate. Don't even think of touching another boy. To think of a sin was a sin. And to sin was to put a mark on the soul. Sin—led to hell. There was no way around it. If you sinned, you were doomed.

Realizing I was gay wasn't an easy task. Although I knew I was attracted to boys by the time I was about eleven, I didn't connect this attraction to homosexuality. I was not queer. Not I. I was merely appreciating a boy's good looks, his fine features, his proportions. It didn't seem to matter that I didn't appreciate a girl's looks in the same way. There was no twitching in my thighs when I gazed upon a beautiful girl. But I wasn't queer.

We sat through endless English classes, and history courses about the wars between men who were not allowed to love each other. No gay history was ever taught. You're just a faggot. Homosexuals had never contributed to the human race. God destroyed the queers in Sodom and Gommorrah.

---

[3] *Ibid.*

I resisted that label—queer—for the longest time. Even when everything pointed to it, I refused to see it. I was certainly not queer. Not. I.

Near the end of my junior year in high school, most of the teasing and taunting had let up. Now I was just ignored. Besides, I was getting a reputation for being a hippie, since I spoke up in social studies classes against the war, and wore my hair as long as I could without incurring the wrath of the administration. When your hair reached a certain length, you were told to get a hair cut. If you didn't, you were sent down to the vice principal's office where you were given a hair cut.

I had a friend toward the end of junior year; his name was Joe. He introduced me to Jay at the bowling alley in South Philadelphia. I knew immediately I was in love with Jay.

A relationship developed. It was all very daring; neither of us understood what was happening. I still rejected the label. I wasn't queer. He wasn't queer. But I knew I was in love with him. I told myself that all the time. Yet I wasn't a homosexual.

Franny was a queer. He lived a few blocks away. He used to dress in women's clothes and wait for the bus on the corner. Everybody laughed at Franny. Everybody knew he was queer.

Then, one night, Halloween, a chilly October night, Jay called:

SCENE SEVEN:

. . ."What?"

"It's wrong."

"What's wrong?"

Tossing in my sleep—sweating. It was the winter of '69. The heavy woolen cover became a thick shroud on top of me. The heat pricked me like so many needles.

"Why can't I see you tonight?"

"We can't see each other anymore. . . ."

My heart was an acrobat. It leaped like a frog. Landed in a deep puddle. Help, it shouted. It was going down for the third time.

"Why?" I felt nauseous. I was going to vomit.

"We can't. I've got to go."

"Wait—!"

"What?"

There were tears running down my cheeks in streams that left a salty residue at the corners of my lips. The record player in the background shut off, closing me in. The walls of the room collapsed. I was entombed.

"Please, talk to me. I can't let you go like this. I want to know what's wrong. Please. . ."

"I can't see you anymore. It's over. It was a mistake."

"It wasn't a mistake, Jay. I—I love you."

"Don't say that." Voice quivering; don't force me to see things I don't want to see right now.

116

"But I do. And you love me. Admit it. Don't break it off now. Admit it. Admit that you love me."

"I've got to go."

"You can't go. Admit it!"

"Goodbye."

"Jay?"

Silence.[4]

We learned about Michelangelo, Oscar Wilde, Gertrude Stein—but never that they were queer. They were not queer. Walt Whitman, the "father of American poetry," was not queer. No one was queer. I was alone, totally unique. One of a kind. Except for Franny who wore dresses and makeup. Where did Franny go every night? Were there others like me somewhere? Another planet, perhaps?

In school, they never talked of queers. They did not exist. The only hint we got of this other species was in religion class. And even then it was clouded in mystery—never spelled out. It was a sin. Like masturbation. Like looking at *Playboy* and getting a hard-on. A sin.

Once a progressive priest in senior-year religion class actually mentioned homosexuals—he said the word, broke the silence—but he was talking about homosexuals as pathetic and sick. Fixated at some early stage; penis, anal, whatever. Only heterosexuals passed on to the nirvana of sexual development.

No other images from the halls of the Catholic high school except those the other boys knew: swishy faggot sucking cock in an alley somewhere, grabbing asses in the bathroom. Never mentioning how straight boys craved blow jobs, too.

It was all a secret. You were not supposed to talk about queers. Whisper maybe. Laugh about them, yes. But don't be open, honest; don't try to understand. Don't cite their accomplishments. No history faces you this morning. You're a faggot. No history—a faggot.

EPILOGUE:

The boy marching down Spruce Street. Hundreds of queers. Signs proclaiming gay pride. Speakers. Tables with literature from gay groups. A miracle, he is thinking. Tears are coming loose now. Someone hugs him.

> You could not control
> the sissy in me
> nor could you exorcise him
> nor electrocute him
> You declared him illegal illegitimate
> insane and immature
> but he defies you still.[5]

---

[4] *From the novel* Deaf Mute's Final Dance, *by Tommi Avicolli.*

[5] *From the poem "Sissy Poem," published in* Magic Doesn't Live Here Anymore, *Spruce Street Press, 1976.*

COLLARED QUEER

Louie Crew

He could preach about his ghetto
till his cracker bishop wept
guilt dollars into his parish coffers;
he could shout about the city managers
till his people marched affirmative action
through every municipal office;
he could narrate their family history
till his boy and girl joyfully plodded
through the books grandparents had been denied;
he could presage his weariness
till his wife calmed him with her care;
but because he could share with no one
the fact that he was queer,
he hitched a hose to his VW exhaust
and quietly went to heaven.

FAY

Louie Crew

My one earring stores my powers:

It charms my lover into bed.
Worn aisle-side on buses and trains,
   it reserves me a doubleseat until
   all others are filled.
On campus it keeps me off all but
   the most enlightened committees,
It is 99 percent foolproof in protecting
   me from conversation wasted on racists.
At times it has made otherwise sane folks
   dangle from dormitory windows to giggle,
   "Where's your husband?"
Worn with a cap and gown, it wards off
   any threat of Respectability.
In class, it assures that students will
   question what is said and not vainly
   agree because of who said it.
In church, it has made stranger priests
   spill me a double portion of the Mass. . . .

When I take it off, people take me
   for any other mortal.

Chapter 6:
Work: Fulfillment or Desperation?

THE POWER OF MONEY IS IN THE SPENDING, NOT THE EARNING

Richard Haddad

Do we mean then, when we say that men wield most of the economic power in our society, that they earn most of the money? I can't quarrel with the fact that men earn more than women, but I do have some problems absolutely equating the male's earning ability with power. It has always seemed to me that the power of money is in the spending, not the earning. And I understand that the very men who favor other men when it comes to earning money aim the majority of their product and service advertising at women. To put it another way, there are apparently an awful lot of men whose very jobs depend on the spending power of women.

Why do we continue to nurture the illusion that men hold the power in society? Is it possible that the power they do hold is really a trifle? That if it were acknowledged to be a trifle, men would become offended or disillusioned and would no longer be willing to do their duty—which is to work? Is it possible, in other words, that the *illusion* of power is what the male gets in return for doing his job—feeding, clothing, and housing his family? Remember that whether his job is making laws or enforcing them, running a business or deliv-

120

ering the mail, he does it for one simple reason—to earn money to support himself and his family.

How on earth did he get suckered into that deal? If men are so powerful, why do they spend a lifetime supporting themselves and other people? Why aren't women supporting *them*, the way kings are supported by their subjects?

No longer willing to be defined by what they do for a living, or how successfully they do it, many men *are* developing different attitudes about career. They are finally acknowledging what women will learn in time—that most jobs are neither glamorous nor exciting nor rewarding; that they frequently kill their practitioners either by consuming them or by boring them to death. Even if they are lucky enough to have a job which does offer a measure of satisfaction, a measure is not sufficient to compensate for what most men give up in slavish devotion to their jobs.

THE SEMISPLENDOURED NIGHT

Jim Sanderson

In the begining he had stood intent with her, listening to the throb and smell of fearful excitement, tensed with the heightened awareness of his new body, the future suddenly made present, as if each touch of skin and each limb lived in their own right.

And now he lay old and quiet in a dark weak bed which sagged in the middle, making a kind of seat for this thickness, but which he would not forsake as he would not his wife because it understood and indulged him, and he was grateful. He lay with his wife, who was not old as he was, not really old, and he did not sleep but simply lived in another place.

For a moment or two, some time in the last hour, he had thought to make an effort, to ask his wife how she felt about oldness. But he had got up and gone to the bathroom instead. Sitting on the toilet he had thought—that's what it's all about: you can't stand your feet on cold tile anymore. And he had drifted away on his river of unreality.

In bed he had refrained from putting his feet on his wife. Her sleep-murmured endearment irritated him vaguely. A pleasant evening with the family; and yet the forty candles and the jokes seemed now a bit gratuitous. And so too the discussion of money which had crept in and had been carried on over the heads of the children. It was mostly my fault, he thought, accidently giving her a poke with his elbow.

Money. Money. The root of all pleasure. Or is it? He thought for a while whether it was, and then he attempted to remember what evils money had brought him. He could recall none, and resolved to make a list some day of money priorities. He was good at making lists, but somehow in recent years they had never gotten very long. It was a luxury of uncompleted internal projects that he had begun increasingly to allow himself, not without an occasional bout of reproach.

Earlier in the bed he had tried to raise a wave of disgust at his inability to *think* on any one subject for some time. It's just that I don't care any more. Is that it? Don't care or can't *feel* about things? Was forty really some kind of watershed of feeling? But what was there to feel, really?

Flesh unprovoked, perhaps unprovokable; the majesty of spirit unexercised, still untried, frequently denied. Many demands unmade, many self-sins shrugged away with casual forgiveness until perhaps they now passed unrecognized. Who or what was there to feel for? Old visions hazed by fears, hopes long dulled by the learned, enforced pattern of caution. Yes, caution had become his name, his private disaster, because all the world thought of him as a bold, even slightly reckless man, and he was tired of this illusion and its failure. Most of his unlife had been connected with this illusion.

He lay lumpish, angry in a bleak night like all nights, aware vaguely, unable to go further, cursing even this awareness and yet wanting more. Wanting more? And bored with wanting.

They had been playing kick the can in the hinter block of back fences and family garages. Casual trash piles and garbage cans, a crude boy-mown lawn and giant-high untended spires, a gnarled deep-barked oak which dropped its acorns on a tarpaper garage roof, a transmissionless Model A coupe left aground on cinder blocks, a yapping possessive dog guarding a chicken-wire rabbit hutch: the poor back-lived world behind the guant, respectable, peeling house fronts, a leisurely loving jungle of preadolescence barred to parents, a warren of trails and hideaways, a young strength of power and contempt, inpenetrable to them, unknowable, the real world.

Her name was Genevieve, pronounced in the French manner. A hawk-nosed high jumper who insisted upon her turn at riding him upon the crossbar of his own bike, which made a painful and unmanly crimp in his legs, at which he had finally to protest, and insist upon his primeval right; and also because there was an as-yet-only-suspected, ill-defined pleasure in riding her between his pedaling thighs. Sometimes during the year when he was twelve he had grown bolder and stood up to pump against her spinal flesh and he thought she had not known. She had understood, of course; they always did.

"But to the girdle do the gods inherit, beneath is all the fiend's;" he had recited it with large wickedness several years later to several girls, and they had not caught his sense, or pretended not, except for the word girdle, and the man laughed now at the precocious Shakespearean, so malely cynical in his near virginity, and put his hand upon the devil's due.

Jarvis sat in that office, that large, walnut-veneered office with scarlet window panels of gold-threaded Dacron which opened only to unwalnuted brick because his status was just short of windows's august rank; he sat in that office like a young toad with its warts not yet fully developed. Not seeing, not knowing but all-watching; Jarvis's eyes never closed during the day and at night counted, with a mathematical cunning, the moths, bats and small night deer which crawled upon his walls. And made mathematical precisions upon the energy expended and the logarithmic ledger cost of each staring, which thus negated the effort of all because the cost of the account-keeping alone would overwhelm the budget.

He began to stir in anger in the bed, making mechanical motions which the bed understood. A rapid montage of five or six company faces flittered across his mind's screen but as always the image of Jarvis returned in a slow dissolve of angry reds and yellows. He was sleek and round-faced and groomed and young, and he had a great future in the company they all said. He could sit and stare at you for a frozen two minutes without once blinking his eyes as other people did, and his mouth kept itself in perpetual crouch ready to spring into self-righteous attack. Still, the secretaries twittered that he was handsome; his contemporaries conceded that he had a brilliant analytical mind; and all intoned that he had a great future in the company. A great future, a great future, an acid hymn which burned its own fiery cross on his chest and he thrashed angrily in bed, alarming his wife because he seemed to be pressing her arm against the headboard.

He apologized contritely and this action of control, the control which in the early days had come with such anguished straining inside but had now become automatic, drove out the vision of Jarvis for an instant. When the image drifted up again Jarvis was smiling, the little smile of Christian charity which he really seemed to believe, and the vigor of hate somehow drifted from the man in bed. He noticed that it left him, seeped away in what he had once thought to be maturity and had later estimated to be a loss of vital male juices, and he was a little saddened to once again find it so, and almost reached out after it, grasping at a thin vapor of care.

But instead a sweet vision of the creature in the fencepost came over him, and he was kind and gentle-touching. He wondered sometimes about this scene; a damned silly senseless bird in a fencepost nest. Once at a cocktail party he had almost asked a psychiatrist about it: a scene of pathetic terror that he almost enjoyed. Occasionally he even elaborated memory's detail so that the sun warmed him with an animal heat of spring, and the boy lived in the bright gaiety of Columbus-like discovery; and the grass of the boulder-strewn cow lane was celery green, new green and tender to the soft cool noses of the spring calves.

Tender too the bird who lived in the hole in the top of the fencepost, the rail-split post beaten and weathered by twenty or fifty storms. From his earliest memory it was always the sixth post. Or perhaps it was the seventh. He bestrode one of those scoured black basalt boulders, higher than his head, master of all the fields, of the lustrous crows, the inch-high sprouts of wheat, the hummocked pasture beyond, and almost rising to the great symmetrical grandfather maple which stood at the crest of the lane, over all the farm and the farm people who lived on it. He stood high on the rock, immobile, watching the bluebird.

She fluttered uneasily on the post top and paused, studying him. He was a faun, half-unmasked but he did not betray his nature. The bird dropped, invisible, into the top of the fencepost and he slipped, skinning his gentle chest, from the basalt boulder. Sure-footed, he approached the fencepost with his mouth open in delight.

He was still, sensing that the bird would rise again in fear but she did not, and then in a sudden inspiration of daring he strode to the post and clapped his hand across the top of it. For an instant it was triumph as the frightened bird beat and pecked against his palm, and then it was fear at what he had unleashed, fear and anger, but when the fear became great enough he released her. She flew away in wild apprehension and then circled back as if she would attack him and he waved his arms in scorn and the anger took over in him for having been made to enter shame and he shouted an unnamed shout. Shout. Shout. He did not know he was shouting at a bluebird, because she had a nest to protect and he was an aggressor, and then she was gone and he was left in sad possession of the world.

He peered, dimly, into the posthole to see two eggs of the most exquisite turquoise-green, a color which he was ever after unable to forget. But the eggs had never hatched. When the snow came he put a stone over the hole in the top of the post and did not look at it as he drove the cows past, switching their impassive bodies with his grandfather's old thick buggy whip.

And so, avoiding the always painful penetration of this final image, he came back to Jarvis, the symbol of his present frustration, of his great present concern, of his life, the life of men, vital and important. He was not kind; damn you, he cried at one time in the bed, damn you.

It had been a great idea; everyone had thought so. From H.B. on down, from the executive v.p. on down, from the high mogul on down, from the man in 1502 on down, from the balding, white-fringed, pompous bromide-proclaiming old man, the cunning acute little man who lived in the psyche of the consumer, who had never guessed wrong (or never allowed wrong guesses to be remembered) in his red leather chair and his glass-walled private outhouse on the roof, glass-walled because it was higher than any other building in town, from this little big little man down.

They had all known it was his idea.

He had conceived it on a night such as this, busy with connubial concerns. Change us and make us great, make us rich, the little man had said, and on a night such as this he had had the idea, a loathsome simple unheeded unneeded product but a *thing* that millions might buy, a sheer convenience stupid arbitrary product that might strike a woman's fancy. Oh they knew it. Jarvis knew it, and H.B., the great man, the old high man knew it.

Then how could they be so obtusely wrong? How could they slant product research surveys for predetermined answers? How build upon a false, internally conceived eggshell foundation? It was to be his product. He was to be the brand manager. He felt strong for it, physically strong, as if in TV commercials he could lift thousand-pound gymnasium barbells and tow two-thousand-pound cars in demonstrations uphill with a steel cable across his chest, and push over mountains of sandbags stacked ten bags wide into a raging flood below. He felt strong in the bed now. He felt strong and brutal and angry, and he took out his anger against the faceless mob and he smashed all the windows of their offices

124

and slapped alive all the smug young females who knew who was important and leaned on their typewriters smoothing their tight sweaters tighter than the smiles of those empty, crimsoned, shell-like, crablike, cunning little faces, the faces of the secretaries and the administrative assistants who sat idle, making phone calls and watching as they talked, and sent their work down to the secretarial pool.

He disliked secretaries. He could not dictate and this annoyed them. He was always asking them to read what he had dictated and to start over. He writhed in the knowledge that he needed to begin again and in the knowledge that they were repeating his name under their masked faces and that he was known as the man who had forgotten his head and oh, let's try it again.

There could be no rapport between him and them and they had taken Miss Biebighoffer away from him. The old girl—he was the only one who had taken the trouble to learn how to pronounce her name—had been 160 pounds of flab and girdle but she had known shorthand, and had never allowed herself an erasure in a letter and she had sat kindly, sympathetically patient as he thought, as he thought how to phrase the important words that he had within him. Sometimes, pad upon her thick, wool-covered knee, she had escaped in reverie with him.

It had taken a month to compose the first memo; a painful month of week-ends and 4 A.M.s, of nights awakening, of product examinations, of efforts with the kitchen blender in the middle of the night, product placed to freeze in the ice-cube tray overnight and then left to thaw slightly and tested on the neighbors, who in their sophistication had to make jokes. But the product was right, the idea was right, and they were tearing at his essential, they were weighting him down with little men who nagged, with little girls who smiled knowingly and wrongly, as he attempted to put all of the information together. My trouble, he thought, is that I cannot sell. They see me in many pieces, some contradictory, some foolish. I cannot spend all of my time impressing them. I have work to do.

But he was not a failure. They did appreciate him. In seven years his salary had almost doubled—not as much as some, but not bad; he had no grand titles to shower upon strangers; but he was more than an assistant. They knew him and if they did not like him they respected him; his memo had reached the highest level, on 1502. The man there *knew* what it takes to build a future for this company. He *knew* that strange ideas, unique combinations, a certain fantasy of the ordinary is essential to develop new consumer products. He did not laugh.

Rather, he stood in the office door, a suddenly descended Jove-like cherub, angry it seemed at first in his abruptness and then smiling as if to reassure the mortal's fears; and he had pronounced the idea genius. A bouncing awkward little man who had insisted upon slapping him upon the back although he had not known how, as if he had never done it before, but so obviously pleased with himself for having discovered a new idea that for an instant it almost seemed that he had created the idea himself and the world owed him kudos.

The genius of managing people is always of a higher order than the genius of creativity, he had mused darkly, and behind the great enthused little man he observed the simpering face of agreement and subterranean attack, Jarvis.

Jarvis the young toad, Jarvis who shared and seemed to absorb and radiate the momentary glory of a new idea but who was obligated by his nature to sabotage until his negative soul was fulfilled; except that negatives, in a kind of corporate algebraic fallacy, were never converted into positives but were combined instead into greater and greater negatives.

And so they were going to do it to him again. They were going to be so judicious, so meticulous, so niggling, so literal-minded—when the product cried out for fantasy and the grand gesture—that it would fail in its test market. And it would be his third failure. He was forty and he had been associated with three new products which had failed, all of them in a certain sense marked out as his future in the company. Of course, of course, they smiled, nine out of ten new products fail. They must; it is only the tenth we need to make us grow. But each time it got harder because he was older and the dazzling promise of youth no longer rode in his vanguard. He was creative, naively creative at forty, and he did not believe, really believe in it any more, although it was all he had to sell. He was a loser.

Jarvis, the all-seeing Jarvis, kept the count for the company and amassed the negative power which could never be identified as corporate error. The premature wisdom of the safe old had lived in Jarvis from the womb, and it was the anger, the frustration of his own normal birth which broke wave after wave over the man in bed this night as he turned and thrashed in dulled sensitivity and no physical glory.

From side to side he rolled, little knowing, little caring about his wife, as he paced the corridors, shattering the partitions and the fragile beings, the negative beings, with a giant shining metal ball weight on a heavy link chain, flailing over his head and with a whistling whip crashing again and again through the flesh and metal and resistance, smashing them down, smashing them down, flailing wildly and blindly, crushing them, mauling them, revenging the positives, shrieking and laughing, trampling them into the inlaid rubber tile floors until, gasping and triumphant, the building had been cleared and he stood sweaty, naked and strong, calmly before the old man, and H. B. asked him to sit down, and he had. . . .

But his anger lacked the power of sensual attraction and slowly, quietly he began again, once more as a kind of last reserve with Genevieve on that fall evening, that smokey fall evening just before supper, squeezed in the eight inches between the double garage doors with muscular, stringy brown-faced Genevieve, pronounced in the French way, three inches taller than him but pressed flat between the doors side by side so closely that their flanks touched. She wore slacks and a heavy corded black sweater, a plaid scarf and a fierce lock of hair, which she angrily puffed out of her eyes.

They waited, closely and yet apart, sharing a tension as the cries of the game echoed outside and the pursuit raced around them. Many times their names were called and the shouts became more distant, and the game began to break up under the adult female super-summoning shrill voices, and suppertime came and the game was over.

Still they waited, poised, caught in a frozen moment of anticipation, ready to dart out from either end of the double doors, and yet knowing that no need remained. They were alone. They did not know what they were waiting for. Leaves, newly raked, smouldered and flamed fitfully several yards away. A dog padded about the garage, a large incurious dog sniffed at the doors for a long instant and went away. The dark between the doors deepened. It was now more than suppertime. Neither of them moved.

The tension mounted unbearably, and for no reason the boy began to count her exhalations. Suddenly they both stretched their arms in cramp and their hands came in contact briefly and dropped away in embarrassment, as of two grown men touching hands on a busy street. They settled into immobility; it seemed to him a purposeful accident.

He did not know how long he had dreamed in this condition, every sense challenged and every part of the intellect narcotized. He heard her groan, the mere suggestion of a groan as she breathed. "I feel funny," he had croaked aloud, shocked at the sound of his voice. The words were absurd and regrettable and in an anguish he pressed his forehead into the wooden panel of the garage door until from the sharp edge of the panel he imagined somehow that he had driven a crucifixion spike into his head, for he was at this time reading the lives of the martyrs.

"So do I," she had breathed heavily and dramatically, her voice lower, more masculine than his. He swallowed again and again, afraid she would make an action. Again they were suspended between hell and earth, between no movement that was intolerable and unparalysis which was worse. At last with a huffing snort she clawed her way out from between the doors. He was beside her in an instant, apologetic.

"Where shall we go," he asked. "Here," she said. They stood staring at each other, their mouths open. "Well," she breathed. "What," he asked. She put his hand on the three white pearl buttons at the side of her thin chino slacks. Slowly, with infinite care and wonder he began to undo them. At the second button she tugged down the slacks with both hands, and with a gasp of overexcitement he half-closed his eyes in aroused embarrassment not to look at the pinkness of her forbidden underwear, which he had long studied on the iron washline behind her house.

She turned half away in the darkening gloom and made the swift motion which disposed of it. Hastily he made his own preparations and approached her. She wheeled to embrace him so tightly that his lips were bruised but still she insisted, pressing, pressing, with her steely muscles. He resented her strength, which made her very good at scissoring over fences and useful even in tackle football, so that in the choosing of sides she was often second or third, ahead of him.

He almost became angered, and then he surrendered and she helped him to understand how his role was to be accomplished, and he was immensely grateful, then and thereafter, to women who took it as a kindness to assist in the conjoining.

The sudden warmth and security of her overwhelmed him; he could only stand and gasp, marveling. They stood clutching each other in the middle of the garage not far from a crankcase oilspot, in the gloom of the almost dark. A cherry-patterend kitchen chintz, yellowed with light behind it, registered in his mind indelibly through a small dusty pane of the garage window over her shoulder.

"Well," she hissed in his mouth, "why don't you do something?" Do? He moaned in sincere bewilderment. Do? What was there to do, in what way could this unknown voluptuous quiet be perfected? Her undulating motions seemed crude and violent to him at first, bruising at the point of contact, but he began timidly to imitate her, unsure whether his male pride required harmony or counterpoint. In the end he compromised. For a few moments it was unbelievably exciting and then it seemed to grow routine and he was conscious again of being bruised but was in no way willing to stop. She seemed to become angrier as time went on and he could not understand why, although he attempted to please her in various ways that occurred to him, and when this did not seem to help he gave up the effort.

Suddenly he wanted to talk to her, to ask about this phenomenon, to discover where she had learned it, but, "Shut up," she had muttered darkly, increasing her own pace; he needed his breath to keep up with her. "Watch out," she cried, and she bit him. It hurt and it angered him, and he bit her back, not daring to bite quite so hard. "For what?" he muttered. "For what happens." "But what happens?" "You'll know," she uttered from the back of her throat.

But he did not know and could not know, until a sudden gripping began to take hold of him, and a terror of the sensation threw him into a shiver and he wanted to stop more than anything he could remember wanting but was swept on by the fierceness of her clutch and an unleashed curiosity of his own, demon-daring that had once led him to ride his bicycle through a roaring ten-foot bonfire and on occasion to jump from a diving board, without taunts, although he had no knowledge of swimming.

He was whirled away into the sky and tossed feet over head, constricted in the hand of death and yet freed beyond all measure, something inside of him seizing him, as in a fit, breaking through until in a panic he cried to her to stop, before, as it seemed to him, he crossed a barrier which he could never again remount, and which might mean the end of his body as he had known it. In real fear he fought with her but she was bigger and stronger with compulsions of her own and he could not escape and then with a wild shriek he hurled her backward and fell on top of her on the cement floor and together they slid in the oilspot, unknowingly, and lay there for an apocalyptic second that he was to seek again all his life.

Even the memory of it was so rare that at this age he did not often allow himself to use up a bit of what remained. It was a memory based on child flesh, so distant and roseate that once in a while still it overwhelmed him, while a conscious adult mind said that he was a fool, infantile and self-hypnotized.

Reason said these words now, the calm rational mind untied by the relaxed hand of flesh; but he put away the reproaches and began to think, in a kind of

128

mindless fear, of what he would do at work tomorrow, what new point of attack he could use in the research department, what new study of adult versus teen-age attitudes toward allied products he might devise, and what it could prove. He patted his wife affectionately on the stomach, and after a time it came to him without exceptional surprise that he had made love to her, and this event had almost passed without his notice.

MID-LIFE TRANSITION

Eugene R. August

In the middle of the 70s I turned forty years old and entered into what I now recognize as a mid-life transition classic for American males. I have since learned to recognize this transition as a normal and natural passage which most forty- to forty-five-year-old males must negotiate, and to cherish it as an opportunity for reappraising one's past and for recovering aspects of the self which have long been neglected. But at its onset I was like most men in our society—totally unprepared for it. Popular wisdom on the subject was a compound of ignorance and callousness: mid-life males were ridiculed as "middle-age crazies" suffering from "second adolescence" or "male menopause." In my own case, reading came to the rescue: especially valuable were the insights in *The Seasons of a Man's Life* by Daniel J. Levinson and his colleagues (New York: Knopf, 1978). Although I was thus able to make sense of my own era of transition and to convert its confusions into constructive changes, I made some bitter discoveries. Men in mid-life could expect precious little understanding or help. While mid-life women were encouraged to emerge from the empty nest and to find new vocations and interests in life, society had a vested interest in keeping the mid-life male locked into his traditional roles and responsibilities. Everyone —his family, his employer, his community—was actively interested in his *not* changing his life significantly, in his *not* making any waves at all. In short, I discovered that our "male-oriented" society was sadly ignorant of the rhythms of men's lives and markedly insensitive to the needs of men as they moved from one phase of live to another.

MALE HELPLESSNESS

Tom Williamson

Rape is the one emotionally charged issue about which few people (male or female) can keep a calm head. The word is the very embodiment of profound feelings of helplessness. But feelings of profound helplessness can be communicated in other ways besides the sexual act of rape. For men, three ways this gets communicated are through unemployment, underemployment, and the fear of unemployment. For men, work means survival, and the lack of work can cause an individual to commit suicide, or, at the political level, topple a government.

This is why affirmative action for women terrorized many men, given that men were being shoved aside without an orderly means of transition. It still is the case that only a lucky few men can talk about self-fulfillment the way they hear the women's movement talking.

IMAGINE IT

Rand Harris

You are sitting with your boss in the deputy commissioner's office. Plush. Just one step from the real seat of power. The two women are chatting amiably. Nothing special. You are not included in their conversation, nor are you excluded. Then there is some subtle, perhaps predetermined cue, some final decision, and they turn their attentions to you. "As you may have guessed, Mr. Harris, you are not to be recommended for retention in your position."

Not fired. Nothing personal. Just not recommended for retention. "Your abilities are well recognized. But it has become increasingly apparent over the past months, that your special contributions are not exactly what is required." Well rehearsed. No blame. Very civilized. "You have time to make decisions about your future and we intend to give you every assistance."

Decisions about my future. Indeed. And questions about the past. Anger. How in the hell did I get to this place? And what on God's earth shall I do now?

Years ago there were all those odd jobs—laundromat attendant, bank teller. Then school, a stint in the Air Force, and travel. I earned a graduate-level degree in a profession—a career with high ideals. A first supervisory-level job. Promotions. Greater responsibilities on a larger stage. Finally, there was the private office, private secretary, car whenever I wanted it, freedom to manage my own time, create my own programs, and a good salary.

But there were also vast disappointments in the caliber of my managers, reduced hopes that the situation would ever significantly improve, sickness when I awoke, pervasive sadness, disillusionment. Isn't this what can be expected, though, in a position of responsibility, especially when it is new? And the hazards of working for government certainly were not unknown to me. Time would take care of these bad feelings, I hoped. And time sure did. Overtaken by the barely hidden ambitions of others in my profession, never bothering to tinker with the intricate machinery of politics, my choices were reduced to "stay and fight" or "get out." I got out. I was sick and I was tired. Now I realize I was lucky in many ways.

There on God's next block was something to do. Something good to do. A job to help heal the damage. A job with a very multinational corporation, doing work that was definitely "feet on the ground." Not nearly as much money, a much smaller stage, no secretary, no car. A job that was convenient, that came at the right time, that would see me through. A job with the company that for thirty years had given regular paychecks, family medical care, paid vacations and security to my father.

He was overjoyed. I think he has never been happier with me. My feelings were satisfaction, restraint, quiet. Somehow a very large circle I had been traveling had closed. At the point where it closed stood my dad, still slim and erect, awkward in his love for me, pacific. Since I was a child my path had curved away from him until we were diametrically opposed. In order to define and know myself, I stood opposite him. Much later I became more my own person, with a stronger sense of myself, more able to be adventurous and to be routine. Without my knowing, it became acceptable to acknowledge my likeness to my father and, later, to embrace it. Now for the rest of our lives it remains for my father and me to celebrate that circle and each other in it.

Lucky, too, are my friends and I, who now have new opportunities to be with each other. We discover new ways to entertain ourselves without great expense. We are less easily distracted by spectacle and more lavishly entertained with our own stories, talents and ideas. We find there is a very substantial grace in the simple meal well served and the elaborate conversation well turned. We indulge ourselves in these things orgiastically.

More practically, there is no noticeable decline in the style of life to which I had become accustomed. The reduction is easily offset by the prodigality of simple pleasures, by the new-found time to completely consume and enjoy them, and by learning how to better steward my new income. I no longer shun investments and am rewarded by refining my investment strategy. Also, stepping down several rungs on the tax bracket ladder represents no small savings.

Most important (and for the first time), it is I who have control over the direction and speed of my life. Like my father, I can now imagine doing substantially the same work for a long time. I can also see the opportunity to progress to more responsible positions, if I choose to accept them. More than likely I will do a combination of both. Certainly I will never be able to give the time and energy I now have for more important occupations—to be creative, to write, to decorate, to entertain and to love. And never again will I find it necessary to define or to prove myself in terms of a career.

The speed and direction are now mine because my life is mine, and work has taken its rightful place in a rewritten personal scenario. These are not accomplishments fought for and hard won. They were thrust upon me; I stumbled and discovered. I do not think ambition vulgar and, yes, I thank goodness for all those who, for whatever reasons, aspire highly in their careers and who seek to manage, supervise, and lead the rest of us and our mutual enterprises. Nowadays I mostly smile a lot. I walk so that I can notice what is around me. I listen so that I can hear all that is being communicated. I try to make a habit of frequently casting my eyes forward and up.

Imagine it.

MEN WHO WEAR "PINK COLLARS"

Mike Kelly

In the beginning, Delroy Salmon felt he had to keep reminding himself he was a man.

For one thing, he was the only man. All of his co-workers were women, and everybody seemed to be asking whether he was strange.

Worse, he constantly encountered disbelievers: "You're really a doctor, aren't you?" Salmon remembers people asking.

"No," Salmon would reply, "I'm a nurse."

Salmon, a registered nurse at Greater Paterson General Hospital in Wayne, is one of a small group of American men today working in so-called "pink collar" jobs, positions that are traditionally filled by women. To them, the raised eyebrow, the open-mouthed stare, and the prying question are commonplace. So are the low salaries that characterize jobs in nursing, secretarial work, child care, maid service, or as telephone operators—all fields in which men are now working.

Some of these men are motivated by humanitarian devotion to certain kinds of jobs, such as nursing or child care.

Some just need a job. Still others are hoping to start at the bottom, say as a secretary, and then move to a more powerful corporation job. One local business school, in fact, reported that a male secretarial student used his office organizational skills to help gain acceptance to the army's officer's training school.

Many of the men explain, however, that their biggest fight is not low salaries or prying questions. In almost every case, they say their hardest job is combating the poor image that society gives them for taking these jobs.

In many cases, men in these fields are perceived as unaggressive, unmasculine, and not career-oriented. On the job, some men say they feel they have to perform better than women. And they are constantly chided for doing "women's work." Many such men say their most difficult fight is proving they are not homosexuals.

"Generally, male secretaries are perceived as being gay," said Warren Schimmel, vice president for academic affairs at the Berkeley School, a business school with six branches including one in Ridgewood, and a former secretary to the president of the New York Central Railroad. "The same goes with hairdressers."

One northern New Jersey hospital administrator, when asked whether he had any male nurses working for him, laughed, then replied: "We've had a few of them, and there's no question they're as queer as three-dollar-bills."

Next to low pay, the homosexual stereotype is the largest factor in keeping men out of traditionally female jobs said Jerome M. Rosow, president of the Work in America Institute of Scarsdale, New York, which conducts labor research studies for corporations, government, and unions.

"Customs and practices die hard," said Rosow. "Society sends out a lot of hidden signals. You see a male nurse and the assumption is that he is a homosexual or there is something wrong with him for wanting to do that kind of work. You have to have a strong ego or be very confident of your work."

The number of men entering traditionally female jobs increased when affirmative action rules were established in the early 1970s, but since then the number has leveled off. On the other hand, large numbers of women are now working in traditionally male jobs, primarily because the pay is much better.

During the seventies, the number of men in predominantly female jobs rose by thirty-six percent, to 375,000, according to the Bureau of Labor Statistics. Still, only 2.5 percent of America's employed men worked in these kinds of jobs in 1980, compared to 2.1 percent in 1971.

During that same period, the number of women in traditionally male jobs in heavy industry, computers, law and medicine increased by more than one hundred percent to over five million. The proportion of women in male-dominated jobs also rose from 8.4 percent in 1971 to 12.2 percent in 1980.

Ironically, in a time of high unemployment, traditionally female jobs are plentiful. The Work in America Institute, for example, says there are more than one hundred thousand job openings for nurses in America. The federal government predicts that more than three hundred thousand job openings for secretaries and office clerks will go unfilled during the 1980s.

The poor image of traditionally female jobs, however, stops even unemployed men from applying for openings.

"Many men think of secretarial work and nursing as women's work," said Samuel M. Ehrenhalt, New York, regional commissioner of labor statistics for the federal government. "You see this in some places of the country where there are big layoffs. Would an unemployed steelworker become a nurse? Not likely!"

Among the men who have entered traditionally female jobs, however, there seems to be a singular pride in combating so many stereotypes.

"Why am I a secretary? Because I'm tops," said Richard Courtemanche, 52, a former Hillsdale resident who had worked for Dart Industries in Paramus and now works as a secretary for a New York law firm.

To Joseph Glover, owner of Better Men, an all-male maid service, pride means being able to clean a house much faster than a woman. "Whereas it takes a lady a day to do it, we can take only several hours," said Glover. "Let's say you've got large furniture in your house. A woman can't move that, but a man can. We even have customers who have maids living in their house, and we still go in and do the cleaning."

For every prideful man in a traditionally female job, however, it's easy to find one who feels afraid or embarassed to admit what he does.

One Lyndhurst man, who became a nurse when he was 50 years old because he felt he wanted to help people in need, asked that his name not be revealed in the newspaper. "I don't want the neighbors gossiping," he said.

Ira Katz, 26, of Palisades Park, a former secretary in Manhattan, said he frequently told friends that he worked as an administrative assistant. "I just felt I could never tell anyone I was a secretary," said Katz, who now works at a theatrical management firm, booking classical music performers in concert halls.

Another former secretary, Marc Semler, 26, of Rochelle Park, said he often told friends that he needed a mindless job while attending school.

"I didn't want to come across as a jerk or a fool by saying I was a secretary," said Semler, who could type more than 120 words a minute and take dictation at the rate of 150 words per minute. "When I mentioned I was a secretary, it really killed conversations. People thought I was some kind of freak."

Semler, now manager of the word-processing center at Hayden Publishing in Passaic, said he became a secretary because he couldn't find any other office job when he was graduated from Bucknell University in 1978 with degrees in psychology and French. "I could type very fast and take dictation," he recalled, "and bosses would kill for my skills."

One problem, said Semler, is that many people refused to believe he was a secretary when they telephoned his boss. "People would think I was the vice president," he said, "and they were in shock when I said I was the secretary."

Such stereotyping often results in outright discrimination against men applying for traditionally female jobs. And the stereotypes are also one of the main reasons behind the predominance of women in certain jobs.

Two local maid services, for example, said they prefer not to hire men. "Men can't do the meticulous dusting," said one maid service manager. Said the manager of another service, "Girls are better cleaners."

One former male secretary said a male employer refused to hire him because he preferred a "buxom blond." Another prospective employer, as a way of trying to discourage him from applying as a secretary, told him he would have to make coffee every morning.

For David Sandborn, however, being a man actually helped in landing a job.

Last year, Sandborn, 19, of Washington Township, was trying to get a job at New Jersey Bell. Instead of applying for a higher-paying job, where his chances of being accepted would be slim, Sandborn asked to be a telephone operator (only 5.8 percent of telephone operators are male).

New Jersey Bell, which is actively trying to recruit men telephone operators, quickly hired him, and Sandborn now works as an operator at Bell's Rochelle Park office.

"I figured if I got a nontraditional job at first, I could always go on to something else." said Sandborn. "Being a male definitely helped me to get hired. It's the same reason that some women get jobs over men in traditionally male fields."

Being a man, says Sandborn, has also resulted in several surprising comments from others, especially women.

"Some of the younger girls ask me for a date when I come on the line," he said.

TABLE 1. MEN IN NONTRADITIONAL JOBS (U.S.)

Occupation:	Percent of men in occupation	Number of men in occupation
Secretary	1.2	33,000
Child care worker	1.7	6,000
Telephone operator	2.9	26,000
House cleaner	3.0	15,000
Nurse, dieticians, physical therapists	5.3	106,000
Elementary school teachers	15.1	225,000
Librarians	18.1	37,000

These figures date back to 1980 and were compiled by the Bureau of Labor Statistics of the U.S. Department of Labor.

Chapter 7:
Finding Our Fathers

GINGERBREAD

Stephen Picchi

Although it's less frequent now, there were numerous times when my parents and I ate dinner together. Sometimes the only noise came from the sounds of chewing. One evening in particular stands out in my mind.

My mother was talking about the high school float I had worked on the year before (it was Homecoming night at the high school I had graduated from); which led to the year before when I had marched with the school's ROTC in the Homecoming parade; which led to old acquaintances who had received ROTC scholarships to various universities; which led to my father saying, with a contented smile, that they would have to pay back the military with a few years of service. I agreed, saying that the people I had known who had earned the scholarships would fit perfectly into the military.

My mother worried about my sister—wishing she would call—tormenting herself with horrible thoughts of my sister lying knifed amid the riots in the student ghetto in Gainesville. She stopped as my father threw the dog some table scraps. She nagged him about feeding the dog (which she did every night), and he retorted by laughing at her (which he did every night).

After a chaotic path back through the sixties my father started talking about an old army buddy of his. At first I noticed a twitch of envy in his tone, but it disappeared as quickly as it appeared. His wife had been lucky that he had been a "bird" colonel when he died of a heart attack on the bathroom floor. She was financially set for life on his pension. He was a good man.

My father surprised me when he said regretfully, "I should have been a 'bird' colonel, too, but I couldn't wait." He paused several seconds, his eyes fogged with time, thinking about what his life would have been like if he had waited to retire as a full colonel. He added softly, as if wondering, "I couldn't wait." His face was red, and he rubbed his eyes and looked self-consciously down at his lap.

His tone of voice made me feel the need to console him. I had never done so before—never been given the opportunity to do so—and was startled when my voice, sounding stilted, murmured, "It's nothing to regret. I'd never have had the. . . patience or discipline to have stayed in as long as you did." I took a sip of my coffee.

I suppose I wanted my father to know I cared about him. For some childlike reason I wanted him to know I was aware of his feelings.

For the first time in my life he looked directly into my eyes. It lasted only seconds, but I saw what I had never seen before in his dark-brown eyes; the disillusionment covered by the blind, competitive drive to make more money and gain more power; the sudden realization that all he had striven for through his life had dovetailed into a decision which he could only blame himself for, and yet he couldn't even do that.

He interrupted my thoughts and said to the salt shaker. "At the time I retired it was necessary. I should have stayed in a few more years. I'd be making almost double the pension I make now, but at that time. . . it was necessary."

I saw my father, age seventy, a man of reason, wondering if his life had been unfulfilled. It hadn't mattered before because there were children to think about—"to put through college." He became disoriented, like an emotionless man suddenly faced with tears, and then he turned to look at my mother. Their eyes met, held, and then fell away.

I pretended I hadn't seen the exchange—my father's bitterness or my mother's realization. There was no verbal mention of what had been silently exchanged, but I knew there would be times when he would again sit and dwell on his sacrifices and failures—wrestling to lay the blame somewhere else—on something defenseless which was past or dead. His many accomplishments seemed irrelevant and unimportant to him—only what hadn't been achieved mattered.

My father bit into a piece of gingerbread, complained to my mother that he only liked the corner pieces. He wanted to know why she hadn't made more corner pieces especially for him. My mother argued that the pan only had four corners, but she'd make gingerbread again at Thanksgiving as she did every year.

HUGGING MY FATHER

Mark Sherkow

I'm thirty-five years old and my father is sixty. I've always been a sucker for movies and even TV episodes that show a father and son who have a conflict or are distant, and who then reconcile with a hug and tears (in the TV shows this is often while one of them is dying). The reconciliation always leaves me crying, and I've known that I feel sad about my own relationship with my father. I can recall only one time when I hugged my father, and I remember it as an emotional high point and an event that tells me a lot about my father and myself and about our relationship.

Ironically, even though my father and I don't hug, we've always kissed each other. We kiss on the lips when we haven't seen each other for awhile and upon parting. We did this when I was a boy, even when I was in high school, and it always seemed natural; my father was interested in what I was doing, and I knew that he cared for me and loved me. But I knew that our kissing expressed something else, too—an emotional inhibition we both shared, an inability or fear to express our feelings in a more physical and involved way, or ever to say, "I love you." Those single pecks, the brief touching of lips, said, "I care for you," but they also said, "I can't or won't show my love for you in any other physical way; this will have to do."

I exchanged these kisses with my father all through high school, but when I got into college, I stopped. I felt that I was too old to be kissing my father. It wasn't "manly." So when we greeted I just shook hands. But I knew that he wanted more than such a cold greeting, and I did too. So after a couple of years I started kissing him again, and we've continued this way of greeting and parting ever since.

To talk about the one time I hugged my father, I'll have to give a little background. I was the oldest of four children, two boys and two girls, and our family did a lot of things together when we were growing up, such as going to dinner or the movies and going on trips. We went to Florida twice, once when I was eight and again when I was ten or twelve. We went during the winter break from school, driving down from our home in Milwaukee. Those two trips were great fun—getting up at 3 A.M. to beat traffic, passing gradually from the snow-covered, cold-ridden Midwest through the curvy hills of Tennessee to the sun and warmth of Florida, and then spending a week in Miami Beach with the ocean/beaches, swimming pools and sun-lovers.

My parents took other vacations to Florida and elsewhere besides those two, vacations where they left us at home. We would rather have been with them, but I didn't mind because I felt good that our parents did so much with us and realized they would want to do some things by themselves. So it was all right.

As I got older, however, something else was happening.

I was interacting more with kids outside the family, and these interactions became more imporatnt to me. In junior high and high school I became involved in a number of school activities and even ran successfully for class president one year. But I had a secret problem that bothered me very much and that I couldn't tell anyone. I felt that I didn't have any real friends and that I didn't know how to make friends. I was unhappy about this problem, but I could barely admit it to myself, and certainly never thought about discussing it with anyone else, especially my parents.

So one day in the fall of my junior year, my father told me that he and my mother were thinking of taking another trip to Florida with the whole family, like we had done several years before. I was shocked. Those Florida trips seemed light-years away, and I knew that a trip now would never be the same for me. I wanted to be with kids my own age, but I was afraid that I wouldn't make friends with any and so be alone. I told my father how I felt, without going into detail: it wouldn't be the same, I was older now and wanted to be with kids my own age, it wasn't enough anymore to be with the family. As I said it, his face and shoulders fell. I had hurt him. He really wanted this trip, really thought it could be "just like old times." Suddenly I felt a tremendous wave of guilt and sadness. I had hurt this man who had cared for and been supportive of me, and I had selfishly thought only of myself.

I started to tell him that I was sorry to make him feel bad, that it was okay with me if he wanted us to go to Florida, but all I could do was to blurt it out, then grab him, hug his chest, hold him and start crying. And it felt so good! His chest felt so strong, so good to hold, the way I guess I had always wanted him to hold me. I think he was stunned. He put his arm around me and said, "That's all right," and just held me for an instant. Then I ran into my bedroom and bolted my back against the door while my mother stood outside saying, "What's wrong?" and I said, "Leave me alone, Mother, everything's all right." She went away, I let the crying continue, and then it was over.

I've never talked with my father about that experience. We did go to Florida, and it wasn't fun for me, though I did meet and spend some time with a couple of boys about my age. What I see as I look back are several things. I see how difficult it was for both my father and I to express our emotions, which remains true today. In particular, we had and still have great difficulty expressing [ourselves] to each other. I see how I isolated myself from my father and from everyone else by not expressing my feelings about not having friends. I also see how this one time when I started to tell my father how I felt, he wasn't able to respond, perhaps didn't want to hear what I was saying and never bothered to find out just what was going on. And I see how my guilty feelings at hurting my father, for being a selfish "bad boy," and for losing his approval made me completely back off from my own feelings about what the trip would be like for me.

So what conclusions do I draw from this episode? For one, the importance of listening, of hearing other people's feelings without reacting or judging. If we're having trouble doing this, so we should learn to take turns. Secondly, the importance of communication, of taking a risk, of sharing our feelings with our friends and those who are close to us. Keeping things inside is a way *not* to deal with a problem, and isolates a person from the people who can help. Thirdly, I see how important approval is to a child, and how setting standards for children can have negative consequences if it means not finding out why a child is acting in a particular way. "Be a good child; a good child doesn't do that," can turn children into approval-seekers rather than helping them to deal with their feelings and communicate with others. Finally, I see how things like hugging and holding—open expressions of warmth and feeling—can have a powerful and potentially healing effect. It's been nineteen years since I hugged my father, but I vividly remember the strength and power of our embrace. It makes me feel good to know that my father and I kiss. And I hope that what I've gained from looking back at that experience will give me the courage to take more risks—to be the kind of person I really want to be, both with my father and with other people.

SWEET POTATO

Arthur Winfield Knight

for Dad

You were the last
of three children,
ten years younger
than your brother,
and you grew-up knowing
you weren't wanted,
always in the backseat
of your parents' car
as if you were
someone undiscovered.
"Children are seen, not heard."
Sick from gas fumes,
you'd vomit by the roadside.

You left home immediately
when you got out of high school.
You disappointed your parents,
going to Heald's Business College.
They'd always known
you'd go to Cal. Instead
you went to see
the Solons play at night
and spent tropical evenings
in the valley playing pool.

Mom says you met a girl
who died an alcoholic
and you never drank much
after that.
She never told me why
you gave up your dream
to write. You worked for
Pacific Fruit and Produce,
taking shorthand
when you weren't
unloading boxcars.
It was during the Depression.
Maybe that explains it.
Maybe not.

When I was born.
you were almost ready
to have a nervous breakdown.
Sixteen-hour days
seven days a week
are too much for any man.
In the evenings you played
the sweet potato,
and I remember you sitting
on the front steps
cutting warts from your thumb
with a jackknife.
There were games of kick-the-can.

When I entered high school
you and mom ended-up
taking care of your parents
because your brother wouldn't
and your sister was dead.

Your father had a stroke
and your mother was confined
to a wheelchair,
and you and mom
only went away once overnight
in the next few years.
Grandpa tried to read the paper
upside-down, and choked
until his false teeth rattled,
living on bananas and baby food.

When I went to college
I smoked and drank too much
—or at least you thought so—
and there were the women
you never seemed to like.
I sent you letters
telling you not to worry,
but you always did.
When I told you
I wanted to be a writer
it was as if
some part of your past
you'd lobotomized came back.
It was an impossible dream.

"Get a job."

I sold the Ford convertible
you'd given me
and went to Europe,
one marriage already behind me.
The first in our family
to be divorced,
making history in my twenties.
I did it again
within three years.
No one was proud of me.
And you said I was
"an educated bum"
before I moved east.
I left a note on your door
saying goodbye.
Mom told me later
you cried when you read it.

It was ten years before
we'd see each other again.
I came back with the woman
who'd be my fourth wife,
sleeping down the hall with her
from the room you and mom shared.
She said you told her,
"Arthur's an adult now."

You'd sold the business you'd had
more than twenty years,
becoming a botanist
because it was something
you wanted to do.
I wondered how you'd managed
to sell venetian blinds and rugs
so many years.
Water on the knee
from laying carpet.
How does anyone survive
meaningless work?

Last weekend you phoned
to tell us
you've finally retired,
that you and mom
are selling the house
and moving here.
It won't be long

before you're teaching our daughter
how to grow things
and describing her daddy's boyhood—
we wore dogtags in elementary school
in case there was a Jap invasion—
and your own.
Born before the radio existed,
you broke your arm
cranking a Model T.

Things change and remain the same.
I can see you at the end of summer
sitting on the swing
as the street lights filter thru
the large maples in our yard
playing my daughter
the same songs you played me
forty years ago
on the sweet potato

MEN EXPRESS FEELINGS, FIND TRUST, CLOSENESS

Roy Aarons

One member reported that he had told his father, who was in the hospital recuperating from a stroke, how deeply he loved him. His father's response was that "of all the things that have happened during my life to make me feel it was worth living, this simple statement means the most of all."

WHAT IS OURS?

Louie Crew

After he had made his dad's bed,
had lotioned his dad's buttocks to prevent bed sores,
and had stared lovingly into the blank, gray, unseeing eyes,
he went to *The Merry Wives of Windsor*
to escape for two hours the old age and dying;
but when Falstaff was trundled off in the laundry basket,
it was his dad's laugh, memorized when he had been 2 or 3,
which he recognized as his own, echoing through the theatre.

Chapter 8:
Parenting: The Greatest Discovery

EXCERPT FROM THE DEBS UNDERGROUND

John Petersen

I don't remember exactly when or how I heard that John and Carol Wilton had split up, but I recall that it was quite a shock to me. They had been close friends of ours for four years. It's strange because they were born-again Christians and I was an athiest. My wife, Sue, stopped short of being an athiest, but wasn't at all interested in any form of organized religion. Perhaps these differences lead to livelier discussions.

As for me, I was glad that the Wiltons weren't completely bored with my Marxist tantrums. For them, we were new people to bring into the good graces of God. Beyond all this, the four of us were very much into the "back to the land" idea.

We had all moved to the great north country within a few months of each other. Sue and I were there more by accident than plan, the Wiltons more by plan than accident. The Wiltons had both been born and raised in the city. John's father had moved from Kentucky to Ohio to escape the coalfields, and went on to spend a good portion of his life in a factory. He considered himself lucky to have done so. When John graduated from high school, he went to work in the factories too and later started working construction. Then, before his move to Minnesota, he was doing both. Working was his prime ethic. John thought work would make everything right in the world.

Many of the rough spots in our relationship centered around the work ethic.

I also felt that working hard was some sort of ethical imperative, but I never let it be the center of my life. Actually, I really didn't like working all that much. If I hadn't had the ethic and a desire to eat, I wouldn't have worked at all. John, on the other hand, lived only to work. It was a competition to him and one that he most generally won. To work with John was to be drawn into this competition. To come out ahead of John was nearly impossible. John made life unbearable if you lost.

John and I started our working relationship as partners in a roofing enterprise. We subcontracted work through a roofing company in Grand Forks, North Dakota. John was a professional roofer in every sense of the word. I knew the difference between the top of the roof and the bottom, but since I thought I knew more than that, conflict was bound to arise. When we weren't roofing, we'd help each other cut firewood and the like. As in all ventures, it seems, somebody always thinks that the one isn't contributing as much as the other. But talking the situation over between us generally got things worked out. In those situations where we feared confrontation, our wives would harangue us until we were close to fighting. Fortunately we both were more afraid of fighting each other than confronting each other on a verbal level.

John and Carol had married before Carol graduated from high school and two children had followed soon after that. Carol felt that these circumstances had left a void in her life, and indeed they had. The Wiltons had bought a forty-acre plot when they moved to Minnesota. The purchase of this land and the move itself had been an attempt to escape the built-in traps of the city. But John and Carol couldn't escape the built-in traps of themselves. John always said, "The only way to keep a woman in her place is to keep her pregnant and barefoot." But Carol was moving into other realms.

During the Wilton's first two years in the woods Carol had been very happy. She had gardened and kept house and looked after the two kids. But after these years passed, both kids were in school and Carol found herself with time on her hands. We were all proud of her when she started working on and finally obtained her high school equivalency diploma. But Carol was fired up now and decided to go further and got accepted into nurses training at Crookston, Minnesota, which was about one hundred miles away. So John and Carol abandoned their homestead and headed once more for the city. Carol's dreams were beginning. John's "back to the land" dreams were ending, though he still was optimistic about the situation. He speculated that when Carol received her nursing license they would move back to the woods, and with Carol earning a steady income John would be free to follow his dreams of backwoods independence.

For two years John drove semitrailers over the road to make house payments and feed his family while Carol went to school. Then when Carol graduated she threw him out of his home because he hadn't been spending enough time with his family. So now he was being denied his kids, his home, and even a sense of his own worth. He came back to the woods alone.

He pulled into the farmyard late one evening. He told me what had happened in brief, and I told him I'd already heard.

145

"Let's go get drunk," he said.

"I can't right now. I've got to milk these cows."

Sue was eight and a half months pregnant with our first child at the time. As I've already said, I was shocked at hearing about John and Carol's separation, but I had other things to think about too. Or so I thought.

"Yeah, I suppose with a kid on the way you have to tend to business. I just thought you might want to tie one on for old times sake."

"I don't have anything against that John, I just need to milk the cows first."

"How long does that take?"

"About an hour."

"I'll pick you up," he said, and drove off.

So I milked the cows and went to the house and told Sue what was happening.

"You're going to go out and get drunk and leave me here alone all night?"

"Well hell, you're welcome to come along. I think we'll just go over to the store and buy some beer and then go down to Ron and Ginny's and get a little crazy."

"I don't like beer, and don't you think you could spend one evening at home?"

"Aw, come on Sue, it'll do you good to get out, and besides John must be feeling low as hell tonight. I think he could really use the company."

"Well, why can't he come here?"

"Damn it, he wants to get drunk out in the woods. You coming or not?"

"No!"

In the meantime John had driven into the yard and was on his way to the house. I met him halfway.

"Ready to go?" asked John.

"Fucking right I'm ready to go."

"What's wrong?"

"Sue is on the warpath again."

We walked back to John's pickup and drove out of the yard.

"Well, what's happening?" asked John.

"Name it."

"Feel like getting drunk?"

"Fucking right."

"Damn; sorry I asked."

"I'm sorry John, but that woman just drives me right up the wall sometimes."

On the way to the store conversation was sparse and small. After buying a couple of six-packs, we were driving toward Ron and Ginny's when John told me he had taken up smoking pot. He'd always been against drugs, but Carol had started smoking again after a six-year sabbatical. John had been taking a few hits now and then just to keep up with what was happening.

"Well, hell's bells," I said, "I just happen to have a toke with me. Care to indulge?"

"Sure, why not?"

So I rolled a joint and we smoked in silence. Then we popped a couple of cold beers. By the time we pulled up on top of the Browns' hill we were both feeling better. Before I opened the door, John turned to me and asked, "How come you and Sue fight all the time? You fight right in front of all your friends, and to tell the truth, you make everyone else real uncomfortable."

"Hell, John, that's just the way we communicate."

"Yeah, I know, and it makes everyone else real uneasy. It's real uncomfortable when you two get started."

"Really John, we don't mean anything by it. It's just the way we communicate."

"Well, if you say so. I wouldn't want to call you a liar. But I think you ought to think about it."

We got out of the truck and went up the path into the woods. Ron and Ginny were sitting by the campfire and greeted us as we approached. The four of us sat around the fire smoking pot and drinking beer, and had a great time. John was very animated, telling dirty jokes and laughing at all the exploits we'd shared in our past. Separations and spousal squabbles disappeared like smoke into the air. But as the flames turned to coals , John's spirits turned to shit.

First he was just silent, smiling occasionally at remarks the rest of us were busting a gut over. Beer and pot will do that to a person. None of us really paid much attention. Then John got up and walked out into the darkness. He came back a few minutes later with tears in his eyes.

"I just can't stand it. I need to go home. Will you take J. P. home, Ron?"

"Sure. Don't you want to sit down for a little while first?"

"Naw, I want to go home. Is that okay with you?" he asked me.

"Yeah, that's fine with me, John."

"Damn it, J. P., I'm serious." He apparently thought I was ridiculing him.

"So am I John. It's fine with me, really."

"Sorry."

"No problem."

John walked off into the darkness. A few minutes later his pickup started and he drove away. The three of us were quiet and in a few minutes I asked Ron if he would drive me home.

Around midmorning the next day, Ron came over. We drank a couple cups of coffee. The conversation turned to the night before. We decided we'd better drive over and see how John was doing.

As we drove into the yard, John was standing by the front door examining the old house.

"How's it going, John?" asked Ron.

"Oh, I'm doing alright. Listen, I'm really sorry about last night."

"Shit, Wilton, you got nothing to be sorry for. Christ, you've been though a lot the last couple of days." Ron's voice had the quality of a cowboy talking to a skittish horse.

"I think you ought to be sorry," I piped in. "I had to ride home with this drunk, stoned fucker." I shook Ron by the shoulder.

John didn't smile. It was only then that I began to recognize his heavy mood. He bent down to pick up a rock and threw it into a marsh.

"You got anything to smoke?" I asked.

"Yeah, it's in the kitchen, up in the cupboard."

I went to get it. When I came back John was leaning against a tree, crying. I looked at Ron and he shrugged his shoulders.

"Anybody got a pipe?"

"Uh-huh." Ron pulled a pipe out of his shirt pocket and I filled it up. I handed it to Ron to light.

"Damn it, I'm losing it, guys. I'm fucking losing it." John sat down on the ground and sobbed.

"Hell, John, you're going to make it. You know that." My consolation made no impression at all. Ron was silent.

In a few minutes John stopped crying and looked up at us toking away on his pot.

"Don't you guys ever do anything but smoke pot?" A sheepish smile crawled onto his face and then ran away. "What the fuck do you all want anyway?"

"We just came over to see how you were," I answered.

"Fuck, too. You just came over to smoke my pot. Why don't you just take it and leave me the hell alone!"

Ron was pushed out of his silence. "John, you know beter than that. We came over to see how you were."

"Yeah, and what about you J. P.? What did you come over for?"

"Oh, I definitely came over to smoke all your pot. I think we ought to fill the pipe again and you should join us. That way you won't make me feel so guilty about smoking it."

"You asshole. Go ahead. I couldn't handle it right now. I always wait till dark. I have too much to do."

An awkward silence followed. Then Ron and I told John to hang in there and that we'd see him later. We drove off down the road.

"Damn, Ron, Wilton has always been a bit paranoid but this is getting ridiculous."

"About the pot you mean?"

"Yeah."

"Well, he's uptight, you know. He's really going through it, isn't he?"

"Yeah. But you know he's mostly feeling sorry for himself. I mean, I know it's really a bitch to have to go through that crap. I really feel for him, but hell, feeling sorry for yourself isn't going to help. Enough is enough. He's tougher than that."

"You take a real hard line, don't you Petersen?"

The days passed and John's emotional state didn't improve. At times his spirits would be high. He'd join right in with what was happening, i.e., smoking pot or drinking beer, or helping the community undergrounders with their daily tasks. Then just when everything seemed to be going good he would collapse into tears. The courage he showed coming back from despair only to plunge down again didn't impress me much. "You're only feeling sorry for yourself," was my only thought on the matter. Not that he didn't have reason to, but what good did it do? All I really saw was a broken man.

148

In the meantime Sue was getting closer and closer to having our firstborn. And when her parents came to visit, pandemonium hit our house. Sue's mother is a nurse and a perfectionist. After Sue had spent days cleaning the house, in anticipation of her parents' arrival, the first thing her mother did was start cleaning house. They bought us a new bed which was unsolicited and unwanted. Her father examined the farming operation and decided it was hopeless. His qualification to make this judgment was that he had once had sixteen head of beef cows on his eighty-acre hobby farm. He read in a copy of my *Hoard's Dairyman* about computerized dairy barns, and was wondering why I didn't have one of those computers. He looked at my equipment and decided I needed all new equipment. At this juncture the furnace quit working and despite the fact that it was the middle of May and we had a woodburning stove anyway, Sue's father totally freaked out, newborn on the way and all. But the final straw started bending when Mommy decided that Sue should have the baby on Monday.

Who knows how long Sue might have gone on being pregnant. What seemed to be important was that Sue's mother only had so long that she could be away from her hospital duties. So Monday morning came and Sue and her parents went to Bemidji to see the doctor. The doctor said that if Sue wanted her labor induced, he'd okay it.

I'd just milked the cows and was in for my second pot of coffee when the phone rang.

"Hello."

"Well J. P., I'm going to the hospital now. They're going to induce labor."

"Is it really necessary?" I asked.

"You know Mom only has a week off from work."

"That hardly qualifies as a medical necessity. Besides, didn't I hear you two talking about how induced labors are generally more difficult?"

"Well, that's true, but Mom is going to be with me. I trust her."

In short, it didn't matter what the hell I thought; the decisions were already made. After nine months of preparing for a natural birth, chemicals were going to tell our unborn child that it was time to bail out. Through the course of the pregnancy we had been practicing the Lamaze method of childbirth. But when labor started Mom started practicing her own method. If I told Sue to do one thing, Mom told her that wasn't right. Inside half an hour Sue's mother was in command. Lamaze was standing somewhere out in the cold. The labor was long and in my opinion gruesome, though there have been worse, I'm sure. It may have been as bad without the chemicals. But neither of us will ever know. Mom was in control.

Finally Sue gave birth to a beautiful baby boy and I was overjoyed. I left the hospital about five-thirty Tuesday morning. The sun was just coming up and was reflected in Lake Bemidji which was just outside the hospital's front door. God! A son and a bright fresh morning. I drove back to the farm intending to milk the cows and get some sleep. But first I had to tell the Browns the good news. They and John had spent a lot of time at the hospital waiting for the birth and giving Sue and me moral support. They had gone home about midnight when it seemed that the labor might go on for quite a while. I thought they ought to know about our baby.

I knocked on their door at about six o'clock, and when I told her, Ginny greeted me through sleepy eyes with a hug and congratulations. Then Ron came rambling down out of the loft and gave me his best wishes.

"How about a joint?"

"I could really use it, Ron," I said, "but I haven't had any sleep and I need to get back and milk the cows."

"Aw, come on and have a toke, and then we'll all go over and milk the cows."

"You twisted my arm."

One toke or two, what does it matter? I've got a son. Three or four tokes, what does it matter, my in-laws are waiting for me at home. Five tokes or ten, what the hell, don't I have a right to celebrate?

Ten or twenty tokes. "Hey Wilton!" John had spent the night there and was sleeping on the floor by the stove. "Hey, you lazy fucker, get up and help us smoke this pipe."

He turned over and said, "Why don't you get fucked. Damn, all you guys do is smoke pot."

"Ron do you want to race the horses?" I asked.

"I've never raced."

We bridled up the horses and had a couple of races. The last race ended with Ron being thrown over the finish line. To no avail, because I beat him anyway.

Ron, Ginny, and I rolled into the farmyard about eight-thirty. When I walked into the kitchen, there were my in-laws. It was the same old story of where have you been, we've been waiting, what about your cows and your responsibilities? In deference to their self-proclaimed importance to my life, I didn't tell them to fuck off. Instead I gave some phony apologies and headed for the barn. Twenty holstein's asses look better than two scowling, judgmental in-laws.

In a few days Sue was ready to come home with our son. Even this special event was not to go by unmolested by Sue's parents. First of all when we went to the hospital, we *had* to take their new Oldsmobile. Secondly, Daddy held the baby on the way home. When I sat down to rock my baby for the first time, Daddy came over and pulled the rocking chair around so that it's position pleased him. I held the baby against me and rubbed his back and felt his warmth and innocence only to be told that I couldn't burp him that way. All of this amongst flashcubes popping off like a Washington press conference. I put our child back in his crib and left. I found Ron cutting firewood out in the woods. We smoked pot till I was ready to pass out, and then I went home and milked the cows.

The next morning there were lectures on responsibility. We were also supposed to be overjoyed at the news that Mommy had called her hospital and would be able to spend another week with us. Get the picture? I made myself scarce.

Finally they left, but not before many people's feelings had been hurt and tempers riled. Sue's parents had in two weeks' time managed to alienate Sue and I from all our friends. Friends who would have been with us and shared in the

150

experience of it all had it not been that "sanitary, sterile" conditions prevailed not only physically, but mentally and emotionally as well.

When they drove out of the lane there was a peace and serenity in the air that had been absent for two weeks. I could walk like I wanted to. I could talk like I wanted to. I could do what I wanted to without the scrutinizing eyes of middle-class righteousness following my every move. Our friends were not long in coming around once the cauldrons of responsibility had left. Pot smoke billowed and beer cans popped and the true welcoming of our son was under-way. Laughter once more permeated the house with it's sweetness. It was all too much for Sue, who sent our asses out of the house.

However, the reality of running the farm quickly came back also. There were many things to do and in the shortness of a Northern Minnesota summer, not much time to do them. I had been hesitant to get involved in these tasks while Sue's father had been there because of his constant interference. He simply couldn't comprehend the magnitude of my tasks but nevertheless always had a word of advice. These words grated on my mind like using broken glass for toilet paper. But in his absence I started full steam ahead.

In the meantime Sue was finding more and more things that I could do for her. She had me bring things down from upstairs that had been stored away for ages. She had me clean up things and straighten up places. She had me change the oil in the car. Then with things in a complete and total state of upheaval I was informed that Sue's sister and her husband were coming to pay us a visit.

So two weeks after Sue's parents left, more in-laws arrived. They drove up in my father-in-law's new Oldsmobile. The next day Sue convinced me that I should go see the banker and get that year's financial business out of the way. This I did. When I came home the Olds, as well as our car, were gone. I didn't think much about it. But when I walked into the house I noticed there was an envelope on the table addressed to me. I opened it and read that Sue had decided to "visit" her parents. She made it sound as if it had been a spur-of-the-moment thing. But then the cannisters missing from the counter started driving a message home. I glanced into the living room and saw that the stereo was gone. As I pieced the puzzle together, I realized that for the last two weeks I'd been helping Sue prepare for an exodus that her whole family had helped plan.

So as I stood in the kitchen trying to comprehend just what had happened, an uncontrollable anger surged through me. The hate I felt was immediately transferred to my in-laws. I thought of all they had done. I thought of the bed they had bought us. I ran to the bedroom and tore the mattress off the bed and threw it out in the yard. I ran back in the house and grabbed the box spring and threw that sucker out, too. Then I went back in for the rest of it. The headboard had to be removed to get the rest out into the yard. I didn't feel the inclination to look for tools so I flattened the fucker. It went out quite easily that way.

My father and brother, who lived just a few miles away, and a visiting cousin showed up and watched while all this was going on. They were unaware of my reasoning, or my lack of it, depending on the point of view. My dad asked, "What in the hell are you doing?" I told him what had happened. "Well, Christ, J. P.," he said, "breaking the bed all to hell ain't going to help."

151

"It sure as hell won't hurt," I said, and headed back into the house to see what else Sue's parents had bought for us. There was the stand our stereo had been on. It was one of those counterfeit pressboard things made to look like genuine imitation wood. I picked it up to make the haul to the front yard. But the sucker fell into three or four separate pieces. This gave me an idea. I picked up the pieces and carried them to the front yard and began smashing them over the head of the now-defunct bed.

My father chimed in again, "You aren't doing yourself any good, J. P. Christ Almighty. I've been through the same kind of thing. If you have to go to court what will this little episode look like?"

"It'll look like I'm one pissed off, long-haired redneck who's ready to kill."

With that statement in mind I jumped into my pickup and headed out the lane, gravel flying, the pickup sliding back and forth and roaring like my rage. I got on the road that ran by the place and headed for the highway, my foot in the carburetor. But at seventy miles per hour I decided that if I was to make it to Missouri I'd have to keep it on the road. When I came up behind a little old couple driving about twenty miles an hour, I slowed and waited for them to get over a hill and then I passed them in second gear with the engine wound tight. At the intersection where the gravel road intersects the highway, I met John. I slid to a stop and asked him if he'd seen either my in-laws' car or my car.

"No, I haven't J.P. What's up anyway? You look real pissed off."

"I am pissed off. That bitch took off with my boy, John. She fucking took off with my boy. I'm going to Missouri and get him back and kill them no-good fucking in-laws."

As I spoke John was getting out of his pickup. When I finished my tirade he was standing by my door with tears in his eyes.

"J.P., what good will it do? Can't you see it doesn't matter?"

"It matters to me goddamn it."

"Listen, I know what you're feeling. I've wanted to do a little killing myself. But these feelings don't matter. You're not going to kill anyone. I'm not going to kill anyone. We've got to go on from here. Come on and turn this crate around. It won't make it to Missouri anyway. We're both just two fucking idiots running around in these woods like we can't find our way out." He was still crying and I was still pissed off. "It doesn't matter J.P. Can't you see that it doesn't matter?"

MEN MUST BREAK THE FEMALE MONOPOLY OVER CHILDREARING

Richard Haddad

The main point in Dinnerstein's *The Mermaid And The Minotaur* is that the only way for us as a society to make any meaningful change in sex-role patterns is for men to break the female monopoly over childrearing. Dinnerstein arrives at her conclusion by combining Freudian and feminist sex-role theory. I arrive at the same conclusion by another application of the Principle of the Should's. The dominant issue of the women's movement has been employment, that sphere which has always been man's domain. The corresponding domain for women has been childrearing, and that is where men must and will muscle in on the action.

Fathering is the central issue of the men's movement, and it is both the easiest and the hardest issue for the individual male parent to tackle. He has any number of daily opportunities to change the way he relates to his children directly and to change the way he relates to his wife on the subject of child-rearing; but he is inevitably intimidated by his own feelings of inadequacy as a parent, the absence of a positive male parenting model, and his wife's reputation (because she is a woman) for knowing best how to parent.

Of course, men *can* parent, and as well as women. As James Levine tells us in his book *Who Will Raise The Children?*, any childrearing researcher who has bothered to ask the question has had it answered with an emphatic yes. Most experts, however, have operated on the assumption that male parenting ability doesn't exist, or if it does, it is naturally inferior to female parenting ability, so they never bothered to study it.

Not only are more men discovering that they *can* parent, but they are also discovering their capacity for intimacy and affection with their children, the excitement of developing their very own parenting styles instead of miming the styles of their wives and mothers, their enjoyment of growing with their children. Clearly, we're not talking here of "helping" with the children—of burping babies or changing diapers on occasion, or of taking junior to the park while mother does some shopping. We're talking of men participating in the rearing of their own children instead of leaving it to the womenfolk. We are talking of men being co-makers of the decisions that affect their children's lives.

Can a man combine career and family? The women who do say it's not easy, but it can be done. There are those men who find satisfaction in being full-time homemaker-fathers while their wives work; and there are others who work part-time, as do their wives, so that each partner gets to spend half the day with the children. Most men who get serious about fathering, however, have to find a way to cope with a full-time job *and* parenting responsibilities. This frequently means a change in attitude about work and career.

MEN AND NURTURING

Jerry Medol

Men are seen as being expendable as long as they fulfill their purpose...and it's like we get ritualized into taking care of other people instead of finding out about ourselves. I'm not saying by this that we get ritualized into being the nurturers; rather, we get ritualized into providing the resources that the nurturers think they need.

CUSTODIAL FATHERHOOD

Ken Pangborn

Many men have fantasies of the Disneyland world they expect in having custody. Fantasies about how it will be all love and kisses, or some such dream. Few realize the great difficulties they will face.

I have seen many men seeking a custody modification who really want their new wives or girlfriends to be baby-sitters or the "parent," and they are not motivated by a genuine desire to *"be"* a custodial parent themselves.

I, like every other noncustodial dad, had all these fantasies. I looked at women I was dating for exceptional parenting skills. I had a dream of how my children would be so glad to see their dad they would jump all over me, that they would remember how close we were before the separation and divorce, and forget about the four years they were not allowed to see me or even talk about me except to say what a "bastard" I was.

None of my fantasies were fulfilled, the day the judge said, "and physical custody is awarded the father." The children cried, and kicked at me and the doors of the car, proclaiming, "I hate you, Ken." For months they didn't miss an opportunity to let me know that they would really prefer to be living with their mother. Acting-out was a sport for them, almost an art form. It was supposed to wear me down to the point where I would give them back to their mother. As resolved as they were, I had to be even stronger, yet I also had to be sensitive to their feelings.

In time the "reverse bonding" started, but in the year and a half it took there was more than one agony for them and for me. The bonding to father is by no means complete as yet. It is a bit easier to see now that we have at least another year or perhaps two, before things really stabilize and the children relax.

Pressure from my former wife has not let up for a second. We have been back to court five times in eighteen months with her attempts to regain custody. I have no illusions that it will end here. The constant war is not only hard on me emotionally but also hard on my wallet.

The constant war over custody as been hardest on the children. Their mother's telephone "visitation" is the third degree in attempts to find evidence to use in court. The direct involvement for the children is a form of torture that has given them many tearful nights.

One of the most important things for me was for the girls to understand that I really loved them. This is an abstract exchange that they are just beginning to understand. But they are learning through example.

Having custody of three young daughters is a mixed blessing. I have chosen not to share the parenting with a woman for the time being. I am not deliberately avoiding women, but I am not willing to share this adjustment time for the girls just yet. I will most likely do so eventually but I have felt that they need time to adjust to their father first, before I throw any other curves at them.

The fact that many fathers do not understand what being a single parent is like should not be counted against them. Almost all mothers have even less understanding of single-parent responsibilities.

My experience with custodial fathers has convinced me that the adjustments that must be made are made more easily and willingly by the male parent than by the female parent. Most men, contrary to popular media and mythology, can cook and sew. These were skills taught to some of us in basic training in the military. Some of us even helped our mothers with dishwashing and cooking chores.

As husbands, before the divorce, we often took care of the 3 A.M. feeding and dirty diaper changing. Contrary to fable, we do a creditable job as single parents. All of the research I am familiar with even dares to suggest that we do a superior job.

Being a custodial father has many rewards as well as demands. There are many special moments. Seeing your child recover from anemia and gain twenty pounds in a year is a significant reward. Seeing children grow from their education is a definite reward. I specially enjoy the evening walks on weekends that are filled with a thousand childlike innocent questions about the world. Some I can answer and on some I must change the subject before my ignorance shows too much.

Being a wise custodial father also means never forgetting how vulnerable your custody is. The merest hint of something less than perfect and you return to being on the outside of the window looking in.

In my case, the prospect of the children returning to their past life is indeed grim. It is hard living under the constant threat of being dragged back into court. The resulting financial mess is one that seems hopeless at times. But somehow I make do, and struggle on being a single-parent dad trying my damndest to be perfect, but realizing I never can be. I still try, despite the popular myth which says that I don't care. I try because I always have cared, and now is my first chance to really show it.

I TOO CREATE LIFE
Coming Home To My Children

Jed Diamond

After the divorce, things became so uncomfortable with Lindy and me that we'd drop the children off at my mother's house so we wouldn't have to see each other. We seemed to fight every time we met, so we worked out the intermediary to funnel the kids between us. It wasn't the best exchange point since my mom lived in a senior citizen's apartment complex and everyone was always worried about the kids making too much noise or bowling over a little old lady as they raced through the hallways.

On one such occasion, the kids got into it as soon as they got in the apartment. Sandy began teasing Gene and jumping up and down on the bed. As I usually did, I tried in my best fatherly, soothing voice to explain to her that jumping might disturb the neighbors. As she often did, she just looked at me and wouldn't respond. Usually her cold stare would get me angry and I'd be on her. But this time something was touched in me and I asked, "Is something going on inside you, Sandy?" I touched her leg and asked, "Aren't you feeling good about yourself?" She looked up, was very present for a moment, then burst into tears and threw her arms around my neck. We sat together, holding each other for a long while. Finally she smiled, then I smiled. No words were exchanged, but something very special had happened between us.

I found more and more often that when I'd try to do what I thought a good father would do, our interactions rarely turned out well. When I reached down from my human here-and-now feelings and acted from that part of me, our interactions began to blossom.

THE ORIGINS OF FATHER'S DAY:
An Affectionate Glance Over Our Shoulders

Tom Williamson

A number of men's movement organizations throughout the country are planning Father's Day events this year, and the Coalition of Free Men is one of them. All this activity aroused my curiosity about how Father's Day got started in the first place, so I consulted a well-rounded and knowledgeable friend who said she thought it was the Hallmark card company that began it all. For some reason I could not—perhaps I did not want to—accept such a commercial explanation. I put on my research cap, determined to debunk this myth. I began with the encyclopedia, which was of little help, although it confirmed that Hallmark was indeed one of the early promoters of the holiday.

Fortunately, my Dad never throws out anything, so I had easy access to the *1948 World Almanac*, published by the New York World-Telegram newspaper. (More recent almanacs only give the date for the event.) That started the ball rolling because this book informed me about the National Committee for Father's Day that was founded in 1936. Its affiliate, the Father's Day Council, was located in New York. From the *World Almanac* I went to the telephone book, looked up the number of the Father's Day Council, and called them. Surprisingly, they had very little informaition about the origins of Father's Day. In desperation I went to my local library, where I should have gone in the first place.

Father's Day was, for the most part, a female invention. The first known Father's Day church service was held in Fairmount, West Virginia, in 1908, the same year that Mother's Day was initiated. In 1908 it was the brainchild of Jessica Clinton Clayton, but it remained a local celebration until somewhat later on, when others in different parts of the country independently hit on the idea. Sonora Smart is recognized as the official "founder."

Ms. Smart knew nothing of Ms. Clayton's 1908 idea, but in 1910, in Spokane, Washington, she felt the desire to create a Father's Day to honor her own father, William. William Smart was a nurturing parent who raised five sons and a daughter alone on a farm after his wife had died in childbirth.

Among the others who thought of it was Jane Addams of Chicago in 1911, herself a prominent suffragette. She said, "Poor Father has been left out in the cold. He doesn't get much recognition. . . . It would be a good thing if he had a day that would mean recognition of him." Harry C. Meek, president of the Uptown Lions Club of Chicago in 1915, was the only man I could find who figured prominently in the founding of Father's Day, quite independently of anyone else. He spent two decades promoting across the country, to top officials and the general public. Alas, it was not until 1972 that a U.S. president (Nixon) signed a bill making Father's Day an official holiday. This law gave Father's Day equal billing with Mother's Day, which had been signed into law 59 years before.

In looking back over the history of Father's Day, it at first seemed strange to me that it was mostly the efforts of women that brought it about, including "reform" women. Where was all the anger against the "oppressor," and how come they were so thoughtful and loving? And then I thought, "What the hell, who cares? What a truly gracious and affectionate gift to men from those members of the other sex who deeply cared about us."

SECTION II: WHEN FEELINGS BECOME ISSUES

INTRODUCTION

Francis Baumli

Sexism cuts both ways. Men are at least as much the victims of insidious sex role conditioning as women. However, until recently the perception has been that the male, who supposedly created the conditions and problems he lives with, has had no right to examine or question the conditions that shape his experience.

It has been a slow, elusive, and arduous struggle for men to disengage themselves from the veils and filters that distort such perceptions and responses. This process of men freeing themselves has had to first be personal in nature. No man could hope to begin freeing himself and others until he could get in touch with his emotions, feel vulnerable with his needs, fears, and confusions, and feel safe enough with his vulnerability to ask other men for help.

Such personal awareness and interpersonal support have been important. But for some men it has not been enough. For example, many a divorced man has spent several years in a consciousness-raising group finding friendship and being comforted because he cannot see his children. But eventually he has realized that feeling and expressing his sadness are not enough. It is now time to go to the attorney, the judge, or the state legislature, and do something about what he has been in despair over for so long. He can no longer be content to allow his feelings of loss over his children to remain only feelings. He must translate feelings into action. An issue is at stake, and he must take a stand.

Many such men, who have been at the forefront of this struggle for men's liberation, have put in long, grueling, and thankless hours of difficult work trying to transform the sexist status quo. Although relatively invisible thus far, many have for years worked a full-time job during the day, and then worked late into the night, seven nights a week, to accomplish whatever gains they have made. In this sense, their work constitutes a revolution by night—late hours during which the writing is done, meetings are held with others of similar concerns, and preparations are made for appearances on radio and television talk shows and for the occasional rallies.

Yes; it is a revolution, but it is very unlike most revolutions. Indeed, it is political in nature, given that there has been a great deal of work with our social structure such as lobbying in state legislatures for fathers' rights, appeals to courts on the sexist draft, dialogue with feminist groups, etc. But this political work is different from most political work in its tenor and approach. It is essen-

161

tially quiet, osmotic and personal, with profound effects, which although pervasive, are not always clearly visible. Those men who spent hundreds of hours and thousands of dollars winning custody battles over the last several years, although they received little or no press coverage, nevertheless set legal precedents. They thereby started a trend, to be picked up by lawyers and other fathers. Eventually it was these relatively inconspicuous actions that set in motion the lobbying, education, and personal rapport between fathers and legislators which made possible joint custody laws and more active participation by divorced fathers in their children's lives.

A divorced dad who gets involved with his kids will likely talk about his experiences with other men. Other men, still with intact homes, may then pick up on the enthusiasm for parenting, slowly realize what they themselves have been missing, and gradually—at a pace so slow we scarcely notice it, but as steady and determined as the progress of the tortoise—these fathers will become more involved. And our society slowly is transformed, with fathers more fulfilled and their children happier.

In this way, the men's movement has been political as well as personal. But the politics have been so gradual, so low-keyed, that we do not readily recognize this part of men's liberation.

Such men, who have been—and are—examining the broader social conditions and personal pressures of living up to the masculine image, have, of course, dealt with more than fathers' rights issues. They have been confronting and redefining many legal, social and psychological forces that oppress men.

In this section, some of these men recount how they have tried to remedy the gender ills they chaff under. They give us an inside view of the difficult, threatening, often painful and lonely efforts they have put forth. They tell us what seems to help, what doesn't work, and most of all, they emanate the courage and joy that is the fruit of their efforts. In this way, other men who also want to free themselves from the social restrictions imposed on masculinity—and the resulting personal constrictions—are given support, encouragement, and most importantly, a sense of community and personal example.

But to encounter the voices of these men (and of the women who share their perceptions) is sometimes a frightening experience, because to read them is to be reminded that, yes, the world of masculinity really is *that* terrible sometimes. And the society we live in really is *that* blind to the masculine condition. Which makes the masculine condition that much more lonely.

But even in the struggle that must accompany such new ideas and new demands, these men have persisted, endured, and even managed sometimes to enjoy the fruits of their efforts. In this sense, reading what these men have to say is also very comforting. It reminds men that their own voices, muted by fears of the masculine wilderness, no longer need remain silent because now there are other voices. Voices of other men who hear and care.

Identifying with the efforts of these men to make changes helps us appreciate, as never before, the truly herculean struggle, the fierce anger, the forgiveness, the gentle caring, and the playful humor, that have all been necessary to transform men's conditioning and men's lives.

Chapter 9:
When Daddy Can't Be Daddy Anymore

DIVORCE

DIVORCED FATHERS FEEL PAIN

Jim Sanderson

"Recently you wrote sympathetically about the problems a divorced mother has in raising her children and rebuilding her life," a man named Dan says. "But I have never heard you, or anyone else, talk about the pain and frustration a father feels in separating from his kids."

It's a small shock when you stop to think about it, but Dan is right. We tend to assume that the parent who left home is the Bad Guy who broke up the family, and thus doesn't warrant a lot of sympathy from us. Even if no Other Woman is visible there must have been some hanky-panky going on. Sinners not only don't deserve the love of little children, they are presumed not to care about it.

But this is grossly unfair and often wrong. It usually takes two to make a ba marriage, and however the guilit is apportioned, the feelings of both partners for their children seldom change.

"A father may actually love his kids more intensely than the mother," Dan says. "But he usually has to make the emotional sacrifice of giving them up because his earning power is superior to his wife's. If somebody doesn't hang in there pushing a career flat-out, part of the family is going to end up on welfare.

"Maybe some men couldn't hack it, but I would love to care for the kids and work part-time the way my wife does. But Peggy could never earn enough to help with child support, even if I could persuade a court to order it, which is doubtful."

The sense of separation is achingly physical, Dan says. "I'm driving down the street and see a boy on a bicycle who looks just like my son. I know it can't be, but I drive like mad to catch up and see his face. The disappointment is always

163

so keen it's like somebody slugged me right in the heart—I can't get my breath."

Dan says he never realized how important it was to him to see his children when he came home at night. "I work with a lot of crazy people and the pressure never lets up. Sometimes I'd ask myself why I'm killing myself like this: but when the kids would come running and climb all over me yelling 'Daddy, daddy!' it was always OK again.

He lives alone now. "I used to call up the kids just before bedtime, but her lawyer won't let me do that anymore. That's harassing Peggy, he says. So now sometimes I just go in the room I have for them and sit on one of the little beds and look at some pathetic bit of clothes or toy they've left here. It's not much."

Visiting days are difficult. "We're strangers, we don't know what to say to each other. It takes most of the day to get warmed up and communicating again, and sometimes you give up trying because you know there will be tears when you take them home and you can't handle it yourself."

"A lot of dads play Santa Claus all the time. You know it's sort of a bribe, but you're afraid not to. It's a kind of desperate attempt to intensify the experience, so you've got something to share."

Many once-a-week dads feel they've lost all parental authority. "Once I discovered my son had stolen some money from my wallet," Dan says. "I was pretty tough on him. The next week when I came to pick him up, Peggy came out and said he didn't want to see me. I explained the situation but she still wouldn't make him come out. He sulked for three weeks and there wasn't a damn thing I could do about it."

In the face of a hostile wife, fathers simply give up attempts to influence fundamental aspects of child development, Dan says. "Unless she'll back you up, you only teach the child to manipulate."

"Joint custody is the ideal," he declares, "but it is easy for a wife to torpedo this. You have to live in the same school district, but in my case there aren't any apartments for rent nearby, and she won't move out of our home.

"Talk about a divorced woman being poor! I can't afford the mortgage and taxes on our home, plus child support, plus my own apartment. But she won't budge. When I suggested we both move to a place where we could share custody, she had the kids attacking me. Why was I going to make them move from their school and their pals and their little rooms that they liked so much?

"I don't have enough money to ask a woman out for a decent date. I either have to cook spaghetti or ask her to pay her own way. Peggy can afford to get married again, but I can't. That's another thing: She had a friend and he moved in. I managed to swallow the idea that I was paying his rent, in part because my son seemed to like him a lot.

"He was teaching Rick baseball, for example. Then suddenly he's gone, without even saying goodby to the boy. I don't know what happened, but I'm in the odd position of comforting my son because my ex-wife's lover flew the coop.

"I'm an outsider looking in. I'm not even as close as an uncle might be, because I can't come in the house. I'm beginning to understand why some men quit their jobs and move to another part of the country. They're not deserters, they just can't stand the pain anymore."

HANDS DOWN

Sheryl L. Nelms

a whole fuckin SWAT team

she called out
a whole
squad

and I didn't do nothin

just cause she
wanted a divorce

and what with
me being
an ex-con
and in the house
with her kids
and that fuckin gun
I didn't even know was there

they sent the whole LA SWAT team

why I didn't give them
no fight
just hands up
on the front porch

why they didn't even file charges

she just did that
to get her
divorce
easier

and by God she did

I wasn't gonna give her
no fight

DIVORCE

Rich Doyle

Probably the most extensive and outrageous manifestation of anti-male prejudice is in divorce. The following may be deemed by some to be contempt of court; but we submit that it is justifiable contempt. Divorce courts are frequently like slaughter-houses, with about as much compassion and talent. They function as collection agencies for lawyer fees, however outrageous, stealing children and extorting money from men in ways blatantly unconstitutional. Job havens for the incompetent and catchpolls, the arrogance and archaic mentalities permeating so many are unspeakable. Men are regarded as mere guests in their own homes, evictable any time at the whims of wives and judges. Men are driven from home and children against their wills; then when unable to stretch paychecks far enough to support two households are termed "runaway fathers." Contrary to all principles of justice, men are thrown into prison for inability to pay alimony and support, however unreasonable or unfair the "Obligation." Dispel all notion that written "law" controls divorce. It has very little impact. Indeed, few judges are even aware of statutory provisions. Judicial whim, or (to grant the pretense of respectability) "discretion," is the actual basis on which decisions are made. Recourse to legal remedies is practically non-existent.

THE DIVORCE

Sheryl L. Nelms

she got
the house
the car
and my little girl

and I got
this fuckin truck

IT'S ALL THE SAME BALLGAME

Tom Williamson

It's all the same ballgame. Men are financially responsible on the date, men are financially responsible in the marriage, so is it any wonder that men are held financially responsible after the divorce?

VISITATION AND CHILD SUPPPORT

OUR PARENTING AND THAT ANGER

Bob and Daphne Bauer

Most of us think that our parenting will continue after divorce, and that things will be fine. We just don't anticipate all that anger and that hatred, and that great little tool for getting back at the other parent—the children.

VISITATION LAWSUIT

33% of the divorced fathers in America have had all contact with their children terminated by their former wives, contrary to orders of the divorce courts. As many as 80% of the divorced dads experience some degree of harassment in attempts to continue a meaningful relationship with their children.

YOU CAN NEVER THANK YOUR FATHER ENOUGH . . .

Gerald and Myrna Silver

David looked up at the front window of the house that had once been his home. He was hoping his son Jeff might see him standing there. Gloria, his ex-wife, had just slammed the door shut after saying that Jeff couldn't go out today because he was busy with homework. This was the fourth time this month David had driven the 80 miles from the small apartment he had moved to after his divorce to see his son. Each time Gloria had found an excuse to turn him away without seeing Jeff.

David stood there with his court order clutched tightly in his fist. He had planned to remind Gloria that he had been given the right to see his son by the judge, but she closed the door before he had a chance to say anything.

Tears of rage and frustration ran down David's cheeks as he drove to the corner gas station and pulled up in front of the phone booth. He had to dial the number twice before he could complete his connection to the local police station. "Sorry," the sergeant said. "There's nothing we can do for you. It's not a police matter. Try calling your lawyer."

In California, section 278.5 of the penal code makes it a felony to conceal a child with the intent to deprive the other person of custody or visitation. Violation of this law is punishable by not more than one year in prison and a fine of not more than one thousand dollars, or both.

In reality, however, the law is applied quite selectively. It is almost invariably used against men who have kidnapped their children from their ex-wives. Rarely is a woman prosecuted for denying visitation rights to the child's father. The law should be applied equally to any parent denying access to the children, but it is not.

On the federal level, the Parental Kidnapping Prevention Act was sold to congress on the theory that it would stop men from stealing their children. But no federal legislation has been put forth to enforce visitation rights for fathers.

When Father's Day draws near, we should reflect upon the role men play in the lives of their children after divorce. It is a dismal fact that society does not value fatherhood with the same fervor as motherhood. Men and fathers are discriminated against in our courts, by the police, and throughout our social fabric.

Father's Day is simply an opportunity to sell shirts, ties, cigars, and cuff links. Last year a major distillery placed a full page ad on the back cover of a national news magazine. The ad did not show a loving father holding his child on his lap or cuddling his infant. It did not show him playing with his toddler or changing a diaper. Instead, the ad displayed a collage of cancelled checks bearing the caption, "You can never thank your father enough, but at least you can give him Chivas Regal." The image of the male as nothing more than a money machine was reinforced.

Bias against fathers is so pervasive that it goes unnoticed. For example, in a 1977 edition of a children's dictionary published by Macmillan, the definition of "abandon" was "to give up completely; leave. The sailors abandoned the sinking ship. The man abandoned his wife and family." Any child that looked up this definition would see a picture of fathers indicted as noncaring parents.

How diffferent it is on Mother's Day. Mothers are pictured holding, hugging, cuddling their children. They are shown as nurturers, caretakers, warm and loving human beings. They cook the meals, dress the kids, kiss the wounds; they are always there. Mothers are sacrosanct and untouchable. Fathers are thing-providers, check signers, givers of money. Where nurturing and loving are concerned, fathers are expendable. The natural result of this attitude is that after a divorce, custody of the children is usually given to the mother. Dad becomes a visitor, on the outside looking in.

Even though California has passed a law which states that joint custody is in the best interests of minor children, and that it is public policy to assure them of frequent and continuing contact with both parents after separation or divorce, many judges still continue to award sole custody.

Fathers' rights groups are working diligently to see that the new law is fully implemented. It is an uphill battle. Many judges and attorneys are simply not convinced that fathers should share the rights and responsibilities of child-rearing. And now, a year and a half later, it is a shock to discover that many attorneys don't even know that this law exists. A dismayingly large number of judges and attorneys continue to see men as nothing more than providers.

In a recent court ruling, a Shasta County lawyer was fined five hundred dollars for filing "an utterly hopeless appeal." The appeal sought to overturn a superior court ruling that denied a father's request for child support from his ex-wife. The judge considered a man asking for child support so unthinkable, that such litigation was considered "frivolous." The child's father is supposed to provide money. The mother only has to provide love.

This kind of sexual stereotyping is felt very deeply by many men and causes them great pain. It is made worse because many men are embarassed to speak openly about their desire to be close and nurturing to their children.

Women's rights activists have gone after runaway fathers tooth and nail to collect unpaid child support. They refuse to recognize that many fathers do not abandon their responsibilities to their children and in fact many pay even when they are kept from seeing their children. The *1978 Child Support and Alimony Report* published by the Bureau of Census (Series p-23, No. 106) says that "almost three quarters of the women due child support payments actually received them." It goes on to state that forty-nine percent received the full amount and another large percentage received substantial but lesser amounts than was due. Only 28.4 percent of the men paid no child support.

Any of the problems of child support would be resolved if society and our legal system worked on finding ways to keep both parents active in their children's lives after divorce. Father's Day will have more meaning when divorced men are allowed to be close to their children more than one day a year.

FATHERS AND CHILD SUPPORT

George F. Doppler

TEXAS: Mike Diehl, research & information coordinator, Austin Chapter, Texas Fathers for Equal Rights, has made an amazing study of 783 divorces which was published in approximately thirty Texas newspapers, and the *Texas Bar Association Journal*. Results of his study are:

1. Of the 783 divorces surveyed, only 18.8% of fathers obtaining custody received an award of child support. No noncustodial mother was required to provide any other continuing service for her children analogous to her role function in an intact marriage.

2. Ninety-six point eight percent (96.8%) of mothers obtaining sole custody received child support. Only one father in five received assistance and help from a former spouse, and over five times as many mothers as fathers received postdivorce help.

3. The average monetary award to custodial mothers was $170 per child per month, with an average award of $253. This did not include direct cash payments; i.e., medical expenses, insurance, schooling, etc.

4. The average monetary award to custodial fathers was eleven dollars per child per month, with an overall average of eighteen dollars per month.

5. Compliance figures: After three years of separation, over 80% of noncustodial fathers were in full compliance with the divorce decree orders. After one year, only 11.7% of noncustodial mothers were paying anything at all.

CUSTODIAL FATHERHOOD

MEN LOSE CUSTODY OF THEIR CHILDREN

Ken Pangborn

Did you know that eighty percent of the men who are awarded custody will lose it again within two years?

THE KIDS GO WITH MOM

Bob Bauer

Over 98% of the kids in divorced families are in the custody of the mother.

CONFESSIONS OF A MEN'S RIGHTS ACTIVIST

Ken Pangborn

Would it be so strange for a man so caught up in the men's movement to admit that even though he has some very strong feelings about the female gender and their less-than-accurate P.R. image, that he really would like to meet Mrs. Right?

I tried marriage once. It ended in 1976 after four years of vain attempts to call a halt to it. I did not remarry, although I have really wanted to. Perhaps I have been overcautious. I certainly still have very romantic notions about what marriage should be like. I have always believed that marriage was forever. If it had been even remotely possible, I would have remained married.

I believe strongly in commitment. I do *not* subscribe to the *Playboy* philosophy of intramural sex. I also do not subsribe to the theory of male dominance, which I see as oppressing me more than it does women. I believe in sharing all aspects of life. (I have found few women willing to do so.)

I would like to have one child with my new partner, when I find her, perhaps two if she wishes. The relationship is the most critical point for me. I need a basically quiet relationship, placing few demands on the other person and allowing for peaceful resolution of all disputes. It must be agreed that this would be a "lifetime" commitment.

I am firmly rooted in the belief that love between a man and woman is the fundamental basis of life. Without that spiritual love, there is little meaning beyond self-gratification. I look to the relationship to be intellectually challenging, and I would hope for a woman as committed to human rights as I am.

While it is not exactly the macho image, I enjoy walks in the rain, and snuggling by a fireplace. I believe strongly in "touching." I am by nature an affectionate person.

I find, however, the facts that I fought for and won custody of three small children (girls), and that I am a militant fathers' rights and children's rights activist are a definite turn off to the vast majority of women. My social life has been less than stellar. Even in Parent's Without Partners, which has perhaps the largest collection of "horny" women[1] under one roof, when it is learned that I have custody of three girls, it is much akin to having contageous leprosy. When I enter a room the women move to the far corner. I think the fact that I am so involved with the men's movement has a great deal to do with it. The first reaction to me at these events is a great deal of female attention, but then when the women learn I have custody, they attempt to persuade me to "give up" the girls, "who need a mother." When I say I think they already have the best Mommy any kid could want, ME!, they run and the word gets out.

---

[1] *Authors's opinion. (There's a lot of horny men there, too!)*

FATHER'S RALLY SONGS

Bob Hirschfeld

I WANT MY CHILD, I WANT MY DAD
(Melody: I want a girl, just like the girl . . .)

> *I want my child, where is that child, who used to call me Dad?*
> *A child who came to me, and sat upon my knee, and made me very glad;*
> *A sweet and gentle child who trusted me, a part of what was once my family.*
> *Don't want a child who's just like my child, it's MINE I want to see!*

> *I want my Dad, where is my Dad, I want my Daddy dear;*
> *My Dad, who loves me so, Oh Mom, where did he go? I want my Daddy here!*
> *A strong and gentle man, a man who cared, who held me in his arms*
> > *when I was scared.*
> *I want my Dad, where is my Dad? I want my Daddy dear!*

> *We want our kids, we'll have our kids, because they love us, too!*
> *The judge, who sits above, can't break that bond of love, there's Higher Power here!*
> *Divorce may break the bonds of man and wife, but our kids love us for the rest of life,*
> *We want our kids, we'll have our kids, because they love us, too!*

THIS CHILD IS OUR CHILD
(Melody: This Land is My Land . . .)

> *This child's not your child, this child's not my child.*
> *This child is our child, and the Law can't change that:*
> *From the child's conception, past divorce destruction,*
> *This child was born to you and me.*

> *And though our marriage, may now be ended.*
> *My hand's extended, to the child who loves us.*
> *Our child is not owned, nor is it just loaned.*
> *This child needs more than Custody.*

> *This child needs fam'ly, this child needs you and me,*
> *This child must know more, than just one parent;*
> *And though we've had fights, this child must have rights:*
> *This child, with Love, will grow up free!*

HOW THE SYSTEM REPRESSES MEN

OUR LADY OF MATERNITY
CHURCH OF THE WOMAN I SERVE

Fredric Hayward

There is another, invisible religion. It is as unchallenged as it is unnoticed. Almost all women serve in the priestly class; judges and legislators compose the nun's auxiliary. The whole world is the church. . . the schools and the theaters, the family kitchens and the singles bars.

The credo, though not expressed in words so direct, is found in an attitude that many women project: "Maybe God created the heavens and the earth, but We created you. Forget Adam's rib. . .you all started as a part of Our body. We Goddesses alone will decide who gets born, and when. We went through nine months of torment for you, just as Christ was crucified for you. We suffered a pain and exertion so great that you mortal men could never survive it yourselves. . .in fact, you can't even *imagine* it! You *owe* Us. Children *belong* to Us and, since you were once children, you know what that implies about you."

This religion is so powerful that it knows no competition. We are the first heretics, and will be treated as such. We must expect to deal with an enemy as explosive and narrow-minded as any other religious fanatic.

When I look at it from this perspective, I see a power more one-sided than power in any other sector that I know. I see the female control of children so complete that it is only recently that some men (not all) are even allowed to cast their mortal eyes on the birth process of their own children, this mystical process, this burning bush of birth.

I see the female possession of children so complete that an embryo need not be "a part of a woman's body" before it belongs to her. In a recent court action, Mr. and Mrs. Del Zio sued a hospital which destroyed the fetus that her egg and his sperm had formed. The embryo had been in a laboratory petri dish, and had never been a part of her body any more than it had been part of his body. Under laws dealing with the malicious destruction of property, Mrs. Del Zio was awarded fifty thousand dollars in damages; Mr. Del Zio was awarded three dollars in damages for the minor inconvenience that a man suffers when he loses his child.

Any female who is biologically capable of reproducing is allowed to do so and, unless she is extraordinarily retarded, dangerous, or young, she is allowed to raise her child. She can be emotionally unequipped, economically irresponsible, ignorant of all child-caring skills, or a drug addict. We will simply trust that her "maternal" instincts will guide her.

Raising children is probably the most important profession which requires no license, no expertise, no examination, no minimal standards—nothing other than membership in the sorority of women.

For a man to get access, he has to apply to a woman for access. This interviewing process is known as "initiating a relationship." Instead of saying, "Hi, do you come here often?" perhaps we should be saying, "Hi, am I good enough to reproduce?"

If she approves your application, she can issue to you a temporary license to be a parent. This issuing process is known as marriage. At some time in the future, if she decides that she no longer wants you to be the father of *her* child, she can revoke your license. This process is known as divorce.

As scary as divorce makes marriage for men, it is the only way to get the license to be a parent. A father's relationship to his children is not a direct one; it goes *through* the mother. If you are an unwed father, you often do not even have the legal right to *seek* custody. Since your relationship with your children is only a legal by-product of your relationship with their mother, when your relationship with the mother is disrupted by divorce or separation, your relationship with the children is automatically placed in dire jeopardy.

Men have been intimidated out of child-raising the way women were intimidated out of auto mechanics. We men really belive that we do not have the innate ability, the parental instinct, that women have. It reminds me of the times women have expected me to fix their stalled cars. I would bend over the engine, push a wire, dust off the battery, fiddle with anything that moved, look intent and wise, and she would sit there and really believe that I knew what I was doing. Similarly, there are millions of incompetent mothers out there, and we really believe they know what they are doing. We are taught that we are too bumbling and too brutal. We are taught that these are *her* children.

We are dissuaded from fathering by self-image, by custom, by media images, by school curricula, by financial necessity, and by employment discrimination.

Supposedly, there are laws and commissions to protect equal employment opportunity. If a company allowed only its white workers leave to stay home with their newborn children, that company would be held guilty of race discrimination. When it comes to employment, sex descrimination is no less illegal than race discrimination; yet, companies can freely deny males the same equal employment opportunity that women have of staying home with their children.

Men have been criticized for being "too late" in caring about children. "Oh, *now* you want custody. Why weren't you spending time with the kids when you were married?" This is unfair, for many men do spend time with their children, in spite of the negative sexist stereotypes we still have about men. But, it is also an unfair charge because divorce is supposed to be a time of transition. Your whole life changes, your roles change, and your needs change. We are certainly not allowed to criticize women for being too late. We are certainly not allowed to say, "Oh, *now* you want a career. Why weren't you pursuing a career when you were married?"

Still, we must demonstrate that custody battles are not the only time when men want to share the joys and responsibilities of being there as their children grow. Demanding parental leaves from our employers is one way to make it clear we are renouncing the system which exiled us from our children's lives.

174

ON ABORTION AND ADOPTION

Rich Doyle

Regarding abortion and adoption—without taking an official position, pro or con, on the morality or legality of abortion per se, the MRA (Men's Rights Association) maintains that prospective fathers, married or unmarried, have an equal right to determine the fate of their offspring, born or unborn; Supreme Court opinions to the contrary notwithstanding. Bread belongs no more to the oven than to the baker.

MEN AND CHOOSING PARENTHOOD

Fredric Hayward

I made up a riddle last night: what would you call it if women lost not only the right to terminate the pregnancy when they wanted to abort it, but even lost the right *not* to terminate it when they did not want to abort it? If she were forced to have a fetus aborted that she wanted to raise? You give up? It would be called *equality,* because that is the present status of men. Whether it is to say yes or to say no to parenthood, the male is totally powerless.

WHEN ALL ELSE FAILS AND THE WAR IS ON: How to Fight Dirty and Win

Gregory P. Robinson

I want to talk about our "attitudinal approach" to this battle. A great deal depends on when you develop it. If the battle is joined prior to the divorce, you actually have an advantage. At least if you are a male. Because you can start doing things at this point to insure maximum contact with your children, and minimum damage to your financial status. You can do things which will mitigate the irreparable rape of your social and financial future. And you can maximize your social and paternal contacts with your children.

For far too many men the battle is joined or awareness dawns too late in the day—after the wife has custody and an award of child support, perhaps an

---

Mr. Robinson is a practicing divorce attorney. This text is from a speech given to Divorced Dads, Inc.

award for maintenance, a lump sum share of the property, and the husband is walking down the road talking to himself. All is not lost at this point, but what we can do is much more limited.

To begin with, we need to focus on the most important person in these proceedings. The most important person is not the wife or mother, not the husband or father, not the legislator that makes the law, not the judge that interprets the law, and not the child; but those bastards, the lawyers. They are the most important. Sad, but true.

There are basically three categories of lawyers that handle child support and custody cases. You want only one of the three categories, not the other two. This applies whether you are just getting into the divorce, or whether you are already in trouble and trying to remedy your situation.

One category of attorney is the silk-stocking-firm attorney, the attorney with the chrome and glass office, the established and prosperous fellow who has a good reputation and is going to charge you a great deal of money to handle your case. Because he is wealthy and established, you believe that he will do a good job for you. Frequently that is not the case. The way attorneys view domestic relations is that they are somewhat less nasty to deal with than rape/murders, or perhaps more so. If you are an attorney, you know that these are the cases that people call you late at night about when they are in the throes of emotional and financial despair. These are the cases that will get you off the golf course. These are the cases that will interrupt your supper. Therefore, the established, wealthy and powerful attorney does not like this kind of case. When he considers accepting one, he will quote you a large fee and ask for most of it up front in an effort to discourage you. You think because you are being charged a great deal of money, he must be good. This is not the case. When he does accept such a case his goal is to handle it as promptly as possible to get you and your spouse dissolved, custody resolved, your money divided, and you out of his files with a minimum amount of problems to himself while getting a substantial amount of your money. When you sit across the desk from this kind of attorney, he will make statements like, "Let's be adult about this." "Let's be civilized about this." "Can't we come to a reasonable understanding about this?" When you hear somebody giving you this line, you want to shoot your antennae up in the air and say, "Bullshit! I am emotionally involved in this! It's my child, my children, my marriage. You're damn right I'm involved. I'm upset. What's this crap about 'Let's sit down, be mature, and try to see if we can't work it out.'" He is telling you, "Let's try and handle it as efficiently as possible for my convenience." Not yours.

Let's go to the second category. The second category is the attorney who advertises in the throwaway shoppers: "Divorces, $150 if uncontested; otherwise, we give you a cheap divorce anyway." This guy also is bad news for you. Not because he does not know the law. He may be a recent law graduate who knows the law very well. He may be an outstanding attorney. He may just be young and beginning practice and not well established. One of the ways he can make a living is doing a lot of domestic relations litigation that more established firms do not like to handle. He has to do a lot of it because if he does not have a big turnover, he is not going to make any money at all because he is doing the divorces so cheap. So if you get hooked up with this guy you are not going to get personalized attention and he is not going to get emotionally and materially involved in your case so that it is customized to meet your needs. He simply cannot afford to financially.

The third category of attorney, the one you want, is the one who does some domestic relations litigation and has done a lot of it, but would really rather not do it. He would rather be doing criminal defense work, insurance defense work, or personal injury litigation. But, he will do it if you can nail him down and get him to do it.

Your job is to find that middle-of-the-road attorney who will listen to you as an individual and customize his time and efforts to meet your needs rather than chop you off to force you into an odd-shaped block to meet his time schedule and his concept of what divorce, child support, maintenance and alimony are all about. This attorney then is the most important person in divorce litigation. Because if your attorney does not go into that dissolution to win something, if he does not go into that custody hearing with the attitude that he really wants to have something done for you, if he is not willing to expend the effort and the energy, if he does not have any gristle in his gizzard and blood in his eye, then forget it. You are going to lose. That is the long and short of it. We can talk about statutes and trends in the law all day long. But the most important thing is your lawyer.

There are a lot of attorneys who do not want to bring up anything sleazy, do not want to bring up anything distasteful, in court. There are attorneys who will tell you, "It does not make any difference that she is a drug addict, an alchoholic, whatever. It does not make any difference. She is the mother. There is a tender years presumption* that favors the mother." Well, the tender years presumption, you should know, is now moot in Missouri and in most states. It is eliminated by statute. Not so with the judge, though. A lot of these old judges who are still on the bench act like they do not know the most recent law. If such a judge rules in your case, you still cannot reverse him on appeal unless you have a really strong case because of the barrier you encounter in the discretion of the circuit court. Put bluntly: the appellate courts will not reverse a lower court unless it is flagrantly wrong.

Which brings me to my second point: do not be afraid to go ahead and appeal if you think you must. But be prepared to fight dirty. Anything worth fighting for is worth fighting to win. It is worth wheeling out all of your amunition, calling out all your friends, seeing who loves you. As the singer Warren Zevon says, "Send lawyers, guns, and money, for the shit has hit the fan." There are some dirty tricks you can pull. We are living in the post-Watergate era. We have a culture where everyone is vulnerable. You are vulnerable. She is vulnerable. I am vulnerable. The question is, are you willing to take advantage

---

*A principle of law in most states that asserts that mother's care is preferable to father's for children ten years and younger (thirteen in some states).

of the vulnerability of the other side? You say, "What in the world are we talkin' about, 'we're all vulnerable'?" Well, I will tell you what I am talking about.

Use the technology that is available. For example, she comes into court and says, "He drinks." Hell, who doesn't drink? Is there anybody in this room who does not drink? Raise your hand! (One person raises his hand.) Are you a health food nut or something? What's the deal? Are you an ex-alcoholic? You never take a drink? (Respondent says, "Well, I drink beer.") You drink beer? Well, you drink then. We all drink. (A brief discussion follows with the respondent about how he drinks only one or two beers a year.) Okay. You don't have to be a hard drinker for her to go into a courtroom and say, "He drinks." Your wife could go in there with a clear conscience and say, "The guy drinks. And when he drinks, he is not himself." You know? "He is not himself!" "He is a drinker, and I am afraid of him." Well, of course she is afraid of him. He is bigger than her. Maybe twice her size. When I had my divorce, my wife said, "I am afraid of the big son-of-a-bitch. He is twice as big as me and when he drinks, he is different." That's right, you know. When I drink, I am different. My inhibitions are down. Okay. So she gets in court and says, "Hey, he drinks. And sometimes, I am afraid of him. Sometimes he is cruel. Either in phsyical action or in deed or in word." If you talk to her on the phone the next day you will say, "Why the hell did you say all those things? I never hurt you!" And she will say, "Because, you rotten son-of-a-bitch, I am gonna clean you for all you're worth and I'm gonna get the kids, too!"

This is a small tape-recording device (indicating). This (indicating) is an adapter with which you can tape-record telephone conversations. All you have to do is slip this on the receiver and plug this (indicating) in the microphone hole. Just think: you do this after she was so sweet and nice and said, "He's been mean to me and he drinks, Judge." Her own lawyer believes this. Her mother believes it. Her family believes it. The judge believes it. Everybody believes it. But if you could go into court after she gets off the witness chair and say, "Hey, wait a minute. She lied. Who is the mean son-of-a-bitch? Me? Or her?" And then you play something like, "I am gonna take you, you SOB." Now you have won a move and she didn't even know she was being tape-recorded.

I tape-record all conversations with people I don't trust. Whenever I say anything on the telephone, I assume the other side is tape-recording me. And, people will say, "Isn't it against the law?" No, it is not against the law. It is against the tariffs of the telephone company. You know what they can do if they catch you tape-recording without the little beep? They can refuse to give you a phone. Big deal.

(Question from audience: "I thought if anything like that was introduced into court it had to be done by a professional.") Let me explain—let me go back and explain how you can use this thing. I could not just go up and say, "Judge, I want to play this tape-recording." He would deny me. What I have to do is put the other party on the witness stand and say, "Didn't you tell my client on the telephone that. . .when he called you?" "I never said that," she answers.

So, then I would say, "Judge, for impeachment purposes, I would like to play this recorder." You can use it for that purpose. See, there are different things you

178

can use it for. Haven't you seen the movie, *The Verdict?* Likewise, there are other ways you can use this. You do not have to use this in the courtroom proceedings. If the other lawyer knows that you have got something like this and you have tape-recorded him lying to you, you can play both ends against the middle and you have got him, too! Ever hear of the Bar Ethics Committee? They don't have any kind of bullshit rule against telephone and tape-recorders. There are lawyers that have been disbarred for lying like that and getting caught.

(Question from the audience: "What about lie detector tests?") No, lie dectector tests aren't worth a bucket of spit. Forget those.

(Question from the audience: "What about writing down the telephone calls I make? What kind of effect would that have?")

Documenting your calls? That helps, of course, because you've got it. But I can document your call. Give me a pencil and a pad and I'll document anything. It might be 1904, before the phone was invented. It's just your word against hers. But, it isn't your word against hers if you have something like this (holding up tape-recorder).

(Question from the audience: "Who would think about something like that, though?")

The lawyer—the one you paid to be a sneaky bastard. That is what you want him for. You want him to win for you. You do not want him to go in there, charge you a lot of money, and give you a bunch of air. You may think you are the most important person in this action, but you are not. It is the attitude of your attorney. And they are just like everybody else. There are good ones and bad ones and better ones. You cannot tell by how much money you pay them. You cannot tell, always, by the results. Because a good one will lose sometimes. But, you want somebody who will give it his best damn shot.

(Question from the audience: "Well, how do you go about finding out who is a good lawyer when you are looking?")

You can ask them straight—a guy is not going to get offended if you ask him up front. Say, "Look, I do not want someone who is just going to charge me and not do anything. I want to know." If he gets offended, then don't trust him. If he is going to get his ego hurt and get angry, well, he is one of the guys you don't want. But if he is willing to listen to your questions and repond fairly, that is the kind of guy you want. If he says, "I see what you mean. You are going to invest a lot of money in me. I don't win them all; I lose some. But, I will give you customized treatment. I will fight for you the way you ask." He should have no qualms whatsoever about talking to you straight like that. And I should say he or she; there are a lot of good women lawyers who feel the same way.

(Question from the audience: "Would a woman lawyer be best in a custody case?")

Oh, they are different—but you are just guessing a lot in that sort of thing. I don't know. I know a lot more good men lawyers because there are a lot more men lawyers. But when it comes right down to it, women are better at fighting dirty because it comes to them more naturally. That is not an insult; that is a statement of fact. It is easier for a woman to fight dirty because guys make rules about fighting, like, "We'll stand toe-to-toe; I'll try to poke you in the nose but

I won't kick or bite." Do not ever get in that kind of fight with a woman because she is going to go for your eyes and your balls. She is going to try and hurt you. When she fights, she tries to win. I respect them for that. Therefore, it is not good to fight with them, whether it be a woman attorney or your spouse, unless you are ready to fight the same way. But too often, men do not know how to fight dirty, and that is often why a lot of them come out of the divorce proceedings saying, "God, what happened?"

(Question from the audience: "What do you think the chances are of a joint custody bill getting through the Missouri legislature this year?")

Let me tell you what you have to overcome to get any kind of joint custody bill through. It was discussed last year, and the bar association opposed it. I was on a committee for the Missouri Council of Churches that endorsed it. I voted for it, but I see why the bar association and the judges are against it. This is why: as long as the parents are living together and everything, there is no problem with the kid going to whatever school and the kid getting permission to go to the hospital or anything like that. When the parents are separated, in space and time, the kid, for example, is here with a broken arm. "I want him to go to Mt. Sinah Jewish Hospital," says one parent. "Bullshit. I want him to go to St.. Theresa of the Blind Bladder Catholic Hospital." And, you can transpose school, college, whatever, and each parent is still wanting to call the shots. They come to loggerheads, and one person want to raise the kid Orthodox Vegetarian, and the other one wants him to be a Hari Krishna. The court is going to be in there saying, "What the hell should we do here? Split him and make him a Presbyterian?" That is the reason the bar association and judges oppose joint custody.

(Question from the audience: "But most people, when you have a couple of parents who are willing to go for joint custody, they are willing to make sacrifices.")

There is your problem. If you have a couple of parents who are reasonable, who give and take and make sacrifices, hell, it does not make any difference if one of them has custody and one of them does not. Right? But the reason I voted to endorse it on the Missouri Council of Churches Committee on Legislation was because joint custody gives a positive psychological lift to the non-custodial parent. Throughout the kid's life he can say, "I did not give up custody. I always had custody. It was joint custody. I was always your father. I never abandoned you." It is a psychological thing, pure and simple. That does not mean it is not real. It is very real.

FEMINIST PERSUASION

David C. Morrow

A few years ago a married woman, using the pseudonym Elizabeth Kane, announced that she had volunteered to become a surrogate mother. At first her husband had opposed her decision, but, she told reporters, *"He finally came to understand."*

But is this the whole story? We hear *her* words: "He finally came to understand." Why don't we get to hear Mr. Kane's story? Are men someday going to be allowed to speak their emotional struggles, or will our voices continue to be silenced by the conspiracy of emotional repression women wield from their domestic stronghold?

Isn't it possible that Mr. Kane's story goes something like this: namely, he understood the realities of divorce court, which is where he most likely would have ended up if he'd continued opposing her desire to commit what was legally adultery. She could have easily divorced him—the courts will accept any reason a woman gives—and he'd have lost his children, his house, at least half the rest of his property, and a substantial part of his future income. Even if he had initiated the divorce, the result would almost certainly have been the same. In either case he would have had to pay all court costs and attorney fees. Finally, if his wife's sperm donor or female customer decided not to take the baby, Mr. Kane, even if divorced, would have had to support it.

No wonder he "understood!" But the question remains, did he ever get to feel than anyone understood him?

REMEDIES AND SOLUTIONS

DIVORCE MEDIATION

Divorcing mediation has caught on as an alternative method to a couple's trashing one another in a courtroom. Services have been established and courses are offered in various cities, but as yet little definite information is available.

A mediator assists a divorcing couple to make decisions by the use of persuasion and tact, whereas an arbitrator simply imposes settlements. Once decisions are reached, a lawyer drafts the legal documents.

Professor Stephen Bahr, of Brigham Young University, studied mediation on the basis of cost, fairness, and overall satisfaction. He questioned persons who had used mediation services, finding that, on the average, couples using mediation services paid $550 less for their divorces than those who didn't. Of those questioned, Professor Bahr found 100% of the mediation clients felt property settlements had been fair as compared to only 50% of non-mediation couples. There were no important differences between mediation and non-mediation couples concerning fairness of custody and visitation. Overall, 90% of those using mediation services were "somewhat" satisfied, while only 50% of the non-users were.

DECRIMINALIZING OUR DIVORCE COURTS

Gerald A. and Myrna Silver

The dehumanization taking place in our divorce courts has been going on for so long that nobody notices it any more, and even the victims take it for granted. Our legal system does not make a distinction between a person being tried for a criminal act, and innocent law-abiding citizens in court to settle domestic differences and divide up their property.

American justice is the envy of the world. We go to great lengths to protect the rights of those accused of a crime. But it is an abysmal failure at dispensing justice in the family law courts. Tradition-bound judges and attorneys use the same trappings and procedures to prosecute a dope peddler as to hear a divorce or child custody matter.

A couple in court to obtain a divorce, or a father whose only desire is to continue as a parent, have not committed a crime, and they should be treated accordingly. It is time to decriminalize our family law courts. Our divorce courts are dehumanizing, and are devoid of privacy and compassion. They must be restructured to deal not only with the legal aspects of divorce, but with the deep psychological and emotional human pain that is an inescapable part of every divorce and child custody proceeding.

There is no need for a young couple whose personal and emotional relationship has died to cower before a judge, while two attorneys battle out their lives and fortunes in an arcane and esoteric verbal and paperwork blitz. These human beings are asking the State to intervene because they have reached an impasse. This does not entitle the courts to treat these people with a heavy hand and a total lack of recognition of their humanity.

Walk into any courtroom and you will find a black-robed judge glaring sternly from the bench high above the attorneys and litigants. To one side is a court reporter, fingers moving like a mechanical robot, immortalizing each word. On the other hand is a bailiff, gun and handcuffs highly visible. This creates an incredibly intimidating atmosphere, instead of an aura of help and caring.

It may be some time before we are willing to take divorce completely out of

Gerald and Myrna Silver are the authors of Weekend Fathers, © *1981, Stratford Press.*

the adversary arena. The present system of hired guns bent on legal shootouts will not disappear overnight. However, many reformers are beginning to recognize that arbitration, mediation, and non-judicial forms of conflict resolution are very effective in family law matters.

Here are some practical ideas which will remove many of the intimidating and dehumanizing elements from divorce proceedings.

Judges should be seated at the head of a rectangular table, at the same level as the litigants, and dressed in ordinary business attire. Bailiffs should wear blue blazers, with their guns and handcuffs not openly displayed. In many courts bailiffs are glorified ushers. Might not their time be put to better use handling routine clerical matters during lengthy proceedings.

Cold and sterile courtrooms should be replaced by facilities more apropos to the matters at hand. Smaller rooms, still open to the public, should be used. These should be decorated in a way which makes people feel at home. Sometimes just putting a few pictures on the wall, or a flower arrangement, can make a big difference in the atmosphere.

There should be more private conference rooms available so that attorneys and clients can negotiate settlements. The present system of negotiating in the hallways does a disservice and is an indignity to litigants and attorneys alike.

There should be a private place where a person in a highly emotional state can cry without being a public spectacle. There should be attended rooms where young children may be left, or where diapers can be changed.

There should be greater use of the telephone for oral arguments and for hearing motions. Attorneys and litigants should be able to resolve routine matters by phone rather than having to be physically present in the court. This could save an enormous amount of money for both the County and the litigants.

Computers should be used to allocate resources, schedule courtrooms, process paperwork and motions, and create more efficiency in the system. This could substantially reduce delays by enabling a flexible appointment sytem to be instituted.

The courts must be more open and responsive to the public they serve. They should periodically produce a "report card" on each judge's performance. Unfit judges should be removed or transferred from family law courts. Others should be given in-service training to improve their ability to handle human relations matters. The public should be kept informed on how such critical new legislation as joint custody statutes are being implemented.

The courts should institute a lay advisory committee. This should be a panel of ordinary citizens, not attorneys. The panel should meet regularly and make recommendations and suggestions for improving the operation of the family law courts.

Ombudsmen should be appointed to help cut through legal red tape. This could help reduce the hostility and the smoldering grievances which now exist between the family law courts and the public.

The use of mediation, arbitration, and conciliation should be encouraged, and the courts should widely disseminate literature about these alternatives, by placing brochures throughout the community and educating the public through the media.

These proposals would save taxpayers and litigants an enormous amount of money. More judges, bailiffs, and court facilites would not be required. Substantial cost reductions would be realized through automation, the use of communications technology, and better scheduling. These cosmetic and psychological changes would still provide an open court. The litigant's constitutional and legal rights would not be compromised and justice would be dispensed faster and less painfully. Above all, these changes would recognize that the litigants are not in court to be punished for a crime, but simply to close the door as gently as possible on a chapter in their lives.

SOME MODEST PROPOSALS

David C. Morrow

Such antimale practices as the automatic deduction of alimony and/or child support from men's paychecks, in combination with the media's endless shrilling about women's "rights," suggest as their logical antithesis the long-ignored need for women's responsibilities. Nowhere is such an oversight more apparent than in divorce law, where the courts encourage women to trample roughshod over men and children.

The careless or manipulative abuse of male visitation rights is typical of women. Laws requiring definite visitation specifications in every divorce decree, and their enforcement by mandatory jail terms, would help solve this abuse. Mandatory sentences for infractions would be necessary, given that the majority of offenders of visitation rights have thus far been women and judicial sexism favoring women could only be eliminated by judicial mandate.

Another problem is misuse of child support. Accounts should be established into which support is paid and upon which the custodial parent writes checks. Court agencies would periodically review each account and the custodial parent's sales receipts, with use of funds for any purpose other than child care resulting in mandatory sentencing, perhaps in accordance with the state's embezzlement penalties.

The parental qualifications of a custodial parent's next spouse is an important matter. If the custodial parent wishes to remarry, a hearing to determine the prospective partner's fitness should be required, with failure of fitness resulting in denial of the right to retain custody if remarriage takes place. Specified reasons for disqualifying a person—specified to avoid judicial sexist favoritism toward women—would include possession of a criminal record, joblessness or possession of a poor work record, history of mental illness, alcoholism, drug addiction, multiple failed marriages, etc. Court agencies would run checks on all information, with falsification resulting in prosecution for fraud and perjury.

JOINT CUSTODY: A WAY TO KEEP FATHERS INVOLVED

Bob and Daphne Bauer

An argument can be made for joint custody by keeping in mind the idea that if you're not participating you eventually drop out. For example, in an organization, if you just paid dues and you didn't have anything to say, how long would you continue coming if no one wanted your vote, or wanted to hear from you? How long would you participate?

A lot of men go on to start a new marriage, to start a new life with new kids, because at least they're kids that they have a relationship with.

WHERE THE JUVENILE DELINQUENTS COME FROM

Bob Bauer

Ninety percent of all juvenile delinquents come from single-parent homes.

THE OPTION OF JOINT CUSTODY

Daniel A. Calvin

As a single parent, I am angry that, with respect to parental capabilities, fathers are assumed "guilty until proved innocent" while the reverse is applied to mothers. In part, my feelings are stimulated by the ways in which I have uncritically accepted and performed under this stereotype without fighting against it.

To suggest that the child custody decision in divorce need not be an adversarial process is new and foreign. This paper presents a case for "joint custody" as a viable alternative to the predominant forms of sole custody, while not overlooking the obstacles that need to be overcome before widespread adoption of the joint custody arrangement becomes a reality.

I. THE AMERICAN FAMILY

In their social, economic and political functions, families are key units in American and other societies. As socializing environments for the development of children and youth, families are highly determinative of the potential the youth can realize. Nevertheless, as we hear more and more lately that "the American family" is breaking down, on the verge of death, or conversely, that it never has been stronger, we rarely ask for a definition of terms. The American family? Just which American family do we have in mind? Black or white, large or small, wealthy or poor or something in between? Do we mean a father-headed, or mother-headed, or childless family? First or second time around? Happy or miserable? Your family or mine?

What we invariably have in mind is a white, middle-class, monogamous, father-at-work, mother-and-children-at-home family living in a suburban one-family house. This is a definition that now effectively excludes more than half the population. It is a family type that is increasingly being questioned by the women and young people who come out of it. Yet it remains the standard conception of what the American family is, the model against which all who live differently are judged deviant.

Therefore, while the norm for American public policies is the nuclear family, the first thing to remember about the American family is that it does not exist. Families exist. All kinds of families in all kinds of marital and economic situations. But the *idea* of the family—what it is supposed to be, what one is supposed to be in his or her role as mother, father, or child—is invariably one of the strongest influences on our lives.

We cannot help it. The picture has been imprinted on our brains since we were tiny, through children's books, schools, radio, television, movies, newspapers, the lectures if not the examples of many of our parents, the speeches if not the examples of many of our politicians. The striking point, in the face of all the propaganda, is how few Americans actually live this way.

Roles in the stereotypical family—man's as economic provider and woman's as nurturing and supportive—are strictly defined. Father works long and hard with great financial success all for the sakes of Mother, Billie, Susie, the new car, house, refrigerator, washing machine, sailboat, and yearly vacation—"seeing America first." Mother will clean and shop and clean, and, along with the schools, help Billie and Susie prepare for their future respective roles in American life as, naturally, breadwinner and homemaker. Late at night Mother will turn into Sophia Loren. And it will all be worthwhile and the economy will flourish.

While we see ourselves as living one way, powerful forces are dynamically affecting the family to respond in complex and myriad ways. The truth of most people's lives, according to the U.S. Bureau of Labor Statistics, is that it now usually requires a working wife to push family income into middle-class status. Talking about "a woman's place" becomes a moot point when one realizes that the vast majority of women have no choice and work out of economic necessity. Nevertheless, although women have been allowed to enter what was

186

previously the male domain, usually at the lowest levels, men have almost never agreed on any large scale to share responsibility for the home. Invasions of each others territory are met with resistance and, in the case of men invading the home, the effort has been minimal and is still in its infancy.

Another significant force affecting the changing American family is reflected in an increasing divorce rate. The divorce rate for 1978 was 5.1 per 1,000 population [1]. On the other hand, the marriage rate for 1978 was 10.3 per 1,000 population. It therefore appears that the (official) American "family" is dissolving through divorce at about half the rate it forms.

Children were involved in a majority (fifty-six percent in 1976) of divorces. Although couples divorcing in recent years have, on the average, fewer children than couples divorcing earlier, a child today is more at risk of being affected by divorce. The number of children involved in divorce per 1,000 children in the total population has grown from 8.7 in 1964 to 17.1 in 1976 [2].

Because the nuclear family remains the norm while in reality it has become a nostalgic dream, many family variations exist for which public policies are inappropriate. Daniel P. Moynihan argued that the black family was "deteriorating" on the ground that about a fourth of black families did not have a male head. The fact that the mother-headed family, known since the beginning of history, could conceivably be another legitimate family form was something few considered. And more recently, Richard Nixon, as president, only months before his 1972 reelection bid, vetoed major legislation for child care because its provisions would impede his most important task: "to cement the family in its righful role as the keystone of our civilization." It is obvious he meant the male-headed nuclear family, since the very next week following the veto he approved measures to provide child care for welfare mothers, so they could be forced to work, because they did not have a male breadwinner at home.

Influenced by rapid changes, a variety of family types exist. Viewed in this matter, families are not structurally determined but are social systems operating within many configurations. Therefore, as one variant, divorce means not the dissolution of a family, but its possible reorganization.

"A divorce does not end everything about a marriage. It severs the legal contract between the husband and wife—but leaves a moral and emotional 'contract' between ex-husband and ex-wife. It shatters the household that was based on the marriage. But it definitely does not break the kinship network that the children of the marriage create merely by their existence" [3].

Nevertheless, public policies, guided by mythical nuclear family norms, treat a mother's and father's parental relationship with their children differently. Although there are few legal guidelines for determining the child's "best interests," and nearly all states legally recognize the equal rights of both parents to child custody, mothers are granted child custody over ninety percent of the time. The explanation for this overwhelming bias in favor of the mother and the disturbing celebration of "mother love" that has accompanied it are not recondite.

II. EFFECTS OF CONVENTIONAL CUSTODY ARRANGEMENTS

Divorce decisions are based upon the extension of assumptions and values which underlie and support the required structure and roles of the American nuclear family. Despite increasing evidence to the contrary, few believe that fathers either can or want to be involved with their children. Once a divorce occurs, popular wisdom has it that not only are children better off in their mother's exclusive care but also that the father in question cannot wait to enjoy his "freedom." Happy man, no longer is he responsible (other than financially) for his children.

It is the fact that children and their fathers are, in effect, also getting a divorce that leads to many problems in the dominant postdivorce custody arrangement—e.g., sole maternal custody and paternal visitation privileges. Ironically, current policy works to break the unbreakable. Although few studies conclude as much, all inadvertently document how our current arrangements tend to make ex-parents of fathers, painfully deprived creatures out of the children, and overburdened persons out of mothers. In short, divorce, as now constituted, victimizes everyone involved. Conversely, from what evidence exists, it becomes obvious that in a divorce the needs of the whole family must be considered in order for any one member to thrive [4].

It is difficult to isolate the responses of any one member of a family to divorce. What affects one member, affects all the rest. Between husband and wife the interdependence is obvious and often negatively reflected in how warring parents handle their children. Less obviously, familial interdependence is largely (and negatively) conditioned by the roles each family member is socially encouraged, even forced, to play. The ways in which the wife is *shut in* with the children and the husband *shut out* are causing many problems.

Beyond the many emotional conflicts, anxieties and pain felt by both parents when they divorce, mothers over and over again report feeling imprisoned by their children. They feel overburdened and experience great difficulty in reorganizing their lives. For long periods of time, they feel depressed and defeated by the situation.

The divorced mother often is harassed by her children, particularly her sons. But she should not be indicted because of the poor relations between herself and her children. Studies recognize she *is* overburdened and suggest that "the importance of positive emotional support from other people cannot be overemphasized when children are a 24-hour responsibility. That is, children cannot provide emotional support—their love is demanding of the parent rather than supportive. A great, and often overlooked strength of the two-parent family is the presence of two *adult* members, each providing the other with aid in decision-making, psychological support, replacement during illness or absence —someone to take over part of the burden. The solo parent not only has to fulfill all family functions, but has no relief from his or her burden" [4B].

While this solo parent is usually the mother, her ex-husband's lot is, in important respects, no easier. The emotional aftermath of divorce that he experiences is very like his ex-wife's, involving feelings of having failed, ambivalence, lingering ties of love and dependence, both grief *and* relief, mixed fears and expectations about the future, rejection, loneliness, anxiety, hostility, and depression.

Differently than his ex-wife, he also feels the disorienting effects of his new life. Bereft of the continued presence of his children and familiar home setting, his sense of continuity is profoundly shaken. "Fathers," said one study, "complained of not knowing who they were, of being rootless, having no structure or home in their lives" [4A]. If *she* is overburdened by children, career and a new, or sought for, personal and social identity, *he* is, in a sense, underburdened. Quite literally, he has lost not only his wife, but also a home, and most of all his children.

The pain felt at the loss of his children is very strong and can cause a previously involved, attached, and affectionate father to spare himself greater pain by virtually ceasing to see his children rather than see them very infrequently. Under conventional visitation arrangements, the father's experience of loss is so deep and his contact with his children so minimal that he often reacts with what one study calls a "Fight-Followed-by-Flight" pattern; "in contrast to a popular myth that fathers walk away from divorce and their families unscathed and carefree, the evidence here is that a majority of these men experience stress severe enough to bring on physical problems. There was also considerable evidence of depression, as well as sense of loss. Many fathers seemed to cope with this loss, as well as their feelings of being devalued as a parent, by limiting their involvement with their children" [4E].

Father's feeling that he is being depreciated and devalued—has become in effect disposable—and his sense of helpless rage and depression is the picture that emerges from every study that bothers to even look at the father at all. Fathers have largely been ignored in the research literature and relegated—in a self-fulfilling way—to the status of "theoretical role model."

Children, however, do not view their fathers as theoretical role models. Quite the reverse: just as there is solid evidence that under conventional visitation arrangements, fathers experience a deep and enduring sense of loss with regard to their children, there is equal evidence that children themselves experience the absence of their fathers as extremely painful. One study documents feelings of loss, powerlessness, confusion, and intense longings for their father's return [4C].

Children are not only deeply pained by their father's absence but they interpret it as abandonment; as a consequence, they feel devalued and guilty with few ways to express their anger and confusion. Also, studies suggest, children who are cut off from their fathers are often subject to the erratic behavior, and sometimes anger, of their overburdened mothers. In fact, mothers with sole custody often develop neurotic attachments to their children, putting sons in the role of substitute father or seeing daughters as appendages of themselves.

In sum, all parties are affected by conventional arrangements during divorce. All studies conclude that the positive or negative magnitude of these effects during divorce are correlated with both the extent of confict between divorced parents and the level of involvement between fathers and children. Fathers want improved relationships with their children. Only children who saw their fathers very frequently—and for some real length of time—were at all satisfied with the new family arrangement [4B,C]. Even more so than in intact homes, how effective the mother's relations with her children are depends in large part on low conflict with her ex-spouse *and* how involved he is with the children. In one study's words, when commenting on the need for additional support systems, "...none of these support systems were as salient as a continued, positive, mutually supportive relationship of the divorced couple and con- ·tinued involvement of the father with the child" [4A]. Thus, all studies report that with minimal conflict between divorced parents, the frequency of father contact with the child is associated with more positive adjustment of the child.

Although those children who fared best after divorce were those who were free to develop loving and full relationships with *both* parents, concerned parties (whether judges, lawyers, social workers, psychiatrists, or, not least, fathers themselves) seem to operate as if there were, in fact, no alternative to the current arrangement in which the father is radically severed, literally divorced, from his children. It is possible to affix an "ex" to spouse, but no parent can become—at least not without great suffering for all concerned—an "ex."

III. JOINT CUSTODY—A VIABLE ALTERNATIVE

It is obvious that there is little understanding that alternatives to sole maternal custody exist. Despite the fact that profound changes in both the family and the ways men and women relate to one another as parents have taken place, these changes are rarely reflected in our institutions. Social change is always swifter than its embodiment in institutional forms. The gap between the world men and women actually inhabit and the one society has been prepared to sanction shows up in painful and difficult ways.

Violent signs of a disastrous public policy are the "kidnappings" that occur between divorced couples, a vengeful game of musical chairs played with chil- dren's lives. Known as "child-snatching," thousands of such cases take place yearly. While hardly a solution to child custody, its increasing incidence is a symptom of the mounting frustration on the part of fathers generally and of despair about the possibility of equity in court [5].

Joint custody is one viable alternative to sole maternal custody. While there are other potential options—sole paternal custody [6], for example—which could also be the best choice for a specific family's situation, I will argue that joint custody, where possible, provides an "optimal" solution. More important, however, is the introduction of choice into the currently deterministic process.

Although still legally precocious and sociologically confusing, joint custody can no longer be dismissed as a fleeting aberration on the national divorce scene. Extensive press and TV coverage and a rash of recent cases indicate that the number of joint custody "families" is growing and that shared parenthood is here to stay. But although famous personalities, press, television, and various state legislatures are increasingly considering joint custody, growth has not been orderly. It may mean one kind of arrangement in one family, and some- thing entirely different in another. Part of the confusion is that joint custody is

190

still in its infancy and not yet adequately defined.

Joint custody has been broadly defined as "that postdivorce custodial arrangement in which parents agree to equally share the authority for making all decisions that significantly affect the lives of their children" [7]. In this quasi-legal form, neither the competence of the parents nor the amounts of time spent with each parent is mentioned. It is sometimes called "co-parenting," "joint parenting," "co-custody," or "'shared custody" [8]. In all cases, both parents are involved in the daily routines of living with their children; tasks related to childrearing are divided between parents in a way that makes sense to them; and major decisions are made jointly concerning the health and well-being of the children. There is an attitude on the part of both parents that they are intimately connected to one another through their children and that they respect the other's relationship with their children. This means that one parent does not have the right to move to another city and automatically expect to take the children along. That might indeed happen, but only as a result of a mutually arrived-at decision.

It is essential to emphasize that joint custody is not viable in all divorce situations. Some parents do not have the psychological capacity to be fit custodial guardians under any circumstances. Therefore, when spoken of as a viable alternative, it applies to the majority of situations in which both the mother and the father are fit and capable of becoming custodial parents. Additionally, joint custody assumes four conditions. First, the word "visitation" is never used; whenever a child is with a particular parent, that child is legally residing with that parent. Second, contrary to the common custody dispute, there is no "winner" but shared responsibility and decision-making. Third, children are not thought of as "property" and, therefore, there are no "ownership" rights. And finally, neither parent is required to pay child support.

IV. MAJOR OBJECTIONS

Even though the problems with sole maternal custody are well known, joint custody as a viable alternative is often rejected for one of the following reasons:

A. It is traditionally correct, socially fitting, and psychologically necessary that exclusive custody be granted to the mother.
B. Fathers, by definition, are incapable of being nurturing parents.
C. Sharing custody is an impossible alternative because a divorce situation, by its very nature, is not conducive to the kind of cooperation that this type of arrangement demands.
D. Children are put in an untenable position, dividing loyalties and physical surroundings which minimizes, as a result, their stability.

Each of these objections is discussed below.

A. The Myth of Mother's Love

Until the beginning of the twentieth century, "patriarchy" almost exclusively determined the legal status of children [9]. Before the nineteenth century the response was, "the children belong to their father." During the nineteenth

191

century and the early years of the twentieth, customs began to change until, in approximately 1920, the rights of the father ended. From the 1920s on, mothers were virtually assured of the custody of their children even though the mother's paramount claims are not now, nor were they at any time, based on law.

The decisions are largely based upon a presumption of "mother's love." In 1921, one court expressed it as follows: "For a boy of such tender years nothing can be an adequate substitute for mother love—for that constant ministration required during the period of nurture that only a mother can give because in her alone is duty swallowed up in desire; in her alone is service expressed in terms of love. She alone has the patience and sympathy required to mold and soothe the infant mind in its adjustment to its environment. The difference between fatherhood and motherhood in this respect is fundamental" [10].

While these Victorian-sounding sentiments are used as justification for custody decisions, there is neither scientific data nor rationale for the presumption in favor of the mother beyond an amorphous but strong conviction that women are, by nature, nurturant creatures, and by instinct filled with love for their children. In different economic circumstances—World War II for example—this presumption was overlooked only to be rediscovered when order was reestablished. What is often "instinctive" or "natural" in humans is invariably tied to what a particular culture requires of them.

Industrialization, which split the wage labor of men and the private labor of women, was behind the exaltation of motherhood and the invention of maternal instinct. That is, maternal instinct came along precisely when it was required, making a virtue out of what seemed to be a necessity. Its enshrinement paralleled the development of a new—not God-given—family form which came to be called the "nuclear" family, characterized as a refuge from the world and the social—but not economic—center of personal life. As our culture became both urban and industrialized, the father's activities moved away from the house and thus left, for all practical purposes, the raising of the children in the hands of the mother.

Given that this *was* the situation (nuclear families in 1920), it was not long before a new ideology about both the family and motherhood arose. Sociologists such as Parsons who speak of the father's instrumental role and the mother's expressive roles in family life fairly ossified the options open to adults. Because the child was raised by the mother, psychoanalysts *assumed* her influence was paramount not because anyone could prove it was intrinsically so, but because it was *de facto* the case. The tendency of other researchers has been to concentrate attention upon the mother as *the* influential parent and to minimize, as a result, the influence of the father, peers, and the larger social network.

Maternal love must be recognized as a sentiment, a conscious attitude rather than an instinct. The mother's paramount role in the child's life was discovered (and the father's denied) in order to justify the status quo. Ironically, both men and women helped create an ideology that now—with different "families" and economic conditions—victimizes both. The measure of the sexes' equal

192

victimization is that the stereotype provides social and legal barriers to the mother's desire for *economic* parity at the same time that they operate to prevent the father from obtaining *parental parity.*

B.   Non-Nurturing Fathers

Essentially, the assumption of the male's inability to be a nurturant, caring parent is the converse of the previous issue. Fathers have always been committed to their families but expressed it differently (e.g., dying in wars, earning income); what is being denied is the capability to express it in the same manner as women (e.g., as nurturing parents). Recently, a handful of studies have begun to demonstrate—contrary to stereotypical expectations—that the father's presence can be as deeply felt as the mother's. One summary concludes: "Evidence from diverse studies suggests. . .that fathers can develop the kinds of strong bonds with infants traditionally reserved for mothers. Contrary to long held assumptions, the "mother instinct" is not embedded in the bodies and souls of females alone. Instead, maternal behavior can evidently be produced by male and female alike" [11].

Still other studies have even begun to postulate a "paternal instinct." But this instinct may prove as useless as maternal instinct has proved to be. The fact is that it is cultural bias, not biological imperative, that determines parenting behavior. And increasingly, the changing values of our culture have prompted more and more fathers to seek greater involvement with their children. But, in the usual divorced household, they are denied the chance.

C.   Ex-Spouses' Ability to Cooperate

It is argued that couples that could not get along when married are not going to be able to share their responsibility for raising their children. While plausible enough, it is not what studies of joint custody families have found. They found that: "When couples want to share custody of their children, they are able to isolate out their marital conflicts from their parental responsibilities. In fact, it is not uncommon for joint custody parents to frankly admit their antipathy toward one another but to maintain, at the same time, that they do not intend to harm their children just because they might like to harm one another." [12].

In effect, co-parents seem to truly consider the best interests of the child. What often begins as a front—an appearance of minimal conflict in the children's presence—becomes in time a reality of self-fulfilling prophecy.

Contrarily, under sole custody, conflict is not minimized. The studies previously cited about sole custody households all pointed out the value of the father's continued and solid involvement with his children and the virtues of low conflict. That is, sole custody seems to work best when, in fact, it is pretty much akin to joint custody. Usually though, sole custody appears to exacerbate parental conflict and it is often used by the mother as a club, forcing the children into a bind in the middle.

Another reason joint custody may, in time, minimize parental conflict is because it appears to more fully satisfy the needs of both parents. There is a combination of "time off" and (if anything) enhanced involvement in childcare. It is obvious enough how time off might well suit many mothers. As for the fathers, studies have overwhelmingly shown that among the divorced, it was the joint custody fathers who were most satisfied. Those fathers who had more contact with, and joint custody of, their children were significantly more satisfied than fathers with less contact and no custodial rights of their children. This finding, that it is not just the fact of having children, but the experience of an active ongoing relationship with them that is ego enhancing, supports the work of Erikson, Biller and others who have noted the importance of such involved parenting for healthy adult development.

D. The Child as "Yo-Yo"

A major objection to joint custody is that the child's loyalties are divided and stability is undermined by shifting living arrangements. From actual experience with joint custody situations, no evidence of negative impact has been found. As one joint custody father stated: "I think it is certainly more damaging for a child to have only minimal contact with one absent parent than it is to have two sets of clothes, books and toys."

Nevertheless, a book which has been widely influential because of the stature of its authors—*Beyond the Best Interests of the Child* (BBIC)—asserts the opposite of these and previously discussed findings [13]. The authors state that "psychoanalytic theory. . .calls into question those custody decisions which split a child's placement between two parents or which provide the non-custodial parent with the right to visit." Further, they advocate that custody be irrevocably awarded to one parent with total authority. In other words, "the non-custodial parent should have no legally enforceable right to visit the child, and the custodial parent should have the right to decide whether it is desireable for the child to have such visits."

But—and this can hardy be overemphasized—there are virtually *no* social science data to support the proposition that a single official parent is preferable to two. In fact, *BBIC* does not contain a single reference to any empirical study in the extensive literature on adoption and foster placement and does not consider data from recent divorce research. It uses but one single citation from nonpsychoanalytic literature. Moreover, psychoanalytic data are used in support of the authors' position without acknowledgement of the major criticisms that have been leveled at the studies from which they derive.

Regarding the desirability of one parent, the authors observe: "Unlike adults, children lack the capacity to maintain positive emotional ties with unrelated or hostile adults. They will freely love more than one adult only if the individuals in question feel positively to [sic] one another. Failing this, children may become prey to severe and crippling loyalty conflicts." In rebuttal, critics state: "Yet children *do* have existing relationships with *both* parents and given any change at all, they show remarkable tenacity about continuing to love them both. Moreover, I know of no studies which show that the legal death of one parent, and the complete subordination of the child to the other's possibly distorted view, is a preferable step for the child's future development. If anything, there is much more evidence—not mere opinion—that it is potentially damaging to the child to be completely subject to one parent's will and that by

194

maintaining close and continous contact with both parents, the child is afforded in-depth exposure to two points of view, which I believe to be constructive" [14].

V. *JOINT CUSTODY AS A LEGISLATIVE PRESUMPTION*

Although most state statutes, like New York's Domestic Relations Law, assert that there shall be "no prima facie right to the custody of the child in either parent," the spirit of the law is generally ignored and the presumption is heavily in favor of the mother. It is therefore argued here that joint custody needs more than encouragement; it needs to be the legislative presumption. During divorce proceedings, the presumption would therefore be in favor of sharing the children. Instead of the parties trying to prove which parent is the most fit, they would have to show why joint custody will not work.

Various state legislatures have instituted or are beginning to consider joint custody statues. Seven states (Iowa, North Carolina, California, Kansas, Nevada, Oregon, and Wisconsin) already have joint custody legislation pending. And in New York, during November 1978, the New York State Standing Committee on Child Care held hearings on the subject.

The Oregon law became effective in 1977. It simply provides that the judge may decree joint custody. Joint custody is neither expressly encouraged, nor does it set forth the criteria for when it would be appropriate to decree joint custody.

More to the point is the California law which became effective January 1980: ". . .Custody should be awarded in the following order of preference, according to the best interests of the child: (a) to both parents jointly pursuant to Section 4600.5 or to either parent. In making an award of custody to either parent, the court shall consider which parent is more likely to allow the child or children frequent and continuing contact with noncustodial parent, and shall not prefer a parent as custodian because of that parent's sex" [15].

It could be argued that to call for a presumption in favor of joint custody is coercive. But the current bias in favor of the mother is also coercive. Courts must not only reflect prevailing social standards but must also be the arbiters of the justice inherent in these standards.

Equally, by making joint custody, as opposed to sole maternal custody, the norm, it will become so for many. Realistically, it simply suggests the capacity for, and importance of, shared parenthood and the powerful social sanction for such an arrangement. When joint custody would not work (where the parents themselves say it will not work), no court in the land will make it happen. This presumption differs from our current bias, which coercively sanctions an arrangement that not only may damage all those involved, but that people are nearly powerless to change. As things now stand, it is very difficult—financially, socially, and emotionally—for men and women to do anything but conform to the irrational bias in favor of the mother. Under joint custody, on the other hand, both parents are equal. If they do not wish to adopt a joint custody arrangement, all they need to do is to say so.

Even, however, if a presumption in favor of joint custody became the uniform law of the land, in and of itself (as the aftermath of the civil rights legislation made clear) the change in the law would not be enough. Without modification of the social system and services that both institute and support the legal changes, no joint custody law can work.

Roman and Haddad have developed a set of recommendations designed to change what was previously identified as the source of our regressive child custody policies. The recommendations are conceived as a package, and it does appear that nothing short of a wholesale assault on present conditions, underlined by changes in the law itself, is required [16].

1. We need to establish a nationwide network of family counseling and mediation services within, but not limited to, the domestic or family court systems. (Such supportive services should be free, or on a sliding-cost scale, and voluntary, unless a custody dispute is involved).

2. We must institute long-term, extensive research on both the impact of divorce on families and the effects of different types of custody arrangements.

3. We must enforce and strengthen laws that grant the sexes equality in employment and income. Encourage split work shifts. Make day-care facilities available to all who want them at fees that reflect a sliding scale, proportionate to family income.

4. We should incorporate into the school curriculum, nationwide, nonsexist family courses in marriage and parenthood, and courses in alternative lifestyles, at all school levels.

5. We should stress and make mandatory interdisciplinary courses in marriage and divorce for all those engaged in working with families—teachers, psychologists, lawyers, and social workers, among others.

6. We must remove family law from an adversary climate and redefine the role for the matrimonial lawyer as advocate for the full family and not one of its members.

7. We need to expand community programs for the divorced.

VI. CULTURAL AND POLITICAL REALITIES

Although this analysis should lead to a rational and comprehensive change in policy, the political realities and constraints are such that there appears to be little chance of full implementation. In crucial ways, what people think about themselves and believe to be their options are the most formidable barriers of all. Thus, our sexist cultural assumptions and their internalization by the majority of men, women and children present the overwhelming obstacle to change. These obstacles can be examined where least expected, in the vanguard of the women's movement itself.

In analysis of the original [17] and today's [18] feminist movements, the focus on issues outside family life and the failure to achieve changes in domestic life have been pinpointed as reasons why women's lives have not been seriously altered. It is striking that feminist literature says not a word about the custody

196

of children after divorce. If child custody is mentioned at all, the tendency is to call for more stringent enforcement of child-support payments, the creation of more and better day-care facilities, and split work shifts for women. This implies that maternal sole custody is taken for granted and, thus, the very conditions feminists decry within the intact household are encouraged in the divorced one.

By sanctioning the entrapment of divorced mothers in the home while advocating the liberation of women (and men) from sex-prescribed roles, the women's movement is caught in a grave contradiction. As everyone knows, it is a central tenet of feminism that fathers ought to be more involved with home and child care, mothers less so. But what has not been recognized is that feminist theory is largely restricted to intact families. There is near complete disregard for the father of the divorced family and the need for his continuing serious participation in the life of his children.

As in other areas of contemporary life, this schizoid response to experience is not wholly unrealistic: there is an understandable reluctance to relinquish the one area of power that women now have. Since women are inadequately prepared for what is in any event a discriminatory job market, many feminists believe that women can ill afford to lose the admittedly problematic status that exclusive parenthood now affords them. Or so goes a largely unspoken argument, complicated by feminist fears of alienating what it regards as its natural constituency. These feminists believe that because shared parenthood is seen by many women as a threat, the issue is a political hot potato best dropped so that what support middle America now gives to the women's movement is not lost. Should the movement advocate what many women have been led to believe will harm them? A similar paradox has plagued ERA proponents.

At the same time, it is surely true that feminists (along with psychiatrists, social scientists, and others) are not themselves free of cultural stereotypes. Not only does the most liberated women often feel guilty about less than full-time child care; she is apt, upon occasion, to exhibit a "reverse sexism" of her own. This sexism takes the form of doubt or negativity about the capacity and commitment of fathers to care for their young. Even in a revolution, rhetoric often outstrips action; it is far easier to talk a good line than be comfortable living it.

These culturally induced attitudes are strongly resistant to change. When, from the very vanguard itself, there is a reluctance to confront the need for the revolution to extend into domestic life, then how much more resistance will be found in the less politically sophisticated who are, after all, the vast majority?

For most adults, parenthood is still parcelled out in sex-described roles, and the old cliches prevail: many women still feel that less than full-time devotion to their young will brand them as bad mothers, unnatural, selfish, cold and rejecting; many men do not regard nurturance as their proper sphere. Because child care has traditionally been "women's work," the suspicion lingers that for men to engage in it is unseemly, indeed unmanly. The result is that many women who do combine a career and children feel guilty, and many men are fearful or reluctant to even try. It is hard, in fact, to overemphasize the amount of guilt and fear that is involved. Nor, in this connection, can we afford to forget how sexist parental roles often are neurotically incorporated into the way men and women relate to one another.

Sharing child care is, in may ways, a threat to both parents: her feminity is threatened and his masculinity undermined. This threat may not be consciously recognized, but it is often at work. It makes the woman ambivalent about her husband's involvement—experienced at times as an infringement, a loss of her control—and it makes the man, who is beset with doubts about his capabilities, equally ambivalent and no less fearful of a loss of control, particularly in his career—heretofore, a source of his security. The magnitude of changes required and, therefore, the potential resistance to them are extremely significant. Invasion of the previously exclusive female domain of child care by men has broad implications [19]. The issue of joint custody is only one block in the building of an entire foundation. Truly shared parenthood involves men in a critical situation in a manner which cannot help but have impact. How much impact will depend upon the extent of involvement and how successfully resistance is overcome.

REFERENCES

1. National Center for Health Statistics, "Births, Marriages, Divorces, and Deaths for 1978," *Monthly Vital Statistics Report: Provisional Statistics,* DHEW Publication No. (PHS) 79–1120, Volume 27, No. 12, March 15, 1979.
2. National Center for Health Statistics, "Final Divorce Statistics, 1976," *Monthly Vital Statistics Report: Advance Report,* DHEW Publication No. (PHS) 78–1120, Volume 27, No. 5, Supplement, August 16, 1978.
3. Bohannan, Paul, "The Six Stations of Divorce," in *Divorce and After,* ed. Bohannan, Paul, Garden City, New York: Doubleday and Company, Inc., 1970, pages 33–62.
4. The section which follows relies heavily on five recent studies which are more fully discussed in Chapter 2, "The Impact of Divorce on Families," in Roman, Mel and Haddad, William, *The Disposable Parent,* New York: Holt, Rinehart, and Winston, 1978, pages 48–84. The studies are as follows:
   A. Hetherington, E. Mavis; Cox, Martha; and Cox, Roger, "Divorced Fathers," *The Family Coordinator,* October, 1976, pages 417–427;
   B. Wallerstein, Judith and Kelly, Joan, "The Effects of Parental Divorce: The Adolescent Experience," in Anthony, E.J. and Kaupernik, C., eds. *The Child in His Family,* Volume III, New York: John Wiley and Sons, Inc., 1974, pages 479–505.
   C. Wallerstein, Judith and Kelly, Joan, "The Effects of Parental Divorce: Experiences of the Preschool Child," *Journal of the American Academy of Child Psychiatry,* Volume 14, No. 4, Autumn, 1975, pages 600–616.
   D. Gersick, K.E., "Fathers by Choice: Characteristics of Men Who Do and Do Not Seek Custody of Their Children Following Divorce," unpublished doctoral dissertation, Harvard University; 1975; and,
   E. Greif, J. B., "Child Absence: Fathers' Perceptions of Their Relationship to Their Children Subsequent to Divorce," unpublished doctoral dissertation, Adelphi University, 1977.
5. Lewis, Ken, "On Reducing the Snatching Syndrome," *Children Today,* November–December 1978, pages 19–21, 35.

198

6. Contrary to popular perception and publications, sole paternal custody is not increasing in proportion to sole maternal custody—e.g., the bias toward awarding children to the mother appears to continue unchanged. Between 1970 and 1978, the proportion of all children living in two-parent families decreased by eight percent. While children living in single-father families increased by 31.9 percent, those living in single mother families increased by 43.9 percent. Therefore, "although both situations have increased in number, contrary to some speculation, the frequency with which a child in a single-parent family is living with a father has increased no more in proportion to the number living with a mother." *Marital Status and Living Arrangements: March 1978*, Bureau of the Census, Department of Commerce, Current Population Reports No. 338, Series P-20, May 1979, page 6.

7. Roman and Haddad, 1978, pages 20–21.

8. Galper, Marian, *Co-Parenting*, Philadelphia, Pennsylvania: Running Press, 1978.

9. For a fuller development of these ideas which are, of necessity, summarized, one should see:
   A. Roman and Haddad, 1978, Chapter 1, "Child Custody and the Law," pages 22–47;
   B. Levine, James A., *Who Will Raise the Children*, Chapter 1, "Mothers, Fathers, and Experts," New York: Bantam Books, 1977, pages 1–15; and,
   C. Segal, Julius, and Yahraes, Herbert, *A Child's Journey*, New York: McGraw-Hill Book Company, 1978, especially Chapters 5 and 6 on "Mothers" and "Fathers" respectively, pages 73–134.

10. Quoted in Roman, Melvin, "The Disposable Parent," a presentation at the Association of Family Conciliation Courts, Minneapolis, Minnesota, May 11–14, 1977, page 3.

11. See especially Segal and Yahraes (1978), Chapter 6, "Fathers," pages 105–134.

12. Roman, 1977, page 19.

13. Goldstein, Joseph; Freud, Anna; and Solnit, Albert, *Beyond the Best Interests of the Child*, New York: The Free Press (MacMillan Publishing Company, Inc.), 1973.

14. op. cit., page 22.

15. Section 4600 (a) of Civil Code of California as amended (Chapter 915, AB 1480).

16. Roman and Haddad, 1978, pages 179–196.

17. O'Neill, William, *Everyone Was Brave*.

18. Howe, Louise Kapp, *The Future of the Family*, Touchstone Book, New York, 1972.

19. See, for example, Dinnerstein, Dorothy, *The Mermaid and the Minotaur—Sexual Arrangements and Human Malaise*, New York: Harper and Row, 1976.

DESPERATE MEN—THE FAILED MIRACLE: JOINT CUSTODY

Ken Pangborn

Since 1979 the men's movement has taken the concept of joint custody and clutched it to it's bosom. However, I contend that the promise of joint custody to solve all of our problems with respect to divorce and children is a narcotic.

No one can deny that much of the evidence on joint custody or shared parenting, offers a lot of desirable advantages over forced sole parent custody. But what has escaped most of joint custody's ardent fanatics is that its success had a lot to do with the fact that both participants up to a very recent date had to agree to joint custody and actively seek it.

The concept of imposing joint custody on unwilling participants is quite a different story. The impact on children is a disaster because it prolongs their continued vulnerability on the battlefield of the parent's animosity. In fact it has been shown that the anger of many women becomes so intensified when joint custody is "forced" upon them that a host of problems ranging from violence to child snatching has been the result.

The table below shows how the divorce "system" has reacted to the emerging men's movement.

TABLE 1. CALIFORNIA DIVORCE CUSTODY STATISTICS

YEAR	Mother award %	Father Award	Joint Custody	Others
1970	90%	8%	0%	2%
1980	90%	2%	6%	2%
1981	91%	1%	6%	2%

My reaction to these figures is that the judiciary of California has used joint custody as a means to avoid what otherwise would have been sole father custody. You will note that the estimates for 1981 show that women gained one percent and fathers lost one percent. Even the most simple-minded person can conclude what'is happening if they function in the real world and not California's Disneyland mentality. As you can see, women did not give up a single percentage point of their custody monopoly.

In addition, many men have been "duped" into thinking that joint custody will be more easily enforceable in court than visitation. *W-R-O-N-G!!!!* Much to the dismay of men, courts have taken an even more cavalier attitude toward joint-custodial fathers seeking contempt judgments for denial of joint custody access than they have toward fathers seeking to enforce their own visitation rights. We all know that past attempts to interest judges in denial-of-visitation cases was much like trying to hold a conversation with a hibernating bear! If you do wake him up and get his attention, boy, will he be pissed! (But at you, dummy!)

It is becoming increasingly clear that in cases where joint custody has been "imposed," the children have become even more the pawns of spousal warfare.

Joint custody appeals to desperate and *lazy* men who cannot or will not bear the burden of proving themselves worthy as custodial parents. Fathers can and do win custody of their children under even the most adverse of circumstances. I have never met a worthy male candidate that we could not win custody for. I have heard tales of super-prejudiced judges. A very experienced leader in the movement knew the judge my case was tried before. In conversations over the lengthy period of my ordeal, all he could do was relate how "terrible" the judge was, and how no father won custody before this judge. I was also told that no father in America had ever won custody under the circumstances upon which I was requesting it. But I did get my custody order.

I make no apologies for being the custodial dad of three girls of "tender years." And it was done *without* proving my former wife unfit.

Joint custody has an appeal to the obvious sense of fairness in people. But, as all narcotics, it distorts perceptions of reality. Joint custody works well when there is cooperation of both parents, and the children. But it is horrendous when there exists that level of belligerence that makes such an agreement difficult.

A large segment of our movement is marching to the drum of joint custody. It is seen as the "new" solution to all of our problems. It isn't! It is neither new nor the solution to our problems with our ex-wives. Many hard-line "tender years"[1] adherants boorishly state that joint custody is a new and experimental idea. Proponents hope that the "new" concept shows great promise for the future. Both sides are ignorant to the fact that joint custody is hardly new. It was the "law" in several southern states in the nineteenth century. It didn't work then, and it won't work today. One need only look at the legislative process that took place when joint custody was "dumped" by those states as a dismal failure. Remember, there was no vociferous women's movement then.

I am not embarassed to say that the track record of custodial fathers is vastly superior to that of women. I have frequently been asked by the fanatics of joint custody not to mention sole custody fathers. They fear the reaction of women's groups. Hell, I welcome their feeble attempts to attack my statements. Every single study of single parent dads versus the women has given us a wide margin of superiority *if* the final product, successful and happy children grown into productive and happy adults, is worthy of mention.

The strain which results from imposing joint custody on unwilling parents in the futile hope that they will be educated to it's benefits, and come to love it, is an absurd denial of basic human psychology. Few Americans come to love something "forced" upon them.

The trouble with cramming such laws down everyone's throats is that it has caused a negative reaction in the "power" system that dumps on innocent men and their children, in the form of "punitive" decisions. Men are most frequently the victims of judicial anger in property settlements. which have been escal-

---

[1]*See Robinson, When All Else Fails and the War Is On, footnote, p. 177.*

ated. Children have suffered by being forced to live with mothers who otherwise would not have been rewarded custody. In short, the plan has backfired. I hope we have learned.

LIVING WITH MOM AND THEN DAD: A MATTER OF PERSONALITY, NOT GENDER

Lee Zukor

Just a few years ago I was living with my mother. My father lived a few blocks away, and I was just beginning to understand the meaning of the big word in my life: Divorce. Although it is a big thing for a little kid to cope with, it didn't seem too hard to handle.

Just about eight months ago I moved from my mother's home to a new one—my father's. My dad now does his job, as well as my mother's, just as it was the other way around for my mother. I continue to live a very stable life. Every once in a while I joke with him, saying things like, "Shouldn't the woman of the house be doing that?" (which he answers, "She is!") and "A woman's work is never done—especially when she's a man" (which he doesn't answer at all, usually).

LIFE WITH FATHER

My friends sometimes ask me if I feel strange living with my father and not my mother, and I say, "No." It seems like these eight months have been forever, and yet I still clearly remember my parents together (that stopped almost six years ago), and then living with my mother.

Living with my father has its ups and downs. My father works sometimes when I am around. His job as a psychologist requires a fairly neat house (I sometimes neglect to give him help in getting it that way), and a few fairly quiet hours (in which I usually do my homework). One good part is that for boys, sometimes it is easier to talk to their fathers about certain things such as problems in school and girls. I know that kids usually talk to kids, but lots of times the conversation goes like this: "Should I ask her out?" "She's a tramp, she flirts with everyone." "But she's so pretty!" "How can you like that ugly thing?" "But she always helps me with math!"

All of this can easily confuse a child. With my father, I can discuss these things without being embarassed or confused. Together we relive (in a manner of speaking) his childhood—his reputation with the guys and girls, his first date, and other things like that.

After thinking for weeks about all the differences between living with each of my parents, I discovered that all of the differences (other than what I've already mentioned) were because of personality and not sex.

I think my new life is going to work out O.K.

Chapter 10:
Violence and the Male Victim

THE BATTERED HUSBAND

BATTERED HUSBANDS: A HISTORICAL AND CROSS-CULTURAL STUDY

Suzanne K. Steinmetz, Ph.D.

My wife started out hitting me and when I restrained her she started kick-ing and that's when she did the damage. . .what I remember was her kick-ing the bottom of my foot, kicking my legs, it did hurt. . . I have always felt more powerful than her and knowing that if I started hitting her I could hurt her, I made a conscious effort. . . to rule out physical violence (Brown, 1982)

Discrimination against minorities has been an area of great concern these past two decades. This concern has focused on discrimination against Blacks, Chicanos, Indians, and women. Little by little a new picture of what really happens is emerging—namely, one cannot discriminate against another group without suffering losses. We all pay for discrimination. When we discriminate against others, we not only lose potential talent, but suffer increases in crime, lack of personal security, and costly and inefficient welfare programs. Males, however, are usually not considered to be discriminated against; therefore, research in this area is notably missing.

HISTORICAL OVERVIEW

Women are not the only ones who have endured abuse. Historically, men have been given the right to control women through abusive means if neces-sary, since women and children were often seen as chattel, along with farm animals and property. There were, however, instances when society considered the wife justified in using physical force against her husband.

The charivari, a postrenaissance custom, was a noisy demonstration intended to shame and humiliate wayward individuals in public. The target was any behavior considered to be a threat to the patriarchal community social order. Thus, in France, the husband who allowed his wife to beat him was made to wear an outlandish outfit, and ride backwards around the village on a donkey while holding on the tail (Shorter, 1975).

The Britons treated battered husbands by strapping them into a cart and parading them through the booing crowds. The assaultive wife was also punished by being made to ride backwards on a donkey and being forced to drink wine and then wipe her mouth with the animal's tail (Shorter, 1975).

In colonial America, Joan Miller was charged with "beating and reviling her husband and egging her children to healpe her bidding them to knock him in the head and wishing his victuals might choke him." (Demos, 1970:73)

The bumbling husband, or the "Dagwood Bumstead syndrome," is another way in which depreciation of men by women has been permitted in our culture. It is revealing that a systematic examination of domestic relations as pictured by comic strips during the 1950s revealed that males were considerably more likely to be the victims of marital violence!

A favorite theme of the turn of the century comic strips such as "Katzenjammer Kids" and "Bringing Up Father" was the husband who endured physical and verbal abuse from his wife (Table 1). The popularity of these domestic relations comics was most likely sustained because they approximated, in comic, nonserious manner, common family situations, perhaps thus allowing men and women to carry out in fantasy actions which they were not able to carry out in reality. (Steinmetz, 1977–1978).

TABLE 1. MARITAL VIOLENCE IN COMICS[a]

	Perpetrator of Aggression	Victims of Hostility/attack	Initiate Violence	Recipients of Violence
Husbands	10	63	10	14
Wives	73	39	7	1

[a]Data adapted from Saenger (1963)

These comics often depict the husband as deviating from the cultural idea of masculine strength, self-assertion and intelligence, and assuming the character traits which have been culturally ascribed to femininity. The wife in the comics, while justified in playing the dominant, chastising, physically violent role, since her husband did not fulfill his culturally prescribed roles, is simultaneously described in undesirable, "unfeminine" terms.

STREET VIOLENCE

An examination of street crime suggests that while rates for female perpetrators of criminal violence are increasing dramatically they are still considerably lower than comparable crimes for men. As the data in Table 2 indicate, men are more likely than women to be perpetrators or victims of a wide range of violent activities (U.S. Dept. of Commerce, Bureau of Census, 1977, 1978; U.S. Dept. of Justice, 1978). More than eighty percent of the cases of criminal homicide and about eighty-five percent of all aggravated assaults are committed by men. Women are offenders in less than eight percent of robberies and in less than one percent of forcible rape.

With one notable exception, rape, in which women constitute over ninety-nine percent of the victims, men are also more likely to be victims of street crime. Men constitute about eighty percent of the homicide victims, nearly seventy percent of the robbery victims and about seventy percent of the victims of aggravated assault (U.S. Dept. of Commerce, Bureau of Census, 1979).

*TABLE 2. WOMEN AS VICTIMS AND OFFENDERS

	Victims of Violent Crimes[b] rates/100,000		Offenders of Violent Crimes[c] rates/100,000	
	Males	**Females**	**Males**	**Females**
Murder[d]	16.0	4.4	7.4	1.3
Forcible Rape	20.0[e]	200.0	12.6	0.1[f]
Robbery	1000.0	400.0	54.5	4.3
Aggravated Assault	1400.0	600.0	92.2	14.3

[a]Except for victims of murders, all data are for 1976. Data are converted to rates/100,000 for comparability.
[b]*Statistical Abstract of the United States.* U.S. Department of Commerce, Bureau of the Census, 1978. p. 180, Table 291; p. 183, Table 297.
[c]*Statistical Abstract of the United States.* U.S. Department of Commerce, Bureau of the Census, 1977. p. 177, Table 294.
[d]Rate for 1975.
[e]Rate too small to be statistically significant. Rate of 0.2/1000 reported in *Sourcebook of Criminal Justice Statistics,* 1978, U.S. Department of Justice. p. 401, Table 3.37.
[f]Total number of cases reported was 184. *Sourcebook of Criminal Justice Statistics,* 1978, U.S. Department of Justice. p. 484, Table 4.6.
*Source: "Women and Violence: Victims and Perpetrators." S.K. Steinmetz. *American Journal of Psychotherapy* XXXIV, (3) July, 1980 p. 338.

There has been considerable speculation about the causes and implications of the dramatic increase in crime rates among women. However, the greatest increase in female criminal activity parallels the increasing number of women who hold positions of trust in the business world.

One explanation for these trends is expansion of the opportunity structure

(Simon, 1976). If women are not part of the Mafia, there will be no women involved in "contract" activities. Furthermore, if women do not hold high administrative positions with considerable power, then women are not available to participate in Watergate-type activities. As women gain access to areas traditionally reserved for men, we may expect a wider range of criminal behavior to be exhibited.

HUSBAND ABUSE

Abuse of men, as a topic of investigation, has received very little attention. Likely this is for two reasons. Men will go to great lengths to avoid reporting that they are abused, given that such admission would stigmatize them in the eyes of others. As a result, men tend to report only the most extreme abuse, and would not dream of reporting lesser abuse—such as slapping or kicking—which women routinely report. In other words, a greater percentage of women are likely to report less severe injuries, and as a result, the highly visible evidence would suggest that women are abused more often than men, whereas this actually is not the case. A second factor is that men often have greater resources (money, credit, status, power), which allows them to utilize private sources of help and avoid reporting their victimization.

Studies of infanticide (Radbill, 1968) and homicide (Wolfgang, 1958) clearly indicate that women have the potential to be violent. Ian Oswald (1980) examined the histories of patients admitted to the Royal Infirmary of Edinburgh because of parasuicide [near suicide]. During 1977 and 1978, 592 admissions of women who were married (or living with a man) and between twenty and forty years of age answered thirty items which contained questions on victim and perpetrator of violence. They found 299 reported domestic violence; and 263 were victims of violence. Of this number, 124 (46%) reported that they themselves were excessively violent and thirty-six (12%) had been perpetrators of violence but were not the victims of violence.

Since society does not generally recognize the woman's right to chastise her husband, there is little likelihood that society will be aware that the wife sometimes takes violence beyond the norm. As one male respondent, who had been terrorized by a knife-wielding spouse, and had gone to work with deep fingernail gashes on his face, related, "I never took the fights outside; I didn't want anyone to know. I told the guys at work that the kids did it with a toy" (Steinmetz, 1977–1978).

Why has husband abuse been ignored? There are probably four major reasons: lack of collected data, selective inattention by both the media and researchers, reluctance of men to acknowledge abuse by women because of the stigma, and greater frequency of reported physical damage to women making their victimization more visible.

The concern men have over reporting their female abuser also has affected the official statistics collected on husband-wife violence. Curtis (1974) reported that while violence by men against women was responsible for about twenty-seven percent of the assaults and 17.5 percent of the homicides, violence by women against men accounted for nine percent of the assaults and 16.4 percent of the homicides in his study. While women commit only about one-third as many assaults against men as men commit against women, the number of cross-sex homicides by the two groups are nearly identical. Wilt and Bannon (1976) warn that caution should be applied when interpreting the Curtis findings. They note that "non-fatal violence committed by women against men is less likely to be reported to the police than is violence by men against women; thus, women assaulters who come to the attention of the police are likely to be those who have produced a fatal result."

Although the documentation on husband beating is not as extensive as that on wife beating, we do know that over three percent of 600 husbands in mandatory conciliation interviews listed physical abuse by their wives as a reason for the divorce action (Levinger, 1966). While this is far lower than the nearly thirty-seven percent of wives who mentioned physical abuse, it is consistent with some other data which suggest that there is about a one-to-twelve or one-to-thirteen ratio of abused husbands to abused wives.

It should be noted here, however, that this ratio is gathered from police statistics (see Table 3) and only reflects abusive situations which were reported by the victim, or were sufficiently visible to others, e.g., neighbors, so that the police were brought in. Other data, however, gathered from sources less selective and more comprehensive than police files, suggest that the ratio of abuse between husbands and wives is nearly equal in most respects (see Table 4).

Based on police records and a random sample of New Castle County (Delaware) families during 1975, it was estimated that seven percent of the wives and just over one-half percent (0.6) of the husbands would be victims of severe physical abuse by the spouse (Steinmetz, 1977a). Statewide data collected between January 1, 1981, and June 30, 1981, revealed that there were 423 reported incidents of wife abuse and 33 reported incidents of husband abuse. Thus, while the actual number of reported abuses grew considerably, possibly due to increased services and wide advertising of their existence, the ratio of twelve or thirteen abused women to one abused man remained constant in police records (see Table 3).

TABLE 3. COMPARISONS OF MARITAL ABUSE RATES OVER TIME

Study	Date	Male Abuse	Female Abuse	Ratio
Levinger, Divorce Petitions	1966	19	222	1:11.7
Police Statistics, N.C. County, 1-year period	1975	2	24	1:12.0
Police Statistics, N.C. County, 6-month period	1981	18	262	1:14.5
Police Statistics, State-Wide, 6-month period	1981	33	423	1:12.8

But an examination of the data presented in Table 4 suggests that in most studies for most types of violent interactions, the results obtained for husbands and wives are quite similar. While husbands slightly exceeded wives' "use of any violence" in all but the National Survey (Straus et al., 1980), wives exceeded husbands in the frequency with which these acts occurred. Only Gelles (1974) found husbands to exceed their wives in use of physically violent modes. He found that eleven percent of the husbands and five percent of the wives engaged in marital violence between two and six times a year, and fourteen percent of the husbands and six percent of the wives used violence between once a month and daily. Wives exceed husbands in one category, however: eleven percent of the husbands, but fourteen percent of the wives, noted that they "seldom" (defined as between two and five times during the marriage) used physical violence against their spouse. The average violence scores of wives as compared with husbands were all higher in the Steinmetz studies: 4.0 vs. 3.5 (1977a); 7.8 vs. 6.0 (1977b); and 7.0 vs. 6.6 (1977c). The Straus study found that wives committed an average of 10.3 acts of violence against their husbands during 1975, while husbands averaged only 8.8 acts against their wives.

TABLE 4. WOMEN AS VICTIMS AND PERPETRATORS OF SPOUSAL VIOLENCE[a]

STUDY	N	THROW THINGS		PUSH/ SHOVE		HIT/ SLAP		KICK		HIT WITH OBJECT		THREATEN WITH KNIFE/GUN		USED KNIFE OR GUN		USE OF ANY VIOLENCE		MEAN FREQ.	
		H	W	H	W	H	W	H	W	H	W	H	W	H	W	H	W	H	W
Gelles (1974)	80	22	11	18	1	32	20	25	9	3	5	5	0	–	–	47	33	–	–
Steinmetz (1977a)	54	39	37	31	32	20	20	–	–	10	10	–	–	2	0	47	43	3.5	4.0
Steinmetz (1977b)	52	21	21	17	13	13	13	–	–	10	12	–	–	–	–	23	21	6.0	7.8
Steinmetz (1977c)	94	31	25	22	18	17	12	–	–	12	14	–	–	–	–	32	28	6.6	7.0
Straus, Gelles and Steinmetz[b] (1980)	2,143	3	5	11	8	5	5	2	3	2	3	.4	.6	.3	.2	12	12	8.8	10.3

[a] Adapted from Steinmetz, 1977–78.
[b] Incidents occurring during 1975, all other studies reflect incidents occurring through the duration of the marriage.

A CROSS-CULTURAL EXAMINATION OF HUSBAND ABUSE

Aggressive family interaction in the United States appears to be quite different from that found in a country such as Japan, where physical punishment is not sanctioned, and child abuse seems to be relatively uncommon (Goode, 1971), or in Sweden, which recently passed laws prohibiting the spanking of children. If there are social/cultural factors which influence levels of aggression, then it would appear that one could reduce aggression by changing these factors. For example, a change in ideology could effect such a change. In preliberation China, physical abuse between husband and wife, mother-in-law and daughter, parents and child, and the landlord and peasant was common. Oppression of the weak and less powerful had a long tradition in Chinese culture, and this oppression fostered physical abuse. However, the equalitarian ideology of the People's Republic of China does not support the use of physical force to resolve interpersonal confict; as a result, physical punishment is rare and child abuse and wife beating are unheard of (Sidel, 1972).

Although caution must be taken in the linking of societal levels of aggression to interpersonal and familial levels of aggression, there is both theoretical and empirical support for this relationship.

Studies based on the data in the Human Relations Areas files found that the incidence of wife beating in seventy-one primitive societies was positively correlated with invidious displays of wealth, pursuit of military glory, bellicosity, institutionalized boasting, exhibitionistic dancing, and sensitivity to insults (Slater and Slater, 1965). These descriptions sound curiously similar to the macho male's attempts to dominate, which are often linked to wife abuse in the United States.

Lester (1980), also studying primitive cultures, found that wife beating was more common in societies characterized by high divorce rates and societies in which women were rated as inferior. Societies which experienced not only high rates of drunkenness, but also high rates of alcohol-related aggression, also had higher rates of wife beating.

In another study, data on marital violence were compared from six societies—the United States, Canada, Finland, Israel (with city and kibbutz subsamples), Puerto Rico, and Belize (British Honduras)—with subsamples of Spanish-speaking Creoles and Caribs (Steinmetz, 1981).

While analysis of these data must be considered preliminary, it appears that the percentage of husbands and wives who use violence apparently did not predict the severity and frequency of the violent acts (see Table 5). Finland, in which over sixty percent of husbands and wives were reported to have used violence, had the lowest mean frequency scores of actual violent acts. On the other hand, the kibbutz sample from the Israeli data had the fewest number of husbands and wives using violence, but those who did use violence were extremely violent.

In each society, the percentage of husbands who used violence was similar to the percentage of violent wives. The major exception was Puerto Rico, in which twice as many husbands used physical violence to resolve marital conflicts as did wives.

Wives who used violence, however, tended to use greater amounts. For example, although twice as many husbands in Puerto Rico used violence than did the wives, the frequency scores of wives was greater (X = 5.78 vs. 6.60). In the kibbutz sample, almost equal percentages of husbands and wives used each type of violence. However, those wives who resorted to violence used considerably more than did the husbands (X = 12.56 vs. 9.91).

The data suggest other interesting questions. Whiting and Child (1953) found less wife beating in societies which lived in extended family forms; thus, the levels of violence in the kibbutz sample as compared with the nuclear family (city) sample were surprising. However, Demos (1970) notes that to survive the cramped living quarters, early colonists went to great lengths to avoid family conflict. It appears that they vented their hostilities on neighbors, and conflicts between neighbors were extremely high. Is it possible that preserving the community tranquility is of extreme importance, and therefore, the kibbutz family keeps conflict within the family to preserve the more important communal tranquility?

TABLE 5. CROSS-CULTURAL COMPARISONS OF MARITAL VIOLENCE[a]

COUNTRY	N	THROWING THINGS %		PUSHING SHOVING %		HITTING SLAPPING %		HIT WITH SOMETHING %		USE OF ANY VIOLENCE %		MEAN FREQUENCY %	
		H	W	H	W	H	W	H	W	H	W	H	W
Finland	44	20	23	18	14	16	14	9	9	61	64	2.19	2.18
Puerto Rico	82	28	16	22	11	25	11	22	11	49	25	5.78	6.60
British Honduras	231[b]	24	21	25	23	23	22	19	18	39	38	6.83	6.38
Spanish Speaking	103	23	22	27	26	25	20	20	19	40	39	5.85	5.73
Creole	79	24	21	19	17	22	18	15	15	34	29	7.78	7.17
Carib.	37	31	30	30	27	24	27	22	19	51	54	7.37	6.20
U.S.A.	94	31	25	22	18	17	12	12	14	32	28	6.60	7.00
Canada	52	21	21	17	13	13	13	10	12	23	21	6.00	7.80
Israel	127	14	14	13	12	15	14	13	13	22	20	8.42	8.65
Kibbutz	63	16	14	16	14	17	16	14	14	21	16	9.91	12.56
City	64	13	13	11	9	13	13	13	11	22	20	7.59	7.38

[a]Source: "A Cross-Cultural Comparison of Marital Abuse." S.K. Steinmetz *Journal of Sociology and Social Welfare.* Vol. 8 (2) July, 1981, p. 411.

[b]Contains twelve cases additional which were mixed families.

CONCLUSION

The critics of research on battered husbands have labeled women's violence against their husbands as "usually insignificant physical attacks" (Field and Kirchner, 1978). However, I contend that physical violence between spouses is never insignificant. While an initial attack may be mild, it is often a precursor to more violent attacks, and may serve as a later "justification" for a husband's violence toward his wife.

In my original article, "The Battered Husband Syndrome," I concluded with the following: "Although the data discussed do not represent, for the most part, a systematic investigation of representative samples of battered husbands, it is important to understand husband beating because of the implications for social policies to help resolve the more global problem of family violence. . . .When the focus remains on the battered wife, the remedies often suggested revolve around support groups, crisis lines, and shelters for the woman and her child. This stance overlooks a basic condition of violence between spouses—a society which glorifies violence if done for the "right reasons," the good of society, or that of one's family. It is critical to shift at least some of the blame from individual family members to basic socio-cultural conditions so that more resources will become available to help families and a greater emphasis will be placed on changing the attitudes and values of society." (Steinmetz, 1977:507–508)

Over eight years have passed since that first article on battered husbands appeared. Knowledge in this area has expanded and we realize more than ever the importance of reducing all forms of domestic violence.

BIBLIOGRAPHY

Brown, R. "Battered Husbands Need Help." *Sunday News Journal,* Wilm., DE) October 10, 1982, pp. 1 and 4.

Curtis, L. A.: *Criminal Violence: National Patterns and Behavior.* Lexington, Mass., 1974.

Demos, J. *A Little Commonwealth.* Oxford University Press, New York, 1970.

Field, M. and Kirchner. "Services to Battered Women" *Victimology* 3 (1–2) 1978.

Gelles, R. J. *The Violent Home: A Study of Physical Aggression Between Husbands and Wives.* Sage Publication, Beverly Hills, Calif., 1974.

Goode, W. J. "Force and Violence in the Family." *Journal of Marriage and the Family.* 1971, 33 (Nov.):624–636.

Lester, David. "A Cross-Cultural Study of Wife Abuse." *Aggressive Behavior.* 1981.

Levinger, C. Sources of Marital Dissatisfaction among Applicants for Divorce. *American Journal of Orthopsychiatry,* 36:5, 1966.

Oswald, Ian. "Domestic Violence by Women." *The Lancet.* Dec. 6, 1980, p. 1253.

Radbill, S. X. A History of Child Abuse and Infanticide. In R. E. Helfer and C. H. Kempe (Eds.), *The Battered Child* (1st Ed.) Chicago: University of Chicago Press, 1968.

Saenger, G. Male and Female Relations in the American Comic Strips. *In the Funnies, An American Idiom,* White, D. M., Abel, R. H. (Eds.) The Free Press, Glencoe, Ill, 1963; pp. 219–23.

Shorter, E. *The Making of the Modern Family.* Basic Books, New York, 1975.

Sidel, Ruth. *Women and Child Care in China.* New York: Hill and Wang. 1972.

Simon, R. J. American Women and Crime. *The Annals of the American Academy of Political and Social Science.* 1976, 423 (Jan.) 31–46.

Slater, P. and D. Slater. "Material Ambivalence and Narcissim." *Merrill Palmer Quarterly,* 1965, 11:241–259.

Steinmetz, S. K. *The Cycle of Violence: Assertive, Aggressive and Abusive Family Interaction.* Praeger, New York: 1977a.

Steinmetz, S. K. The Use of Force for Resolving Family Conflict: The Training Ground for Abuse. *Family Coordinator,* 26 (Jan), pp. 19–26, Secondary analysis of data. 1977b.

Steinmetz, S. K. United States-Canadian Comparison of Intrafamily Conflict. Canadian Conference on Family Violence, Simon Fraser University, March 12, Secondary analysis of data. 1977c.

Steinmetz, S. K. The Battered Husband Syndrome. *Victimology* 2:503, 1977–78.

Steinmetz, S. K. "Women and Violence: Victim and Perpetrators." *American Journal of Psychotherapy,* 1980, 34 (3):334–350.

Steinmetz, S. K. A Cross-Cultural Comparison of Marital Abuse. *Journal of Sociology and Social Welfare,* 8 (2):, July 1981.

Straus, M. A., R. J. Gelles and S. K. Steinmetz. *Behind Closed Doors: Violence in American Families.* Doubleday, New York, 1980.

Tiger, Lionel. *Men in Groups.* New York: Random House. 1969.

Whiting, J. W. M. and T. L. Child. *Child Training and Personality: A Cross-Cultural Study.* New Haven: Yale University Press, 1953.

Wilt, G. M., and J. D. Bannon. *Violence and the Police: Homicides, Assaults and Disturbances.* The Police Foundation, Washington, D.C., 1976.

Wolfgang, M. *Patterns in Criminal Homicide.* New York: Wiley and Sons, Inc. 1958.

U.S. Department of Commerce, Bureau of the Census. *Statistical Abstract of the United States,* 1977, p. 177.

U.S. Department of Commerce, Bureau of the Census. *Statistical Abstract of the United States,* 1978, pp. 180, 183.

U.S. Department of Justice. *Sourcebook of Criminal Justice Statistics,* 1978, p. 401.

MEN ABUSED BY WOMEN

Dan Logan

Because men are taught to act strong emotionally and suffer in silence, we hear little about male assault victims. The National Institute of Mental Health and other experts say men are abused as frequently as women—physically weaker women are more likely to use weapons.

These studies have found that men are almost always too embarassed to report these crimes: it stigmatizes them as rape does a woman.

THE MURDERED HUSBAND

FAMILY VIOLENCE AND WOMEN'S LIB

Ken Pangborn

We have been criticized from time to time for our statements regarding our disenchantment with some of the activities of the women's movement. We have been sharply critical of some of the extreme politicalization of "family violence" by the women's movement, and of the bizarre antics displayed on this subject.

213

It has long been a concern of ours that the women's movement, even supposedly responsible national leadership, have been inaccurate in their presentation of the issue. Former MEN (Men's Equality Now) Chairman Richard Doyle has emotionally referred to the "license to kill" which has seemingly been handed to wives and girlfriends.

A case in point was recently carried on the national news wires about the murder of Henry Szelog by his wife Priscilla. Ms. Szelog admitted killing her husband. She was acquitted. Her defense was that she was *driven* to the brink by psychological and physical *threats* by her husband.

As the story demonstrates, she was *not* battered, but "threatened." This represents a major danger to justice. Until this time, a woman must have alleged physical abuse by the male. Now all she must do is allege a "threat" to abuse. Women's groups, who had funded and planned the defense at the Manchester, New Hampshire, trial, applauded and cheered the verdict.

Ms. Szelog must live with what she has done. Whatever political forces influence the courts, she has fallen victim to a psychological disease that is shredding the fabric of civilization and regressing human society to a jungle mentality.

It does not take a super brain to see a dramatic increase in the number of women who have murdered husbands and boyfriends. Our "sophisticated" media has ignored the trend and the danger it presents to civilization.

The lack of sophistication in our society is of concern to everyone. Domestic violence is not on the decline, but on an incline. We are not finding answers to the problems of society. The actions of some women's groups is appalling and disgusting. The developing gender-based anger is a serious factor that is being largely ignored.

Lesbians announced in a New York confab several years ago a strategy to heat up the battle of the sexes to the point of "armed combat." Their announced objective is to destroy the traditional heterosexual orientation of our society by creating a situation of hate and distrust between men and women, so that ordinary people will fear relationships with the opposite sex, and more women will then become sexually available to them.

We see a cult attacking the minuscule rights of children. In California a few years back, women's organizations lobbied for the passage of an extending clause on the abortion laws providing that *women* should be granted the final legal authority to decide for 72 hours following delivery of a child if the child is allowed to live or must be surgically terminated. The proposal failed then, but would it today?

Have we become so desensitized that human life has no value? We have noticed a complete restructuring of how we view human life. We are beginning to see human life as a "lump of protein" and nothing beyond that. I am not a religious fanatic and have personal disdain for the "born again" cult, but to ignore human intelligence and the human spirit, both so unique, is a sad regression.

It is a fact that our society becomes more outraged at the accidental death of a cat or a dog than it does at the senseless and brutal deaths of more than 2,000 children (from child abuse) each year. And I must point out that it is *WOMEN* or their agents who are killing 90% of these children!

For the simple-minded, let me explain now what you have failed to understand in the past. Our anger is *NOT* at women. It is at what is being done *to* women! We are as eager as anyone to shed unreasonable sex role stereotypes, and in that we join responsible women. However, we have concern for women who are bing made the victims of people who do not really have their interests at heart.

The fundamental difference between us and these dangerous, immoral, and sick segments of the women's movement is that we cry and suffer when a man murders a woman or batters her. We do *not* applaud and cheer. We take no joy in a woman's suffering nor do we countenance contribution to it. We condemn all violence against children, including that perpetrated by males. We do not rationalize it or excuse it.

I hope that we can build bridges with *responsible* women's organizations to work for real solutions to the problems we *both* face. Men and women need not be natural enemies. If you read this as anger toward women, then you have seriously misunderstood what we have said.

HE WASN'T SUCH A BAD GUY

Priscilla Szelog, 38, of Milford, New Hampshire, shot and killed her husband of 20 years because he'd pulled her hair and slapped her. She let him have it with a shotgun, reports the Syracuse *Herald Journal,* because she'd grown afraid of him. A jury found her innocent of second-degree murder charges.

"The verdict is fine," she told reporters, "but now I miss my husband."

THE MASS MEDIA PEEP SHOW

MAN BEATEN TO DEATH. . .FILM AT 11:00

Fredric Hayward

As another boxer lingered near death, another National Hypocrisy Week was spent in his honor. Almost every sports section in newspaperland and almost every local sports reporter on television devoted a piece to expressing dismay at the savage sport of boxing.

The sympathy for the stricken Korean was real, and the sadness that watching brutality is such a popular pastime was genuine. What bothers me, however, is the inconsistency which sports commentators and enthusiasts maintain. A fight which gleeful reporters called "great entertainment" was belatedly labeled "brutal" and "senseless" only after word leaked out of Kim's terminal condition.

Roberto Duran, another boxer, is a name that lives in infamy in the minds of Duk-Koo Kim's mourners. Duran, you might recall, committed an unpardonable sin: he quit a fight without spilling an obligatory stream of blood. In his rematch with Sugar Ray Leonard, Duran simply stopped fighting in the 8th round. He asked himself, "If I can't win, why risk serious injury," and could come up with no convincing answer. Why get hurt, Roberto? Because That's Entertainment!

The condemnation was virtually unanimous, and especially scathing. If a ballplayer turns in a poor performance or stops trying, he is criticized as an athlete. Duran, on the other hand, was criticized as a man. Athletes play ball; men fight.

To deprive the sports world of a vicarious feeling of nobility (It is far more rewarding to watch another man choose death before dishonor than it is to make the choice oneself) not to mention depriving us of 7 more rounds of the thrill of combat, was extremely cruel, Roberto. Millions of men who sit in their bucket seats in the morning as they drive to their offices, and sit on their executive swivel chairs in the afternoon as they dictate and dial, and sit on their easy chairs at night as they watch the fights, pointed a finger at this Panamanian peasant, who battled his way to a world championship, and dared to label him "unmanly."

I was in a taxi with a hotel PR man from Las Vegas and an immigrant driver from Nigeria. We talked about Kim, and they reached a quick consensus that the fight should have been stopped sooner. Actually, I had thought the fight was relatively close until the one-punch knockout/execution, but I wondered what these two sensible men had to say about Duran.

"No, that's different," these two strangers from opposite sides of the globe responded in unison. "He wasn't even hurt."

"But, why should he have to get hurt?" I naively persisted. "He knew he lost the fight and had nothing to gain. Why should he risk ending up like our new Korean vegetable?"

"He quit! It's completely different!" As far as they were concerned, Duran was so utterly and obviously wrong that there was nothing to discuss.

The problem for losing boxers, finding that narrow ground between getting hurt enough but not too much, is that they can physically stand while being mentally unconscious. Supported by the ropes, uppercuts, and conditioning, they can remain as upright as a sleeping horse. The good news is that a real man never quits. The bad news is that, to be a real man, one is never allowed to quit.

The night before Kim provided his entertaining death, there was a different championship fight. Alexis Arguello remained standing as the referee stopped the bout; but he also remained unconscious for 4 minutes after the bout. These minutes were used to show replays of a battering even more brutal than Kim's. As Arguello's eyes rolled around in slow motion, several vicious punches before the fight was stopped, it became clear that luck, not the referee, had saved

Arguello's life. Duran, that coward, refused to entrust his life to luck.

Although violence against women is a source of concern, violence against men is a source of entertainment. An unfounded rumor claiming the existence of a movie that showed a woman being killed brought immediate governmental action. But "Boxer Dies. . .Film at 11:00" brings only an increase in ratings. The snuff movie was condemned, but the snuff news clip was repeated from every angle and at every speed.

Feminist demands to be treated like men, and feminist demands to curtail violence against women, are mutually exclusive. If women ever did "rise" to the status of men, the first thing they would learn is that this world is an even more dangerous place for men of their size and ability. That infamous villain, the double standard, is the only thing that stands between many women and extinction.

Women's groups are demanding that women be able to walk the streets without fear. . .like men. They do not realize that, if men walk without fear, it is not because men face less danger. Rather, it is because fear is one of several emotions which are prohibited under the rules of masculinity. The man "who walks the streets without fear" is statistically four times as likely to be murdered as the woman who commands our attention. It is easy, ladies, to feel no fear. Here's the trick: simply learn the manly art of suppressing your emotions.

TELEVISION AND THE MALE IMAGE

Robert Keith Smith

I recently read where the Los Angeles chapter of the National Organization for Women gave their annual turkey awards to several TV commercials felt by the chapter to be "antifemale" or "degrading to women." Two examples: Pepsi-Cola commercials for "depicting women disrobing, while the men in the same ads do not." Also, jeans commercials "for presenting a view of women from the rear. . .and encouraging the misconception that women always dress to please and entice men."

For years, I have been angry over the way commercials demeaned men, but those commercials seemed to go unnoticed by women's groups. Why is it we hear about "antifemale" books, movies and now TV commercials, but never a word when they are "antimale"? Think of the TV commercials for men's underwear. Fruit of the Loom commercials portray an elderly lady holding up men's shorts while several men dressed as various fruits surround her. The male sex is made to look as foolish as possible. Or how about the Hanes underwear commercials? One features "the invisible Hanes Man"—a pair of undershorts and undershirt walking around and being captured by two policemen. Another shows a man in an elevator being stripped by several women. The man stands there, a simple look on his face, and lets it happen to him, encouraging the notion that men would let such a thing happen to them. As for TV programs, nothing degrades women as much as the male sex is degraded by the popular show, "Saturday Night Live." Nearly every weekend, the show has at least one joke about the male anatomy. Penis, circumcision jokes, even erection jokes are made on national TV, yet no one complains. Well, I'm complaining, complaining about TV shows and commercials which degrade men and about the failure of women's groups to acknowledge that men as well as women can be offended by the way they are portrayed in the media.

THE IMAGE OF THE MALE IN TODAY'S FILMS

Robert Keith Smith

Since feminists have been charging that films of the last few decades are degrading to women in the areas of sex and violence, I couldn't help but wonder why no one has made the same complaint about what has been the male image in films. Not just recent films, but ALL films. For every film that shows a woman being killed, there are dozens that show men being slaughtered.

The most recent film to anger women's groups was Brian De Palma's *Dressed to Kill.* In one scene, Angie Dickinson is slashed to death in an elevator by a man with a straight razor. The scene is very graphic; and yes, it is shocking and terrible to watch something like this. But how many war films have been made that have shown thousands of males being slaughtered? How many westerns have been made with men shooting each other to death? Not only do people not object to war films and westerns, but many people hold them up as heroic behavior! But just think about it—is that famous scene in *Dressed To Kill* really more horrible than all the thousands of war films featuring young men being killed? I don't see how anyone can say it is.

However, if something is accepted in real life, then it makes sense that seeing it acted out in film is accepted. Many people don't object to sending young boys off to war in real life. How can we expect them to get upset by seeing violence toward men on film? Clearly, a new appreciation of men must come about in our society. Men are going to have to start demanding that they be treated with the same respect and dignity that women are. Since films are a reflection of life, and often influence how we think, I think it is very important to examine films that are degrading to the male sex in the areas of sexuality and violence. I want to here discuss these two topics, and go on to offer some hope, by looking at a few films in recent years that have presented the male in a positive light.

Hopefully, this article will make men (and women) think about films they have seen that I haven't mentioned, and think about how males were portrayed. Was there violence against men as well as women? Was the male body and male sexuality presented as a joke? These are questions men should ask themselves after seeing a film.

218

PART ONE: VIOLENCE AGAINST MALES

I'm not going to wirte about all the thousands of war films and westerns that have been made. First of all, there are so many that it would be impossible to deal with individual scenes from them. Since most war and western films are so much alike anyway, it's possible to generalize about the violence in them. In the second place, I don't watch war films anymore, and I see very few westerns.

But think about all the war films you've seen. The thousands of young men being killed aren't pictured as living human beings. They are merely "things" that are used up on each side. In a film, the slaughter of these men is simply referred to as "action scenes." Talk about no respect for human life!

The same is true of Westerns. John Wayne always killed the bad guy, and the scenes of fighting and shooting are just good old all-American fun. I can't remember the question of morality coming out in any of those films. Fistfighting is usually played for laughs. It's presented as "okay" behavior for males. And yet I've never heard or read about men objecting to these films. But women are out there protesting hundreds of films because of violence toward women. The odd thing is, many of those same films feature males being killed, too. But nothing is ever said about that.

There are a whole list of thrillers that feature gory killings. Some of the most famous are *Halloween, He Knows You're Alone, The Silent Scream, Happy Birthday To Me,* and, of course, *Dressed To Kill*. All of these films have been condemned because of their explicit violence toward women. And yet in *Halloween, He Knows You're Alone* and *The Silent Scream*, there are men killed as well as women. And in *Happy Birthday to Me*, most of the victims are male, and the killer is a young woman.

I am not able to see all the films that come out every year. I did not see the following three films, but I have read many reviews of them. In all three, there are scenes of graphic violence toward men. The Swedish film, *I Am Curious Yellow*, a box-office hit, included a fantasy scene in which the female lead groups her male lovers together and castrates them. The French film, *The Last Woman*, ends with a man cutting his penis off with a carving knife. Many critics praised this film and excused the horrible violence by trying to say the man's self-mutilation was simply his way of saying he was sorry for "using" so many women. And the Japanese film, *In the Realm of the Senses*, includes a scene in which a female castrates her lover and carries his sex organs around the town with her. Many critics called the film "beautiful." One New York Times critic (a woman) wrote that the castration should be viewed as the man's total love for the woman. Can you imagine saying that a rape scene should be viewed as a woman showing her total love for the rapist!

Violence toward men has been shown on film in several ways other than castration, murder and war. For instance, I've noticed a disturbing number of recent films showing boys and men being hit or kicked in the groin. This is usually played for comedy. What I find most disturbing is that audiences—both male and female—usually laugh at these scenes. In the 1969 hit, *Butch Cassidy and the Sundance Kid*, Paul Newman is ready to fight a man, but instead kicks him as hard as he can between the legs. The scene is supposed to be funny, and sure enough, the audience burst into laughter when I saw the film. On a recent Academy Awards show, the same scene was used along with others to open the show. I can't imagine anyone daring to use a scene that showed a woman being hurt—there would be too much protesting. In the hit film *Little Darlings*, Kristy McNichol kicks a young man in the groin. He grabs himself, falls over in pain, the music starts and the credits roll. When I saw the film the entire audience was laughing so hard I could hardly hear the music. "Why?" I asked myself, as I always do when such a scene occurs.

In the 1970 film *Myra Breckinridge*, the most telling scene has Raquel Welch tying a naked young man across a table and raping him with a dildo. This film was considered a "comedy." Isn't it interesting that when a film degrades a woman, we recognize it as the degradation it really is, but when a film degrades a male, it's not considered as such. Instead, critics and the public call it "satire," or simply, off-color humor.

I think it's quite clear that in the movies, the male sex has suffered the same degrading scenes of violence that women have. The difference is that women are vocal in their anger toward films like this. The time has come for men to become aware and speak out against how we have been portrayed in films over the years.

PART TWO: THE MALE BODY AND MALE SEXUALITY AS A JOKE

While it is true that the female body has long been exploited in films, at least it is usually exploited in a complimentary manner. Let me explain. The first film that I am aware of which featured female nudity and played to a wide audience was the French film *And God Created Woman,* with Brigitte Bardot. Yes, the nude female was put on display. Yes, this is exploitation. But think about that title: *And God Created Woman.* The female body was being presented as a beautiful object. A decade later (1968) the same director (Roger Vadim) presented his then-wife Jane Fonda in *Barbarella.* Once again, there was female nudity. The female was presented as a sex object. But always in a complimentary way. This is true of many films.

But on the other side of the coin, how has male nudity and the male sex drive been presented? Nine out of ten times, the male is presented as crude, oversexed, and willing to do anything for sex. In 1971 the hit film *Carnal Knowledge* told us that all males are slobs out for nothing but sex, and all women are poor innocent victims who are nearly destroyed by the male sex drive. Even though this film was offensive to the male image because of its one-sided approach, at least it was well acted and tried to make a serious statement. But more shocking and offensive is the endless series of so-called "comedies" about high school and college men who seem to take pride in being slobs. *Saturday Night Fever, Grease, Summer of '42,* and National Lampoon's *Animal House* all picture boys and men as totally out of control sexually. In these films, the male sex is neither modest nor gentle. They are all pigs who will have sex with any female and will do anything to get it. Yet all four of these films have been smash hits. I keep hearing that women want kind, loving and gentle men. Yet they go to these films and seem to enjoy them. And what about the men in the audience? Do they identify with what they see on the screen? Do men really find it funny to see their own sex begging a woman to have sex? Don't they feel the least bit foolish?

What is so disturbing and frustrating to me is the huge public acceptance of this type of film. The most shocking example and the most degrading film to the male sex is also one of the biggest money makers in film history. The film is the 1982 hit *Porky's*.

The film is supposed to be a comedy about young boys and everything they will do to have sex. This film keeps the stereotype going that all males are over-sexed animals. There are too many scenes to write about in detail, but here are a few examples. The very first scene shows a boy in bed asleep. The camera moves down over his body to show he has an erection under the blanket. When he wakes up, he reaches for a ruler to measure his penis. He keeps a "growth chart" under his bed. The audience in the theatre where I saw the movie was laughing hysterically through this entire scene. I tried to discover what every-one was laughing at, but I still don't know what was so funny.

This scene made me think of Martha Saxton's biography, *Jayne Mansfield and The American Fifties*. In the book, Ms. Saxton tells how the late film star was exploited as a sex object because of her large breasts. This is, of course, true. But after seeing *Porky's*, I couldn't help but feel that when a woman is exploited as a sex object it's considered a terrible, degrading thing. When a male is exploited it's all considered a big laugh.

I felt nothing but anger as I sat through this film, but the rest of the audience laughed all through it. This film reduces the male sex to nothing more than a joke. Two of the characters are named "Pee Wee" and "Meat" because of their sex organs. I can imagine the public outcry if two female characters were given degrading names relating to their vaginas.

The most degrading scene in the entire film is also the one most people think the most funny. The scene shows three boys looking through holes in the girls' shower room. One boy stands up and puts his penis through. He doesn't know the female gym teacher has come in. She pulls on his penis and the camera cuts back to the woman pulling on him. At the risk of sounding like a prude, I have to say that the scene angered me unlike anything I've ever seen in a major movie.

But my anger wasn't just due to what I saw on the screen. As I sat watching this movie, I looked around at the audience. The theatre was filled. There were only a few women. The rest of the audience was all male. Most of them were high school boys, the rest were younger boys. They were all laughing hard at the scenes I've just described.

I thought of similar films that made boys and men look foolish in a sexual way. The audience response at other films like this was always the same. How-ever, *Porky's* is much more explicit and degrading than any previous film about high school boys. Here was a film that showed the male sex acting like fools.

Every male in this film is presented as stupid, immature and concerned only with sex. The naked male body is shown not for erotic effect, but for belly laughs.

And the males in the audience go right along with it. When I left the theatre and heard all the young boys who were leaving saying what a great film it was, I wondered if men would ever start taking pride in themselves. Couldn't they understand that what they just saw made the male sex look ridiculous?

Surely there are men in audiences around the country who are offended and even angered by how their sex is pictured in films like *Porky's, Grease, Saturday Night Fever,* and all the other films with the same theme. Yet, already there are sequels to *Porky's*. No doubt hundreds of other such films are already in the making.

Hopefully, what I've written will start men thinking about what they see on the screen. Hopefully, men as well as women will start to object to being pictured in degrading ways and in degrading situations. If the men's movement is going to grow, it must be concerned with the way men and men's lives are portrayed on the motion picture screen.

PART THREE: THE MALE IN A POSITIVE IMAGE

Although they are few and far between, a handful of today's films are presenting men as loving, decent human beings. To people who don't go to films often, that sentence may sound strange. But anyone who goes to films on a regular basis will understand it.

Very seldom have men been presented in a way that makes us look like intelligent people. But the exciting change of attitude among some writers and actors has helped present the male in a favorable light in several films over the last ten years. Those of us who could never identify with John Wayne now have such actors as Jon Voight, Dustin Hoffman, and Al Pacino to identify with.

The first time I became aware of this was in 1973. I went to see a film called *Scarecrow*, with Al Pacino and Gene Hackman. I didn't know too much about the film before I went to see it. But what unfolded on the screen was the most beautiful film about male friendship I had ever seen. Pacino and Hackman, two drifters, met on the road and became the best of friends. As their friendship developed, one could see how important friendship is to the total development of a person. In their past, both men had had many problems, either with the law or with their relationships with women. Perhaps if they had known each other before, they could have worked out their problems simply by talking with each other and supporting each other. *Scarecrow* is the most beautiful film, alongside *Julia,* about friendship ever made.

The next year brought *Conrack* with Jon Voight. The film did not do well at the box office, which was amazing. Here was the true story of a young man who teaches black children in a grade school where they previously have learned nothing. Here was a man on film who didn't get drunk and rape women and didn't go around beating up other men. Here was a young man interested in the welfare of young black children.

Jon Voight was excellent in the role and he brought the same feelings of love, tenderness and kindness to his Oscar-winning role in *Coming Home* with Jane Fonda. Voight's role of a decent man forced to do terrible things in Vietnam showed that the true strength of a man is in being able to say, "War is wrong, killing is wrong."

In 1979, Voight made a third film that presented the male in a positive manner. *The Champ* told of a father fighting to keep custody of his little boy. As the father fighting to keep his child, Voight brought all the pain and anguish to his character that any man would experience if he thought he were losing his child.

That same year brought another film with the same theme. *Kramer vs. Kramer* was a smash hit with both the critics and the public. It was wonderful to see Dustin Hoffman win the best actor Oscar for his performance as the father fighting to keep his little boy. The fact that the film itself won the Oscar for best picture was an extra bonus. At long last, fatherhood was being acknowledged as being a man's rightful role.

One could hardly expect more films like *Kramer vs. Kramer* to be made. After all, look how long it took for the few films I just mentioned to be made. Yet in 1980 Robert Redford directed his first film, *Ordinary People*. This is a beautiful film that tells of a young man (Timothy Hutton) who is suicidal because of the accidental death of his brother and the strained relationship between him and his mother (Mary Tyler Moore). After seeing young high school boys depicted as oversexed animals in so many films, it was wonderful to experience the character played in this film by Timothy Hutton. A sensitive young man who feels pain over his brother's death and wants desperately to reach out to his mother, Hutton gave a brilliant performance that was rewarded with an Oscar. And Donald Sutherland was truly excellent as the father. Like *Kramer vs. Kramer,* this film pictured a father and son expressing their love for each other. The end of the film, with father and son expressing their love and need for each other in the morning light, was an encouraging sign that at long last some of the men that make films are seeking a new image for today's man. *Ordinary People* went on to win the Oscar for best picture.

Maybe somebody is listening.

Chapter 11:
The Sexist Draft

THE DRAFT

M. Adams

Me: Do you think women should be drafted?

Woman: No! that would be horrible.

M: Why is it any more horrible than drafting men?

W: Because!

M: Because what?

W: Well, because! You mean I have to *tell* you? How can you even *ask* that?

M: It's my childlike curiosity. Why is drafting women any more horrible than drafting men?

W: Well, you *can't* just send women into war.

M: Why not?

W: What?? Why are you doing this? You're upsetting me.

M: I'll mention it in confession on Sunday. Why can't we send women into war?

W: *Because!!* You know why! It just isn't right!

M: Why isn't it right?

W: God! Because...women would *have* to stay behind...because, well, they're the childbearers.

M: That not what you said last week.

W: What are you talking about?

M: Last week, when we were talking about jobs. You said, and I quote, "It's disgusting when men look at women as the childbearers of society, as though women aren't good for anything else." Then you went on to say that no woman should be regarded as a childbearer, and that that perception of women should never stand in the way of her getting any job for which she's qualified. Well, I agree. Fighting in the infantry is a job, and I say if a woman is qualified, then she should *not* be regarded as a childbearer, that that perception of women should *not* stand in the way of getting the job—through conscription or otherwise.

W: But that's different!

M: How is it different?

W: Well, a job is one thing—but fighting in the army is *dangerous*. We can't send women out to be killed in war—who would be left to have the babies?

M: But you believe that baby-having should be voluntary, right? Society shouldn't *expect* women to have babies; it should be the individual woman's choice. . . right?

W: Of course!

M: How about after a war? Should it still be completely voluntary, even then?

W: Yes, of course.

M: So you're saying that we should exempt *all* women from this dangerous obligation, based on the fact that someday, *some* of them *might* decide to have babies. Is that it?

W: Yes, I suppose so.

M: O.K. Let's extend that idea. Lots of jobs are dangerous, too. Being a cop is dangerous. Being a coalminer is dangerous. Being a psychiatrist is dangerous since so many of them commit suicide. Your logic would dictate that society *deny* these and all other dangerous jobs to *all* women, based on the fact that someday, *some* of them *might* decide to have children. Does that sound good to you?

W: It's not the same thing!

M: Sure it is.

W: No, it's not! Not *all* women would have those kinds of jobs.

M: And not *all* women would be drafted, either. They would simply be considered as *candidates* for the draft, right along with men. Then, those individuals judged most able psychologically and physcially to survive the experience would be chosen to serve, regardless of their gender.

W: (A long pause) But. . . if you draft all the strong people, you leave behind a weak populace to reproduce.

M: O.K.—so we throw in a few weaklings from *both* sexes and leave behind a few strong ones from *both* sexes. No need to discriminate there.

W: But. . .men are *stronger* than women. . .everybody knows that! They have greater upper-body strength. . .and they can run faster.

M: That's not what you said last week, either.

W: *Now* what??

M: Last week you said and I quote again, "Women are just as good as men, and can do anything that men can do, and it's presumptuous and chauvinistic for men to think otherwise." When we were talking about sports, you said something like, "Why won't men compete against women? Are they afraid the women might *beat* them?" You read passages from Ashley Montague to me and gloated over the theories that women are physically superior to men: that they have higher thresholds of pain, higher resistance to extremes in temperatures, and better stamina in general. You showed me pictures from a magazine of women bodybuilders and became quite smug—and you said that I'd better watch myself, that women aren't the "weaker sex" any more. I agreed with every point you made and I still do. Many women would make better soldiers than many men. Those women should be drafted in place of those men.

W: But the vast majority of women *wouldn't* make good soldiers. So it seems practical to institute a policy that applies to the majority.

M: Actually, to do so would be *impractical* as well as inconsistent with your other views. The vast majority of women wouldn't make good cops or coalminers or construction workers, either. Does that mean we should institue a policy that applies to the majority and deny all strength-oriented jobs to women?

W: No. . .no, of course not. If an individual is qualified, there is no reason to deny her a position.

M: So, not only is your characterization of women inconsistent, but your manner of dealing with that inconsistency is inconsistent. When rights and privileges are the issue, you say, "Let the qualified individual come forth." When responsibilities and risks are the issue, your philosophy changes to, "Let's institute a policy that applies to the majority." As far as being practical, it would be most practical to

226

choose the fittest people from the entire populace to fill the quota, rather than taking them all from one group and winding up with a lot of under-qualified troops. For every unfit male draftee—and there are always lots of them—there is a woman somewhere who could do the job better. Universal candidacy for conscription works out to be more practical, too. You lose.

W: Well, I guess that all sounds logical, but you can't always be logical about things in life. This is more of an *emotional* thing. It just doesn't *feel* right to send women into war. It's always been that way.

M: "Male chauvinist pigs" could just as easily say that "it doesn't feel right to have women in the workplace. . . it's always been like that."

W: Look, you're really starting to make me angry. This whole conversation is ridiculous. It's an *emotional* issue. It just *feels* right, emotionally, to have men be the ones who fight our wars. Our whole society thinks so.

M: Nazis used to think that it just felt right, emotionally, to commit genocide. Their whole society thought so.

W: Are you comparing me to a Nazi??

M: That got me in trouble with someone else, once. . . so I guess I'll answer *no* to that.

W: Logic just doesn't enter into it. Most men would agree with *my* point of view, anyway.

M: And when they *do* agree, feminists call them "chauvinistic." Feminists go nuts any time a man says anything to the effect that women shouldn't fight in the army.

W: Well, if a woman *volunteers,* that's different. Of course, women should be allowed to fight if they *want* to.

M: Oh, I see. This is another example of "a man's obligation is a woman's right." I've heard that somewhere before, it seems. It's one of the high points of phony-humanist insanity.

W: Still, men seem to agree with it and accept it.

M: Fewer and fewer men do every day. Since women raised the issue of sexual equality, the idea is beginning to creep into the minds of many men that liberation works both ways. Why in the world *should* any man accept your unfair terms? How are men *supposed* to feel when society tells them, "You've got to do this and women don't?" Why should any rational being welcome discrimination against itself? *Women* don't! Feminists won't stand for *any* form of discrimination against women, however trivial it may be. You expect men to gladly accept life-and-death discrimination against themselves, while women are rallying against gender in pronouns! Te, tes, tir, turds! If women can get riled up about things like that, why should men agree to your sexist terms about the risk of life?

W: I don't know. . .because men are *supposed* to feel that way. . .I mean, you're supposed to protect women—to *want* to protect women. You know?

M: And what is it that women are supposed to *want* to do for men?

W: What?

M: Are you willing to have women compensate men for this "wanting" to do something for women? What things could society impose on *women,* on the basis of their gender, for them to "want to do" for men? Is there *anything* that you could tolerate as a form of discrimination against women? Could there be *any* parallel custom that would involve women serving men that you could accept?

W: I *guess* so. . . .

M: Name *one.*

W: What?

M: I said *name one.* I'll give you five hundred dollars if you can name *one.*

W: Oh, stop it.

M: Go ahead! Name one! It doesn't even have to be anything important! Name one silly little thing that you would allow society to impose on women as a group.

W: Well, I'd have to think about it.

M: I'll wait.

W: You're being really awful to me.

M: Feminists have been really awful to me for fifteen years. I'm still waiting.

W: Oh, *I* don't know, for God's sake!

M: Well, let's see. Let's think of something really minor. . .or at least minor when compared to the draft. I remember a few weeks ago you were screaming about how when banks print the names of the depositors on checks, they "automatically print the husband's name first." You talked about how chauvinistic it is. You were so angry you could hardly eat your dinner. Anyway, that seems pretty insignificant next to being exclusively obligated to fight wars. So how about that? Could you accept *that* as a social custom in your society? Would you allow men that small compensation for being the only ones drafted?

228

Having their names printed first on checks?

W: Listen! That sort of thing makes me really angry because it's like the woman is somehow less important than the man. It's like she's some kind of sub-entity to the male.

M: If you, in your own beliefs, obligate men to protect you with their lives, you *make yourself a sub-entity* to them. In *any* life-situation where someone is *responsible* for something else, it always follows that the someone should have a *measure of control* over the something else. If men are to be responsible for women, then it follows that they have that measure of control. And, as I have said, having their names printed first on checks is damned small compensation. Well, how about it? Could you accept top-billing on checks for men as compensation for your belief in an all-male draft?

W: No—that doesn't even make sense.

M: O.K.—then pick something else.

W: You're driving me crazy with this shit! How can you be so deliberately antagonistic and mean to me?

M: I was never cuddled as a baby. I'm still waiting to hear about your compensatory obligation for women.

W: This is stupid! Men are supposed to *want* to do these kinds of things.

M: Ah! Chivalry. Oho! Is that it?

W: Well, if you want to call it that. . . .

M: Call it whatever. The point is that *you* believe in a society in which men are expected and *required* to take dangerous risks for the sake of women, risk that can ruin them physically or psychologically or both, or kill them; and you believe that men should do so *without any form of compensation* from the society or reciprocation on the part of the women. Even chivalry originally had its compensations. Chivalry developed as a response to the female role, as compensation for women for being the childbearers and for being domestics. The male and female roles *attempted,* at least, to compensate for one another. I'm not saying they succeeded—and I certainly don't believe in them. But the idea of give-and-take was very much a part of them. *The female role was chivalry's only reason for existence.* If you take away the female role, there is no longer any reason for chivalry to exist, no longer any reason for men to feel any chivalrous desire to protect women or pay any other form of stigmatic tribute to them. You've said yourself that childbearing should be voluntary and *not* stigmatically imposed on women, and that society should *not* see women as childbearers. Feminists have equally renounced *every single aspect* of the female role, down to the smallest detail.

229

How are men supposed to *want* to make this enormous sacrifice for women? You were even complaining once about preference for veterans in hiring for jobs. Are men to get *no compensation at all* for the obligations your beliefs would impose on them? What the hell do you think chivalry was all about, anyway? In fact, you once said, in a completely different context, that chivalry was a "chauvinist plot designed to keep women in their place." How does *that* fit in with your thinking that men should *want* to protect women? What the hell *do* you believe, anyway? Have you ever really *thought* about any of this??

W: I don't know! Look, you're really being vicious. This conversation is really upsetting me, and you don't even seem to care.

M: I suppose *that's* against the rules, too. Not only can you not *draft* women, you can't upset them, either. Actually, that's the *real* reason we don't draft them—it would upset them too much.

W: You're terrible!

M: Last week you said I was cute.

W: Hmpf! That was before I knew you had such strange ideas about women.

M: Strange ideas?? I believe in sexual equality! I thought that's what *you* believed in! You said it was *so hard* to find a man who believed in sexual equality! Well, you've found one! Equality has reared its ugly head, and you don't seem to be very happy with it.

W: Look, you can only carry equality so far.

M: How far? To the point where it stops being convenient for women?

W: No, that's not what I meant.

M: That's *exactly* what you meant, and you don't even realize it!

W: No, you're wrong!

M: All right, then I ask you again: Name *one* inconvenience which you would allow society to impose on women—*one* point of inequality which would go against women that you would accept.

W: I can't think of anything right now. Look, in a war, it's different. Millions of people get killed all at the same time. A society couldn't let its women be killed in great masses like that. . . the women have to stay behind, so that the population can be built back again. I mean, it's the rule of the barnyard! It's as simple as that!

M: Rule of the barnyard??

W: Of course. Everybody knows *that*! All it takes is one male for any number of females to procreate as fast as possible. That's why we need to protect the women.

M: Procreation, is it?

W: Yes—and it's really not the kind of thing you can use this "equality logic" of yours against. It's a practical matter, an emotional matter. . .a survival matter. There are no logical arguments against it.

M: Actually, there are *four.*

W: Four what?

M: Four logical arguments against it.

W: You can't be serious!

M: I'm deadly serious. The "procreation" argument—or as you so demurely put it, the "rule of the barnyard" theory—is always the last refuge of a Mariologist scoundrel. People always fall back on this argument whenever they are desperate to protect women from true equality. They always think it's their ace-in-the-hole. In reality, it is probably one of the greatest hoaxes ever to be put over on the Western civilization.

W: Hoax? What are you talking about?

M: The whole idea is nonsensical and inappropriate.

W: It is not! That's just a fact of biology, whether you like it or not!

M: But as far as implementing a discriminatory social practice based on that fact, it's nonsensical and inappropriate.

W: How?

M: As I said, for four reasons. First of all, in a conventional war, it is highly unlikely that the population would ever be that seriously threatened. No one society would be in such danger of extinction that it would have to take such drastic procreative measures. The only thing that might threaten a population to that extent would be a *nuclear* war, and in that case we can't control *who* gets killed. Everybody gets zapped, and there's nothing that can be done.

W: But that's not true about conventional war. Look at poor Russia. After the war, seventy-five percent of the men were dead!

M: I'm glad you brought up that example, because it doesn't make any sense, and, if anything, supports my argument. I'll explain in a minute. The second reason is one that almost nobody ever thinks of. You said that "we would have to hold the women back in order to rebuild the population"—that it was the "rule of the barnyard." There's another name for that practice. . .can you think of it?

W: Procreation?

M: No—there's another name for it. A name to which Western civilization doesn't react nearly as reverently as it does to "procreation." Can you guess?

W: Propagation...? Breeding...? I don't know!

M: No, it's none of those.

W: Well, what is it?

M: It's *polygamy.*

W: What do you mean?

M: Just what I said. That practice is called *polygamy.* Western civilization despises it and has *never* practiced it, *not even after wars.* When you say things like, "We have to hold the women back to rebuild the population" and "it's the rule of the barnyard" and "all it takes is one man to any number of any women," what you're saying is that *we must begin to set ourselves up for the practice of polygamy*—a practice which has been repugnant to Western society for two thousand years, and which, consequently, it has never practiced. It is patently illegal and has been for centuries. It is against every religious, moral and legal dictum regarding reproduction, and will undoubtedly remain so. So it becomes ridiculous that society has always fallen back on this idea of "protect the women in times of crisis so that we can rebuild the society," and then it turns around and declares the mechanism for doing so immoral and illegal, and refuses to practice it! *Even after the worst wars!* The only exception was the Mormons in the nineteenth century out west. After they were practically wiped out by Indians, they practiced polygamy to rebuild their population. Of course they did so illegally, and they eventually got in trouble for doing it and were made to stop. So the same society that screams, "We must preserve our women for procreation" turns around and prosecutes the only group of people in its history who ever tried to fulfill the idea! Everyone has always gotten into this "save the women" fervor and has jabbered about "procreation," and then no one has ever followed through on it.

W: But that's because it's just never been *necessary....*

M: Which was my *first* argument...remember?

W: Oh....

M: You're arguing for *me!*

W: Still, it seems like the safe thing to do...protecting the women, I mean.

M: Not really. My first argument was that such drastic procreative action would probably never be necessary, even in the worst cases. The *fact* of my second argument is the best support for my first argument. The fact that modern society has *never* practiced polygamy—together with the fact that all the modern societies are still with us—is proof that it has never been necessary. You mentioned Russia, and the fact that after the war, seventy-five percent of the men were dead—a pretty severe case in point. You offered that as an example of why we need to stockpile women for procreation. Well...did the Russians practice polygamy after the war?

W: No, of course not.

M: And are the Russian people still with us?

W: Yes.

M: What happened to the "rule of the barnyard?" It wasn't needed.

W: Yes, but the excess of females left over after the war surely must have helped to repopulate, even without polygamy.

M: Incorrect! Proponents of chivalry always blurt that out—they claim that keeping all the women around is procreative even without polygamy. That's totally false! Which is my third argument: In a society which practices monogamy, it is actually *anti*-procreative to create a disproportionate number of one sex. The most procreative situation in a monogamous society is to have the most *equal* proportion of men to women possible.

W: Are you sure?

M: Of course! Let's take a simplified example. Let's start by making everything symmetrical, even. Take a sample population on a desert island, of one thousand people—half men, half women. For the sake of argument, let's say *all* of them are capable of reproducing. Say there's a terrible war, and only the men are drafted. Let's use your Russian example: after the war, seventy-five percent of the men are dead. Out of an original five hundred men, 375 are killed. That leaves 125 men left to procreate. But this society is monogamous, which means that each of the 125 men can only procreate with one woman at a time. Therefore, at any given time there can only be 125 couples procreating for that society. Now, suppose, *both* sexes had been drafted. Once again, for the sake of argument, let's say half of the casualties were women and half were men. Assuming the same number of total fatalities as before—that is, 375—that would leave behind, in society, 625 procreators, roughly half male and half female. That means that instead of 125 fertile couples there would be *312* fertile, monogamous couples left to rebuild society. Drafting both sexes shows a 150% increase in procreative efficiency over the male-only system in a monogamous society.

W: But the numbers wouldn't add up so neatly in reality.

M: That's correct, but the system still works out pretty well. Men are capable of reproducing later in life than women, so we would not want to draft as many young women as young men. But remember that we would draft *only those individuals* who represent the best x number of military specimens from the society in the first place. Due to the fact that *on the average,* men are bigger and stronger than women, *more young men would be drafted anyway.* The percentages are probably about the same: the surplus of *young,* fertile women would just about parallel the *older* men who are still able to be fathers at an age when most women could no longer be mothers. So, the greater average male strength, by coincidence, takes care of the fertility period offset. Monogamy loves equality, it seems.

W: So why hasn't anyone ever thought of all this before?

M: I'd like to know, too! Historically, of course, there were *other* reasons—political and social reasons—why it would have been unfair to draft women. But today, with all of the reforms in social customs and laws that are aimed at freeing women from their role, and with all the talk about protecting women for one reason and another, we're so wrapped up in Mario-chivalry that we really can't think straight—literally! The "procreation" argument is always invoked with great sanctimony, and everyone dutifully reacts with great deference and guilt, and *nobody* for two thousand years has ever bothered to think it through to the end. . .that society would *never* follow through on the idea, and, in fact, that because we *don't* follow through on it, it actually is *anti*-procreative and defeats its own purpose due to monogamy.

W: Did you say you had a fourth reason?

M: You mean you're actually *interested* in hearing it? I thought this discussion was upsetting you.

W: I'm sort of numb at this point, I guess.

M: The fourth reason is simply that the procreation cop-out is completely at odds with the current trend towards women's rights. Implicit in the protect-the-women-for-procreation argument is the idea that after a war, women will be *responsible* for rebuilding the population—that childbearing would become their *role.* We've already discussed how you and feminists in general are dead set against *that* idea. First of all, feminists decry polygamy as a "chauvinist" institution which degrades women. But polygamy needn't even be brought into it. Even after a war, women would continue to demand their "right to choose." You know very well that *you* would!

234

You've told me that you don't ever plan to have kids, right?

W: Right; I don't want any. I want to live my own life.

M: Well, suppose there were a war? Would you feel any differently *after* a war?

W: Who knows *how* I'd feel? That's just empty supposition.

M: O.K.—there *was* a war. There was the Viet Nam war. That wasn't supposition. We did not draft women into that war, and the procreation argument, as always, led the pack of reasons why we didn't. If, back then, someone had asked you to explain why women were not being drafted, you would have surely gotten around the procreation excuse, just as you did today. Your feminist philosophy of the right-to-choose and your desire to "live your own life," however, *also* developed during that war. When the war was over, did you feel any differently about your right-to-choose?

W: No.

M: You *still* wanted to live your own life and not have any kids!

W: Yes. But it wasn't really necessary to obligate women to have children or to enter into polygamy after that war.

M: Right. I know. It never has been. That's my argument number one, remember?

W: Yeah, I remember.

M: And suppose there were another war like World War II? After that war, would your plans for your personal life change?

W: Probably not, but *that's* supposition . . .

M: I'll grant you that, but I'm not even necessarily talking about personal preferences. I'm talking more about your general philosophy regarding women's right-to-choose. Would *that* change after a war?

W: No.

M: There you have it! Women would surely continue to demand the right to live their own lives and choose whether or not to procreate. And they would undoubtedly point, as you did, to the fact that it isn't really necessary to obligate women to reproduce and enter into a childbearing relationship—whether it was polygamous *or* monogamous—that the population isn't really in any danger and will replenish itself on its own . . . which is my first argument!

W: But . . . we would *still* need to keep women around, just for the ones who *do* decide to have children.

M: Not a good enough reason—especially in the face of the other three

235

W: arguments—to rob men of their civil rights by giving women such incredible comparative freedom. The whole procreation argument simply *isn't good enough* to justify discrimination against men in this horrible way. Frankly, I'm not sure *any* argument ever would be.

W: Hmm. . . .

M: You've painted yourself into a corner with your demands for 'equal rights. *Any* argument that you use to demand equal rights can be used to mandate equal responsibility. Conversely, any argument that you use to *exempt* yourself from equal responsibilities can be used to *deny* you equal rights. There's no escape. The logic is immutable. That's just plain, remedial morality. You can't have your cake and eat it too.

W: But wait a minute—there's another aspect to the procreation thing.

M: Oh?

W: Yes. It's true that we don't—and shouldn't—practice polygamy. But we don't necessarily have to practice *polygamy* in order to procreate with an excess of women in society. We can protect the women, and *still* use procreative measures without actually practicing polygamy per se. . . .

M: We *can??*

W: Sure. All we'd really need is a sperm-bank. . . .

M: WHAT!??

W: A *sperm-bank!* That's all that's really necessary.

M: *Shit!!* Do you realize what you're saying?

W: I'm talking about artificial insemination.

M: But do you realize the *implications* of what you're saying??

W: I'm saying that protecting women can *still* be procreative without having to resort to polygamy if we use artificial insemination.

M: *Resort to polygamy!??* Chirst!! I don't believe you! You've got the *nerve* to bitch about how men "reduce women to childbearers and domestics," when you've just reduced men to the *suppliers of sperm-banks. . .!!!* After which society can dispose of them in war at its convenience! I'm really sorry I compared you to a Nazi before. . . it was an insult to the *Nazis!!*

W: All right, calm down! Look, you've obviously given this issue a great deal of thought. Most other people haven't.

M: That's my whole complaint!! Nobody bothers to think about it!

W: In any case, you've got to be more tolerant of people who haven't thought about it as much. The things you're saying are very touchy and disorienting to a woman, and you've got to be patient when someone doesn't quite understand your point of view....

M: The way *feminists* have been tolerant with people who haven't thought about *their* issues as much? The way *feminists* have been patient with men who are disoriented by the woman's point of view and "don't quite understand it?" Yes, you and your movement have set such a fine example for us!!

W: O.K., O.K. The point is that you have some exceptional thoughts on this subject. It must have taken you quite a while to think about all of the things we've talked about.

M: I thought it all through one afternoon when I was sixteen years old. I was sitting under a tree eating a tuna-fish sandwich. It took me about two or three hours to figure it all out. You could have figured it all out, too, if you had bothered to think about it for five minutes. Sperm-bank! Shit!

W: I'm sorry, but you'll just have to learn to accept it when someone disagrees with you. I just don't happen to believe that women should be drafted.

M: Right—I'll "accept" that the same way *you* always "accept" it when a man disagrees with one of your feminist ideas. You always pop your cork and start screaming, "chauvinist." What should I call *you?* Feminists have corrupted the meaning of the word "chauvinist" to the point where it practically means nothing; perhaps we can corrupt it a little more to include women who think the way you do.

W: And exactly what is *that* supposed to mean?

M: It means women who go around babbling about "chauvinism" and something they call "sexual equality" who wouldn't recognize the true meaning of sexual equality if it fell on their heads.

W: You certainly don't have a very high opinion of women.

M: I certainly don't have a very high opinion of *you.*

(Needless to say, it was our last date.)

THE MALE'S UNPAID ROLE: BODYGUARD AND PROTECTOR

Fredric Hayward

What would you pay someone who agreed that, if he was ever with you when you were attacked, he would intervene and try to get himself killed slowly enough to give you time to escape? What is the hourly wage for a bodyguard? That is your job, you know, every time you are with a woman...*any* woman, not just your wife. Men have not yet begun to investigate our own unpaid roles. There are many.

FEMINISM AND THE VETERAN

David C. Morrow

Consider tomorrow's war veteran, returning home psychologically and perhaps physically wounded, to find he must pay for a divorce secured by his draft-exempt wife after he's spent two years away from her—most probably not through his own desire. Since alimony and child support are to be deducted from his paycheck, he is ordred to find a sufficiently high-paying job within thirty days or go to jail. His ex- then shares half his hard-earned military pension with the succession of men she lives with in the house he bought and is probably still paying for (each of these men possibly subject to later palimony), keeping her alimony by avoiding remarriage and setting a fine "liberated" example for his children. He is allowed to see his kids only at certain times, although their mother often leaves them in taxpayer-supported day-care centers, long after she gets off work, so she'll have enough time to shriek at City Hall about how oppressed she is.

WE WHO ARE ABOUT TO DIE

Fredric Hayward

Through poignant headlines and distraught commentary, the media makes it clear when women are killed. The woman/victim unit is etched in our collective mind. When men are killed, however, we tend to use other labels: soldiers, miners, workers, people, and often, just numbers. **"Scaffold Collapses. 18 Plunge to Death."** It disguises the monotonous pattern of male death, and keeps us from interrupting the flow of antimale rhetoric and asking, "How come so many *men* are dying?"

War is also typical, because no one talks about *why* it is typical. Later, when the smell of explosives and death has drifted away, we will return to the inequity and sympathize with the mothers who have suffered the loss of a son, and the wives and girlfriends who have suffered the loss of a provider and protector.

We are not supposed to pity the male soldier. He deserves to die, we are told, because "men make wars." But, of the 56,886 Americans killed in the Vietnam War, there were zero lawmakers. . .and six women. Korea, World War II, same pattern.

The American men who were shot up, sliced up, or shredded up in the wars had no greater role in "making the war" than the American women who stayed home. It is wrong to blame all blacks for the crimes of a few; it is racist. It is wrong to blame all men for the wars of a few; it is sexist.

I am tired of hearing that men cause war. Politicians, perhaps, but not men. I swear, Ms. Steinem, I've never caused a war in my life. Politicians declare the wars, and female prime ministers have a near-perfect record in the War Declaration category. Golda, Indira, now Margaret. Until the Equal Rights Movement abandons its rhetoric, simplifications, and fingerpointing, the only change it will bring will be that the power of women to have men fight and die for them will be exercised politically, as well as socially. It is not the feminine morality of women generals, but the specter of women casualties which will do most to encourage the peaceful resolution of international disputes.

I am tired of hearing that the ones who suffer most in war are women. Docile males seem to get killed, while angry females seem to scream about bombs they never heard and rapes they never suffered. If "it is the women who suffer most" in postwar Indochina, it is only because it is mostly the women who are left. Feminism has given a cruel, new meaning to the phrase "lucky stiff." The only thing that post-war societies have in common is not the luck of men, it is the lack of men.

WOMEN IN COMBAT

Dan Logan

Asked about women in combat at her confirmation hearings, then–Supreme Court nominee Sandra Day O'Connor said she'd hate to see them come home in coffins. Why are men expendable in her eyes?

WOMEN WANT TO SERVE

A poll of women between 18 and 35 has revealed that almost 70% believe women should be drafted if men are, especially in the event of a crisis. 60% don't think military women should be kept out of combat. 61% would consider joining the military. The poll surveyed 1,007 readers of *Glamour* magazine.

THE EXPENDABLE MALE

Fredric Hayward

When someone says, "Women are not equipped as men to handle construction work," there is an outcry. When someone says, "Women are not equipped to be police officers," there is an outcry. But, when someone says, "Women are not equipped to be soldiers," there is only a murmur.

We all know that women have proved effective in positions formerly restricted to males. We also know that women in the Viet Cong, P.L.O., and Red Brigade make highly effective soldiers and killers. We have all seen films of ninety-pound, Asian female laborers routinely lifting heavier objects than combat requires. We all know some women who are stronger than some men and some men whose personalities are more gentle and nurturing than some women's. We all know that treating people as stereotypes instead of considering their individual strengths and weaknesses is unjust to those individuals and inefficient for the country. Finally, most of us are committed to equal rights. Yet, there is still no outcry, only a murmur.

The reason there is still no outcry is that women's military competence has little to do with our opposition to equal treatment in the draft. The opposition is really based on our conditioning to protect women. Women are too fine, too innocent, too valuable to risk.

THE PEACE MOVEMENT AND THE SEXIST DRAFT

Francis Baumli

It is very difficult to talk about a sexist draft when dealing with people who are part of the peace movement. Their comeback usually goes something like this: "Maybe the draft is sexist, but that is not the issue. The *real* issue is that there should not be *any* draft at all, because war is *never* justified. So let's not talk about drafting women. Let's work to end the draft."

To their comeback, I usually reply with arguments to the effect that maybe

240

defensive wars sometimes *are* necessary. For example, how is it morally objectionable that a military force should have gone into Germany to release the Jews from Dachau in WW II? And when the Pol Pot regime in Kampuchea, from 1975 to 1979, eliminated 3 million people out of a population of 7½ million, wasn't Vietnamese military intervention which halted the mass murder justified?

But when I say such things, our arguments seem to go on endlessly, and perhaps rather aimlessly. No doubt about it, we all would like to see all wars, all military preparedness, and all killing stopped. The problem is, we get lost in our separate, "if only's." And we do not seem to get anywhere.

And the question remains: Is the draft sexist?

Yes, I say. Even if you are the most committed pacifist in the world, even if you could have out-peacnicked Gandhi himself, if you still refuse to discuss the sexism inherent in the military draft, then you are being unfair to men. If indeed all war is wrong, then that, in my opinion, is all the more reason why *everyone,* male and female, should be drafted for military duty. Because then, in the true spirit of democracy, we have not placed gender restrictions on the kind of draft resistors the government must contend with. This way, if a war is entered into by our country, and our citizenry is drafted without regard to gender, then both women and men have an equal stake in deciding whether or not it is an unjust war, and whether or not they should fight it.

Truly, women, we men appreciate your participation in peace rallies, your educational efforts, your pain, and your own unique, valuable, and indispensable resistance to war. But we want something more.

We are tired not only of being the chivalrous warriors when it comes to fighting wars, we are also tired of being heroes when it comes to resisting war. And we believe that it is a sad but inevitable truism about human nature that people usually get more involved in a moral issue when it is their own ass they are saving. We therefore believe that judgements about the justice of any war, and the resistance to unjust wars, would be a lot more reasonable, fair, and effective if it were your ass, as well as ours, that you are trying to save.

So, women, as much as we appreciate the impact of your peace vigils, and the sincerity of your mourning after men die, we would prefer your more direct involvement right now. Why sit by while men do the dirty, heroic work? Why don't you insist on your *right* to register for the draft? That way, when the generals hand down their orders, and both men and women decide to hold out for peace, we will all be in it together—with the same self-interests and shared hopes that we will all come out of it alive.

241

Chapter 12:
Reclaiming the Body

HOW BOYS START OUT UNHEALTHY

Tom Williamson

One way to teach a little boy to hold in his emotions and to take risks is to have someone he is dependent upon for acceptance (parent, teacher, etc.) express disapproval, withhold love or acceptance, deprive or humiliate him, and/or lash out at him with corporal punishment, when he cries or exhibits fear. In addition, the boy can be rewarded for enduring pain, as is often done in sports.

What this amounts to is a formula for masochism, which, when taken to its logical conclusion in the adult, can lead to workaholism, the ignoring of all symptoms of ill health in order to live up to the expectations of others, and the battle to conquer stress, which can lead to a heart attack or stroke, or some other form of premature death.

KIDS ARE SMOKING—WHY DON'T WE CARE?

Jim Sanderson

I suppose I'm not smoking cigarettes today because Mr. Steinbrenner made it so tough for me that I quit before I learned to inhale. Most kids did their experimenting with "butts" stolen from their parents, but I didn't have a relative within a hundred miles who smoked. The only convenient source was a vending machine located some 15 feet inside the front door of my favorite hamburger hangout.

I had one of Mr. Steinbrenner's deluxe hamburgers every day after my paper route. We had a tacit pact that when I was an "eating customer" I wouldn't try to hit the cigarette machine, and Mr. S. wouldn't have to watch me. So I'd hang around out front at odd hours, and when I could see that he was busy over the grill with his back turned, I'd bust through the double doors on a dead run, frenziedly shove my 15 cents into the coin chutes, and pull the first plunger I could get my hands on. Mr. S. had been a football star in his high school days, and although he must have been 40 then, he could still put one hand on the counter and vault over it with no more than a single angry grunt. Our scenario always went *crash-bang* through the door, *clink-clink* into the coin chute, *chaang* with the plunger, followed by a "hot damn!" from Mr. S. and the *whoomp* of his feet hitting the floor on this side of the counter.

He never quite caught me, although once a single swipe of his paw ripped down the pocket of my jacket as I escaped. Also he sometimes made it over the counter before the pack of Old Golds or Twenty Grand dropped into the mouth of the machine, so I'd have to tear away empty-handed. Mr. Steinbrenner always picked up the pack triumphantly, put it in his pocket, and we chalked that up as one for his side. We must have run through this cigarette Olympics 20 times, but we never talked about it when I came in and slipped onto the stool for my Special Deluxe with extra mayo. He didn't seem to hold it against me for experimenting, and for my part I understood that he was acting in the place of my parents. He just didn't want me to develop a habit that might kill me.

I finally decided that all the lying and sneaking around plus fighting a war with Mr. S. was too much trouble. Smoking was expensive, made my clothes smell awful, and my best friend was howling every time I dropped ashes in his newly recarpeted Model A. Also I couldn't get the hang of holding a cigarette in the corner of my mouth like Bogart without the smoke drifting in my eye. So, while I never admitted anything to my parents, I did confess one day to Mr. S. that I was giving up the filthy habit. He looked at me to see if I meant it, then sighed with relief. "This counter isn't getting any lower," he said, and that day he gave me a free chocolate shake with my burger.

It all sounds rather sweetly quaint now, right? My neighbor Ted today makes no objection to his two teenagers smoking at home; in fact, the family cigarettes are purchased at the supermarket out of the food budget. "If there's no way you can stop them from smoking, why be hypocritical?" he says. "Anyway, we ought to be glad they aren't smoking something worse."

I don't buy this reasoning. For one thing, you get absolutely nothing out of a marijuana cigarette unless you are a trained smoker who really knows how to draw the smoke into your lungs and keep it there for several instants without choking to death. Secondly, while medical researchers are beginning to suspect that heavy pot smoking may be dangerous to your health indeed, we nevertheless know with absolute certainty how deadly cigarette tobacco is. How can we worry so much about our kids taking up with demon Mary Jane and yet be so callously calm about cigarettes? Just the other day the World Health Organization reviewed all the studies since 1975 linking cigarette smoking with heart disease, respiratory diseases, lung cancer, other cancer, and birth defects. Calling the evidence "overwhelming," WHO proclaimed a worldwide campaign to get young people to quit the cigarette habit before they start. This trumpet call to common sense was greeted by the usual massive apathy. But why? Just because the injury lies years in the future, does that mean we don't care? If our kids were drinking some kind of slow poison instead of smoking it, wouldn't we be crying out in protest?

In the recent election several states voted on the question of raising their alcohol-drinking ages above 18. How come nobody is proposing some new laws about selling cigarettes to kids aged 14? Or 10? Or enforcing the old laws still on the books? Of course no law does any good unless parents are willing to take some action to support it. We are not going to alienate our sons and daughters if we tell them, with great love, that we don't want them to smoke because doctors say it's dangerous. It's not old-fashioned over-protectiveness. It's modern and "with it"—based on the latest scientific evidence. If enough parents had the guts to take a stand maybe we'd find some Mr. Steinbrenners out there to support us. I know a few honest merchants who would cut off the kiddie trade if they thought it would make any difference.

But in any case, Mr. S., wherever you are, thanks for saving my life.

HOW YOUNG MEN DIE

Tom Williamson

When looking at a specific age segment for young people, in 1977, 80.25 percent of all premature deaths for males between the ages of fifteen and twenty-four were because of accidents (56.43), suicide (12.61), or homicide (11.21). While the leading three causes were the same for both sexes, they accounted for only sixty-three percent of the female group. All three are related to life style or mental instability and not to infectious disease. Part of the differences between the sexes in these statistics indicate that boys are under more pressure than girls to take risks and to perform.

MEN AND THE MACHO IDEAL

Jay Smith, Ph.D.

Macho behavior affects virtually everything we males do. There is a macho way of driving a car. We males, expecially during adolescence when we are the most insecure about our masculinity, learn to drive fast and recklessly. There are macho ways of drinking and eating, both dangerous to our health. We males are expected to have second and third helpings and to see how much booze we can put away, while for women it is socially unacceptable to overeat or to get drunk. Combine the macho pressures to drive fast and drink heavily, and you have the potential for tragedy on the highway. The macho way of working brainwashes us into believing that the longer we work and the faster our pace, the more we accomplish. And the macho pressure to win and achieve at virtually any cost causes us males to continue playing in a football or basketball game when we are hurt, or to not take a day off from work when we are sick. The net result of these and many other self-destructive behaviors which seem to emphasize speed, power and excess in our lifestyles is physical and psychological damage.

HEALING MY BODY/HEALING MYSELF

Jed Diamond

I began doing a meditation whenever I started to feel sick, and I "asked" my body what it was trying to tell me. I felt foolish when I began—what would people think if I told them I talked to my stomach—but what I heard when I listened made it all worthwhile. I've had stomach problems since I was a kid. As an adult the doctors always thought I was about to get an ulcer. I drank Maalox like milkshakes and always carried tablets with me. Now when my stomach begins to hurt I ask, "What's the message you want me to get?" Recently it told me I was under increasing stress and I needed to cut back on my work. It consistently tells me to slow down, to eat more slowly, usually to do everything more slowly. I had always accepted stomach problems as part of being a man. I certainly don't anymore.

I'd learned that colds and flu were messages that I needed to rest, though I still had to fight the feeling that I should be well in a short time, as if I was allowed only a certain amount of time off. I often felt like life was a big basketball game. To win I had to run from the first whistle to the last. We were allowed a few two-minute time outs along the way, but no one could ask the referee to extend the time out to three minutes because we needed a little longer to rest.

I always saw life as a team sport. Being alone was cowardly and not even in the rules of the game. In all the years with Lindy, I never felt free to take time for myself. I always felt I had to be doing something useful. I even decided that I went to all those dull evening meetings for my job because it was the closest I could get to being alone, and still feel I could justify my actions.

Sleep was also a suspect activity, only to be engaged in if the purpose was to get you ready for the next day. Sleeping late on Sunday was acceptable only because by God I'd earned it by driving myself all week, and I needed my rest to fight the new wars on Monday. I learned early on to "never, never, never be caught sleeping at unauthorized times!" I couldn't even count the times that Lindy would come in while I was dozing in a chair or sacking out on the couch in the early evening. I would rouse myself as soon as I heard her footsteps. "Were you sleeping, hon?" "Oh, no, just resting my eyes." I even remember being wakened from a sound sleep at midnight and finding myself feeing guilty, saying cheerfully, "No I wasn't asleep, I was just reading."

I can't believe I lived with such insanity for so long. I still tell my wife I feel fine driving even when I'm dead tired, but I've been working on that one too. It's felt like a very long road, but I was glad I began to listen to what my body was telling me, and began to be strong enough to act on what I was hearing.

COCK SURE
THE WISDOM OF THE PENIS

Jed Diamond

The discomfort I felt when I'd piss was another lesson in listening to my body. It began shortly after Lindy returned from her trip to South Dakota with Dena, although I didn't see the connection at the time. I also felt some discomfort when Lindy and I made love.

It was so vague I wasn't even sure it was real. I couldn't really remember how it felt when I would come in the past, but in some way it didn't feel as good as it had. I saw Dr. Roberts several times and got all kinds of different medications for the infection. I asked him if the infection could be affecting my sexual response, but he seemed a bit uncomfortable and said he didn't know. For some reason I didn't feel comfortable talking about it with Lindy. She seemed to be enjoying herself just fine since she got back from South Dakota.

I'd always trusted doctors to know what they were doing, but I was beginning to wonder about Dr. Roberts. He'd been giving me one medication after another and nothing seemed to be helping. Finally he suggested a "small" operation to remove part of my prostate gland which would clear things up. The thought of being cut into scared the shit out of me. When I suggested to him that I'd like to get another opinion he seemed offended, although he told me to go ahead if I didn't trust him.

I went to the medical library at the hospital and read what I could find about prostate trouble. I found it was generally more prevalent in older men, though it could be a problem at any age. What really scared me was a line that said viewing the prostate under the scope was a tricky business. Many physicians who were inexperienced would make the mistake of saying the prostate was enlarged when in fact it was not. I had this image of Dr. Roberts, who had done most of his work with older men, thinking, "Now I've got a young one I can try out my new toy on and see how it works." What scared me the most was knowing that I had come close to trusting the "doctor" over my own intuition because he was a "specialist" and must know the best thing for me.

I finally went to a different urologist, feeling a little guilty to have deserted Dr. Roberts. To my relief and surprise, Dr. Evert took me off all the medications. The burning and discomfort disappeared after a few weeks, leaving only the vague feeling that my ejaculation wasn't as strong. Dr. Evert acknowledged that he didn't know that much about sexual problems and referred me to a specialist in San Francisco. For once, one of these goddamned doctors had been honest enough to say, "I don't know" instead of getting out his knife to cut the problem away.

I met with Dr. Finkle in San Francisco, a specialist on urology and sex. He was very straight with me. He told me he could make a lot more money doing surgery than talking to people about their sexual problems, so he needed to be paid in advance. There was no guarantee that my sexual relations would improve, but after one session we could decide together whether to go on. He did a complete physical with real gentleness, unlike my other doctor, who seemed to delight in watching me cry out when he stuck his finger up my ass to "massage the prostate." Finkle seemed reassured when I told him that neither of us had an affair during this time when our sex had been so unsatisfying. I told him I'd been having the prostate trouble for about a year, and he seemed interested in what was going on in my life during that time. "Nothing that I can think of," I told him. His prescription was simple, almost too simple for a $50-an-hour specialist. "Drink two gallons of water a day to flush out your system, then have no sex for two weeks. When you do have sex again make the setting romantic and conducive to good lovemaking."

"Jesus, doc, I can handle everything except the two gallons of water a day. I won't ever be able to leave the bathroom." He just smiled and said to do it. He said not to worry if our lovemaking didn't improve immediately, but to give it a little time. After a year of urinary discomfort, disinterest in sex, unsatisfying sex when I would come almost before I could get my cock inside, and anger and impatience from Lindy, I was ready to try anything.

"Give it a try and come back in two months," he said. I left the office with more hope than I'd felt in a long, long time.

After seeing Dr. Finkle I began to wonder if anything had happened during the time I was having "problems." It began to dawn on me that there was a connection between my problems with my cock and my feelings about the events in my life over the past year. When I began thinking about it, it was all so obvious. Of course there was a connection. After Lindy returned from her trip I felt much more pressure to perform. I needed to keep pace with the unknown men she may have met—men I was too afraid to ask about.

In my fear I had deadened my feelings. But my cock wasn't dead and it had been expressing my inner feelings all along. "I'm scared. Lindy returns from her trip all excited and wants to be more sexual and wants me to do it more often. I'm not sure what this is all about and I'm not sure I want to 'do it bigger and better.' I'm not even sure I like sex as much since she's become more aggressive. She calls it 'premature ejaculation'; I call it 'I want to get this over with as quickly as possible.' Now she wants to act on that 'head tripper' Jed's idea to have an 'open marriage.' Well, let me tell you. Your head may think you want an open marriage, but take it from someone who is closer to the center of things. Your cock knows you don't, and you're scared shitless. And what thanks do I get for having the guts to speak out? They want to cut a little bit out of me. I ought to just keep my head down and my little mouth shut."

WHY JOHNNY CAN'T HAVE KIDS

Michael Castleman

The great American sperm crisis came in 1975. Actually the crisis began sometime in the 1920s, but it was not until the mid-70s that reports appeared indicating that American men's sperm counts had declined drastically over the past 50 years. At first, the reports were published not as hard news but as filler material, often ending in light-hearted speculation that the downward trend might be caused by either increased sexual activity or tight-fitting jockey shorts.

In September 1979, however, the levity ended when a Florida State University chemist suggested that toxic chemicals—not sex or underwear—were responsible for the decreased sperm counts. Dr. Ralph Dougherty examined semen samples from 132 student volunteers and found alarmingly high levels of four toxic chemicals; DDT, polychlorinated biphenyls (PCBs) hexachlorobenzene and pentachlorophenol, the first three of which are known or suspected carcinogens and teratogens (substances that cause birth defects). The students' modal sperm count (most frequently occurring) was 20 million per milliliter (ml), compared with modes of 60 million/ml in a 1974 study and 100 million/ml in a 1929 study. Dougherty reported that thirty of the students, twenty-three percent, had sperm counts so low that most doctors would consider them effectively sterile—below 20 million/ml. Subsequently, Dougherty and his co-workers identified another carcinogen/mutagen in seminal fluid: Tris, the flame retardant once added to fabrics that failed to meet government flammability standards. Tris is now banned.

Some epidemiologists challenged the extrapolation of Dougherty's findings to the general population, saying that the students may have been exposed to higher concentrations of seminal pollutants than the general population. Dougherty retorts that, if anything, the students' exposure was less than average: "Most toxic chemical exposure is occupational, but these men were in school, not in factories. Florida is a relatively clean part of the country. There is no chemical industry here, and the major agricultural product around Tallahassee is timber, a low-pesticide crop." Dougherty said his findings were suggestive, not definitive.

Genotoxins is a term coined to refer to those substances that, in men, may cause one or more of the following: fertility impairment, testicular cancer, structural sperm abnormalities or birth defects. The catalog of known genotoxic substances includes pesticides, herbicides and industrial chemicals. It also includes a number of substances that have less widely known adverse effects on men's—and sometimes on women's—genetic health; tobacco, marijuana, certain antibiotics, diethylstilbestrol (DES), lead, X-rays, some forms of artificial light and plutonium. Video display terminals have recently become suspect.

The most notorious testicular assailants are the halogenated hydrocarbons. These complex chemicals have figured prominently in recent workplace sterility scandals. Dibromochloropropane (DBCP), for example, sterilized almost all male workers who handled it at Occidental Petroleum's Lathrop, California, factory. California banned DBCP in 1977, and after residues of the chemical were identified in samples of a variety of fruit crops, the Environmental Protection Agency (EPA) banned it nationally in 1979 (except for use on pineapples, where it supposedly leaves no residue). Despite the ban, DBCP persists in the environment, and chances are it recently crossed your lips. Two years after the California ban, the pesticide turned up in water samples from hundreds of wells, many of which supply drinking water to communities in the San Joaquin Valley. California health officials ordered the most seriously contaminated wells plugged, but DBCP-contaminated water continues to flow into California homes and into the irrigation systems that supply water to the leading fruit- and vegetable-growing region in the United States.

The pesticide Kepone sterilized workers involved in its production at the Life Sciences Products Company in Hopewell, Virginia, in 1975. Kepone was also discharged into the James River, which empties into Chesapeake Bay, where it later turned up in commercial fish. Virginia instituted a "cleanup campaign," which concentrated less on cleaning up than on improving the image of Chesapeake Bay fish. Kepone was later discovered in rodents near the bay, having worked its way up the food chain.

Dioxin, an ingredient of the Vietnam War herbicide Agent Orange, causes severe reproductive deformities in mice and monkeys at extremely low concentrations (less than 500 parts per *trillion*). Experts acknowledge it to be one of the most toxic substances on earth. Unexpectedly high birth defect rates have been found among children of Vietnam veterans, more than one million of whom are conservatively estimated to have been exposed to dioxin. Among these birth defects are spinal malformations, a defect that is also appearing in record numbers in Vietnam. The herbicide 2,4,5-T, which also contains dioxin, was sprayed for years on power-line and railroad rights-of-way. Seven million pounds a year were sprayed until 1979, when the EPA restricted its use because it was implicated in high rates of miscarriage among Oregon women living near sprayed areas. The EPA still permits annual spraying of two million pounds of 2,4,5-T on rice and range lands.

DBCP, Kepone and dioxin had long been known to cause sterility and other genotoxic effects in mice. But the industries involved in their manufacture either suppressed the information or argued that the effects could not be extrapolated to humans. Today, however, there is general scientific agreement that substances known to be genotoxic in mice can be presumed to be genotoxic in humans.

Other widely used pesticides and industrial chemicals with proved genotoxic effects in mammals include ethylene dibromide (EDB), malathion (the pesticide sprayed around the San Francisco Bay Area to kill the medfly), lead, cadmium, mercury, nickel, carbaryl, dinitrotoluene, vinyl chloride and chloroprene. The list will surely grow. According to a recent report for the Council on Environmental Quality (CEQ), at least twenty common industrial chemicals have been linked to human reproductive impairment, and of the 55,000 industrial chemicals currently in use, "few have been thoroughly tested for reproductive effects."

In recent years, considerable attention has been focused on the risks to unborn children from pregnant women's use of over-the-counter and prescription drugs. Considerably less attention has been focused on the genotoxic effects of drugs on men, but ample new research shows sperm to be highly susceptible to damage from drugs long considered "safe."

DES, for example, the synthetic estrogen known to cause vaginal cancer and other reproductive abnormalities in some daughters of women who took it while pregnant, has been shown to cause a variety of testicular abnormalities and possibly cancer, in many of the nation's estimated 1.3 million DES sons.

Ten antibiotics—among them penicillin, tetracycline and trimethoprim (brand names Bactrim and Septra)—also temporarily suppress sperm production, an effect seldom discussed in medical literature. And you don't even have to take antibiotic drugs to have them reach your testicles. Large quantities are fed to U.S. livestock for epidemic control in crowded feedlots. In 1979, the General Accounting Office reported that fourteen percent of the nation's meat and poultry was contaminated with illegal chemical residues, among them, the antibiotics, hormones and pesticides already mentioned.

Other drugs have similar effects. Among stress-related illnesses affecting men in their reproductive years, ulcers and ulcerative colitis are two whose incidence is fast increasing. The drugs commonly used to treat them, cimetidine (Tagamet) for ulcers and sulphasalazine (Azulfidine) for ulcerative colitis, both temporarily impair fertility. The *New England Journal of Medicine* reported that Tagamet, which recently replaced Valium as the most widely prescribed drug in the country, reduced men's sperm counts an average of 43 percent. The journal suggested that Tagamet should be used with caution by "young men who wish to maintain their fertility."

The list of spermatotoxic drugs continues to grow. The CEQ reported that at least forty drugs in current use are known to impair reproduction, and thousands of others on the market today have never been tested for genotoxicity.

Radioactivity is also a major area of concern. Radioactive substances ingested by mammals tend to collect in specific organs. For example, iodine 131 gravitates to the thyroid gland; plutonium, the main ingredient of atomic weapons and one of the most potent carcinogens on earth, accumulates in the testicles. Before 1940, no trace of this synthetic element existed, but above-ground atomic weapons tests and releases from nuclear facilities have dispersed an estimated 10,000 pounds of it into the atmosphere. Today, every person on earth is believed to carry detectable traces of plutonium in his or her body.

In 1979, epidemiologist Dr. Carl Johnson, then Health Department director for Jefferson County, Colorado, surveyed cancer rates around Rocky Flats. The Rockwell International factory there produces plutonium components for nuclear weapons. Rocky Flats has recorded many routine and accidental plutonium releases in the past twenty-five years, including one in 1957 that was about 19,000 times today's permissible limit. Using National Cancer Institute data, Johnson compared cancer rates upwind and downwind from the plant and found an excess cancer rate of twenty-four percent in men living downwind. The most striking difference occurred in the incidence of testicular cancer: seventeen cases upwind, forty downwind—an excess rate of 140 percent.

Plutonium is not the only source of ionizing radiation aimed at the testicles. X-rays have long been known to cause sterility and structural changes in sperm. Whose testicles are at greatest risk from radiation? Nuclear industry workers certainly, but hospital workers are also exposed, according to *Radiation on the Job*. Health care accounts for a staggering ninety percent of human-made radiation exposure. In the United States alone, some 700 million X-rays and 70 million nuclear medicine procedures are prescribed each year, an average of 3.4 per person. As a result, many medical personnel are classified as "nuclear workers" by the EPA Office of Radiation Programs; health workers, in fact, comprise forty-nine percent of workers classified as such. Nuclear workers are allowed to be exposed to ten times as much radiation per year as non-nuclear workers. The problem is that most hospital workers have no idea that they may be classified as nuclear workers, and a federal government survey showed that most hospitals offer inadequate staff training on the hazards of radiation and how best to avoid exposure.

Twenty years ago, doctors said ten percent of couples were unable to have children and men's organic problems accounted for ten percent of the infertility. Today the situation has changed dramatically. Dr. Bruce Rappaport, director of the Infertility Clinic at San Francisco Planned Parenthood, reports that an estimated twenty percent of couples are unable to conceive and that men's organic problems account for about 50 percent of the infertility. These estimates, however, should be viewed with some caution, Rappaport adds, because until recently infertility was almost always automatically blamed on women. Higher rates of infertility in men may therefore reflect either a new biological trend or a belated recognition of facts long ignored. Rappaport says he leans toward the former explanation: "The problem is environmental pollution. Doctors often say, 'Well, there's better detection nowadays.' And there is. But there has also been an explosion of spermatotoxic substances into the environment."

Testicular cancer rates have doubled among whites and tripled among blacks since 1950, according to the National Cancer Institute. Although it accounts for only one percent of cancers in men, testicular cancer has become one of the most *common* solid malignant tumors in men aged fifteen to thirty-four. It has also been striking men increasingly earlier in life. A century ago, testicular cancer was virtually unheard of in men under fifty. By 1969, men under twenty-five accounted for twelve percent of cases. Today, they account for more than twenty-six percent.

The testicles are so sensitive to toxins that several authorities in the field have suggested that the sperm counts of workers be used to test the safety of industrial chemicals. If workers' sperm counts fell after introduction of a new chemical into the workplace, it could be presumed hazardous. "It may sound like something out of a Woody Allen movie," Rappaport says, "but spermatotoxic substances are everywhere. There's an enormous population exposed to known spermatotoxin every day. Without adequate monitoring of the context and

251

quality of semen and of men's reproductive health, this country could be in big trouble quite soon."

Implementation of Rappaport's suggestion would surely provide hilarity among the nation's workers, but the guffaws would in many instances give way to eerie silence when the results came in.

Every man alive is being exposed to pollutants that impair men's reproductive capabilities. Some of these substances may one day even be used as chemical contraceptives for men. But to be acceptable in a democracy, birth control must be practiced voluntarily.

Use of the most notorious spermatotoxic substances (DBCP, DES, dioxin) has been restricted, but even when banned, these substances tend to persist in the environment. They work their way into the food chain, and as they move up the chain, their concentrations tend to increase. Humans occupy the highest position in that food chain, a perch that appears increasingly precarious. Unless genotoxins are removed from the environment, the generation now in its infancy may have considerable difficulty obeying the Bible's first and most fundamental edict: Be fruitful and multiply.

PROTECT YOUR FERTILITY

A permanent solution to the sperm crisis would require sweeping political and social action, which appears unlikely in the near future. Nonetheless, men can take significant steps at an individual level to safeguard their fertility and genetic health:

• Do not panic. If this article has caused a dull ache between your legs, you do *not* have testicular cancer. It appears as a *painless* lump or swelling in the testicles. Even if you have been exposed to one or more of the spermatotoxins mentioned, bear in mind that most fertility impairment effects tend to be temporary, unless you have received a high dose of the toxin. Dr. Bruce Rappaport says that sixty percent of the couples who visit the San Francisco Planned Parenthood Infertility Clinic conceive a child within six months.

• Research the genotoxicity of substances where you work that you think may be harmful. Write or call the *National Institute for Occupational Safety and Health. NIOSH* has a large library and through its health hazard evaluation program can send teams of medical workers into the field for medical testing and sperm samples at workplaces where employees are believed to be exposed to toxins. Contact Dr. Philip Landrigan, *NIOSH,* 4676 Columbia Parkway, Cincinnati, Ohio 45226 or call (513) 684-2427 for help.

• Report exposures to genotoxic substances to co-workers, union reps, local media and state and federal *Occupational Safety and Health Administrations.*

• Learn how to perform a testicular self-exam. This quick, simple, painless procedure—similar to a breast self-exam for women—can detect testicular tumors early, when treatment gives best results. Free how-to brochures may be obtained from the *American Cancer Society* office nearest you.

• Ask your mother if she took DES when she was pregnant with you. If she does not recall, ask if she had any miscarriages before she became pregnant

252

with you. If so, she may have taken the synthetic hormone. DES sons should be examined by a urologist. For more information, contact *DES Action:* in the east, at Long Island Jewish-Hillside Medical Center, New Hyde Park, New York, 11040; in the west, at 1638-B Haight Street, San Francisco, California 94117. Include a stamped, self-addressed envelope. *DES Action* will send you an excellent pamphlet on DES sons. The organization also publishes the best newsletter on DES exposure, *DES Action Voice,* quarterly, available for fifteen dollars per year.

- Eat foods rich in zinc. This trace mineral is particularly important to men's fertility and reproductive health. The typical American diet is zinc-deficient because processing removes most of it from foods. High-zinc foods include peas, carrots, eggs, milk, whole grains, nuts, and sunflower seeds. If you eat a balanced diet, you probably do not need commercial zinc supplements sold at health food stores. But if you take zinc supplements, do *not* exceed the recommended dose; toxic reactions are possible. If you are curious about your zinc level, you might consider hair analysis, a relatively new medical test that is increasingly popular with holistic practitioners. The test, which costs about forty to fifty dollars, involves the analysis of a lock of your hair to measure levels of many minerals, including the spermatotoxic heavy metals.

- Take vitamin C. It helps eliminate lead and other heavy metals from the body.

- Wash fruits and vegetables carefully *with soap* or soak them for a few minutes in a mild solution of water and vinegar. This will not eliminate all pesticide residues—systemic pesticides are in plant pulp, not on the skin—but it still helps.

- Drink only in moderation. Alcohol depresses production of testosterone, the male sex hormone.

- Don't smoke anything. Tobacco and marijuana have been linked to reduced sperm counts and structural abnormalities.

- Ask physicians and pharmacists about the reproductive effects of *any* prescribed drugs.

- Avoid unnecessary X-rays. The *Health Research Group* publishes *Medical and Dental X-rays: A Consumer's Guide to Avoiding Unnecessary Exposure,* $3.25 from HRG, 2000 P Street, Suite 708, Washington, D.C. 20036. And every health worker should read *Radiation on the Job: A Manual for Health Workers on Ionizing Radiation,* three dollars from the *Committee Against Reproductive Hazards* of the Coalition for the Medical Rights of Women, 1638-B Haight Street, San Francisco, California 94117.

- If you are trying to conceive, keep your scrotum cool; no tight underwear, no hot baths; heat kills sperm.

- If you work in an operating room, try to have "gas scavenging traps" placed on all anesthesia machines. These reduce worker exposure to waste anesthetics.

- If you are concerned about your sperm count and want medical advice, consult a urologist or a family-planning clinic.

253

GETTING A VASECTOMY

Jed Diamond

It took a long time before I was ready to hear what my cock was trying to tell
.me. For years, I had been thinking about having a vasectomy. It had been clear
to me for some time that I didn't want to father any more children by design or
by accident, and I wanted a form of birth control that I could count on. I
couldn't justify telling myself it was the woman's responsibility any longer. Yet,
since Lindy and I had been in an open relationship and had been sexual with
other people, I had had two pregnancy scares and one actual pregnancy. When
I read the letter saying she was sure that the night we made love was the night
she conceived, I was terrified. What would this mean for my life? What did she
want from me? I breathed a sigh of relief when I continued reading and found
that she was happy she was pregnant, wanted nothing from me, and that she
and her boyfriend had decided to have the baby and put it up for adoption.
Then I felt hurt. There would be a child I helped conceive somewhere in the
world and I'd never have a chance to know her. Somehow, I even knew it would
be a girl.

I read everything I could find on vasectomy and talked to friends who had
them. I knew in my head they were safe, relatively painless, and easy. What it
got down to was my terror at the thought of being cut into. When I realized that
was the fear, I did a meditation, feeling somewhat foolish, and asked my cock
what it thought about having a vasectomy. The answer I got was to go ahead
and have it done. It was right for me.

A week later, I was sitting in the waiting room of the doctor's office. I had
taken the tranquilizer he had prescribed two hours before. I was still terrified,
but drowsy. I brought my mother along for moral support and to drive me
home afterwards. I knew I wasn't one of those macho men who would jump
back on his Harley afterwards and ride off looking for someone to try it out on.
I planned to take the weekend plus Monday off if I needed it and just lie in bed
and take care of myself.

I went into the doctor's inner office with him and the nurse, pulled down my
pants and got up on the table. The air was cold where I'd shaved myself in preparation for the "operation." The actual procedure was minor, even for someone
like me who was terrified of doctors, and particularly doctors with knives. The
tranquilizer had made me drowsy. The shots into my balls were much less painful than I was sure they would be, certainly less than novocaine in the mouth.
I couldn't even feel the two little cuts in my scrotum, and within half an hour
I was walking proudly, though a bit gingerly, back to the waiting room.

The healing went quickly. I took the extra day even though I felt fine, wore
a jock strap as directed to give the added support I needed. Two weeks later I
returned, shot a specimen in a tube, and they confirmed that I was "shooting
blanks." Shortly thereafter, I tried it out for the first time, with a little trepidation

254

ιhat it wouldn't work right. It felt great, and I had the added bonus of being told that my come tasted better than before.

THE CRIPPLE AND THE MAN

Jai Noa

In the first and second grade at the school for the handicapped, Joey and I were the normal ones. The other students had big hearing aids (with boxes in their shirt pockets), or talked funny, or wore leg braces, or drooled a lot. Surrounded by kids with such obvious differences, we seemed normal. We each had a mild case of cerebral palsy; but I had no idea what that was or how it applied to me. I wore "nightshoes," and I went to see nice old Dr. Phelps who let me pick out a lollipop before I left. But I was naive about my social status as a cripple.

"Why are you walking like that?" (Was I walking differently from all the other kids?) This was the first question I had to confront the next year on the playground of the regular school. I decided to stand still in one spot so no one would notice how I walked. But then, "Why are you standing like that?" (Oh no, it must be that I even stand funny.) I began to spend recesses sitting by a telephone pole.

The surprise and shame that came with the sense of myself as a freak were some of the most intense and dreadful feelings of my childhood. This was only the beginning of a growing awareness of the ways I wasn't normal. Many of the most significant differences were gender-specific. More and more, I shared a vague affinity with Pinnochio in his yearning to be a real live *boy.*

The boys played sports. I could have played with them, but they and I both knew that I couldn't play very well. Every year as they developed their athletic skills, the gap grew wider. Boys play sports to win. What was the point of playing if I couldn't contribute to their victory?

I spent my time with the few other boys who didn't play ball. My one close friend was named Ross. We soon staked out our own territory. We were separated from the boys' playground by a street full of girls. We called our club the Secret Silent Service System. In the words of our club song we were "the best club in the world; there are only two members in it, but we still think it's the best. . . better than all the rest." We vowed to "fight off all our enemies." While the other boys played sports, we engaged in fantasy adventure, like righteous terrorists in exile. Still, we were uncomfortably aware of our status as outsiders.

At times Ross would flirt with being admitted to the mainstream of boydom. One day he was engaged in playful rivalry for a basketball with a few other boys. I chased the ball and knocked it away from him. He began to pummel me in the face with his elbows. He was furious. Not so much because I had hit the ball, but because I had tried to follow him into the boy world. His blows caused

255

my head to jerk back, and his voice was meaner and tougher than I had ever heard it. My head was pushed into the electric meter once, and then again. I put my hand to the back of my head and realized it was bleeding. I went into the school with blood down the back of my white shirt. And I lied to the teacher so my friend wouldn't get in trouble.

My overwhelming experience during middle childhood was as a boy who was incompetent at virtually every activity which was a mark of male identity. At Boy Scout meetings, when I did play baseball, someone would run the bases for me when I hit the ball. My carpentry attempts were crude, and it didn't occur to me that I might improve with practice. And Brandon, who picked a fight with me a few times, landed the sharpest jab by jeering, "You fight like a girl!"

In the eighth grade a couple of boys made an attempt to include me in their games. I was told how to hike a football and I could do this well enough. But I had neither the physical self-confidence nor the agressive "instincts" to rush an opponent. I also served as a first-base umpire for a time. Since both my knowledge of baseball rules and my ability to make quick accurate decisions were pretty lousy, I was soon ejected from the game. By the time I was thirteen, my inexperience—probably even more than my physical limitations—had a decisive impact on my chances of breaking into the sports of my classmates.

Exclusion from sports means exclusion from the comaraderie, rites, and secrets of the world of young males. As a result, the male cripple is a sissy by the time he reaches puberty. Throughout adolescence, he suffers an anguished search for affection, intimacy, and sexual fulfillment. Before I try to describe the nature of this suffering, it will help to examine the paradigm for the expression of passionate affection in this society.

Romanticism as an ideology asserts the primacy of a human ideal in the quest for interpersonal fulfillment. The three general traits which characterize the romantically ideal man are handsomeness, strength, and self-confidence. Other more specific attributes such as "noble" facial features, muscular build, physical strength, and engaging personality can be a part of a romantic ideal.

Romanticism, like all creeds, provides its adherents with a false sense of security against the uncertainty and lack of perfection in the real world. When the romantic man finds his object he thinks, "I have fallen in love." He has succeeded in essentially reducing another person to a set of fixed ideals. He begins to surrender all other values at the feet of this idol. This process is usually quite subtle and not clearly recognized, but the series of self-betrayals (and the self-deceptions used to mask them) are not less compelling because they are disguised. Furthermore, everyday experiences which should suggest that the beloved one does not measure up to the romantic ideal are usually not enough to immediately break the self-imposed spell.

The male cripple is the antithesis of the romantic ideal. He is viewed as physically unattractive, weak and insecure. Having been largely removed from the male social scene, he tends to lack social poise. Often he does not project qualities conventionally thought of as masculine. In any case he is rarely thought to exude virile allure. As a life-long member of an inferior caste, he finds stability and serenity elusive. Emotionally he is at war with a society which alternately treats him as a monster, a child, or an asexual nice guy, but hardly ever as a man.

During high school, a number of girls were the objects of my romantic daydreams. I did not date or become friends with any of them. And the communication of romantic feelings was furtive. For example, when I was out of state with my family, I mailed an anonymous note to Jeanne. Another time, I slipped a ticket to a Valentine's dance on Kathy's table in the cafeteria. It was most important for me to avoid detection, even though I also wanted to make myself known. But my interest in various girls had to remain a frightening secret because I perceived myself as an unacceptable candidate. I had little doubt but that rejection and embarrassment would accompany any expression of sexual desire, however tentative. The stereotypes I had learned about myself had become self-fulfilling prophecies. Women were taboo to me, although they remained my most significant preoccupation. Thus the social and psychological basis existed for my transition from sissy to creep.

I use the idiom "creep" in a very special sense. "Creep" refers to the *ashamed sexuality* of most men, which is an inescapable fact of our social life, and one which each of us must confront sooner or later. It is ironic that if there is an almost universal manner in which men share a common crippledness, it is in the realm of sexual expression. Conversely, it is primarily through his sexuality that the male cripple comes to participate in the universal male world. Thus, the man as creep is a cripple, and the cripple as creep becomes a man.

A creature of low self-esteem, the creep feels he cannot develop sustained intimate friendships with others. Despairing of intersubjective happiness, he takes the other as an object to exploit as best he can. This is a cynical attempt to validate himself through domination. The delightful joys of erotic pleasure are turned into their opposite by a guilt-ridden quest for power. The creep then is a voyeur, a pornophile, and an exhibitionist. He enjoys not only invading the sexual space of others, but also feeling that his penis has the power to cause a reaction, even if only one of discomfort or disgust.

The heterosexual male creep tries to reduce all women to whores, i.e., to what he thinks of as dirty sluts who are so low they would fuck someone as contemptible as himself (and thereby elevate him)! He may cruise bars or parties in search of a drunken easy lay. In his masturbation fantasies, he chooses a woman who is "too good" for him and envisions her as a slave of sexual passion.

The creep is the man who fails to live up to the romantic ideal, and who feels crushed, bitter and resigned to this failure. And since most men suffer defeat in the romantic meritocracy at one time or another, the cripple can find an identity partially located in the world of men. Increasingly, during his teenage years, and for an indefinite period of time thereafter, the cripple can find a bond with any men who indulge in misogyny.

Yet, while most other men are able to find reassurance in a degree of conformity to the manly ideal posited by romanticism (a brief escape from creepy desperation), the cripple is not so sure to. The predominent social message he has received is, "You are a pitiful soul who needs help." It is this attitude more than

257

overt hostility or fearful avoidance which is the cripple's worst emotional scourge.

Adults, including my parents and teachers, always seemed to exaggerate and distort the limitations stemming from my disability. My mother always expressed the view that activity beyond my usual routine would be too tiring for me (and my father never disagreed). My teachers would make special allowances for me, suggesting that I was not capable of the quantity or quality of work the other pupils did. It was embarrassing and humiliating to hear adults, time and time again, instruct my peers to "Do this for him," or "Help him do that." It was also effective. I learned to let others do things, since I was presumably incapable or incompetent.

Increasingly, I grew resentful of this form of "being nice," of protecting me from myself. I became distrustful of almost all friendly overtures since they so often were a subtle and condescending form of social invalidation. Altruists offer untender sweetness in presenting themselves as "good" persons. However, the cripple soon realizes that such people remain unavailable and inaccessible to him.

Their liberal attitude seeks to assimilate him into the cultural mainstream by pretending that he's just a normal person, and by wishing away his subjective and objective reality with good-cheer preppiness. Good-hearted positivists would train the cripple for a job, make a few more building entrances accessible, and provide counseling services. Anything to make him feel like one of the gang. But behind their smiles it is painfully obvious how sorry they feel for us. And such pity betrays their profound ineffectuality.

Perhaps the most revealing sign of the fake consciousness of the liberal is the recent correct-speak term, "physically challenged." It is true that persons who are suddenly afflicted by a disabling illness or injury may face extraordinary physical challenges for a period of time. But after a while, the physical dimensions of the affliction become relatively routine, while the psychosocial and interpersonal dimensions are challenging, or more precisely, taunting. In the case of men who have suffered combat injuries or sporting mishaps, the term "physically challenged" suggests that a macho will-to-power (a prime source of past fulfillment and identity for many of these men) can make everything all right. The inference is that if they have the stamina to reconstitute themselves in an athletic fashion (e.g., to become wheelchair jocks) they can salvage a place in the world of normal men.

The only real hope for the crippled male is a social movement which is willing to mount a radical challenge to the everyday lives of men. We need a men's movement that is as unsettling to conventional masculinity as cripples are to normalcy. It is not helpful to moralistically denounce and ostracize (repress) the creep. The creep can only undergo a metamorphosis in the light of day. All men feel creepy from time to time. Moreover, if it is true that this feeling lurks in our groins, then it is also true that all men sense that this kind of suffering is a high price to pay for emotional survival.

We need to develop circles of support which will challenge our creepiness in a manner that will ensure its obsolescence. But none of this will be enough if we continue to keep one foot in the ideology of romanticism. Here is where understanding the cripple's subjectivity is most valuable. Because he continually confronts his outsider status vis-à-vis the male world, the crippled man's negativity toward male culture is not merely analytical or ideological, it is experiential. On the one hand, he experiences himself as an ironic salvation from stale maleness. On the other hand, he sometimes feels like a trapped victim—a powerless sissy in macholand.

Sometimes my own stake in the male culture feels very small, and the potential for realizing my desires very great. I scamper about as if I were in the midst of an erotic cartoon of my own invention. The soldier, the policeman, the boss, and the boyfriend can neither understand nor suppress me. All they have to offer me is my crippledness, and I toss it back in their faces.

We cripples are beginning to refuse the roles of "handicapped," "retarded," and "crazy." We are breaking free of the emotional shackles these roles imply. We want a world where our value is not measured by standards of "productivity," but where satisfying activity can become an end in itself. A world without false oppositions of beautiful and ugly, strong and weak, manly and wimpy. For if loving communities of proud people desire to create a world in which they can live as free, autonomous, guiltless persons, they will have to embrace us too.

Chapter 13:
Men and Women's Issues

ISSUES WITH WOMEN

MEN HAVE ISSUES, TOO

Robert A. Sides

My experience is that the public is not ready to hear about things male, though anything from Working Woman Wok Techniques to Makeup As The Billionth Example Of Male Oppression gets front-page coverage in the *New York Times*.

THE CLICK TOCKS FOR MEN, TOO

John Gordon

Some time ago, the quite excellent writer Jane O'Reilly became famous in feminist circles for an article defining the phenomenon she designated as "click." "Click" is a female recognition of incongruity—the moment when a woman suddenly sees for the first time the sexist import of some statement, action, or mode of behavior which she had formerly taken for granted. Gloria Steinem gave a good example: She was watching "The CBS Evening News" as it was showing a clip of President Nixon reporting on his search for a Supreme Court justice: "We are seeking," he said, "the best man for the job." The best *man* for the job! Click! She threw her pillow at the television, called up her friends, and started the ball rolling.

That was all about ten years ago. We have our woman justice now, and many another change in the same direction. The "NO COMMENT" section of *Ms.*

notwithstanding, just about everyone must acknowledge—Betty Friedan, for example, *has* acknowledged—that the occasions for those feminist "clicks" are much fewer and fainter and farther between than they used to be.

But. Last June 30 *I* was watching "The CBS Evening News." It was the terminal date for the ERA, and about a third of the broadcast was devoted to speeches by women saying, on the basis of no evidence whatsoever, that the amendment's defeat was the work of chauvinist men wanting to keep them in their places, that it all went to show how oppressed and discriminated against American women still were. Then came the next news item. The next news item, delivered with no acknowledgement whatsoever of incongruous juxtaposition, was about the first young man—the first, doubtless of thousands—to be prosecuted for failing to register for the all-male draft.

Then I opened a newspaper and came across the information that Helen Reddy was suing her husband for divorce and demanding property and child support. Helen Reddy, of course, (the newspaper did not consider the fact fit to print), is the one who made herself famous and quite rich by warbling about how she was Woman, strong and free, and through with depending on men.

Then I opened my mail, which included the clipping of an adverse review of my book from the *Los Angeles Times,* the gravamen of the criticism being that my book whines about men being sent off to be killed in wars, whereas everyone knows that men are the ones who make wars. This was, as I say, on June 30, at the end of a three-month period during which the main news event—covered, I presume, by the *Los Angeles Times*—was the Falkland Islands war, as waged by one Margaret Thatcher.

What I mean to say is, *click.* I am a teacher of literature, and one of my main jobs has always been to make students aware of a text's possible irony—aware, for instance, that when Swift's Gulliver waxes enthusiastic about English civilization and gives as his example news about the latest thing in munitions, there is a discrepancy between the way he sees things and the way they really are which is not inadvertent—which is, in fact, the main point. Such recognitions are essential for an intelligent reading of literature. And also, I think, for a nondeluded life. As I recall myself when I was the age that my students now are, for instance, what I'm afraid I see is a Gulliver, thinking myself quite sharp but actually blind to the grossest incongruities. In the summer of 1967 I was traveling around Europe with a girlfriend; we had a fight, decided to split up, and divided our pool of money between us, and in spite of our other differences agreed that she should get almost two-thirds of it, because everyone knew that women needed more comfort than men. Gulliver! Gullible twit! And during the same period, when I was busy thinking up every conceivable argument against the draft laws, including the fact that they tended to discriminate against minorities, it never occurred to me, not once, that they discriminated absolutely against the minority of which I was a member by birth. Deluded dolt!

Anyway, I have since had my consciousness raised, and come to see that at the moment we inhabit a culture which is just fruity with incongruity of the kind Jane O'Reilly once wrote about, with the critical difference that by now almost all of it pertains to the lives of men. Under the abortion laws, pregnant women have sole power to decide whether or not to have the babies for whose upkeep, under the divorce laws, the fathers will be held accountable. Click. The same people who twelve years ago insisted on the resignation of a presidential adviser when he suggested that premenstrual tension might limit the capacities of some women are now demanding that premenstrual tension be an admissible defense in the trials of accused women murderers and child abusers. Click. The people who find pornography intolerable because it reduces women to their genitalia line up reverently for Judy Chicago's "Dinner Party" table of stylized vaginas. Click. The same people who coined the term "sexist" have been supporting and encouraging a hate-literature industry dedicated to demonstrating that all males are rapists, Nazis, and child molesters. Click.

Men have historically been slower than women to pick up on the nuances of the changing social contract, but the incongruities of which I speak are well past the stage of nuance, and spotting them is like picking blackberries: as soon as you see the first one, you start seeing hundreds. Our job now is to help our fellow man to see that first blackberry. After that, the clicks will start coming on their own. It's bound to happen sooner or later, and the sooner, the better.

MEN ARE DISADVANTAGED, TOO

Richard Haddad

It does appear, upon examination of some of our laws, that women have been accorded a "second-class citizenship," a popular phrase today. And there's no denying that a goodly number of male lawmakers, past and present, have had some fairly rigid opinions about the "place" of women in our society. However, you don't have to do much research to discover that they've had some fairly rigid opinions about the place of men in our society as well.

The same lawmakers, for instance, who denied property rights to women also mandated alimony payments for men and set up a social security system which mostly benefits women. The same lawmakers who frowned on working women also frowned on vagrant men. The same lawmakers who will pay a woman through the welfare system to stay home and raise her children won't pay a man to do the same thing. And exactly who was it who decided that only men should die fighting in war?

UNEQUAL EQUALITY

Frank S. Zepezauer

For married men the beginning of the school year was the most irksome. It wasn't because we faced two more semesters with the often provoking American teenager or because summer salary negotiations had disappointed us again.

No, what irked us were the September reports of the jet set, those teachers who had flown to Europe for the summer or had toured the Orient or had checked out the latest Broadway season or had picked up college credits in the Sierras. Their return to campus in fall re-opened the daily chit-chat about their travels. They exchanged tips about restaurants in Florence, boutiques in Paris, pensions in Vienna. They gossiped about colleagues they bumped into at the London American Express. They compared exchange rates and Eurail prices. Some had grown so sophisticated that they no longer bothered to talk about Europe at all. Everyone went there. Now, a trip to Sri Lanka, *that* might deserve comment.

Gathered almost defensively at one cafeteria table, the family men munched away on their sandwiches listening to infinite variations on the same theme, dreaming that maybe some day, when the kids were a little older and when we'd moved up the pay scale, we might have enough put aside to take the wife and kids over to Europe for a few weeks, some day maybe, if something didn't happen like it always did to families and if college expenses for our oldest didn't hit us too quickly.

We differed in other ways, too, we family guys, and the funny thing is that we were part of a system that was relatively rare in the fifties, is fast becoming the norm in the eighties, and represents for cultural reformers the ultimate utopia. In our district on the San Francisco Peninsula we had a gender-balanced workforce where everyone—man or woman, single or married—got equal pay for equal work. This equalitarian setup nevertheless discriminated against married men and their families, putting them at the bottom not only in economic means but in social and professional status as well.

I can tell you about it because for the first twelve years in our marriage my wife stayed home with our four children while I supported them with my pay from high school teaching. This happened between 1954 and 1966, the beginning of the end of the "traditional" family's domination of our private lives, a period now widely cursed for its oppression to women.

From a male breadwinner's point of view, what was it like? If you taught in the public schools, you lived in a multilayered society. Clustered at the top you found married women who added their salaries to already handsome incomes brought in by Mr. Executive or Mr. Physician or Mr. Businessman. The best off, those without children through chance or choice, joined the affluent upper-middle class. They left school in the afternoon to return in big cars to homes in nearby high-rent districts. They exhibited fashionable wardrobes, saw their hairdressers every week, enjoyed the cultural amenities, spread an expensive table and travelled frequently, in jets. Those who combined career and motherhood—today's most fretful predicament—still had relatively comfortable joint incomes to help resolve the dual role problems.

At the next level you found male teachers with working wives. The best situated had wives who also taught school, enabling them to share not only the doubled income but the discretionary time allowed by the academic year.

At the same level you found unmarried teachers who shared household expenses with one or more other parties. Unmarried teachers living alone were not as well fixed but did well enough to join the jet set.

All of these groups—married women, men with working wives, unmarried teachers living alone or with others—formed the upper layers of the socioeconomic scale in our school district. Below them you found a gap and then you reached the bottom layer composed of breadwinners, male or female, but mostly at that time, male.

Supporting a family on a teacher's pay brought these men close to genteel poverty. To appreciate their situation, you have to know something about teacher pay scales. Teachers advanced in salary by acquiring years of service and college credits. In 1962–63 in our district a beginning teacher with only a bachelor's degree earned $5,316. To reach the highest possible salary, $10,464, he had to earn 66 more credits beyond the B.A. and work twelve years. He might improve his salary by getting work elsewhere, but school districts seldom allowed more than six years of transferred seniority. That mean that teachers in the middle and upper pay ranks actually lost money by shifting to better-paying jobs.

This system bound older teachers to their jobs and forced younger teachers into an endless scramble for college credits. Year after year they took night and summer courses to reach that coveted 66 credits, almost what you need for a Ph.D.

While they struggled up the pay scale, teachers had to make do with salaries that put them at the bottom of college-trained professionals and behind nearly all skilled trades. For family men that wasn't enough. Thus, in addition to working off-campus for college credits, most of us also worked at part-time jobs. The man who wielded the chalk in math class that morning could be seen that night swinging a watchman's nightstick, or pumping gas, or ringing up retail sales, or officiating at an athletic event. After waiting five or six years to break in—there was a long waiting list—many of us eventually joined the male majorities who staffed night and summer schools.

Our local experience followed national patterns where male schoolteachers formed the bulk of moonlighters. Figures that held steadily from 1958 through 1978 show that twenty percent of male teachers, compared to five percent of females, took extra jobs. In the late sixties University of Illinois investigator Harold W. Guthrie discovered that in large school districts, eight percent of female teachers took extra work as compared to forty-five percent of all males and sixty-six percent of married males. Incidentally, this pattern is matched by nonteachers. In 1982 among all workers three times as many men as women worked at second jobs.

Consider also that in spite of talk about our having to work only nine months, many of us had heavy take-home loads. A nearby consulting firm discovered that academic teachers and coaches in our district put in fifty-five- to sixty-hour work-weeks, enough to squeeze eleven months of work into a nine-month academic year. Nor have I mentioned the work required of a family man when he went home to his wife and children, a minor point but worth looking at during a period that dramatizes the domestic burdens of the working wife.

Consider finally that married men did most of the union work during this period. The leadership of the California Teachers' Association affiliate in our district and the local branch of the American Federation of Teachers had large male majorities. That was not by choice, surely not because of prejudice. We encouraged women to join and to serve as legislators and executives. But despite their equal distribution among the faculty, women did not appear in equal numbers in the professional organizations. This happened, I believe, because married men were goaded by stronger needs to take up union work.

This situation produced other ironies. The growing number of male breadwinners pushed up salaries as school boards slowly recognized that a teacher's income was increasingly more likely to support a family. But the drive that sent breadwinner salaries upward also propelled married women and single teachers into the jet set. Such facts made salary increases harder to come by. Since 1970, when the economy cooled, school boards have been granting only cost-of-living adjustments that have failed in most cases to match inflation. By the midseventies male breadwinners were in worse shape than before.

Something else widened the cleavage between the jet set and the breadwinners. It was status, an intangible that affects each of us deeply. Married women in those days—and to some extent in these days also—achieved or enhanced their status by assuming the social rank of their husbands. Few of them flaunted their position. Male teachers suffered little snobbery. But outside the school most men and women went home to different socioeconomic worlds and seldom mixed.

At the same time, even though they had the same job and salary, men and women experienced differing professional status. Public school teaching placed men far down in job prestige, lower than most other male professionals, lower than their female colleagues. Men in the schools had to cope therefore with feelings of reduced status and self-esteem. Such feelings varied with the individual and the district. Among the male teachers in our district, for example, there were enough former officers and noncoms to staff a regiment and enough talented academics to staff a small college. But nationwide so many people believed that a man in teaching was a loser that it affected how we felt about ourselves. That was one of the reasons why most male teachers I know would not select the same career again and would not recommend it to young men.

Before I wrap up, let me anticipate some objections. I have so far not allowed for exceptions. Each teacher, male or female, had in fact a separate story. Some male breadwinners had handsome inheritances and lived well. Some childless married women supported a houseful of relatives. Some wanted to get married and have children, but for one reason or another could not. Single-parent females were probably in worse shape than male breadwinners. And happiness, however you define it, visited or ignored teachers of both sexes at every level of the multilayered society we lived in. I grant the exceptions but reaffirm my point: everything else more or less equal, a gender-balanced equal pay system discriminated in several ways against family men.

I also acknowledge that my claim about a gender-balanced staff applies only to teachers and not to administrators, nearly all of whom were married men. Nationwide the percentage of male administrators reached above ninety percent as late as 1973, one sign, presumably, of the prejudice women encountered in those days. Where prejudice existed, it was wrong and had to be stopped. But imbalance in the number of male and female administrators does not necessarily reveal prejudice. In some cases women chose not to pursue administrative positions because they had less to gain than men. If they were married, they also had something to lose. Long before flex-time scheduling became an issue, public-school teaching offered a rare opportunity for women to match their work hours to the in-school schedules of their children. Eleven-month administrative jobs cut into their at-home time with their families. Married men, on the other hand, had greater incentives to work toward higher-salaried positions. As late as 1975—five years into the Women's Liberation era—males still had twice as many advanced degrees as females, one sign of their more deliberate effort to reach administration.

Finally, it could be said that I have pushed the word "discrimination" beyond the range of normal usage. Of course, I have, as does everyone who uses it to describe how an essentially neutral system sharply divides people into differing personal circumstances. I would not have used the word during the period I discussed; it would not have occurred to me to do so. Male breadwinners may have had to operate on tighter budgets and may not have liked it, but none of us claimed he was being discriminated against. I nevertheless use the word here for several reasons:

• So much retrospective indignation has been aroused over the way men presumably oppressed women in the bad old days that it's worth looking at how one group of men really worked and lived and how they dealt with the status system around them. That won't resolve the endless debate about who had it tougher, men or women, but it will help correct a now popular stereotype about the royally privileged preliberation male. In this context, the idea of "oppression" itself derives from a particular way of looking at what happened. But other equally valid perspectives are available. Thus, if we say that according to a special way of viewing it, society discriminated against women, we can also say that according to a different way of viewing it, the society of my school district discriminated against married men. And, I suspect that if we examined other subsocieties, looking closely at the actual lives of men and women, we would find that the word "discrimination" could often cut both ways. It was tough being a woman in those days, and it was tough being a man. The collective challenge of that reality was called the "human condition" which, by and large, is an equal opportunity employer.

• Using the word "discrimination" also helps focus on the different meanings of "equality." Those who mouth the word as a political slogan suggest it has one meaning, so simple a toddler could grasp it. It doesn't. In fact, it names a complex idea whose meaning shifts according to how and where you use it. We've already heard about the distinction between "equality of opportunity" and "equality of result." And we have seen how one kind of equality suffers when another kind is imposed. However you justify it, reverse discrimination still discriminates.

We also need to look at "equality" obtained by accommodating an organization to the private decisions of its members. Some people rule flatly against the practice. In our school district, for example, any suggestion that breadwinners be compensated for their heavier domestic responsibilities provoked immediate protest. Equal pay for equal work was the strongest absolute this side of the speed of light, and if a man was squeezed financially because he chose to support a family, that remained his own business. He was not to presume he could ask other employees to subsidize the results of his decision.

Yet, in effect, that's what we do when we require employers to adapt to the decisions of female employees to have children. When the overall salary pool is diminished to pay for day-care centers and maternity leaves, or when quotas are established to modify otherwise gender-blind hiring and promotion policies, the rest of the employees do, in fact, subsidize the private decisions of their colleagues.

• To say that adapting to such private decisions helps women compete more equally and promotes our common welfare by stabilizing their families is a good argument. It says what feminists constantly argue, that their gains are our gains. But whatever its merits, such an argument would not have served the married schoolteacher in the fifties and sixties. He could have, nevertheless, made an arguable point, which is another reason I use the word "discrimination." For example, men forced into moonlighting could not compete on equal terms with those who could use their out-of-school time to work on their teaching or to improve their qualifications or simply to find relief from the daily hassle with teenagers. Nor could they afford all the available methods of professional advancement. Although the district provided generous sabbatical leave plans, for example, most breadwinners did not have the money to take advantage of them, not, at least, until the late sixties when they reached the top of the salary schedule. Even then, sabbatical leaves remained too costly for many married men.

By the same token, such men could claim that the money supporting their families also contributed to the common good. A functioning family is an efficient educational and social welfare agency performing essential services for all of us. Thus, "private" decisions to build families have important public consequences. Consider also that however they are disparaged today, older conventions derived from the belief that it was necessary and proper to create families by having mothers stay home with small children while fathers supported them. Those fathers who became teachers thus paid a heavy price for doing what most people at the time expected them to do.

By pointing out the complexity of words like "discrimination" and "equality," I am not saying we should abandon the rule of equal pay for equal work or deny equal opportunities to women. I accepted the system then and accept it now. I have no complaints against the circumstances that influenced my life; I don't feel complaints are justified. I chose to teach in public schools, chose to get married, chose with my wife to have children, and recognized that such decisions brought their own consequences. Nor am I here disputing that in the strictest use of the term, women were, in fact, discriminated against in many areas of our society.

But I am saying that for all the reverence we now grant the ideal of "equality," we often find that when we try to achieve it in practice, it turns into a will-o'-the-wisp.

SPEAKING OF FEMINISM

WOMEN'S RESPONSIBILITIES AND THE E.R.A.

Robert A. Sides

You've seen that ad for the E.R.A. about the woman who was alive after her husband died? The message is, you, know, "poor her"; she wasn't his economic equal until she died eight years after him. . .a "grave" concern for women who seek equality. There then follows a barrage of exhortations from celebrities to "Help pass the E.R.A.!" But here is what is interesting to me: nowhere do they talk about why the guy dies so much younger than his wife. Was it due to the fact that he had to pay for her, too? Was his economic burden unequal?

Again, it was a tactical error by feminists: *the poor woman.* And women wonder why the E.R.A. won't pass? Feminists may not have high opinions of men, but they don't think we're *that* stupid, do they? Feminists should have said to Joe Sixpak, "Hey, Joe, were you goin' without that E.R.A. in your hand. . .to an early death? Maybe you'll live eight more years if your wife shares the monetary load as well as lode. And maybe you can take some time out to golf, oil paint, and be around the kids and family while she gets her M.B.A. at night school." But it seems they didn't want to scare women off by showing them the new responsibilities they'll have to shoulder. They only wanted to point out the "rights," the good stuff.

FEMALE CHAUVINISM

Richard Haddad

Feminist ideology is becoming more dogmatic than ever. One who does not agree that men oppress women, even if that one supports women's rights, is branded antifeminist. Commitment to the objectives of the women's movement is no longer enough; a friend of the movement must pledge allegiance to feminist sex-role theory or else is not friend but foe. The concept of men's liberation is lauded, but the way to the liberation of men is through the liberation of women! Feminism is being transformed before our eyes into female chauvinism. The very idea of an independent men's movement is denounced as misogynistic and is actively resisted.

I HAVE A FANTASY

John Gordon

I understand that I am addressing an audience composed mainly of people who already know the score—preaching to the converted, as the saying goes. In a way that's nice. It means that for once I can expect a minimum in the way of sharp intakes of breath and other signs of indignant incredulity. It also means, probably, that at the end I will not be told that I'm just as far out as the extremist feminists I attack and that the truth must lie in between—midway between those who say that all men are despicable and those, like myself, who say that those who say that are despicable. (This is a reaction which never fails to remind me of a 1950s Jules Feiffer cartoon in which President Eisenhower is shown responding to the desegregation riots in Little Rock, Arkansas with the words, "We must guard against the extremists of both sides: those who want to blow schools up and those who want to keep them open.")

In a way, as I say, that's nice, because for once I can assume a certain community of shared perceptions, a common knowledge of certain facts. You don't need to be give the figures on suicides or mortality rates or child-custody decisions, or be reminded of the draft. It isn't necessary to explain to you, for instance, why pension funds which discriminate against women (because they live longer) are being rewritten according to sex-blind standards while life insurance policies which discriminate against men (because they die sooner) are not, or to spell out for you how it is that the same people who twelve years ago yodeled for (and got) the scalp of Dr. Louis Berman when he wondered out loud whether premenstrual tension might incapacitate some women for positions of high authority, can now demand the acquittal of murderesses on the grounds that premenstrual tension incapacitated them for any responsible

269

action.

I assume from the start that all this and more is a given, for here and for now —they're things that most people don't know or won't face, and our biggest job is to keep repeating them until people do know them and do face them. But not here, and not now.

Which of course is my problem. What *am* I going to tell you? The only answer I've been able to come up with is that I should give the kind of talk appropriate for such a setting—one where everyone pretty much sees eye to eye from the start. In other words, a pep talk. And I thought of the most successful pep talk of modern history, Martin Luther King's "I Have a Dream" speech. The problem is, we've all gotten more cynical in the twenty years since that speech was made. Few of us have that sort of dream anymore. What we have instead are fantasies. So:

I have a fantasy.

I have a fantasy that I'm on a ship along with the entire editorial staff of *Ms.* magazine, and that for five days they've been kvetching at me about how oppressed they are by the patriarchic chivalric code, and how they've figured out that it's all a subtle way of keeping them in their place. Then the ship starts to sink, and I make a little bet with myself about which of them is going to be the first to crack: from whose lips will the words "Women and children first!" be introduced into the discussion?

I have a fantasy that Gloria Steinem, or some recent clone, finds herself on the stage of the Apollo Theatre in Harlem, explaining in her plummy accent how women have been oppressed just like blacks except of course that it's been going on a lot longer, and that therefore, when you think about it, women have really been *more* oppressed, and so all those black males in the audience ought to stop *whining* and send their unemployment checks to her Madison Avenue office. . .at which my fantasy draws the curtain on the ensuing mayhem.

I have a fantasy that Nancy Reagan wakes up one morning and finds herself turned into a *man,* which means that for the first time in her parasitic life she has to earn her keep by means more strenuous than she has so far been called upon to employ—the purchase of expensive china and expensive clothes, the mouthing of vapid pieties, the dewy-eyed gaze at her husband when in public, and the disagreeable but mercifully infrequent obligation to lie down and intone "Oh, Ronnie! Oh, Ronnie!" on occasion. In my fantasy, she wakes up as a man one morning to discover that Ronnie is not at all charmed any more to have her gaping at him in that way, realizes by degrees that when you're a man you have to really *do* something if you want to get anywhere, and winds up wildly casting about for a dramatic gesture which will make an impression on the media the way she used to.

I have a fantasy in which women leaders who declare silly wars automatically turn into male soldiers. It lifts my heart to imagine Margaret Thatcher suddenly finding herself strapped into a parachute harness and descending through a cloud of flak toward Port Stanley. I am delighted at the thought of Queen Victoria, sending her Tommies off to die pointlessly in the Crimean War with the words, "Oh, that the Queen were a man. . .I should give those Russians such a beating!" getting her wish.

270

Not all the fantasies are so violent. Sometimes when I'm walking along a city street or driving along a highway I take a survey of the cars going by with couples in the front seat, and count the ones in which the male is driving. So far, it's always turned out that in about four cases out of five, the man is behind the wheel. In my fantasy, that situation is evened out or, better yet, reversed. Because face it: driving is a bore and a strain. It has nothing to do with power— it's a menial mechanical chore for which chauffeurs and cab drivers quite rightly demand financial compensation, and here are all these men doing it, without thinking, for nothing. How many of them, I wonder, have gotten lectures about what chauvinists they are from their passengers? How many of them have been trained *not* to walk around the car at the end of the trip and open the door for their rider, because *that* would be sexist? Sexist, my foot. The fact is that opening a car door and getting out yourself is a snap, whereas driving a car through traffic is a drag, and *that's* the reason that feminists have made an issue out of the former but not the latter.

I have lots of time-machine fantasies, most of them involving cross-temporal confrontations between the girls—that's what I called them because that's what they called themselves—I dated or wanted to date in the pre-feminist sixties and their liberated counterparts of today. Why is my timing so lousy, I ask myself? Fifteen years ago I was forever being told that if I didn't *take charge,* if I didn't assert myself and act manly and all that, then I wouldn't get anywhere with women. It was *women* who told me that, and who demonstrated how true it was. I think almost any man who remembers that time can at least understand Holden Caulfield's rueful explanation for his perpetual virginity: "The problem with me is, when girls say stop, I stop." I think almost any man who remembers that time remembers that absolutely the *worst* thing a woman could say to you was that you weren't like other men, that you were sweeter and more understanding and so she thought of you as a *friend,* even as a *brother.* God, those fatal words, *friend* and *brother.* What they meant, of course, was that now she could confide in you about her beastly boyfriends, who weren't so accommodating and were therefore getting laid. Anyway, in my time-machine fantasy, a posse of modern feminists gets sent back to 1967 to explain to those women that it's *good* for men to be sensitive and caring and attentive to their wishes, and a similar posse of 1967 women gets sent to 1985 to testify on my behalf against those convinced that Gordon, as a heterosexual male, must *ipso facto* be at best an unindicted co-rapist. Why is my timing so lousy? I advise the men in the audience, even today, not, however, to take this too seriously, because everything I've heard from the men and women I've talked to over the last year indicates that the Harvey's Bristol Cream ads are a bad joke, that by far most women still want to be called up, asked out, squired around, and paid for, that it's still true that a man not willing to *take charge* is going to spend a lot of Saturday nights watching television. I'm reminded of a recent cartoon in the *New Yorker,* in which a woman says good-bye to her date with words to this effect: "Thank you for the wonderful evening, Fred. You were the most sensitive, thoughtful, open, feeling, caring, vulnerable man I've ever met. It's too bad you're a wimp."

I have yet another science fiction fantasy, this one modelled after H. G.

271

Wells's *The Invisible Man,* in which feminists who complain about how men reduce women to their physical components are made invisible and allowed to listen to a gaggle of their sisters reducing men to their financial components: "What's he *do?*" "Where'd he go to *school?*" "What's he *drive?*" "Where'd he take you to *dinner?*" Someday I would like someone to explain to me why seeing people in terms of tits and ass is any more degrading than seeing them in terms of dollars and cents.

Mainly, though, I have one big fantasy, which sort of sums up all of them. I was recently on a talk show tour promoting my book, being asked all kinds of questions by audiences and interviewers. Some of them went better than others, but what with one thing and another, none of them went as well as I would have liked. So when I came home I constructed for my own amusement a fantasy interview, with which I'll conclude. In the following, "Q" is the ideal interviewer, and "A" is the ideal me.

Q: Do I know you from somewhere?

A: Probably not, but it's possible. A few months ago I was doing a lot of talk shows. I was on "Donahue," which is a real zoo, and "Charley Rose," which is more relaxed, and a bunch of local shows, including some in Boston.

Q: What was your gimmick?

A: Feminism.

Q: It's been done. To death.

A: Let me explain. I was on as a critic of feminism, or rather. . .

Q: That's been done, too. About twelve years ago, George Gilder wrote an antifeminist tract called *Sexual Suicide,* and Midge Decter came out with a couple of works about the same time. And today—just take a look. *Real Men Don't Eat Quiche, Conan the Barbarian,* John Travolta and Sylvester Stallone! Macho is back in. Meanwhile the ERA is down in flames, and the army has discontinued coed basic training because it says the women can't hack it, and Betty Friedan and Colette Dowling and Susan Bolotin and it seems just about every other issue of the *New York Times Magazine* have been coming out with reports about how the troops are waffling or defecting to Harlequin romances, Lady Di haircuts, and Nancy Reagan frocks. Now there's even a book out called *The Compleat Chauvinist* by Dr. Edgar Berman, the same character who was forced to quit a national advisory board years ago when he said that women's menstrual periods incapacitated them for positions of authority. If *he's* being let back into the *zeitgeist,* you just know feminism's in trouble. And so now here you come along, going on talk shows and all, just to help dance on its grave. You scumbag.

A: Let me explain. I'm not getting on the bandwagon with any of that stuff. I *hate* all that stuff, except for *Real Men Don't Eat Quiche,* which is genuinely funny. They're all giving one message, which I just abominate. They're all saying that men and women are genetically programed to be, respectively, apes and marsupials. The Berman book, for instance, is mainly one long panegyric to testosterone, which it coyly calls the "hormone of champions." It even pretends to estimate the testosteronic levels of various prominent women, with Bella Abzug scoring high and Sophia Loren at rock-bottom. I mean, really.

Q: Sounds gruesome. So you're against those guys, but here you say you've been going around attacking feminists. What's your gimmick?

A: My gimmick is free will. I think people can change if they choose to, and that those who do not live in a police state are obliged, after a certain point, to take responsibility for the lives they've made for themselves. I dislike male chauvinists who tell me that I'm denying my essence if I don't live up to the latest sociobiological data about how packs of male screamer monkeys behave in the wild. I dislike feminists who tell me that everything I may have done or may try to do with myself is secondary to the fact that I was born male, which means that I am part of everything that's wrong in the world, which means that if I really want to do the world a favor I'll go stick my head in the oven. It seems to me, in fact, that when you get down to it both groups are saying the same thing.

Q: Oh, come on now. Aren't you being a *little* paranoid? What feminists have you known who believe that?

A: Some, but not many. Obviously, the ones who believe that do not tend to consort with the likes of me. But I have *read,* and heard, and heard of, lots. If I may be permitted to quote from the introduction to my book:

> By my own estimate, in the last twenty years the four feminist books that have had the widest impact have been *The Feminine Mystique, Sexual Politics, Against Our Will,* and *The Women's Room.* Of those four, three operate from the assumption that women's woes are traceable to the nature of the male libido: *Sexual Politics* is about heterosexual pornography, and how it is paradigmatic of the relation between men and women; *Against Our Will* is about rape, and how it is paradigmatic of the relation between men and women; *The Women's Room* opens with an attempted rape and concludes with a successful one, and features a cast of men who typically dabble in writing sadistic pornography and sound like this: "Hey, come here, Mommy, Baby wanna suck your boobs. Little Billy cold, Mommy, need little Blissy come play with him."

Add to that list the following: Adrienne Rich, Robin Morgan, Mary Daly, Kathleen Barry, Phyllis Chesler, Joanna Russ, Alice Walker, Germaine Greer (sometimes), Gloria Steinem (sometimes), Ti-Grace Atkinson, Andrea Dworkin, Shulamith Firestone, Margaret Atwood, Sally Kempton, Flo Kennedy, Bella Abzug, Jill Johnston. . . .

Q: Excuse me for interrupting, but the names that I recognize sound rather dated to me. Aren't they mainly the shock troops from the early days, when feminists had to make wild statements in order to get attention? And weren't they entitled to a few excesses along that line, considering all the crap they took from men all those years?

A: No and no. The reason the names sound dated is that feminism as a whole has come to seem more and more out of touch, and the reason for that is that it's failed to come up with sensible people to replace that other crew. In fact, if you take a look, you'll see that the screamers are as much in front as they ever were, that if anything they're gaining ground. It's the handful with a sense of balance—Jane O'Reilly, Karen DeCrow, Elizabeth Janeway—who are being left behind.

Q: I seem to have overlooked these screamers that you claim are everywhere these days. Give me some examples.

A: Oh, for instance in academe, which is where I make my living, teaching English. If I open the latest copy of the most prestigious journal in my field, *PMLA*, I come across an article about George Orwell's *1984* and how it's all really a parable of male chauvinist politics. And if I look at the trendiest journal in the field, *Critical Inquiry*, I find this, from the feminist Susan Gubar:

> Not a few of the most exciting experiments of women artists, moreover, grow out of a self-conscious attempt to obliterate aesthetic distance. . . . It finds a kind of culmination in the performance art of Mierle Laderman Ukeles, whose "Maintenance Art Activity" consists in washing museum floors with a damp mop, over and over again, and even more to the purpose here, Carolee Schneemann, who reads from a long scroll she removes from her vagina in the performance of *Up To and Including Her Limits*.

Q: Oh gag. Surely you don't mean to tell me that this sort of stuff is typical?

A: I mean to tell you that Susan Gubar is a co-author of the single most influential book of feminist criticism around, and that it is full of that sort of nonsense, and that like all such books it received a benediction from the *New York Times*, and that its disciples are everywhere in academia, teaching courses at which male students are often made to feel most unwelcome, the reiterated message of which is that as males they belong to a contingent of fascist rapists. I mean to tell you that in the name of feminism, statments about my sex are daily being indulged and subsidized which were they about any other group would be instantly dismissed as the rankest bigotry.

Q: Well, look. Even accepting your scarifying report from academia—I mean to say, hasn't it always been a preserve of zanies? It's not as if we're talking about the real world?

A: Well, what *is* the real world? Judy Chicago on the road, peddling her platefuls of stylized vaginas? Jane Fonda, at the top of the best-seller list, telling everyone that it took her twenty years to figure out that dieting and exercise were good things because all that time male doctors kept the truth from her? Robin Morgan, in the recent movie *Not a Love Story*, wailing that "to be a woman today is to be in a constant state of rage?" Joyce Carol Oates, one of the least underexposed writers of all time, going on about how because she's a woman writer she hasn't been paid the proper kind of attention?

Q: No, that's all media hype. Besides, these women are just reacting, as I said before, to "all the crap they took from men all those years." Sure they're extreme—so what? So was Thomas Paine. They're stiking back, after centuries of abuse, and aren't they entitled to get carried away now and then?

A: They would be, if there really were something for them to strike back *at*. But where is it, this great historical body of anti-female propaganda that's supposed to justify all the lashing back?

Q: Oh come on. Everyone knows how misogynist western literature has been.

A: Everyone *says* that, but the truth happens to be almost exactly the opposite. Kate Millett's *Sexual Politics,* which first presented the case, is just a joke; no one who's actually *read* the books she runs through her mill can consider it anything but a fraud. She set the pattern. Take a good look at the works that are always cited—the Bible, Milton, Swift, Freud, Lawrence—and you'll find that they occasionally say bad things about women because they often say bad things about the human race, in which they include women. Sift out the misanthropes, and what you're left with, maybe, is Strindberg, Philip Wylie, and a couple of Rolling Stones songs. Hardly the cumulative weight of western culture. In *fact,* the great propaganda campaign in the war between the sexes has been, for at least one and a half centuries now, against men.

Q: Come again?

A: Let me recommend a book to you, Ann Douglas's *The Feminization of American Culture,* which documents the history of two of the most popular and influential *genres* of the nineteenth and early twentieth centuries, the antimale novel and the anti-male tract. These works—thousands of them—were part of a campaign to represent men as barbarians whose urges had to be leashed in by the forces of decency—meaning women—if civilization were to survive. Some of the consequences of that campaign were Prohibition, Comstockery, and the laws against abortion and birth control. The ongoing flood of antimale hate literature isn't a *reaction* against anything, it's a *continuation* of an old campaign. Men are the main targets these days because they always have been.

Q: You're the English teacher, and I don't want to get into a lit. crit. debate with you, so let's forget the nineteenth-century novel, if you please, and look at the way women are depicted today. It seems to me that there's still a lot for them to be angry about.

A: Like where?

Q: Television, expecially commercials. Degrading hard-core pornography, which is everywhere these days. The wave of gory "women in danger" movies, which specialize in female victims being terrorized and butchered. All of this has a hell of a lot more to do with the image of women today than any Victorian novel.

A: As for television commercials, I challenge you to give me an example of any female depicted more "degradingly" than that man with the obsession for squeezing rolls of toilet paper, or that other male character in the yachting outfit put-putting around in the toilet for Ti-D Bowl. I mean, can you *imagine* what Gloria Steinem would have to say if it were a *woman* in that toilet? As for pornography, the standard image of a typical hard-core movie is of a man and a woman together repetitively engaging in intercourse, and although you can be consistently squeamish if you want and say that such an image "degrades" that man and that woman, or the human race, I can't for the life of me see how it can be said to "degrade women," period, which is what I hear all the time.

275

Q: Well, a lot of those movies involve a lot of S & M, where women are tied and beaten, don't they?

A: As for the S & M subgenre of hard-core pornography, yes, it's disgusting and disturbing, but it's hardly normative, as these people would have you believe; according to the best-documented studies, about ten percent of pornography features violence, not all of it by any means women-directed, and even that is a small portion of the total body of media violence, the great majority of whose represented objects are and always have been male.

Q: Well, you can pooh-pooh it all you like, but the fact is that there has been an increase in media violence against women, and that it corresponds with an increase in *real* violence against women nationwide, especially rape.

A: The *fact* is that the notion that rape has increased dramatically over the last decade has everything to do with Susan Brownmiller and her cronies and nothing to do with F.B.I. or Department of Justice figures, which show it holding steady since 1973 at a rate of two-tenths of one percent of the population. On the other hand, one area of violencce in which there *has* been a big jump is in child abuse—a despicable crime which we don't hear much about from feminists for the sufficient reason that about two-thirds of its perpetrators are female.

Q: Boy, you really *are* out for your pound of flesh, aren't you? Don't you even have the common compassion to recognize that any mother who would brutalize her own child has to be deeply disturbed and in need of help?

A: Whereas wife-beaters are just beasts, huh? This venerable chivalric distinction explains why we have counseling services for child-abusers and prison cells for rapists; and, incidentally, why men in prison outnumber women by twenty-five to one. It also explains why you get so upset about "women in danger" movies—the idea that a *woman* should suffer physical harm seems just . . .well, *worse* to you, whereas male victims are strictly ho-hum. The same sexist sentiment was shared seventy years ago on the deck of the *Titanic,* when eighty percent of the female passengers escaped in lifeboats and eighty percent of the males drowned, and of course in the wars that followed, in which American men died by the millions while their womenfolk stayed home knitting socks, rivetting rivets, playing the black market, and cheering them on from afar.

Q: Now you're not going to blame women for *wars,* are you? Everyone knows that men make wars.

A: It's amazing—do you know I was being told that even as the Falkland Islands war was being waged by Margaret Thatcher? That the *Los Angeles Times* ran a review dismissing my book on the grounds that "Men make wars," while on the front page of the same issue Margaret Thatcher was shown welcoming home the survivors of her "boys?" It's just amazing. World War II, the Korean War, and the Vietnam War were entered into by this country's representative councils at the behest of an electorate, fifty-two percent of which was female. And that business of women sending men out to defend them or their honor or to grab more goodies for them is an old story: there were the eighteenth-century battles where ladies of quality perched with parasol on shady hillocks overlooking their men at war, and the southern belles who egged on their swains into duels of honor with the words, "Better a *dead* hero than a *living* coward." It's the oldest sexist message in the book—that men are just lower and therefore more expendable in the interests of the common good in a way that women aren't, and its continuing currency can be measured by the fact that men commit suicide three times as often as women, that they die eight years sooner, that they are more prone to stress-related diseases, that they are statistically less likely to apply for admission to hospitals and more likely to have something seriously wrong with them when they get there.

Q: Look, you want to do statistics; I can do statistics, too. There's one little figure which pretty much says it all, and which explains a lot of that bitterness you find so distasteful. It shows that women earn . . .

Q and A (in unison): *"fifty-nine cents for every dollar a man earns."*

Q (solus): So you *have* heard of that fact, eh?

A: It would have been hard not to, since it is probably the most widely publicized set of numbers in circulation; sometimes I think the *New York Times* must keep a special row of typeface containing just those numbers, so it can bung them into every third issue or so. The only problem is that the moral drawn from them, that women continue to be horrendously discriminated against, is bogus.

Q: *What?* I happen to know that the conclusion comes from what even you must recognize as a reliable source, the U.S. Commission on Civil Rights.

A: To whose chairman I recently wrote, requesting clarification about those very figures. And his assistant, Ms. Caroline Davis Gleiter, was kind enough to write back, referring me to a number of studies of the subject, one of which, Solomon W. Polochak's *Discontinuous Labor Force Participation and its Effects on Women's Market Earning,* spells out the main reason for discrepancies between male and female earnings: it's that women are many times more likely than men to leave their jobs to care for children instead of staying on to build up seniority and higher salaries. Among the two groups of males and females to whom that differential does not apply—childless singles—salaries are virtually identical.

Q: Well? But doesn't that just show that women are almost always loaded with the kids, and isn't that a form of discrimination?

A: Even if it were, it wouldn't be the form of discrimination that the people who parrot and preach and sing and editorialize about that fifty-nine-cents-on-the-dollar mantra pretend it is. You asked me earlier for examples of the influence of the kinds of feminists I'm challenging. Well, here's a big one—that you and millions of others have committed to memory a datum which is, fundamentally, a gross distortion of reality, a pro-feminist lie, even though the truth has been available for years.

And no. I don't consider the fact that more women than men take care of the kids a form of discrimination in any meaningful sense of the word. For one thing, I'm not at all convinced that child-rearing is such a bad fate, compared to lots of the jobs out there in what you call the real world. Please remember I said I believe in free will. No one *forces* those women to have children or to enter into marriages the terms of which, implicitly or explicitly, are that they shall have primary responsibility for raising whatever children result. Recently many women *have* been asking, successfully, for an equal sharing of child-rearing responsibilities, and the anti-ERA backlash constitutes one big piece of evidence that among those that haven't many don't want any such thing, that they want their men's lives devoted to bacon-bringing, rather than parenting. In any event, what legal pressure there is in this realm is all directed against men, who are routinely required by the courts to one, stay away from, and two, pay for their children, according to paternity and child support laws the patent unfairness of which most feminists have not thus far been conspicuous in protesting.

Q: Well why on earth should they? They've got plenty of inequities of their own to fight.

A: Such as?

Q: Well, for instance the withdrawal of federal funds for abortion.

A: Sorry, but that seems to me a pretty marginal grievance at best. During the Vietnam War I protested on behalf of the principle that citizens ought not to be taxed against their wills to fund a policy if they sincerely believed it was tantamount to murder, and I don't see any reason to abandon that principle. Feminists ought to be the last people to demand of others that they choose between violating their consciences and breaking the law.

Anyway, even granting that as an issue, it's pretty small potatoes. What, after all, would *you* say is today the single most flagrant case of sex discrimination around?

Q: (Silence)

A: Well?

Q: Oh, all right, all right, I'll say it: the all-male draft registration law. Which N.O.W. and other feminists' organizations are on record against, by the way.

A: Good for N.O.W. The point is that at a time when the country was noisily overturning every vestige of legal discrimination against women, in the name of equality, it could blandly order young males to sign up for a program which in the past had discriminately maimed and slaughtered their fathers and grandfathers, and that while all this was going on we kept hearing about how oppressed women were by dirty movies and offensive television commercials. *There's* a testimony, if you want another one, to how pervasive is the influence of those feminists that you considered so quaint and eccentric. I'm not sure how, but it looks to me as if they've done a pretty good job of determining what people notice and don't notice, what gets considered unfair and what is taken as a matter of course.

Q: Come on, drop the conspiracy theory, will you? The conventional expendability of males, in war or otherwise, was around long before anyone ever heard of Betty Friedan.

A: Exactly, and that's my point: Feminism, for the people I've named, hasn't been a conversion experience; it's been a confirmation, into the old codes of chivalry. These people haven't eliminated stereotypes; they've cemented them.

Q: You're making an awful lot out of this draft business, which may be gone soon anyway. Can you give any other examples of the oppression of males?

A: You mean aside from the suicide and mortality and disease and hospitalization and imprisonment statistics, and the paternity and child support laws, all mentioned previously?

Q: Yes

A: Sure. The fact that by a Supreme Court ruling a man can be guilty of statutory rape but a woman can't. The fact that the father of an unborn child has no say in whether it gets aborted but is required to support it if it isn't. The fact that heterosexual rape is not the only felony charge, in some states, for which the presumption of the accused's innocence has not been significantly qualified. The fact that, Jean Harris notwithstanding, in the last few years a number of women have gotten away with murder on the basis of their unsubstantiated testimony that their victims abused them. The fact that I have a file full of letters from men, in response to my book, recounting job interviews in which they were told flat-out that they weren't being hired because the company or university was looking for a woman.

Q: Are you *really* telling me that *women* are oppressing men?

A: I'm telling you that that statement has at least as much validity as what we hear all the time, that men are the oppressors of women. Actually, though, I think that in this context the word "oppress" is silly. I think that if our old friend the Martian, trying to fit in, were to come down to the U.S.A. and look around, seeking to figure out which of the two sexes was a better deal for it to adopt, it would have a hard choice. And I think that would have been more or less true ten or twenty or thirty or forty or fifty or a hundred years ago, although I'd be willing to bet that in 1943 it would have opted for Rosie the Rivetter over G.I. Joe. The fact is that over the centuries the sexes have done a bang-up job of making things more miserable for one another than they had to be. There was a time when it seemed as if feminism were going to be the force to make that state of affairs better, were going to help liberate both men and women from the old encumbrances. But no more. The single clearest thing about feminism today is that it has become a lobby, tactically and morally indistinguishable from the American Dairy Association or the National Rifle Association. It looks after one special interest group, fudges and lies and wheedles and bullies in that group's interest, and doesn't give a fig for any idea of fairness. It's too bad; I suppose my one-time hope that it might be otherwise derived from some residual chivalric notion that women couldn't be quite as shitty as men. So much for that fairy tale.

Q: And has this disillusioning experience led you to any other conclusions?

A: Yes: the unpleasant one that men need their own lobby too—because we're really getting screwed, guys, and we've been shown that the only way to change that is to organize, raise a few million consciousnesses, and start making with the squeaking wheel.

Q: How is it going?

A: Better than you might think. The memberships are still relatively small, but just wait. Historically men have been more obtuse in these matters than women, but we're not *totally* oblivious, and the reality around us is just too

279

strikingly at odds with the popular feminist version for most men not to start recognizing the discrepancy sooner or later.

HYPOCRISY IN WOMEN'S LIBERATION

Robert A. Sides

What makes me angry is this: I walk around and see women who deny up-and-down that they have *any* power at all. Yet they're very careful to wear clothes—mini-skirts, thigh-slits, whatever—that they casually *say* shouldn't affect men. They play dumb around the power such things have over men. We are to believe, I suppose, that they employ makeup, stockings and perfume to enhance their minds. Strange "thinking." They say it's not their responsibility if men respond excitedly, then turn around and expect mere "eye contact" on their part to be considered assertive! Are we to believe that a "look" is a power-ful shaper of male behavior but protruding nipples are not? One senses that these same women want all the CONTROL, all the powers of being the judges of social mores, but none of the real-life risks of meeting their needs.

Meanwhile, if I am going to get my social and sexual needs met, I have to, at some point, let a women know I HAVE those needs. (Lo that I could *halve* those needs and take care of just myself and not her at the same passive time!) I have to be direct. I have to be vulnerable. I have to ask the questions that get a yes or no answer. I must be specific about days and times and how much money I carry with me. But I can walk by any ten thousand women and not one will do the same. I cannot tell, except by lending them the "special treatment" women say they don't want (because it treats them as children and not "equal" adults), who is looking for men and who isn't. I'm supposed to read nuances, read minds, and yet ignore blatant body and clothing signs. It makes me furious. It's a losing game for men. It's not equal.

No wonder men are beginning to say, "Stop feeding me that crap!" If equality means that we have to give women more, that they don't have to give or do any-thing, well, "equality" just isn't going to happen.

CONCEPTS AND OVERVIEW OF THE MEN'S LIBERATION MOVEMENT

Richard Haddad

I want to present some ideas on the nature of the men's movement—a presentation that will include a re-examination of feminist sex-role theory. I will refer to feminism frequently and not flatteringly, and it is important for you to understand that I draw a very sharp distinction between women's rights (or equal rights in general) on the one hand, and feminism on the other. Equal rights is a concept with which I presume few will quarrel. I support the concept and its application without reservation on any subject you care to name.

I do have some problems with feminism—not with feminist advocacy of equal rights, but with feminist sex-role theory, feminist portrayal of men, feminist rhetoric, and feminist naivete. My problems with feminism extend to feminist men because of their blanket adoption of feminist sex-role theory, their acceptance of the negative portrayal of men which feminism advances, their parroting of feminist rhetoric—which for some reason sounds sillier coming from a man than from a woman, and their equally naive posturing about how society is currently ordered or should be ordered.

True confession: I was once a feminist. I stopped considering myself a feminist several years ago, shortly after an incident in which an acquaintance who was an officer of a local chapter of the National Organization for Woman was refused entry to a local feminist coffeehouse because he was a male. Denying him entry on the basis of his sex was a violation of the county human rights law, and on threat of legal action the coffeehouse sponsors ultimately rescinded their women-only rule. The incident, however, had a big effect to me. It was not THE reason or even the major reason I abandoned feminism, but it occurred at a time when I was doing a lot of thinking about how relevant feminism was for men, and the incident was very symbolic for me—mostly of the hypocrisy I had begun to sense in feminist women.

Since then, as a result of much reading on the subject, a lot of talking with friends, a lot of reflection on my own life, and my observations of the lives and behavior of other people, I have developed some fairly strong opinions on the origins of sex-roles, the nature of what I call the sex-role contract which has existed between men and women, the role of the feminist movement in what I feel is an unprecedented and extremely significant period for our society, and the inevitability of a men's movement which will complete the sex-role revolution which feminism began.

My thinking has led me to conclude that men as a class do *not* oppress women as a class. Nor do I believe that women as a class oppress men as a class. Rather, I feel that men and women have cooperated in the development of contemporary male and female sex-roles, both of which appear to have advantages as well as disadvantages, but which are essentially restrictive in nature, growth

281

inhibiting, and, in the case of the male, physically as well as psychologically lethal.

I argue that in a society in which the roles of both sexes have not only been rigidly defined for so long, but originally complemented each other as well, it is ludicrous to hold either sex responsible for the condition of the other. It seems somewhat obvious to me that women have traditionally been reared to be the nurturing, sensitive, noncompetitive people because these characteristics were most suited to the domestic, child-rearing role they assumed in the order of things. It seems equally obvious to me that man, the hunter, the physically stronger of the sexes, has traditionally been reared to be the aggressive, unemotional competitor because these characteristics were vital to his early role as protector and provider.

The problem, I think, is that somewhere along the line, we (men and women both) lost sight of the purpose of stressing different characteristics in the rearing of our male and female children. And so, for instance, long after physical strength ceased to be a major factor in providing food and shelter, women continued to rely on men to take care of them; and long after it was unnecessary for men to be away from their families much of the time, they continued to rely on women to raise their children and keep their homes. Even today, after almost two decades of modern feminism, men jealously guard their economic and political roles, resenting and ridiculing the intrusion of women into "man's business"; just as women, who jealously guard their child-rearing role, only lately assigning men to "helper" status in the home, will undoubtedly resent and resist the full and equal participation of men in the child-rearing process.

I argue that men do not dominate society—do not have a monopoly on power, nor do they rule the world. They are certainly over-represented in decision-making positions in certain of our social institutions like government and industry, but that is because it has always been their role to perform in those arenas. And I argue that they have no more used their position in these institutions for their own benefit as men, than women have used *their* position as the primary parent for their own benefit as women.

As far as power is concerned, a dictionary definition is "a position of ascendency; an ability to compel obedience." Someone defined it for me once as the ability to say no and get away with it. Either definition seems to have very wide application to both sexes. But if that is so, then why do we generally associate power with men and not with women?

I think the answer is two-fold. For one, we frequently fail to modify the term power by the set of social transactions we are labeling. For another, we do not look for power everywhere it exists. Maybe we are afraid.

For instance, if the subject is political power, we might conclude that men have more of it than women. And if we are discussing economic power, we might come to the same conclusion. But aren't there other kinds of power? Don't we generalize about men and power based on the apparent political and economic power they have?

How about domestic power—power in the home, where virtually all of us spent our most formative years? And what of the female's power over men by virtue of his more socially acceptable (i.e., expected) sex drive? We are all familiar with the manner in which women are perceived as using sex to reward the male for good behavior—and to punish the errant male by withholding it. I ask you to consider which kind of power it is—economic, political, sexual, domestic—that has the most significant impact on us as individuals and as a society. Does the chairman of IBM have more power over you than your wife? Is our president's imprint on you stronger than your mother's? Doesn't it seem to you also that the power wielded in interpersonal relationships makes all other forms of power seem puny in comparison?

I argue that men do not enjoy a life of privilege. Far from it, a look at the life of the average man is a fairly depressing sight. What kind of privilege is it that bestows on men a ten-year-shorter lifespan than women, and a higher incidence of disease, crime, alcoholism, and drug addiction? What kind of privilege is it that blesses men with a frequently self-destructive need to achieve? What kind of privilege is it that honors a man with the duty to spend a lifetime supporting others, more often than not at an unsatisfying job?

Whether or not we choose to look, the effects of sexism are all around us, in plain sight. What the feminists, in their proper concern for women, have neglected to point to our attention is that for every woman who is discouraged from working (by the whole of society, not just its economic or political components) there is a man forced by social convention to work; and for every bored and unfulfilled woman, there is a man burdened with the responsibility that only a primary wage-earner knows, who will die early, in part, from sex-role poisoning.

Men's liberation recognized that society lays oppressive roles on *both* sexes, a fact which feminism tends to ignore. Because its subject is men, not women, men's liberation is no more likely to dwell on the way society oppresses women than is feminism likely to dwell on the way society oppresses men. The objective of the men's movement can only be to free men of the restrictive roles in which they find themselves, and to foster the conditions under which they can define and choose for themselves the behaviors and relationships with which they are most comfortable and free. This simply cannot be done within the context of feminist theory, which proposes an oppressively negative view of men: the dominant gender which has it all and keeps it by exploiting women.

Next time you visit a large bookstore, go to the women's studies section and page through as many of the hundreds of titles on the subject as you can. Try to find *one* which acknowledges sexism as a double-edged sword. Try to find *one* which is based on the premise that for every women's issue, there is a corresponding men's issue; that for every sexist dictum about what women shouldn't do, there is a corresponding male imperative; that for every assumption that women should behave in a certain way, there is a corresponding male "shouldn't." Find a title which says that men and women are equally oppressed —that they are jointly locked into socially mandated sex-roles; that as women have suffered economically and politically, men have suffered in more personal ways: physically, emotionally, socially, and psychologically.

If you cannot find that title in the women's studies section, ask for the men's studies section; and when you are told that the store does not have a men's studies section (you will probably be told that *everything* is men's studies), make your way to the sociology section. You would think that what the rhetoric of feminism ignored, the social scientists could not! Among the titles on the origins and development of sex-roles, try to find a title which denies that men have a superior position in society; a title which acknowledges the enormous power the female of the species has traditionally wielded through her trusteeship of future generations: her child-bearing role. Look for a title which has discovered that men and women have traditionally interacted in ways which preserved a balance of power among the sexes—a title which describes men not in terms of the power they have but in terms of their traditional economic role in society's scheme of things.

And when you find that title, if you find it, proclaim its author a calm head in a sea of hysteria; a thoughtful person who observes well what is and what we are; men and women *both* playing out a script which we did not write and do not particularly like, but who play it anyway because it takes enormous courage for us to ad-lib and extraordinary circumstances for us to do it successfully.

The calm heads are rare enough as it is, and in an age dominated by feminist theory, they are not likely to have been published anyway. It is fashionable to subscribe to the theory that men oppress women. It is also convenient to do so if one happens to be a woman, and flattering if one happens to be a man. What is fashionable, convenient, and flattering has, of course, a much larger audience than what is unfashionable, inconvenient, and unflattering.

And so it goes until enough men tire of the flattery and turn back to the reality of their lives, and find something different than they did the last time they looked. First one, then another, asks himself why he is supporting his wife. . .or why he got married in the first place. . .or why he had children. . .or why he doesn't spend more time with his children. . .or why he continues to labor at a job which bores him. . .or why his wife got custody of the kids after the divorce. . .or why he pays alimony. . .or why his sons will go to war but not his neighbor's daughters. . .or why his wife will probably outlive him.

And suddenly, what flattered him yesterday angers him today. He turns further inward to examine his life, and feminism becomes irrelevant to him, as it should, because he is a man and feminist theory does not comprehend the male experience nor does it address his problems.

As the media has only recently begun to notice, something unusual is happening to men. And because there is no comprehensive theory to explain it all, the media is perplexed by it and leaves us (for a change) to draw our own conclusions, except to suggest that what is happening looks like a reaction to feminism. The social scientists are mostly skeptical. They are still grappling with the impact of feminism on social structure and are not yet ready for another upheaval. Besides, they are somewhat comfortable with feminist theory—it *is* a man's world, isn't it?—and are not terribly inclined to entertain a new perspective.

So the sociologists (as well as the anthropologists and the biologists) say there is no precedent for it, and the psychologists explain it away as a reaction to stress; and every day another man realizes that if women are not in charge, then *no one* is running the social machine because he is *sure* that men are not in charge; and all of the theories about his behavior be damned, he will live the rest of his three score and ten exactly as he pleases.

And *that* is what the men's liberation movement is all about.

I am an angry man. Not quite as angry as I was a few years ago, but still angry. What is at least as important as my anger, however, is the fact that I am comfortable with my anger—comfortable with feeling it and with expressing it—and am not the least bit inclined to apologize to anyone for that anger.

I am angry because of the way I lived my life for some 30 or 35 years—the way I was conditioned to behave, the advantage that was taken of me in my conditioned state, the many self-destructive games I was taught to play, the life decisions I never got to make, the control over my life I gave generously to others, the guilt I allowed to be instilled in me, and my tolerance of exploitation through manipulation of my guilt.

Very specifically, I am angry because my father, who was conditioned in precisely the same manner I was, was so preoccupied with his role as breadwinner that he never had the time—or maybe the inclination—to develop the relationship with me I needed and wanted so badly.

I am angry because in my rush to select a career—or at least to find a job—right after finishing school, so that I could start earning a good living so I could get married so I could have a family so I could demonstrate to my parents and relatives and the rest of the world that I was a "mature and responsible adult male," I abandoned some dreams I am now sorry I never pursued.

I am angry because I was never really convinced that I had the option of not getting married, and never really convinced that once married I had the option of not having children. I am also angry because no one ever prepared me in the slightest for either marriage or parenting, and so not only feel that I was forced by social pressure into getting married, but was also led to believe that no special skills or preparation were required to function and to be happy in that esteemed institution.

I am angry because of the sometimes defensive and sometimes self-righteous denial of most of the women in my life that they had anything at all to do with my conditioning and the reinforcement of my conditioning to think, behave, and react in certain prescribed ways, and that they have benefited as well as suffered by my conditioned reactions.

I am angry because women have been blaming and dumping on men for close to fifteen years now, harping on the privilege and power we theoretically have and have used to exploit them and keep them subservient, forgetting and overlooking that our so-called privileges and powers were foisted on us by social customs which *they also* helped to maintain, and that these same customs have exacted from us an outrageous price for a very questionable male advantage.

I am angry that in the name of eliminating sex-stereotyping, feminism has reinforced some of the most fundamental and devastating stereotypes of all: the man as predator...stalking...powerful...base and insensitive...exploitive and untrustworthy. . .driven by uncontrollable and animalistic urges; the woman as victim. . .noble. . .pure. . .caring. . .selfless. . .loving. . .trusting . . .sensitive. . .suffering. . .used, battered, and reused for man's unspeakable purposes.

I am angry over the hypocrisy of too many women I know—their assertion of stength and independence *except when it is convenient* to be weak and dependent; their insistence that I and other men change, but *only* in ways and to a point which will please them; cries for affirmative action in employment but not in the domestic relations court; a thousand press releases from NOW on abortion but "Let's not press the draft issue because that's 'politically unwise.'"

I am angry because of the broken bodies and spirits of good men who spend their lives locked in a death dance, driven by compulsions they do not understand, filled with fear of not meeting the masculine ideal, buffeted by the frequently contradictory expectations of the women whose approval they desperately need.

In *The Hazards Of Being Male,* Herb Goldberg suggests that just as the women's movement did not have the impact it did on society by encouraging women to sit on their anger, men must understand *that* they are angry and *why* they are angry if they are to break out of the binds that are strangling them. With pathetically few exceptions, those men and women involved in the women's movement show little to no inclination to recognize, much less deal with, the anger of men.

Feminist theory, I am afraid, is one of the culprits here. For a feminist, agreeing that men can be angry at all, much less angry at women, is like saying that the king has a hard life, or that the master should be supported in his anger by his slave. But there is another factor—anger in men is frightening, to the men themselves and to the women in their lives. The mere thought of it is enough to send everyone running.

So let's pretend that anger in men does not exist. Let's pretend that it doesn't contribute to violence if it's not expressed in other ways. Let's continue to tell men that they have the good life going for them; that they should be grateful for their privileges; that they need to learn to appreciate women more, and to spend more worshipful time with them; that if they would only stop oppressing and exploiting women, all of the problems of the world would be solved and we would all live happily ever after.

Ah, fantasy!

So the men's movement in which I am involved will have none of the nonsense about oppressed and victimized women; no responsibility for the condition of women, whatever that condition might be; none of the guilt or self-loathing that is traditionally used to keep men functioning in harness.

It does not buy the line that men rule the world or that, all things considered, they have any more power than women do.

It will hear nothing of the male's life of privilege, or of his advantages as a male unless those advantages be balanced against the disadvantages of the male role.

The men's movement is rooted in the male experience, not the female experience or the female perception of the male experience.

It is positive, not negative, on the subject of men, and is supportive of men who dare to break out of self-destructive roles.

It is assertive, even arrogant, sometimes even obnoxious. And although it may someday be a "loving revolution," it seems to me that the men involved have a lot of anger to work through first.

Additionally, the men's movement is not a backlash movement—a reaction to women's rights. In fact, it seems to me that if a genuine backlash to feminist advances ever develops, it will come from *women,* not from men. The overwhelming majority of men have little to lose in a successful sex-role revolution —and a great deal to gain in the way of relief from their own stifling sex-roles. I believe a relatively small percentage of women would be delighted with a successful conclusion to the revolution: men and women raised and treated equally in *all matters* social, emotional, legal, economic, and political. But I think many more women, who do not choose to give up the advantages of the traditional female role, may certainly have something to say to the feminists when and if, for instance, their husbands throw them out of the kitchen and tell them to start earning their own keep.

The men's movement, however, is most certainly *not feminist*—that would be a contradiction in terms. Feminism will have nothing of the male experience and will not recognize it as valid. It downplays the relative importance of male concerns and insists that women's problems and struggles be given top priority.

Nor is the men's movement anti-sex. A random review of feminist literature could easily lead one to conclude that women would prefer that every male child were castrated at birth if only science could figure out how to manufacture semen artificially. More than one prominent feminist has been quoted as saying that men are all rapists at heart. They are animals, properly housed in cages. They view women only as sex-objects; use them for their own hedonistic purposes. They cannot even keep their hands off women on the job.

We are told that prostitution exploits women. We all know by now, of course, that *Playboy* exploits women. And most recently, we are advised that pornography exploits women. What amazes me is that I have always thought just the opposite; that if anyone is exploited by prostitution, skin magazines, and pornographic films, it is the consumer—the man who pays to get laid, who pays to look at photographs of naked women, who pays to watch other men with clownishly large penises cavort with women with watermelon-sized breasts.

Who is exploited or exploited more, however, is not the point. Any woman has the right to be as neurotic about sex as she likes, but the men I work with want nothing of those neuroses—we have enough of our own, thank you; few of them, fortunately, involving sex. We like sex! It is fun! And we are not about to make hypocritical asses of ourselves by jumping on the anti-sex bandwagon.

The men's movement must not be anti-business. It is so fashionable today, especially in feminist circles, to talk about the evils of the corporation—that horrible, white-male-oriented, dehumanizing beast which ravages our once virginal country in its quest for profits, exploiting women (of course) and sometimes even men. Most ironic of all is that the government itself, theoretically

287

representative of the people, and which is responsible for creating the legal entity we call the corporation, has been engaged for some fifteen years in a masochistic ritual of punishing private industry for having difficulty operating in an environment which, as Sears noted in its lawsuit on the subject, the government itself created.

I use the word masochistic to describe the government's behavior because I regard the government and industry as arms on the same public body—tools which we, the people, have created and use to help us function as a society. We speak contemptuously of "The System" as if it were something the government or industry or both have created and maintain primarily to exploit the citizen-worker. The government does not run the system. Neither does the corporation. The system runs both, and we—men and women—run the system. And if we believe that the system is out of control, we have no one but ourselves to blame.

Lastly, the men's movement must not be aligned with any particular political party or philosophy. I feel I have to say this because it looks more and more like the women's movement has aligned solidly with left-of-center Democratic politics, and because most male feminist groups have a very silly habit of mixing leftist politics and an anti-corporate attitude with men's issues.

The men's movement can no more be Marxist in its orientation than it can be capitalistic; no more liberal than conservative; no more Democratic than Republican. Men of all political persuasions, of all income levels, of all classes, the black and the WASP and the Catholic and the Jew; the laborer and the corporation executive; the urban and the rural dweller; all suffer the same conditioning as men, the same self-destructive tendencies; the same need to achieve at all costs; the same provider burden; the same guilt; the same dependence on women and distance from other men.

We can afford no illusions about panaceas, political or structural. It makes not a damn bit of difference whether I am for or against nuclear energy. It matters not a bit whether my sexual preference and my lifestyle and my views on abortion and my opinion on the oil crisis are compatible with yours. The issues which *bind* us began to influence us before we could read, before we had any concept of race, before we knew anything important other than that our mothers existed.

We need to listen to each other for the cries of pain and to recognize the fear we all have. We need to approach each other cautiously but steadily, holding out a hand of understanding and trust and support. We need to acknowledge our anger and help each other turn it into a source of energy for positive change. We need to talk with each other openly and stop worrying about how "cool" or knowledgeable we will appear. We need to forget what women will have us be, and to figure out first *what we are* and what *we* want to be and how *we* choose to live our lives, and that—and only that—is what will make for a genuine men's liberation movement.

FEMALE EMOTION AND FEMINIST LOGIC

M. Adams

Women came to that land of cold, hard (and often specious) logic the same way they came to so many other traditionally male realms: through that one-way gate that allows women to become more masculine while barring men from becoming more feminine. Just as women can wear pants and men can't wear dresses, just as women can remain single and have careers while there are no such things as "house husbands," women can now wax logical while men look just as strange as ever waxing emotional. And no man ever wielded logic as viciously as your average feminist. As a result, men don't stand a chance against the combined onslaught of female emotion and feminist logic.

If a man questions a feminist premise, he is immediately hit with a barrage of analysis and theory that would take anyone five years to untangle. It is sufficiently laced with truisms and platitudes to appear, especially to the guilt-based male perception of women, to be irrefutable. Men buckle under the bombardment of feminist logic, the same way that *women* used to feel helpless when men used logic to manipulate *them*. Feminists have turned that table on men, but the difference is that feminists can still cry. Feminists can still pout. Feminists can still use emotion and emotional arguments against men whenever they want to. For all the angry logic in the world, feminists are still women, and women have still got squatter's rights to the domain of emotion.

FEMINISM AND MALE GUILT

M. Adams

In the humanist community, feminism is like a never-ending ideological "ladies' night." All sociological theory and rhetoric are on the house. And if that's not enough, then a woman can always hit on the male-feminists to treat her to some more. "Hey, sailor. . . buy me a rationalization for being angry at you and treating you any way I want, and I'll show you a good time by relieving some of your guilt." And the sailor trades away his own relationship with himself for a little sign of approval from some angry women.

TODAY'S MALE FEMINISTS

Richard Haddad

Today's male feminists are largely men filled with self-loathing who expiate their guilt through the worship of a goddess who gets her kicks out of dumping on men. They ignore or belittle the role restrictions men have lived with, and rigidly follow the feminist party line on issues. Although they represent themselves, and are represented by the women's movement, as men's liberationists, they attract few men and have virtually no lasting appeal among those they do attract. Their arguments simply do not register with the average male's experience, and they can't hold his attention for long.

Chapter 14:
Making Changes

THE STRUGGLE

THE TROUBLE WITH MEN'S ISSUES

M. Adams

Nobody wants to listen to men's issues. They don't want to listen because men's lib doesn't sell perfume. It doesn't sell pantyhose. And even deep inside, they still don't want to listen because we're not women. We're not pretty. We don't have cute smiles and bouncy hair and remind them of their mothers and sisters and first girlfriends. We're not sexy and exciting when we're angry. We're not a challenge to suitors. *We're not the recipients of chivalry.* Who are we? We're complainers, crybabies, wimps, nerds, cowards, weirdos.

MEN ARE ISOLATED

Tom Williamson

Men are isolated. They aren't just isolated individually, they are isolated in groups. For example, they are isolated by occupation. I keep hearing that police are a very tight group, that they don't really come out of their shell and relate well to people outside of their occupational sphere. Then one day I saw some statistics on police—they have a high rate of suicide, of drug addiction, and family breakups. Then, on another day, I was attending this course about computers and I heard the teacher, who is a programmer, going on about alcohol addiction and family breakups among computer people. *Computer World,* the principle trade journal for computer people, even ran a front-page article about the disastrous effects of job-related stress on data-processing managers and how they must learn to be more communicative. Next, I found myself listening to a late-night talk show and the psychotherapist being interviewed tells the audience that psychotherapists have the highest rate of suicide of any profession. Until then I thought it was the police.

All these people seem to think that it's only happening either to computer people, or psychotherapists, or police. Well, the problems are not occupationally compartmentalized, because whatever it is that's happening is going on all across occupational lines. It is primarily affecting men. Men are the ones most apt to be found in stress situations and to have been brought up to deny that they suffer any stress or have any feelings. So it's not cops, psychotherapists, or computer programmers who are at risk. It is men.

Somebody needs to bring this all together, and do something about it.

MEN DEALING WITH THEIR PAIN

Robert A. Sides

As long as men are themselves afraid of emotions, or are themselves afraid of *real* emotional displays, they aren't likely to help someone else whose emotional dams have finally burst, be they male or female. Such displays are too-painful reminders of their own buried pains.

MEN HIDE THEIR PAIN

Bob and Daphne Bauer

Why aren't there more men's advocacy groups? It's because men try to deal with these problems by themselves, rather than associate with other men and share their hurts. They keep their hurts to themselves, or they just try to avoid them. And this doesn't work, of course.

FIRE

Will Watkins

Three times
You fanned fire
As you sat
In the male circle.
"I drive other men
Away," you said
(And your words
flared the fire red.)
"I am lonely,"
You said
(And your words
forced the fire yellow.)
"I am consumed
by longing," you said
(And your words
fused the fire white.)
"This heat can char
the soul," someone cried
(And the fumed circle
exploded suddenly,
taking flight
like a kicked bonfire.)

THE MEN'S MOVEMENT AND MEN'S DIVORCE SOCIETIES

Tom Williamson

There are two large groups or organizations of men in particular where there's a lot of hurt. One is with the veterans—in particular, the Vietnam veterans. And another group is the divorced men. Now it's true, as Herb Goldberg has pointed out, that the guys who go to these divorced societies are often the most angry individuals; but when you look at their cases, they have every right to be as angry as they are. What's difficult about the whole thing is that men cannot ask for help until it is either almost too late, or it is too late. Unfortunately it is those for whom it is almost too late, or it is too late, who are the guys who end up in the divorced societies. The divorced societies have two principal problems, as I see it, that prevent their effective functioning. One is their frequent shows of rage which become misinterpreted as attacks on all women.

And the second problem is that very often these guys are so demoralized by the legal system which they are fighting that they end up in an extreme state of depression where they can't function properly. Depression is very immobilizing and it ruins incentive and focus. I think there is a need for a men's movement organization that will be cognizant of these issues, and will try and work with all different aspects and angles of this thing. There is no reason why those who are concerned with civil rights' issues should be considered at odds, or labeled in a derogatory way as "angry," as though there is something wrong with that, and put over in the corner as deviants who are opposed to men who are trying to fully develop their human side. I maintain that before we are going to get large numbers of men who are capable of dealing with their lives more or less in a planning arrangement, rather than in a reactive way, who are capable of asking for help when it is reasonable to give them help, and for whom something can still be done, we are first going to have to develop a movement that focuses very heavily on our human side, on men becoming more sensitive not only to being in touch with themselves, but also, to being in touch with other men. Once we can identify with the problems of each other as men, then the legal side of this movement will gush forth with a flurry. But as long as men deny their own pain, and therefore the pain of other men, little will happen. The key is to reach the emotions. Behind *every* legal issue lies the emotions.

STEREOTYPED AT 13: THE FRUSTRATIONS OF BEING A YOUNG MALE

Mark Zukor

I feel that there is much discrimination towards boys in several ways in society. First of all boys are treated poorly in schools for no reason whatsoever. I have experienced this primarily in elementary schools. During my schooling through grades 1–6, I have been degraded because of my sex. "Boys are rough, troublemaking liars" is the typical stereotype by many people. Therefore boys get treated as though they are meaner. Many, in fact, are just the opposite, but they get treated as the other half does. Girls, on the other hand, are "sweet, gentle, and honest," another typical picture by society. The girls get treated as if they are angels and would not do anything spiteful. This hurts both sexes because the boys who do not fit in with the rowdy group get angry at the way they are treated. They begin to think of themselves as worse than others, and may change drastically because of this pressure. The girls will go through life as if they are the highest quality stuff around. And because they are treated like they are, they will think less of boys and look down on them as they were influenced to do when they were young.

The teachers who tend to do this the most are the women teachers. They might do this because they feel that women are usually discriminated against and they want to stop that by treating the girls as superiors. Or, the boys represent the men who have put down women, and the teacher wants to brainwash them into the opposite, that women are superior. Also the teacher might have had a bad past, and has suffered a lot of prejudice because of her sex. She doesn't want "her girls" to feel this so she treats them better than she had been.

Finally, the teacher may just be one of the people who think that boys are troublemakers and should be treated with more discipline. The men teachers feel as the boys do, and have warned me not to touch any girl. "If they hit you or start a fight," my male gym teacher said, "just don't do anything; you'll be the one to get into trouble, even if you did nothing. That's just the way it goes."

BOYS BREAK AND STEAL

Not only does this occur in schools; it occurs in stores all over. While in a local shopping mall with my brothers, I was watched like a hawk. I am sure the woman in one store felt that we would break or steal something. She even told us to not touch a thing if we weren't going to buy it. I was angry and we just left, saying, just loud enough for her to hear, "Gee, since they don't treat us like regular customers, we should go somewhere else to spend our money." Another time I went to a candy store where there were aisles of small toys, cards, etc. I spotted a 20-year-old man watching my every move. If I went to one place, he went there too. I then decided not to buy anything there, but to have some fun with the guy, anyhow. I stared at him for long periods of time, going in and out of the aisles, back and forth. It was fun watching him go back and forth as I did. Then realizing that he was just doing his job, I left.

In conclusion, I feel that boys are mistrusted in common, everyday places in society just because boys have a reputation which is not true for most of them. If this discrimination ceases, it will begin a more pleasant, pressureless atmosphere for many boys and girls all over the country.

DIRECTIONS

SEPARATE ISSUES FOR MEN

Robert A. Sides

I get upset when I hear women talking authoritatively about men's lives. I don't think they know very much about us. Women claim there's a uniqueness to them that we cannot possibly experience because we are men and, in some ways, I believe they are right. If, for example, I stand outside the hospital delivery room just as a laboring woman enters, and say, "I really know what you're going through," she would just as likely and justifiably say, "Are you shitting me? How can you *possibly* know what it's like to birth a child?" Well, in the same way men have to start saying there are certain experiences that women just cannot know about. Men have to insist women stop talking as if they do know, because it demeans and belittles what men live through.

Strange isn't it? Feminism has legitimized the importance of subjective experience, but it seems *only* for women. They still tend to objectify men's lives and play on the conditioned male trait of silent suffering.

MEN'S LIBERATION AND HUMANISM

Tom Williamson

There are the people who have the humanistic approach. On paper it all sounds very nice. They say that we shouldn't have a "men's" movement; that we should have a "people's" movement. Bob Sides is the best one to rebut that. Sides points out that, despite how lovey-dovey all this sounds, we are faced with the problems presented by a gender-specific "women's" movement which is sophisticated, well organized, and which encourages women to express their anger. How come we deny men this opportunity? As soon as we say we want a men's movement, suddenly things get watered down and we have to consider everybody's problems. We have to have a people's movement. We have to be the conciliatory ones. I mean, why can't we examine our own lives and our own space and develop our own issues, and then at some future date sit down with the women's movement.

Men today are getting jerked around. They are in favor of the Equal Rights Amendment because one group of women want it, and they are against E.R.A. because another group of women don't want it. Men, as a gender, have no voice. So, why do we have to jump into this people's thing when in fact, very little is known about men as it is, and we really need an organization that can lobby for funds to get the studies to go out and do the sociological and psychological research that's needed to find out who we really are and what has been happening to us.

BOYS WILL BE...MEN

Fredric Hayward

We have gone far in preparing girls to take on nontraditional roles; we have also done much to prepare society to accept girls in nontraditional roles. The girl who wants to be a doctor, instead of a nurse, is encouraged by affirmative action programs, success stories in the media, proud parents, boys who find her attractive, and school personnel who have had their consciousness raised in equal rights workshops. We work hard to insure a positive environment for the girl who plays baseball, and insist that she be respected.

Sadly, however, we have done precious little to prepare boys to live out nontraditional roles, or to prepare the world to accept a boy who chooses a nontraditional path. The boy who wants to be a nurse instead of a doctor is discouraged by employment discrimination, a lack of models in the media, distraught parents, girls who find something wrong with him (namely, an insufficient promise of future income and status), and school personnel, whose workshops taught them that equal rights means women's rights. We do nothing to insure a positive environment for boys studying ballet.

Today's typical school is like the suburban school in Massachusetts that formed a committee to raise consciousness about what must be done to make equal rights a reality in their educational program. The committee unanimously agreed that living up to *current* gender expectations seemed to place the boys in a more stressful situation than the girls. Today it is even more acceptable for a girl to be a tomboy than it was, for example, in 1954, when Iris Smith was my fourth grade class's best baseball player and most popular girl. It is no more acceptable, however, for today's boy to be a sissy than it was for Bruce Doe in 1954, whose name I have changed because being a sissy was, and is, downright unacceptable.

And the school's committee saw that boys are under continuous pressure to follow a comprehensive code of requirements and limitations. There are certain clothes they may not wear, and certain positions their bodies may not assume. The social code is so restrictive that even certain colors are considered female-only. Feelings are forbidden, roughhouse is mandatory. The ever-present fear is to be labelled a fag[1] and such accusations dominate conversation.

Any failure to measure up brought vicious insults or ostracism from male and female peers alike. Though anything appropriate for a boy is now appropriate for a girl, the reverse is not yet true. The resultant strain on the boys was almost continuously evident in their appearance, conversation, and behavior.

The committee further recognized that disciplinary measures were applied more severely to boys, and that the Student Code of Behavior even specified harsher treatment for boys.

The committee then agreed, almost unanimously, that they would not waste any time discussing these or *any* boys' issues. All attention was reserved for the girls.

Sexism in the name of antisexism has thus been the self-defeating strategy of the Equal Rights Movement for years.

The problem has not gone unnoticed by parents. In various workshops, I have been approached by feminist mothers. Their ideology told them that males have it easy, while girls are denied the range of opportunities available to boys. They took great joy in encouraging their daughters to play soccer, take wood shop, and study law. But what, they asked, should they say when their little boy asks if he could try his mother's lipstick or carry her pocketbook to

---

[1] Or "fem," "queer," "wimp," etc. depending on local vernacular.

the store? Their first reaction had been a frightened no! Then, realizing their hypocrisy, they reconsidered. . .and repeated a reluctant no. What loving parent would send her son out to be ridiculed or beaten up? For boys, the old limitations still apply.

While the old limitations still apply, the old balance is gone. For example, sexism used to create a balanced, if somewhat schizophrenic, self-image: girls used to be sugar'n'spice and everything nice (and weak, irrational creatures who couldn't even change a flat tire), while boys used to be strong, self-confident, and competent (and unkept, unreliable, sex-crazed creatures who couldn't even boil an egg). The Battle of the Sexes continues, the innovation being that we have now agreed on the heroes and villains. Girls have *all* the positive qualities which used to be divided between the sexes; boys are just plain bad.

Boys who were born in 1970 are being taught that they are somehow responsible for, and must atone for, withholding the right to vote from the women of 1870. Boys who have never voted, let alone made laws, are told that it is fitting for them, and for them only, to be forced to surrender their bodies to the military at age 18. . .after all, "they" make the wars.

Most teachers are not aware of their own roles in teaching boys that male is evil. A girl beat up a boy recently at a local junior high school. The teachers smiled over the incident all day. A blow for women's equality had been struck; revenge had been exacted from those males who had oppressed women throughout the ages.

Never mind that this male had an eleven-year-old body and had not yet learned that women's suffrage was not something a doctor could treat. Never mind that the girl had initiated the violence and struck first. Never mind that a teacher's job includes teaching that violence should be a last resort. Never mind attending to the boy's shame and pain. His only solace was knowing that if he had won the fight, he would have been promptly suspended.

It is no longer true that girls take cooking, sewing, and typing, while boys take wood shop, metal shop, and print shop. Most classes around the country have integrated; everybody takes everything. On paper this looks progressive, but in reality, there is something missing. Too often, the new programs are presented as an advancement for the girls and appropriate degradation for the boys. That is, girls now have unlimited opportunity, and (ha-ha) look at those boys in their aprons.

Personally, I must cook every day, I must type every day, and I mend my clothes much more often than I make bookends or utilize all the other wonderful skills I learned in shop. Women's skills are as useful as men's skills, though most men do not find this out until they have been divorced and reduced to a steady diet of TV dinners.

My answer to the parents whose sons are curious about dresses and do not know whether to reinforce their ideals of sexual equality or to protect them from the insults and punches that await an "effeminate" boy is "Tell them now! Tell them it is not fair."

Tell them that girls can wear any style of clothing that strikes their whim, but that boys cannot AND IT IS NOT FAIR. Tell them that girls who wear boys' styles are sent to modeling schools, but boys who wear girls' fashions are sent to psychiatrists AND IT IS NOT FAIR. Like the black parents who had to teach their children to sit in the back of buses, you must teach what is required, but you may also teach what should be fair.

The Equal Rights Movement has been very reluctant to raise consciousness about injustice toward males. Research, such as a study of husband battering, has been consciously suppressed. There seems to be a fear of letting men know what is happening to them. While the women's movement is concerned that some men think the movement has "gone too far," I frequently sense in women a fear that the men's movement wants to "go too far." Guilt-ridden men can be easily manipulated, but angry men are more dangerous. Parents, however, should start to raise sons who are aware. We may be forced to deny them opportunity, but we can grant them knowledge.

Stop telling your sons to protect girls. Tell all your children that the gift of protection and responsibility of protection must fall equally. Warn your sons that hitting a girl, even in self-defense, is likely to bring special punishment AND IT IS NOT FAIR. Tell them that discipline, in general, will be more strict for them AND IT IS NOT FAIR.

As you teach that boys and girls can now be equally gentle, tell your sons that they might someday be forced to carry a gun AND IT IS NOT FAIR. As you teach them that they are part of a new age of equal employment opportunity, tell them that only their career and life might be interrupted, or ended, by the draft AND IT IS NOT FAIR.

As you teach them nurturing skills, tell them that only girls will have the security of knowing that, as long as they are not abusive, their children will never be taken away from them AND IT IS NOT FAIR.

Give nonsexist warnings. Daughters hear that boys, if given the chance, will exploit them. But, daughters rarely hear that it is wrong to like a boy because he is popular, or athletic, or strong, or wealthy, or good-looking. Tell your daughters that girls who look for these qualities in boys are just as exploitative as boys who are looking to "score." Warn your sons about these girls, because almost all warnings today, from newspaper advice columns to sex education courses, are intended to help girls and scold boys. Tell boys not to expect sex if they take a girl to the movie, and tell girls not to expect to be taken to a movie.

There is a popular myth that today's girls do not "wait" to be asked. Myths do not require much corroboration, and five assertive girls per graduating class, or two assertive experiences per girl, are all that is required to maintain this one. But, myth it is.

I recently had a college class spend an evening in singles' bars. The men were not allowed to make any of the first moves: no starting conversations, no buying drinks, no asking for phone numbers, etc. The women were excited about going out and picking up new men; they knew that "the new, socially assertive" woman was only a myth, but they did not know that "the man in control" was also a myth. They mistakenly trusted their feminist rhetoric, which had convinced them that the male role of going up to a stranger and making himself vulnerable to rejection is fun and easy.

I watched the men go off, dressed especially nice and practicing their smiles. I watched the women go off, nervously drinking, in search of some last-minute courage. At the following class came the reports: not one man had one conversation all night, and not one woman took any initiative all night. And, another myth bites the dust.

Are you still giving your daughters the impression that "nice girls" do not talk to a boy unless he talks first? Or call a boy unless he calls first? Or ask out a boy unless he asks first? Or kiss a boy unless he kisses first?

Most parents are very reluctant to alter the system that makes boys into predators and girls into prey. This system goes on to drive an unhealthy competitive distance between boys, to force girls to act like objects (and then complain when they are treated like objects), and to lead to an inevitable build-up of resentment in boys toward girls who cultivate the skill of pretending that they share no mutual attraction.

It is very difficult to bring ourselves to encourage girls to stop being the chasee; our conditioning that boys are evil and girls need protection, like most other sexist conditioning, runs very deep. Nevertheless, we will continue the old pattern of dishonest relating unless we begin to face this issue.

Parents must also start pressuring their school systems to examine *all* sexism. During a three-month period, the Boston public school system reported that over seventy-four percent of the students who were suspended were male. Lest the reader think that this is simply a reflection of males being more unruly (Negative sexual stereotypes are still permitted, as long as they apply to males), it is important to note that boys were over four times as likely to be suspended for smoking. . .although statistics (and school bathroom floors) show that more teenage girls smoke than boys, and girl smokers smoke more.

A seventh grade survey in another school system indicated that boys were five times as likely to drop foreign languages and nine times as likely to be withdrawn from the classroom and placed in a learning center. The school system decided not to pursue this matter, and instead, investigated why so few girls tried out for the math team.

Parents should demand that schools present nurturing skills to boys in a positive light. Boys should be told that they are taking cooking and sewing, not to atone for the sins of past males nor to bear an equal share of drudgery, but rather so that they need not depend on a woman in order to have a comfortable home. These boys will be entitled to insist on something never offered men before: the right to full parental relationships with their children, even if divorce destroys their marriage.

Demand that your schools raise our children's consciousness to the problems of boys. Antisexist education should help boys understand that past limitations have damaged males as much as females. Boys should think about questions like, "Am I as close to my father as I would like to be?" "What kind of father would I like to be?" "How do girls take advantage of boys?"

Similarly, girls should be taught more than how to guard against the exploitative male. They should think about the sexist demands that they might be placing on boys. Is a girl who wants to date a boy because he is a football star any better than a boy who wants to date a girl because she has large breasts? Is a girl who expects a boy to pick her up and pay her way any better than a boy who expects a girl to make out?

A girl who decides to become a secretary knows that her social life will not be as limited as her earning capacity. She can still marry her male boss, because men do not rate women by their income. A boy, on the other hand, who plans to become a secretary, knows that a limited income implies a limited social life. Female professionals do not marry "below" themselves. (If women were not still rating men by income, there would not be so many articles along the theme of "Single Shock: Where Are the Men for the Women at the Top," *Savvy,* February 1980.)

Sex education should be life education, and life education must be coeducation. Boys and girls need to exchange honest communication. Most women would be shocked if they learned how so much male behavior (even the violence!) is motivated by a desire to please the female.

As the male learns he must initiate relationships, he learns that money eases his access to women. As the male learns that he has a limited time to overcome her initial aloofness, he learns to describe his value through self-centered conversation. Even demonstrating the intensity of his desire through jealous violence is rewarded more often than not. As the male learns that females feel insecure walking the streets alone, he learns that a willingness to fight on her behalf is also rewarded. From the start, girls reward the boys who spend money on them, fight to defend them, confidently assert a relationship with them, and make the sexual moves on them.

Finally, be patient with the boys who are still showing macho behavior patterns. It is our own fault that we have offered them no viable alternatives. Sometimes, for instance, we tell them, "Now you are free to be sensitive, non-violent, and in touch with your emotions." Then we make it clear through legislation (draft registration), the entertainment media, and our own personal behavior that, when there is an emergency, will all turn to *them* for security. It is a cruel hoax to teach boys to be caring, gentle, and in touch with emotions. . .and then hand them a gun and force them to fight for their lives. Insensitivity, violence, and emotional distance are *positive* qualities for soldiers, and boyhood is clearly still a grooming period for soldiering.

The traditional male roles—providing, protecting, and initiating relationships—are still rather rigidly imposed on men. The traditional male mentality develops as a direct result of this imposition, not as a result of free choice. By showering boys with equal rights rhetoric, instead of dealing with their issues and changing their options, we perpetuate the cycle that is the foundation of sexism.

Fighting sexism by dealing only with women's issues is too much like winterizing your car by putting snow tires only on the left side; it not only represents a failure to see half the problem, but it also insures that your car will swerve off the road at the most inopportune times.

MEN ARE TURNING TO OTHER MEN

Richard Haddad

With less emphasis on succeeding by traditional standards and less concern over how manly society will judge them to be, men are lifting the blankets on their emotional expressiveness and are finding the experience a positive (and healthy) one.

They are even turning to other men for emotional support, and this is an extremely significant development. A combination of conditioned competitiveness with other men and an obsessive fear of homosexuality has traditionally kept adult men distant from each other, cutting off their communication with half the population.

Unlike their fathers before them, today's men are learning, not without discomfort however, to share anxieties and disappointments with other men; to admit weaknesses; to talk about their fantasies. They are revealing themselves as they are and as they'd like to be, rather than as others would have them be, and they're finding that they have much in common with other men—similar problems, similar fears, similar hopes for the future. A spirit of community is building among liberated men, a brotherhood, and it adds dimension to the lives of those who choose to belong.

MEN'S DREAMS OF BONDING

Perry Treadwell, Ph.D.

The rather ordinary man of the eighties comes to a men's group out of some as yet unexpressed longing, hurt or need. He is anywhere from mid-twenties to over fifty, and has found his life disintegrating around him in a female relationship, in a job, or in feeling that he is simply missing something. When asked about his feelings on male bonding he can become very explicit. Words such as "honest," "sharing," "openness," and "trust" are common. One man fantasizes "a loving, caring, open safe kind of bond where men don't feel the need to compete and keep up facades. A place where we could be vulnerable and strong—both. I feel a lot of this with some men but my fantasy is it could happen with all men."

Another man would like to see himself, "exchanging thoughts, sharing experiences in the undemanding way that seems impossible in a man/woman intimate relationship." He sees such an exchange "impossible with a woman because of different psychologies, sexual needs, family demands." Several men express a need for "closeness and caring," "open expressions of affection," but "no sex."

These same men see the barriers to male bonding as competition, female jealousy, and fear of homosexuality. On a personal basis Frank would "like myself enough to be secure to be me and open enough to allow another to be likewise." Such security allows men to "risk sharing" themselves. The barriers of "one-upmanship, the survival of the fittest, and the myth of the superior and super macho man" prevent bonding.

One woman, Peter reported, felt threatened by the men's group, saying, "I'm supposed to be the nurturer and you're getting nurtured somewhere else. It's almost worse than you having sex with another woman."

But the men agree that the biggest barrier is homophobia. Even gay men in the group say they don't want sex getting in the way of brothering.

WHAT'S A WOMAN LIKE ME DOING IN A MEN'S MOVEMENT LIKE THIS?

Naomi J. Penner, M.A.

As co-founder and former vice president of The Coalition of Free Men, a national, non-profit, educational organization concerned with men's issues, I have often been asked what a woman is doing in a men's movement organization. The questions seem to imply that I am a fish out of water, betraying my female sex by supporting men, the "enemy." My response to my questioners has by now become a stock one: "When men will be free, then women will be free; when women will be free, then men will be free; when both are free, children will be free."

In 1969 I founded one of the first chapters of the National Organization for Women in the United States because I needed the support and acceptance of other people in order to feel free to be myself and live the lifestyle I chose. At that time I came in contact with many women who were feeling trapped, confused, frustrated, depressed, angry, and despairing about the condition of their lives. We all pitched in together to create a movement which has since legitimized independence, educational and employment opportunities, and alternative lifestyles for women.

It occurred to me then how dependent we women were on men, yet how often we would consider men the "enemy," to wit, the "opposite" sex, i.e., the battle of the sexes. "All men want only one thing; you can't trust 'em," I would hear over and over again from the women I met. I began to realize how paradoxical and sad it was for me to be expected to love and live in close harmony as a family unit with a member of that "enemy."

"Why were they our enemy?" I asked myself one day. It began to occur to me how differently we males and females had been conditioned from the day of birth. There was pink—sweet, cute, gentle—and there was blue—tough, aggressive, smart. We were encouraged to have different interests: I was given dolls and a tea set; my brother, a truck and a hammer. The career expectations for us were dissimilar: I would become a teacher—a good career for a girl—and a mother; my brother, an attorney. Also different emotions were emphasized in us: I could cry and act hurt, be sweet, innocent, virginal; my brother could act angry and be rough, tough, and sexual (as long as he made sure not to hurt me, for which he would have to feel guilty forever). We were even shown different modes to express ourselves: I was encouraged to express my self through verbalizing; he, through physical outlets. Our clothing and appearance were different; I in my dresses, neat and clean; he in pants, a bit torn and dirty. And many of our values were opposite: I was looking forward to marriage; he was taught that he would be smart if he could avoid it. So there we were, the female and the male, the yin and the yang, opposites blessed with society's crazy expectation that we would eventually grow up and live peacefully and productively in the same household with one of those "foreign species." It indeed seemed to me that members of the "opposite" sex were as familiar and comfortable as a Martian. Yet I knew I had to "get" one of them if I were to be considered a successful female.

So, you ask, what does this have to do with a woman in a men's movement? At first I was typically envious of men—their independence, their initiative, their career opportunities. Then as I became stronger and more aware of my own personal power, I began to realize that it was not only tough to be a woman, but that it was as tough or maybe even tougher to be a man. I couldn't reconcile why men were dying eight years sooner than women and committing suicide three times as often if it was so great to be a man. I found that societal expectations on males to prove themselves as "real men" were overwhelming.

As a woman, I began to see that I had many options. I could choose to work or stay home, to cry or not, to pay for myself or not, to wear skirts or pants, to have sex or not, to be affectionate with both men and women, to call a man or wait to be called, even to have a child by myself if I wished. If I were a man, I concluded, I would be angry at having fewer options. I realized that always having to take the initiative and have the responsibility is very burdensome, and that I would want someone else to do that occasionally and relieve the pressure.

I then came across a study that stated that more people—men and women—would consciously choose to be the male sex if they could because of the seeming advantages. However, the study went on to say, the women, when interviewed by different types of interviewers, were found to be more consistent in their responses and secure in their identity than the men, whose reactions to the questions changed dramatically as the age, sex, and personality of the interviewer changed. This, to me, indicated more insecurity and a desire to please on the part of the men, and I related the results to a quote that says, "Women have their femininity as a birthright; men have to prove their masculinity all their lives." What a way to live a life!

I then decided that if I were going to have good relationships with men, I would benefit by knowing more about what it was actually like to have to play the traditional male role. I decided to risk asking men for their telephone numbers, calling them for dates, and paying the check. I found that it was far from easy to always have the pressure of having to take the initiative and face subsequent rejection. Further, I didn't like having to pay for a man's company. I also realized that as a man the only way I would get sexual pleasure would be to pursue it and face a lot of rejection in the process. I then started observing men more closely. I realized how hard it was for many of them to ask for help and speak their true feelings without thinking less of themselves, and how hard it was for them to keep their heads up if they were unemployed or had less than a status job; in short, how hard it was for them to be accepted for themselves.

Having an understanding of, and sympathy for, the male position instead of envy and resentment which is so widespread among many females, I wanted to educate other women. I also wanted to work closely with men to help them find options. I was aware how little sympathy there was for men. I compared, for example, the sensitivity shown to women and children being killed on the television screen as compared to that shown to men. A man's death was routine and expected. "We men have to be hardened to accept death," one man told me resignedly. "After all, somebody has to be prepared to do the killing and get killed in defense of the country." I met many men who expressed dependence on women for feelings, for affection, for physical nurturing, for parenting their children, for sexual pleasure, for understanding. Many of these men were uncomfortable relating closely with each other.

Thus, finally five years ago in 1980, a few men and I decided to found an organization which we called The Coalition of Free Men. The goals of the organization would be to look at the ways men suffer socially, emotionally, physically, and legally as a result of sex-role stereotyping. Initially, there was a distrust on the part of a few men as to the role of a woman—the "enemy"—in the organization. However, I was soon accepted when the men came to realize that I was sincere, that I liked and supported them, and that I was not there to play games, exploit, humiliate, or judge them.

Despite the fact that I am a woman, I have made a strong commitment to continue working for both men and women. When I am questioned as to my loyalty to my own sex and it is pointed out to me that women, for example, are battered more than are men, I reply that I am concerned only with the fact that there are battered *people*, sex or quantity notwithstanding. And I hasten to add, what about the batterers, who also need help and understanding?

In The Coalition of Free Men we have become more and more aware of the paucity of support services for men because we have found that traditionally men will not seek help until it's often too late. Our goals are to become informed as to the condition of men, to educate the public, and to change a system which is destructive to both sexes. We believe that if a human race is to survive, we must all work together, not as the "enemy" but as trusted partners. To paraphrase Fred Hayward at the National Congress For Men in 1981: "We are not here to *win* the battle of the sexes; we are here to *end* it."

MEN'S LIBERATION AND HUMAN LIBERATION

Richard Haddad

We can hope that human liberation is the pot of gold at the end of the journey, and make that our objective, and have that objective guide our decision-making along the way. We can develop an intrinsic respect for one another—for whatever it is that we want to be in life and for how we choose to live our lives. We can stop saddling each other with expectations based on ancient and long-obsolete notions of how male and female should behave and allow each person to develop according to his or her own individual abilities and interests.

Things will be different in that kind of a world—that's for sure, and different is not necessarily bad—just strange for a while. And I have a hunch that our economy will adapt to whatever happens; that it's a lot more flexible than we think. Just as we are.

WHY IS THE MEN'S MOVEMENT NOT "HAPPENING"?

Herb Goldberg, Ph.D.

The men's movement is by no means a failure or less "successful" than the women's movement. It has just taken a different, less visible form. Any and every man is a part of that movement if he is in the process of recognizing and redeveloping his human side, and is growing away from masculine strictures and definitions of himself. The man who is taking yoga classes instead of playing or watching football; joyously developing a close relationship with a male friend; refusing to accept labels such as "coward," "impotent," or "failure" to describe his responses; and choosing women to relate to who do not expect him to do the masculine dance—to court and take sole responsibility—is part of the men's movement.

SEARCHING FOR MEN'S EMOTIONAL HISTORY

Francis Baumli

In the very heart of Missouri there is a little town called Boonville, population 6,200, situated directly by the Missouri River. Boonville is called a "river town," partly because of its location, partly because some of its commerce—sand dredging and barge traffic mostly—is connected to the river. Crossing the river, which at this point narrows to a width of one-fourth mile, and leading directly into the town, is a seven-span bridge. Before this bridge was completed in 1924,

306

people crossing the river had to depend on a motor-driven ferry called *The Dorothy.*

One day, shortly before the ferry was retired, a Boonville resident was talking to the old ferryman about his job. The old man said that weekdays were quite tolerable since the traffic wasn't too heavy. But Saturdays were very busy since this was the day everyone came to town to do business. And Sundays were as busy as Saturdays, because that was when everyone was out in horse and buggy, horse and wagon, or walking, to do their social visiting.

Asked if he had ever noticed what sort of Sunday socializing people did in those days, the ferryman responded as if the question had indeed occurred to him before. "I've never actually counted it up," he said, "but I think it would be fair to say that nine times out of ten, it was a couple, or the whole family, going to visit the wife's parents." He paused to reflect, and then added, "I don't know what this means, but it must mean something."

I'm not sure what it means either. But there are some possible implications. It perhaps suggests that women were closer to their parents than men were. It may also suggest that women, during those days, were not always the helpless chattel of patriarchal husbands—that perhaps,when it came to domestic decisions, they somehow had the power to get what they wanted. And it further suggests that if the *wife's* parents exercised the most influence over their offspring, and if their daughter was the one who governed her own family's exposure to this influence, then we can suggest that during those times there was a very pervasive matriarchal influence determining the character of personal, family, and social roles. Which suggests that theories about early patriarchy in our society aren't all that pat.

Yes; all this involves drawing quite a few implications from a simple statement by an old ferryman. But these implications do not have to be accepted as conclusive. Rather, they might serve as seminal suggestions to motivate and direct research into what men's *emotional* history really has been. Women for years— perhaps centuries—have reserved the right to tell men what their emotions are. And for the last three decades feminists have been rewriting history as "herstory," and have presumed that herstory will provide the last word on all the gender issues.

While it may be true that the history of politics, economics, and philosophy has thus far been written by men, it does not follow that a true history of men's emotions has been written. No man has yet attempted to chart thoroughly how men's emotions may have been initially oppressed and left to atrophy. No one has explored how perhaps both men and women contributed to, and interacted in terms of, this oppression. And no man has yet attempted to uncover the pain and suffering men have endured for centuries because they have been denied access to their emotions.

I believe that, in the course of men liberating themselves in today's world, one of the most important and enjoyable tasks they must take up is that of reclaiming the right to speak for what their emotions are. Uncovering the true history of male emotions would likely do a great deal toward helping achieve this end.

A HISTORY OF THE MEN'S MOVEMENT

Tom Williamson

INTRODUCTION

The North American men's movement cannot be traced back along one historical line. There have been a number of differing directions which have been characterized by sporadic growth and instability. But with the coming of the women's movement, it became legitimate not only for women but also for men to question gender stereotypes. As this happened, the men's movement began to develop more focus, using some generally recognized concepts which had been pioneered by the women's movement. It is worth noting here that the anger directed toward men by the women's movement helped solidify the men's movement as men reacted to women's anger toward men. This reaction has followed two paths: one accepts the feminist condemnation of men as oppressors, while the other rejects it. The development of these two directions has led to some squabbling over the legitimacy of each to be called a men's movement. As a result, the few attempts to outline a history of "the" men's movement have traced only the development of the faction with which the author identifies, giving the false impression that there is a unilateral movement in this country. This article intends to avoid this approach.

Almost all of the men's movement organizations have been sympathetic to such women's objectives as breaking down sexual stereotypes and passing the Equal Rights Amendment. However, male support of some specific feminist issues is starting to flag. Presently the most controversial issue is joint custody of children in divorce. In some locations the National Organization for Women (NOW) rejects the passage of a joint custody bill in direct opposition to father's rights groups who support it. Other issues which are beginning to cause tension include male concern over the plight of battered husbands, how much corroborative evidence should be required in rape trials, men questioning laws concerned with rape in marriage, the right of an unmarried woman to sue a man in Paternity Court, veterans' job preferences, and male objections to some abuses with respect to affirmative action for women. But on a positive note, the men's movement strongly supports feminist reforms which have removed the sexual concept from rape laws in favor of creating more general assault statutes, supports equal pay for equal work, and supports women entering the labor force.

A CONCEPTUAL BACKGROUND: MAJOR SPLITS

It is noted above that two divisions of the men's movement developed. One accepts the notion of men as "the oppressor," one rejects it. Those who accept the oppressor notion believe that women have suffered more than men from sexual discrimination and refer to themselves as feminist men. Those who reject this notion of the feminist men have no one label on which they agree.

Terms such as "nonfeminist men," "masculist,"[1] or "men's rights groups" have been loosely thrown around with varying degrees of acceptance. Taking these positions are those who resist getting involved with any broad theoretical explanation as to why sex discrimination exists. These men are most often father's rights advocates and insist that all the issues boil down to legalese ("tort," "pro se," etc.). Other men subscribe to the view that the reason men should support the Equal Rights Amendment is because men, more than women, have suffered at the hands of sex discrimination. Still others say that it is no use trying to decide which sex has suffered worse because we have all suffered and it is time to get on with the business of ending discrimination.

The majority of nonfeminist men evolved from men's organizations concerned with legal issues in divorce. Their evolution occurred quite separately from any influence exerted by a women's movement, until very recently when they discovered that concepts like "sexism" and "sex role stereotyping" describe their plight too.

ORGANIZATION OF A MEN'S MOVEMENT AND THE INFLUENCE OF THE WOMEN'S MOVEMENT

There are several very fine works which document the changes which have taken place in male role behavior over the last two centuries.[2] However, almost nothing has been written on the history of male organizations which were specifically formed to examine and champion male gender issues. The two most notable works which have attempted to present a history are *The Rape of the Male* by Richard Doyle[3] (from the nonfeminist men's point of view) and *The American Man* by Elizabeth and Joseph Pleck[4] (from the feminist men's point of view).

People familiar with the men's movement usually have the false impression that it began with the women's movement. There are reasons for this misconception: people may only be familiar with feminist men who trace their roots to the women's movement, or they may be unfamiliar with the nonfeminist men's movement, which in early years received very little media exposure, or there may be some confusion about the nature and relationship of the men's

---

[1] *"Masculist" is a term which has caught on with the Western European men's movement. For the most part this movement consists of men in consciousness-raising groups. Where politics is concerned, flex time in the workplace is the most emphasized issue. Masculists have not yet connected with the father's rights movement. Their first international conference was held in Uthedit, Holland, 1981. For more information, contact, Hugh De Garris, Chausee de Grand 337, 1080 Brussels, Belgium. For more information on European and Middle Eastern father's rights groups, consult the* Single Dad's Lifestyle *directory (see footnote 24).*

[2] *See, for example, Peter N. Stearns, Ph.D.,* Be a Man: Males in Modern Society *(New York: Holmes & Meier Pub. Co., 1979).*

[3] *Richard Doyle,* The Rape of the Male *(St. Paul, Minnesota: Poor Richard's Press, 1976; privately published, 17854 Lyons, Forest Lake, Minnesota, 55025), pp. 259–268.*

[4] *Elizabeth H. Pleck, Ph.D., and Joseph H. Pleck, Ph.D.,* The American Male *(New Jersey: Prentice Hall, Inc., 1980), Introduction.*

and women's movements. Most of the modern-day men's movement has adopted the concept of equal rights between the sexes; thus, much of the rhetoric used by both the men's and the women's movement sounds the same, and gives to some the misimpression that the two movements must have the same concerns. A closer look reveals that each is concerned with many very different issues.

The influence exerted by the women's movement has acted in both positive and negative ways. The notion of equal rights, for example, provided a convenient bandwagon for men's groups to jump on because it fits their attempts to end discrimination against themselves. Nowhere is this more evident than in the father's rights movement. The women's movement was oblivious to this type of male support, rarely articulating why equal rights might benefit men. Instead, they tended to look at equal rights as a single-gender issue and follow a course which blamed men for everything.

By the 1970s men were caught in a bind. For men to complain about the male condition was to appear weak and unstable and to lose credibility. Without credibility there could be no platform upon which to arouse other men to the issues of the day. The women's movement was not willing to provide that platform, which caused many men to form their own groups.

By 1982, with the defeat of the E.R.A., and with men's organizations forming, many men were beginning to question the tactics of the women's movement. For example, the National Organization for Women (NOW) had refused to support joint custody legislation, taking the position that such support would erode women's power base.

But from the very beginning the feminist movement always lacked a certain credibility. A lot of men facing the military draft in the 1960s refused to believe that women really wanted true equality when they were not willing to be subject to the draft. Some of those active in the newly emerging men's movement, who saw themselves as victims of sex discrimination in divorce and the military draft, found themselves unable to gain a platform upon which to call for men's equality with women. Men, feminists were claiming, had *all* the power, and no one was willing to listen to the male spokesman, unless they first contoured their comments to meet the perceptions of the women's movement. During the years he managed *Playboy* magazine, Hugh Hefner tried to spell out sex injustice toward men, but to little avail. In the late 1950s and throughout the 1960s, in the pages of the *Playboy Forum,* Hefner decried the treatment of men as a special class under the law. Beyond this, Hefner's chief concern was aimed at this culture's negative view toward sex. His policy on the matter was set forth in a hard-to-read intellectual treatise called the "Playboy Philosophy," which ran as a series and is remembered by almost no one.

While some books were published on sex equality in the 1960s and 1970s, for the most part they were produced by people outside any formal men's movement.

I: THE DEVELOPMENT OF THE FEMINIST MEN'S MOVEMENT

The social revolution of the 1960s provided the background for a movement centered on introspection, feelings, and emotions. For the first time ever, large numbers of men openly rebelled against the traditional male image of tough, unfeeling warrior. They grew their hair long, altered their dress, and glorified art and poetry. At the same time the key issues of the day centered around civil rights. Were there limits to the government's authority to draft young men to serve in an increasingly unpopular war? And what about the rights of the poor, rights of blacks, Hispanics, the handicapped, and women?

Many well-intentioned men, hoping to help correct what women and minorities were calling the wrongs of the past, jumped on the bandwagon for these causes. It was not the first time men had reacted this way to women's causes. Quite a few men had shown sympathy for the early suffragettes, but they were isolated individuals who never coalesced into a cohesive group to support women.

All that changed in 1970 with the formation of the Men's Center in Berkeley. This marked the beginning of what would become known as the "feminist men's movement." Other such men's centers began to form around the country: some were inspired by a flurry of feminist-styled male authors, and others were outgrowths of local conferences inspired by a growing network of men who wanted to support women's causes and reexamine the masculine role's relationship to patriarchy.

This new movement was quite revolutionary because it united, for the first time, men who had been isolated in their support for women's causes. But beyond this, it gave birth to the provision of an appropriate environment where men could begin to raise some issues of their own. While the basic atmosphere was negative toward masculinity, a forum was at least created where men could begin asking some of the questions about themselves that women had been asking about themselves. These were angry times. The major female feminist leaders often characterized men as "the enemy" and as the "oppressors" of all women. Some men had withdrawn from this hostility. Lacking other alternatives, they joined the newly forming feminist men's movement in search of a place where men could share emotionally and develop male bonding, but for the most part they were unconcerned with philosophy or politics. Others took the accusations that were leveled at men by the women's movement very seriously. They became determined that the "male chauvinist pig" had to change his behavior toward all the helpless victims of a patriarchal society. They saw the primary political function of a men's movement to be supporting women in their quest for equality with men. Any activities which were not politically oriented toward achieving the women's movement's goals were aimed at helping men become more introspective. Even then, the introspective nature of this movement was not free-form. For example, as one group facilitator's manual suggested, a purpose of consciousness raising is, "To find non-oppressive and mutually beneficial ways of relating to women or a specific woman companion, friend or wife."[5]

---

[5]Facilitator's Manual: For Men's Consciousness Raising and Support Groups *(Seattle, WA: Metrocenter YMCA, 1979), p. 4.*

Some feminist men believed that men too had suffered from sex discrimination, but in very limited ways. Several of those who argued that the male role was no bargain did so in the context of a negative view toward capitalism. This view was espoused in one of the earliest and most popular of feminist men's works, the film *Men's Lives* by Will Roberts and Josh Hanig in 1974.[6] Writers also took the view that men needed not only to raise their consciousness, but also to cast off the oppressive patriarchy and its capitalistic underpinnings.

Probably the two best known feminist men's books of early vintage are *The Liberated Man* by Warren Farrell,[7] and *The Male Machine* by Marc Feigen Fasteau,[8] both published in 1974. Both books provided, for the first time, insight into the difficulties men have in trying to live up to their own role stereotypes. As was characteristic of most feminist men's literature, neither book gave a critical appraisal of the influence female behavior has on men. Both Farrell and Fasteau pointed an accusing finger at men as though men had all the power in society. Several other books written by men were soon published which followed this assumption.

As the movement began to grow, an attempt was made toward national unity. The first of these organizations was the Men's Awareness Network (MAN); which evolved into Men Allied for Liberation and Equality (MALE); which, in turn, evolved into M.A.N. for ERA.

For a number of years the main function of these national umbrellas was to organize a yearly conference. As of 1981 there had been seven of them. Locally, men's centers sponsored consciousness-raising groups as their main activity. Feminist men also sponsored crisis centers for women, while any crisis center approach to men was aimed at men who abuse women. Issues involving men battered by wives, women who assist men in the rape of another woman, and false accusations of rape by women were subjects largely ignored. Violence was seen as essentially a male characteristic.

Feminist men have run into several unique problems. For one thing, they have not convinced all feminist women of their sincerity. They have been accused of stealing the women's movement rhetoric in order to gain the limelight, or to trick women into going to bed with them. They have also been accused of adopting a new paternalism toward women by posing as the male protectors of women's liberation.

Among themselves, feminist men have failed to develop cohesive organization and clear spokesmen for their movement because they reject the creation of "male" power positions. This sometimes precludes election of officers and the organizational structure necessary to maintain their groups. Thus, feminist men persist as a loose informal collective with no clear means to achieving their

---

[6] *Will Roberts and Josh Hanig,* Men's Lives *(P.O. Box 315, Franklin Lakes, NJ 07417: New Day Films, 1974).*

[7] *Warren Farrell,* The Liberated Man: Beyond Masculinity: Freeing Men and Their Relationships with Women *(New York: Bantam Books, 1974).*

[8] *Marc Feigen Fasteau,* The Male Machine *(New York: McGraw-Hill Book Co., 1974).*

objectives. Beyond this, their essentially negative view of men as the oppressor has made some men quite uncomfortable.[9]

At least the problem of creating better organization for the purpose of advancing their cause and achieving higher visibility has been addressed. In 1982, a number of feminist men got together and formed the National Men's Organization (later renamed the National Organization for Changing Men), which does elect officers and appoint spokesmen. Rather than attempt to organize the already existing local organizations under one umbrella, they solicited individual grass roots participation from among their members.

To attract members feminist men have to contend with an image problem in addition to their organization problems. Sometimes "radicalism" gets in the way. Freedom from the male stereotype means, to some, the ability to wear women's clothing in public and to allow homosexual organizations a loud and sometimes preponderant voice at their yearly conferences. Also, their rhetoric against capitalism and rather simplistic socialist substitutes, along with their condemnatory attitude toward men who do not share their ideology, alienate many people who otherwise might find them more appealing.

The official organ of the feminist men is *Changing Men: Issues in Gender, Sex and Politics* (formerly *M: Gentle Men for Gender Justice*), a quarterly first published in 1981. Their directory lists approximately sixty participating organizations.[10]

II: THE QUIET MOVEMENT

Feminist leader Betty Friedan, in her book *The Second Stage*,[11] coined the term "the quiet movement" to refer to the whole of the men's movement. This characterization of the men's movement certainly doesn't hold "across the board," as we shall see when we explore its more militant and political aspects. But the term the quiet movement is certainly appropriate for describing a large gray area of male activity.

Here too, the turbulence of the 1960s set the stage for change. The Kinsey Report of the 1950s was alive and well. The Playboy Foundation was challenging outdated sexual codes which made practices such as oral sex a crime. The "humanist" movement in psychology was at its peak, promoting workshop retreats for learning sensitivity. Old Freudian concepts about a special mothering instinct in women were being challenged. And with the unpopular Vietnam War as a backdrop, many young people were openly rebelling against the establishment, shouting such slogans as "Make love, not war." Young men who grew

---

[9]*Robert Charm, "From Macho to Mellow: Conference on Masculinity Explores Liberation, Male Roles," Boston Globe, 5 July 1981, p. A9.*

[10]*The address is: Box 313, 306 North Brooks St., Madison, WI 53715. It should be mentioned here that the official publication for the National Organization for Changing Men is the quarterly, Brother. The address is: Box 93, Charleston, IL 61920. Some affiliated men's centers also publish their own newsletter.*

[11]*Betty Friedan, The Second Stage (New York, Summit Books, 1981).*

their hair long, although they were sometimes called "sissies," helped set trends that were beginning to question and redefine masculinity. Allegiance to the military establishment was no longer viewed as manly. With more and more males open to redefining traditional masculinity, while at the same time being subjected to the influence of the women's movement, many men began experimenting with sensitivity, introspection, and consciousness raising.

The quiet movement was not marked by any one kind of thinking; it did not take on any very clear character until the late 1970s and early 1980s, and is still experiencing a metamorphosis. This includes men who at an individual level began experimenting with change without any affiliation with a formal organization. For the most part these men were unaware that there were formal men's organizations to which they could turn. These men included those who experimented with a more nurturing role toward their children, those who tried role reversal as house husbands, and those who entered occupations such as nursing. Unwittingly, even the Selective Service Administration during the 1960s had contributed to this process by exempting men from fighting in a war who volunteered to go into the traditional female occupation of teaching.

On a more organized level, many men began experimenting with consciousness raising. It is at this level that we see attempts at some organization, even though, more often than not, they were unsuccessful. The small, interactive group process known as consciousness raising has as its chief objective emotional reorientation. But such consciousness raising was frequently chaotic and lacked direction. Learning new emotional and verbal skills is an embarrassing process for many men who feel it calls into question their masculinity.

An added difficulty was that men were not always motivated to take up social change with a positive attitude. Many were forced into social change unwillingly.[12] Some of those who became house husbands, for example, did so because they were unemployed. Some secretly hid their feelings of emasculation as they became dependent on their wives for economic support. In other cases, men responded to the threat that their spouse would leave them if they did not conform to the new liberation philosophies. Others saw their wives walk out the door in search of new options, leaving them bewildered and forced to make unexpected adjustments.

A lucky few found consciousness-raising groups where they could transfer some of their almost exclusive emotional dependency on women to other men. In a few areas, independent men's centers were formed. They tried to provide a physical place or setting where men could come to workshop programs, form more structured consciousness-raising groups, and share informally with other men in an environment where a man would not feel threatened by pressures. The emphasis was on personal growth and increased social awareness.

---

[12]*Eric Skeji, Ph.D., and Richard Rabkin, M.D.,* The Male Ordeal: Role Crisis in a Changing World *(New York: G. P. Putnam's Sons, 1981).*

Examples of individual and autonomous men's center activity include the New York Center for Men (founded in 1981)[13] and the Men's Resource Center of Philadelphia.[14]. Generally, the few local and autonomous men's centers that arose resisted offers to join other groups and resisted politics, preferring instead to develop along informational and interpersonal lines, operating out of a church or someone's living room.

The problems with this quiet revolution is that it is lonely, often represents a pulling back into a shell, and is a passive reaction to social change. It is limited to the awareness of its individual members, rarely exists to do anything more than satisfy their specific needs, and is in a rather poor position to come to anyone's aid beyond the purely emotional level.

III: FORMATION OF A NONFEMINIST MEN'S MOVEMENT

The term "nonfeminist men" includes a variety of groups with widely divergent beliefs. There are "backlash organizations" (formed primarily in reaction to the women's movement), the father's rights groups, and the avant-garde.

A: Backlash

In this article, backlash is taken to mean attempts at completely reversing everything the women's movement has stood for, including the notion that laws should be passed to yank them from the labor force and return them to the home. While there are undocumented reports of men's backlash organizations which existed during the early part of this century, there seems to be only one such group which has opposed modern feminism. This was the National Men's Legion, which existed in the late 1950s.

Almost no information exists about them except for a few pieces of their literature. Basically, they tried to link feminism to Communism and to a decline in American morals. To some degree this group was a product of its time, where conservative leadership was linking any innovative social change to a Russian plot to take over the world.

This National Men's Legion, however, did not thrive, perhaps because no men's group during that time had the political maturity, much less the informed consciousness, to survive. In short, during these times an organized men's movement was the last place from which a backlash was apt to flourish. Were such a backlash movement to emerge today, it would likely come from broader-based political movements such as the Moral Majority, or from women's organizations such as The Eagle Forum or Women Against ERA.

---

[13] *The New York Center for Men, 251 Central Park West, New York, NY 10024. While they are listed in the feminist men's directory, this group insists on and has practiced complete neutrality and is strictly nonpolitical.*
[14] *The Men's Resource Center of Philadelphia, 514-A Randolph St., Philadelphia, PA 19147, is a nonpolitical, independent organization.*

B: The Father's Rights Movement and The Development of a "Generalist" Outlook

The history of the men's movement in North America is riddled with rumors and misinformation about the existence of groups in the early part of this century. If by a men's movement we mean groups specifically organized around the issue of gender politics and how role changes in society may seek justice for men, then the earliest group which has been documented is the United States Divorce Reform, founded in Sacramento, California, by Ruben Kidd and George Partis in 1960.

By contrast, the women's movement can be traced back more than a hundred years in this country, and the questioning of gender roles from a woman's perspective reaches at least as far back as ancient Greece. Throughout this history the women's movement has always had an element of strong male support, even if it did often go against the grain of society at large. For example, one of their most famous supporters in the early part of this century was Sir Arthur Conan Doyle, author of the Sherlock Holmes series.

Doyle was a social activist who produced, among other things, a pamphlet entitled *Divorce Law Reform*. Shortly after its publication he was elected as the first president of the Divorce Law Reform Union in London. The Divorce Law Reform Union had been founded by a small group of prominent British male leaders who set about to effect many of Doyle's suggested reforms, which centered around his outrage over the preferential treatment afforded men under the then-current divorce law.

The men's movement has never enjoyed a similar aid from women. The early men's divorce reform movement, beginning in the 1960s, was made up of men who had been victimized both by an unfair court system, and by ex-wives who hated them and used this system to destroy their ex-husbands. But such victimization did not represent the experience of the average man. Divorce was not something most families went through, and when divorce did occur, it usually did not escalate into full-scale war. This is not to minimize the suffering that some men endured. Many courts awarded impossible sums in alimony as a sadistic punishment, and some courts awarded children to obviously unfit mothers including those who seriously abused their children.

One sad example of injustice during this time is told by Richard Doyle, who recounts the experience of a former all-conference football star from the University of Kansas: "This gentleman developed a terminal disease, lateral sclerosis, whereupon his wife filed for divorce. She openly refused to comply with judicial instructions to honor the visitation portion of the divorce order, left the jurisdiction of the original court and moved to Topeka, Kansas. The dying and immobile man spent thousands of dollars in unsuccessful attempts to see his children. The Illinois and Kansas courts refused to enforce their own orders against the fugitive mother. A Kansas judge declared that it would be best for all if the man would hurry up and die."

Comments Doyle, "Imagine the outcry if the sexes had been reversed!"[15]

---

[15]*Richard Doyle*, Rape of the Male, p. 99.

These kinds of injustices were numerous, and even today the general situation has not appreciably changed. How to deal with these types of injustices became the central theme of the men's divorce reform movement. As the divorce rate soared through the 1960s and 1970s, more and more men were being adversely affected and began joining men's divorce societies.

At first, the central theme centered around strictly legal injustices. Most men, like the courts, believed in a special maternal instinct. The general feeling was that children probably should go with the mother, except in cases where the mother was abusing or obviously unfit. These men thought that the courts should also take this attitude, and enforce it in the best interests of the child; but the courts frequently preferred to look the other way, even in cases where children's rights were being clearly abused.

Slowly it began to dawn on a few men within the father's rights movement that something more was to blame for their plight than merely the routine workings of divorce court. The first to write about this was Charles V. Metz, who wrote *Divorce and Custody For Men,* which was published in 1968 shortly before his death.[16] Said Metz: "Throughout the world, American men are held as prime victims of a female-dominated society."

Metz advanced a theory for sex discimination against men that was nearly 180 degrees to the left *or* right of the women's movement and feminist men. His viewpoint is not hard to understand, for much like the women writers of the day, Metz was writing as an experienced victim of sex oppression. But Metz believed that men were to blame for female domination of men. As he saw it, men, who were in positions of power, were using that power to oppress men via a perverse chivalry which tried to win the favors and approval of women. Says Metz, "We must learn again the business of being the male head of the household." For Metz, the problem was that men had abdicated their power.

By 1968 Metz was an experienced men's divorce advocate, belonging to the United States Divorce Reform, which had been originally founded under the name Divorce Racket Busters in 1960.

United States Divorce Reform was an early attempt to form a national men's movement.[17] It began in Sacramento, California, and soon formed chapters in other states. Its first major project was to try and create a law in California establishing "family arbitration centers." The idea was to take divorce out of the adversarial system which was, and still is, an integral part of courtroom functioning. But their legislative initiative never got enough signatures to be put on the ballot. As Doyle observed, "Although a concentration on California's laws may have been practical, a 'shake-down-cruise' to prepare for taking on all state's laws, non-Californians became restless, and began falling away to form more parochial organizations."[18] Never again would there be a concerted effort by the growing number of men's divorce associations to concentrate their efforts in just one state.

---

[16]*Charles V. Metz,* Divorce and Custody for Men: A Guide and Primer Designed Exclusively to Help Men Win Just Settlements *(New York: Doubleday & Co. Inc., 1968).*

[17]*United States Divorce Reform, P.O. Box 243, Kenwood, CA 95452.*

[18]*Richard Doyle,* Rape of the Male, *p. 260.*

Metz quit the United States Divorce Reform organization and in 1968 co-founded America's Society of Divorced Men, headquarted in Elgin, Illinois.[19] It too was envisioned as a national organization, but has succeeded only to the extent that today it exists as one of almost 200 men's divorce societies in the U.S.

There were several attempts in the 1970s to unite the various divorce societies. Most of them were led by Richard Doyle, who had been a member of America's Society of Divorced Men and who was a disciple of Charles Metz. Doyle expanded on Metz's essential theory, and expanded the issues of the men's movement to include not only divorce but also criminal justice, child abuse, biological gender issues, affirmative action, paternity court, and welfare for unwed mothers in a book called *The Rape of the Male*. This is an extremely controversial work, filled with anger, humor, and Doyle's own brand of socio-biological philosophy.

Doyle is important historically because he figures so prominently in the efforts to bring unity to the men's movement. Moreover, he was the first man in nonfeminist men's liberation to broaden men's issues beyond the narrow confines of divorce. For the first time, men could speak about a "men's movement" rather than simply a "divorce movement."

In 1970 Doyle set about to remedy the factionalism which had developed within the divorce reform movement. The Coalition of American Divorce Reform Elements (CADRE) was formed and met for the first time in February 1971. It was envisioned as an organization of organizations, and to bring about unity the leaders of many of the country's divorce reform groups met in Elgin, Illinois, in 1970. CADRE encountered various problems—including disagreement over how to spend a projected budget—and infighting developed over who would take leadership roles. Three meetings were held before the participants finally agreed that they could not cohere their efforts. This failure set the stage for a recurring theme which was to divide the divorce reform movement and weaken it in future years. This theme, or problem, is "regionalism," i.e., the inability of different regions of the country, and different states—all subject to their own unique divorce laws—to agree on how to confront the variety of prejudices and the complexity of the laws that vary from region to region. Nevertheless, in the following years the divorce reform movement made occasional advances in legal reform within the borders of individual states.

With unsuccessful experiences in the past, Doyle formed the Men's Rights Association (MRA) in May 1973, with himself as president, and Ruben Kidd, one of the original founders of Divorce Racket Busters, as vice president.[20] The MRA limited direct membership to only a few people, preferring to avoid any problems which might arise from disagreements among a grass roots constituency. The organization still exists today, and bills itself as national in scope because its officers are spread out geographically, and because it has been successful in developing an attorney referral service for divorcing men in most major cities

---

[19]*America's Society of Divorced Men, 575 Keep St., Elgin, IL 60020.*

throughout the country, even though most of its lobbying efforts have centered in its home state, Minnesota.

At the national political level, the MRA supported passage of the Equal Rights Amendment. The main reason behind their support was the idea that men, not women, had suffered worse from sex discrimination. By 1976, however, the MRA withdrew its support of ERA because what they saw happening in court decisions regarding equal rights was that it was being justified as a means to benefit women only

C: The Avant-Garde

The year 1977 was big for the men's movement because it was the year Richard Doyle founded MEN International.[21] Also in 1977, Men's Rights Incorporated was founded by Fred Hayward in Cambridge, Massachusetts;[22] Free Men was founded by Richard Haddad, Dennis Gilbert, Allan Scheib, and Allen Foreman in Columbia, Maryland; and the first nationally syndicated column devoted to men's issues was begun by Jim Sanderson.[23] Sanderson's column is not devoted exclusively to men's issues, but when he does go after a men's issue it usually has to do with life-style expectations and relationships. By contrast, *Penthouse* magazine, in 1983, began publishing a regular monthly feature on men's issues which takes a hard look at the political and legal side of men's rights. This feature is authored by twenty-year men's rights advocate, Sidney Siller, who founded the Committee for Fair Divorce and Alimony Laws in 1965.

By 1977 Richard Doyle's efforts were again directed toward trying to get an organization of organizations off the ground. MEN (Men's Equality Now) International was founded and held three conventions between 1977 and 1980. Plans are currently being made for another convention. Primarily, the International has functioned in an advisory capacity to its member organizations, most of them father's rights groups, of which there are approximately forty throughout five countries, with the largest concentration in the United States.

Two main issues have continued to plague the father's rights movement and create internal dissension. One is the fact that problems faced by groups organized on a statewide basis vary from state to state, creating difficulties in coming up with a national focus. The second is that with increased awareness of the more general cultural influences which underscore sex discrimination against men, particularly in divorce court, there is disagreement as to whether it is best to remain strictly a father's rights group, concentrating on legislative changes and court reform, or to take the attitude that discrimination in divorce court will not appreciably change until men come to understand the totality of issues facing them. For example, can alimony be treated as an isolated issue, or is the

---

[20]*Richard Doyle*, Rape of the Male, *p. 259; Men's Rights Association, 17854 Lyons, Forest Lake, MN 55025*

[21]*Men International's current address is Kenneth R. Pangborn, president, MEN International, 2054 Loma Linda Way South, Clearwater, FL 33575, USA.*

[22]*Men's Rights, Inc., Care of Fred Hayward, P.O. Box 163180, Sacramento, CA 95816.*

[23]*Jim Sanderson's column, "The Liberated Man," is nationally syndicated by Sun Features, Cardiff, CA.*

319

real issue that society expects men to be the protectors and providers not only in divorce, but also in dating, marriage, war, etc?

In 1976, Herb Goldberg published *The Hazards of Being Male: Surviving the Myth of Masculine Privilege.* It captured the imagination of four men in Columbia, Maryland, who in 1977 founded Free Men, Inc. The earliest issues revolved around a sense that there was something fundamentally wrong with feminist interpretation of the male experience; the feeling was that men in their own groups had to learn how to articulate their experiences on a wide variety of issues. While many of the early members were married, they sought to extend their message to all men including those who were single and divorced. They formed consciousness-raising groups, held a yearly educational conference, published a newsletter called *Options,* and began to attract national attention as Herb Goldberg referred people to them.

A main tenet of Free Men was that they could not accept the theory of the male as oppressor. To their way of thinking, the father's rights movement, while important, was too narrowly focused. Free Men felt the MRA and other such groups to be too far to the right, and in the beginning, Free Men paid little attention to this "right wing," preferring dialogue with feminist men's groups.

Free Men attracted a goodly number of defectors from the other men's movement organizations. The leadership of the feminist men had not been anxious to inform their rank and file of all the other factions in the men's movement. Thus, to some feminist men, Free Men appeared to be the only alternative to their own philosophy. Because of this difference in philosophy, and because of the many defections, Free Men, as a viable alternative, was deeply resented by the more vocal feminist men's leaders, who came to see Free Men as an enemy.

Meanwhile, the highly politicized father's rights movement was relatively unaware of the feminist men, but because Free Men began extending overtures to the father's rights organizations, the possibilities for cooperation began to be recognized. It is interesting that in the already factionalized father's rights movement, Free Men was *not* viewed as an enemy, and instead, although it was regarded with suspicion by some of the individual father's rights groups, has come to be accepted by many of them.

In the late seventies, in the absence of much media attention, the organizations making up the men's movement remained relatively unaware of each other. The MRA drew up the first list of groups in the father's rights field, which greatly helped to inform different groups of each other's existence. In 1977 there were seventy-nine groups listed in twenty-five states and the District of Columbia. But it should be pointed out here that the list then as well as today omits feminist men's groups, while the feminist men's directory omits groups outside the feminist realm. By 1981 the number of nonfeminist men's groups listed in the *Single Dad's Lifestyle* "directory" had grown to 195 organizations in thirty-three states.[24] Through the creation and use of such directories, a network has begun to grow.

---

[24]Single Dad's Lifestyle. *Contact the editor, Bob Hirschfeld, P.O. Box 4842, Scottsdale, AZ 85281. A more recent, comprehensive list with more than one thousand listings of men's organizations is:* National Congress for Men 1985 Directory. *Write to: COPE, 68 Deering Street, Portland, Maine; Price, $7.00.*

For the most part feminist men are still largely unknown to the father's rights groups, and vice versa. Free Men has remained the one group which has knowledge of, and communicates with, all factions. Between 1977 and the present, debates between Free Men and feminist men have grown hotter, as evidenced in 1982, when the main publication, *M.*, of the feminist men, refused to list Free Men in its national directory.

The debate between Free Men and feminist men has centered around the male-as-oppressor issue. Richard Haddad produced a manifesto in 1979 entitled, *The Men's Liberation Movement: A Perspective,*[25] which crystallized Free Men's position in the movement.

Free Men, in addition to examining the problems of male role behavior, was critical of women and the role they play in helping shape the way both sexes contribute to their stereotypes. As Free Men has proceeded to criticize women, and express its anger against the way men are affected by sexism, the feminist men's leadership has interpreted this as woman-hating and antifeminist. At the same time, to the groups on the right, Free Men's concern with consciousness raising, and talk about role changes, have sometimes appeared too profeminist.

Free Men continued to grow and pursue its own line of thinking until 1980 when it ran into organizational difficulties. Free Men had been gaining membership in states outside Maryland, and it was apparent that eventually the group would have to face the problem of how to administer this growing interest in different regions. By 1980, two new groups were actively seeking to come together as chapters: one on Long Island, New York; the other in Boston, Massachusetts. Free Men, until then, had consisted of one chapter in Columbia, Maryland, with hundreds of men and women from other parts of the country tied into it in the form of a loose network. How to administer these newly forming chapters was one of the issues before the Maryland group when in 1980 they could not decide on how to address this problem, and could not amicably elect an executive director. As a result, the group in Maryland disintegrated.

At the time, Fred Hayward, director of Men's Rights, Inc. was trying to establish a Boston chapter of Free Men which was itself beset with internal disputes. And meanwhile, Tom Williamson, Tom Lynch, and Naomi Penner were trying to form a chapter on Long Island, New York. Both groups did briefly function as chapters before the Maryland chapter folded in September 1980. When the Maryland group ceased to function, so did Boston (Boston was later revived), leaving only a fledgling group on Long Island. This New York chapter adopted the name Coalition of Free Men so that it could legally incorporate as a new group. In the interim, an ad hoc group of former members in Maryland met for the last time in the spring of 1981, and chose an executive director whom they hoped might some day rebuild their segment of Free Men. At the October 1981 meeting of the several Free Men chapters, Maryland's representative chose to be separate from the coalition. He was ultimately unable to revive the Maryland

---

[25]*Richard Haddad*, The Men's Liberation Movement: A Perspective, *originally published by Free Men, Inc., Columbia, MD; reprints available from Richard Haddad, Box 693, Columbia, MD 21045.*

group. What activities he has generated have since concentrated near his home in Washington, D.C.

The Coalition of Free Men has attempted, with noticeable success, to rebuild the Free Men organization. It began by trying to form identifiable chapters and by reaching out once again to those in distant regions who wanted to be part of a network. The organization's main publication is *Transitions*.[26]

For the most part the Coalition of Free Men has acted as a purely educational body, although because of its close contact with father's rights groups it has become political to a degree. The organization, to date, has successfully produced several yearly conferences, and where it has chapters, offers a monthly lecture series open to the public. The underpinnings of its philosophy are based on the learned behavior model and on the idea that the sexes are interrelated through the historic nature of their complementary roles. The Coalition of Free Men neither accepts the notion that sociobiology is the major determination of role behavior, nor endorses scapegoating—where men are deemed to be the sole group responsible for everyone else's problems. The political prototype for Free Men has been Men's Rights, Inc., which, for example, successfully obtained equal life insurance rates for the sexes in its home state of Massachusetts, bringing to public attention the cultural reasons why men are not expected to live as long as women. The relationship between the Coalition of Free Men and Men's Rights, Inc. (M.R., Inc.) has been very close since the time they were both founded.

IV: LATEST DEVELOPMENTS

Social reform is a very old and timeless business that never ends. It keeps evolving, itself becoming the object of reform. Among the feminist men of the sixties and seventies is author, lecturer, and past member of the Board of Directors of the National Organization for Women (NOW) in New York City, Warren Farrell. Farrell has said that in the late sixties and early seventies he foresaw that the feminist movement would act as a voice for human rights. But toward the end of the 1970s, with the National Organization for Women opposing joint custody legislation, the women's movement looked more and more like just any other special interest group. Farrell had expected from them more encouragement for males. He and other male feminist leaders such as Barry Shapiro, chairperson of M.A.N. (Men Allied Nationally) for ERA have been surprised when the women's movement leadership has recently treated them with distance.[27]

In 1980 Richard Doyle, founder of MEN International, still dominated its image. It was an image that certain groups outside of the International were uncomfortable with, given that, as the most visible leader, Doyle seemed to outsiders a dominant one-man show. Furthermore, they feared that the display of anger expressed in his book *The Rape of the Male* would hurt their public image. Also, these groups were unsure as to whether the International would

---

[26]*Coalition of Free Men, P.O. Box 129, Manhasset, NY 11030*

[27]*Telephone conversation between Warren Farrell and Tom Williamson, Oct. 22, 1982.*

ever hold another national convention. Thus lacking any direct voice in the affairs of MEN International, a few of the men's movement leaders decided to explore the possibility of forming another national body to unite organizations across the country.

In 1980 a meeting was held in Utica, New York. Those present were: Joseph and Mimi Babier of Fathers United for Equal Rights, New Jersey; Tom Alexander of Male Parents for Equal Rights, Delaware; and Bruce Gerling, John Rossler, and Jim Taylor of Equal Rights for Fathers, New York. They decided to form the National Congress for Men and used the *Single Dad's Lifestyle* directory of men's organizations to call a convention the following year. The first convention was held in Houston, Texas, in June 1981. A second was held in Detroit, Michigan, August 1982.[28] James Cook of the Joint Custody Association in Los Angeles was elected the first president. The general feeling in the National Congress for Men, and in several smaller groups across the country, was that men were being left out of equal rights consideration. This prompted a number of men's groups in Boston to stage the first equal rights for men rally on Father's Day, June 1982. The rally was sponsored by several nonfeminist men's groups: the Boston chapter of the Coalition of Free Men, Father's United for Equal Justice, Children of Divorce, and the newly formed National Congress for Men under the leadership of Men's Rights, Inc.

A rally such as this indicates the cooperation and possibilities for political focus that are beginning to happen within the men's movement. However, as of this writing, there is no single men's movement organization that has a membership roll or monetary backing that can compare to NOW's. At present, there are questions as to which of the two main umbrella organizations for men's rights in this country—MEN International or the National Congress for Men—will emerge as the more popular or effective. Some people have claimed that competition between the two organizations is hindering the men's movement, but it remains to be seen whether this is true. The National Congress for Men is national in scope, whereas MEN International is international in scope. This difference in focus to some extent reduces the likelihood of a competitive relationship between the organizations. However, in the interests of establishing further unity and cooperation, the officers of MEN International proposed in 1982 to lay aside their charter and join the National Congress for Men, but this proposal was subsequently rejected by the Congress.

Directions for possible unity, however, are changing and remain unpredictable. In the National Congress for Men there is much internal dissension over focus on issues. Certain members of the Board of Directors wish to keep the congress focused on father's rights only; others want to keep its door open to other issues such as working for an equal rights amendment, a gender-neutral draft, aid for disabled veterans, and male health needs. It is not impossible that

---

[28]*The first meeting of the National Congress for Men was hosted by Texas Fathers for Equal Rights, P.O. Box 79670, Houston, TX 77079. The second meeting was hosted by Fathers for Equal Rights of America, 30233 Southfield Road, Suite 208, Southfield, MI 48076. The actual meeting was held in Detroit.*

this conflict over focus on issues will divide the Congress into two smaller groups, or cause it to dissolve entirely. This situation is symptomatic of the whole of the men's movement and at this writing it is impossible to tell which groups in the movement will survive. Meanwhile, MEN International's public image has improved. This is partly because of a shift in organizational leadership; their new president, Ken Pangborn, is very knowledgeable on many issues within the men's movement, and wants the organization to avoid concentrating on father's rights too much and give more emphasis to other issues.

As the National Congress for Men either resolves or succumbs to its current difficulties, and as MEN International tests new terrain, the Coalition of Free Men persists as an educational and resource organization which sponsors lecture series, conferences, and a publication of its own. Men's Rights, Inc., meanwhile, works as a separate but closely cooperative organization, shares the general ideology of the Coalition of Free Men, but concentrates more on specifically legal issues, change via judicial action, and work with political figures in local and national government.

Men of all races need to understand that as human beings they, like women, have unique, special interests. These unique interests may be broken down into three distinct categories: interpersonal, health, and civil rights. The advantage of supporting a local men's rights organization lies not only in becoming better educated as to what the issues are, but in supporting and funding people who will take action on those issues.

On gender issues, men have thus far been the passive reactors to forces of social change which to them has seemed to be inevitable and beyond their control. The time has come for men to begin defining what it is they want from social change, to begin to take the initiative and command some control over the future shape of our society. They need to do it for themselves and their sons. Men, not women, must define what it means to be a man.

About the Contributors

Leroy Aarons is an associate editor of *Washingtonian Magazine* in Washington, D.C.

M. Adams was one of the original officers of Free Men in Columbia, Maryland, and subsequently served as contributing editor to *American Man*.

Ardus is a pseudonym for a free-lance writer and men's rights activist from Ohio.

Eugene R. August is a member of the department of English at the University of Dayton. There he teaches a course entitled "Modern Men: Images and Realities." He has edited a book-length bibliography of writings about the male experience.

Tommi Avicolli is local news editor for the *Philadelphia Gay News*. He has contributed articles to many publications, including *Lavender Culture* and *Men's Bodies, Men's Selves*.

Bob and Daphne Bauer are long-time activists in the father's rights movement, and members of the Long Island League of Divorced Fathers, of which Bob is currently the president.

Rick Blum, Ph.D., is a director for Change Agents Training Institute, and is very active as a counselor in the Hartford, Connecticut, area.

Daniel A. Calvin is an original member of Free Men of Columbia, Maryland. His scholarly work on joint custody, contained in this book, is already a classic within the men's movement.

Michael Castleman is managing editor for *Medical Self-Care* magazine. He is nationally known as a writer on men's health care issues, and is the author of *Sexual Solutions: An Informative Guide*, published by Simon & Schuster in 1983.

Michael Cox is a free-lance writer in the Chicago area, with a background and degree in journalism.

Louie Crew is nationally known as one of the most courageous, and pioneering, of activists for gay rights. He now directs the writing program at the Chinese University of Hong Kong. His recent book of poetry, *Sunspots*, is published by Lotus Press.

Jed Diamond's book, *Inside Out: Becoming My Own Man*, is perhaps the most personal, intimate book published in the men's liberation genre. He is a private counselor in the Bay area, and does self-discovery workshops with his wife, Carlin.

George F. Doppler is one of the most respected, and tenured, members of the father's rights movement. His work began in 1967, and he currently directs the Family Law Reform and Justice Council of Pennsylvania.

Rich Doyle is one of the most important and influential men in the nation when it comes to fathers' rights. His book, *The Rape of the Male*, published in 1976, is already a classic. He founded Men's Rights Association (MRA), MEN International, and the first national attorney referral service for divorcing dads.

David P. Faas is a prolific poet who is a member of The Bisexual Support Group established in New Jersey in 1981.

Herb Goldberg is the most widely read author on men's issues in the world. He has published three books in this area: *The Hazards of Being Male, The New Male,* and *The New Male-Female Relationship*. These books, with an internal organic development and thematic exploration, comprise a trilogy which continues to appeal to every philosophy and faction within the men's movement. These books have been published not only in the USA, but also in Japan, Sweden, Holland, Norway, Germany, France, and England. In addition, Herb Goldberg coauthored *Creative Aggression*, which is a standard text in popular psychology.

John Gordon's book, *The Myth of the Monstrous Male—and Other Feminist Fables*, is the most erudite critique of feminism thus far published. His humor and eloquence as a speaker have earned him status as official "toastmaster" of the men's movement. He is a professor of English at Connecticut College in New London.

Richard Haddad, as one of the founding members of Free Men in Columbia, Maryland, and as publisher of *American Man*, the most important journal in the men's movement, has been spoken of as the messiah of men's liberation. By defining the "generalist" view of men's liberation through Free Men, he has, more than any other spokesman, provided direction for the men's movement as it has taken on strength and momentum.

Rand Harris is a men's activist in the Chicago area and has been an important writer for the Chicago Men's Gathering.

Fredric Hayward founded Men's Rights, Inc., in 1977, and has been one of the most influential men in the nation in working for men's legal rights. He obtained equal life insurance rates for men in the Massachusetts Supreme Court, and has worked hard toward obtaining a gender-free draft.

Bob Hirschfeld is a long-time father's rights activist and for many years published *Single Dad's Lifestyle*.

Brad Hollister is a pseudonym for a computer sciences teacher who is very involved with men's studies programs in Oregon.

Mike Kelly is a staff writer for *The Record*, New Jersey's largest evening newspaper. He has devoted much of his journalistic career to writing about men.

Arthur Winfield Knight is very widely published as a poet and himself publishes *the unspeakable visions of the individual*.

Dan Logan is the current executive director of the Free Men chapter in Washington, D.C. He writes and lectures on men's issues.

Eugene V. Martin is an organizational consultant, adult educator, radio producer, and television host, who has extensive experience in antisexism efforts both as a consultant and as an advocate.

Jerry Medol is a practicing sociologist and community networking specialist. In the Kansas City area, he has helped develop several unique services: the Men's Project, the Delano Project, and the Community Series.

David C. Morrow is a long-time father's rights activist, former editor of *MEN'S,* and a member of the Coalition of Free Men.

Authur Murray is an actor and writer who has extensive experience in the men's movement in England.

Robert D. Nagle is a prolific novelist, with doctoral degrees in both philosophy and psychology. He teaches philosophy at Northwest Missouri State University and is a counselor and researcher in Kansas City.

Sheryl Nelms has for many years been a poet, and is immersed in the network of small poetry journals and workshops in this nation.

Jai Noa is a teacher, political activist, radio host, and writer who lives in Columbia, Missouri.

Ken Pangborn was formerly vice president of public relations for MEN International and currently serves as their president. He has done much to move the father's rights movement beyond the boundaries of the USA to other countries.

Naomi J. Penner, M.A., is an assertiveness and relationship counselor in private practice. She was one of the founding members of the Coalition of Free Men, and founded one of the first chapters of the National Organization for Women (NOW) in 1969 on Long Island. She hosts the radio show, *Man to Man.*

John Petersen is a good example of the "low-profile" man in the men's movement. While not politically active with issues around men's liberation, he stays at home, being what many people would term a "house husband." While his wife works, John takes care of their two sons—ages five and six. John also works part-time as a carpenter, makes toys for children, and writes fiction.

Stephen Picchi writes fiction and poetry. He is a contributing writer for *Empty Closet,* which is published in Rochester, New York.

Gregory P. Robinson is both a minister and a practicing attorney. With a degree in law, and advanced degrees in both divinity and philosophy, he brings an eclectic and original creativity to issues within the men's movement.

Jim Sanderson has published the nationally syndicated column "The Liberated Male" since 1977. He also has authored *How to Raise Your Kids to Stand on Their Own Two Feet,* published by Congdon & Weed, Inc., in 1983.

Roy U. Schenk, Ph.D., is a long-time activist for men's rights and other issues from Madison, Wisconsin. He wrote *The Other Side of the Coin: Causes and Consequences of Men's Oppression,* which was published by Bioenergetics Press in 1982.

Mark Sherkow has worked on men's liberation issues in the Chicago area and has written for *Chicago Men's Gathering Newsletter.*

Robert A. Sides is national secretary and Boston area director of the Coalition of Free Men.

Gerald A. Silver and **Myrna Silver** have published extensively in the area of father's rights in magazines and journals around the nation. Their book, *Weekend Fathers,* published by Stratford Press of Harper & Row in 1981, is one of the most widely read reference books for father's rights.

Jay Smith, Ph.D. is Associate Professor of Education at Adelphi University, Garden City, New York. He has for some years been a leading figure in the formation of men's studies programs at colleges and universities.

Robert Keith Smith is the West Virginia state representative for the Coalition of Free Men. He is the nation's foremost writer on the male image in movies.

Suzanne K. Steinmetz, Ph.D., is recognized as the leading authority not only in this nation, but also in the world, on spousal violence. She authored *The Cycle of Violence: Assertive, Aggressive and Abusive Family Interaction,* published by Praeger in 1977, coauthored *Behind Closed Doors: Violence in American Families,* published by Doubleday in 1980, and has coedited several other books.

Perry Treadwell, Ph.D., is a very involved member of The Men's Experience in Atlanta, Georgia. He is currently writing a book on male friendship and is an expert on the sociobiological nature of the sexes.

Will Watkins is a Boston-based poet whose work has been published in *M.: Gentle Men for Gender Justice.*

Tom Williamson is a long-time activist in the men's movement, belonging to some of the earliest divorce reform and father's rights groups. He was a co-founder of the Coalition of Free Men and is currently their national president.

Frank S. Zepezauer has been a high-school teacher most of his working life. He has written extensively on how feminism has influenced education in primary and secondary schools. A respected educator at Menlo-Atherton high school in California, his writings appear in many scholarly journals around the nation.

Lee Zukor, although he is only twelve years old, is an aspiring writer on men's issues and has published in *Transitions,* publication of the Coalition of Free Men. He is interested in the topic of female "showvanism," does artwork, cooking, and plays baseball.

Mark Zukor, age thirteen and a half, is Lee Zukor's brother, and has also published in *Transitions.* His main interests include artwork, baseball, and computers. He has helped with many projects in the Coalition of Free Men and for *Transitions.*

About the Editor

Dr. Francis Baumli is a noted author on men's issues, whose works have appeared in *American Man, M., The Humanist, Asahi Shimbun,* and many other publications. Best known for his work as the Missouri representative for the Coalition of Free Men, he has hosted the FM radio show, *Men Freeing Men,* and belongs to the National Congress for Men and MEN International.

He received the Ph.D. in philosophy from the University of Missouri–Columbia in 1976, has served on the faculties of several colleges and universities, and has pursued studies in counseling psychology and neurology.

In other professional areas, he serves on the national board of advisors to The Institute for Advanced Philosophic Research and has published widely in professional journals such as *The Philosophical Forum, Contemporary Philosophy,* and *International Studies in Philosophy.*

He lives in central Missouri with his wife, Abbe Sudvarg, a physician in family practice, and his ten-year-old daughter, Dacia.

Index

334

336

To order additional copies of *Men Freeing Men* ($16.95 per copy, fourth class postage paid), send a check or money order for the full amount to:

New Atlantis Press
473 Pavonia Avenue
Jersey City, NJ 07306

Please send _____ copies (payment enclosed $ _____) to:

Name: _____

Address: _____

City _____ State _____ ZipCode _____

(New Jersey residents add the appropriate sales tax. Please allow 4 to 6 weeks for delivery. Price subject to change without notice.)